THE GREAT
CURRICULUM
DEBATE

THE GREAT CURRICULUM DEBATE

How Should We Teach Reading and Math?

TOM LOVELESS
Editor

BROOKINGS INSTITUTION PRESS
Washington, D.C.

Copyright © 2001

THE BROOKINGS INSTITUTION
1775 Massachusetts Avenue, N.W., Washington, D.C. 20036
www.brookings.edu

Library of Congress Cataloging-in-Publication data

The great curriculum debate : how should we teach reading and math? /
Tom Loveless, editor.
  p. cm.
Includes bibliographical references and index.
  ISBN 0-8157-5310-1 (cloth : alk. paper) — ISBN 0-8157-5309-8 (pbk. :
alk. paper)
  1. Education—United States—Curricula. 2. Curriculum
planning—United States. 3. Reading—United States. 4.
Mathematics—Study and teaching—United States. I. Loveless, Tom, 1954–

LB1570 .G72 2001
375'.001'0973—dc21   2001004199

9 8 7 6 5 4 3 2 1

The paper used in this publication meets minimum requirements of the
American National Standard for Information Sciences—Permanence of Paper for
Printed Library Materials: ANSI Z39.48-1992.

Typeset in Sabon

Composition by
Stephen McDougal
Mechanicsville, MD

Printed by
R. R. Donnelley and Sons
Harrisonburg, Virginia

ℬ THE BROOKINGS INSTITUTION

The Brookings Institution is an independent organization devoted to non-partisan research, education, and publication in economics, government, foreign policy, and the social sciences generally. Its principal purposes are to aid in the development of sound public policies and to promote public understanding of issues of national importance. The Institution was founded on December 8, 1927, to merge the activities of the Institute for Government Research, founded in 1916, the Institute of Economics, founded in 1922, and the Robert Brookings Graduate School of Economics and Government, founded in 1924. The Institution maintains a position of neutrality on issues of public policy to safeguard the intellectual freedom of the staff.

Contents

CHAPTER ONE

Introduction

TOM LOVELESS

For the American school curriculum, the twentieth century ended like it began, with an intense debate over what schools should teach and how they should teach it. In 1902 John Dewey, who would eventually become the twentieth century's most famous advocate of school reform, wrote about two "sects" fighting over the curriculum. One group sought to "subdivide each topic into studies; each study into lessons; each lesson into specific facts and formulae. Let the child proceed step by step to master each one of these separate parts, and at last he will have covered the entire ground." The other camp, observed Dewey, believed "the child is the starting point, the center, and the end." Because this view focused so intently on the child, Dewey concluded, "It is he and not the subject-matter which determines both the quality and quantity of learning." A student-centered approach required a particular type of pedagogy, Dewey noted with approval, a teaching style recognizing that "learning is active."

Dewey's observations could have been written in 1999. Nearly a century had passed, but neither side had surrendered. Cease-fires had been fleeting. Decade after decade the conflict that Dewey had observed—and later became an important participant in himself—kept recurring. The terms *education progressive* and *education traditionalist* arose as labels for its partisans, who usually kept their squabbles within the walls of the nation's schools of education. Occasionally, however, the disagreement burst into the headlines, captured the nation's attention, and reminded everyone of the bitterness and rancor in which the politics of education is steeped.

At the end of the century, the debate focused on reading and math. This book is about the public conflict that swirled around these two subjects in the 1990s. The "education sects" that Dewey described so long ago still existed—in reading, in the proponents of "whole language" and "phonics," and in math, in the advocates and opponents of "NCTM math reform," referring to the reform agenda of the National Council of Teachers of Mathematics. The book includes contributions from influential scholars on both sides of the disputes, as well as chapters by distinguished nonpartisans. It examines what fueled the controversies, clarifies adversarial positions, analyzes the politics of the disputes, and investigates how curricular conflicts may have affected policy and practice.

In October 1999 the Program on Education Policy and Governance (PEPG) at Harvard University invited leading scholars to a two-day conference on the math and reading controversies. The meeting was held at the Charles Hotel in Cambridge, Massachusetts, and was jointly sponsored by the John M. Olin Foundation and the Kennedy School of Government's A. Alfred Taubman Center for State and Local Government. A crowd of nearly 100 participants and observers attended.

The papers presented at the conference make up the chapters of this book. They are organized by subject—first math, then reading—and prefaced with an essay by E. D. Hirsch Jr. At the conference, a welcoming dinner was held, with Hirsch as guest speaker. Although Hirsch clearly takes sides in these debates, his remarks offer a philosophical starting place for appreciating all the views expressed in the book. Whether you agree or disagree with Hirsch—or any of the other authors presented here—I think you will see that they agree on one point. The school curriculum is important. What we decide to be the proper content of schooling has significant consequences, not only for today's students and schools, but for tomorrow's society as well.

In the opening chapter, Hirsch argues that the reading and math wars are rooted in an age-old conflict between romantic (progressive) and classical (traditional) orientations toward education. The classical orientation believes in explicit, agreed-upon academic goals for children; a strong focus on discipline and order in the classroom; the primacy of teacher-led instruction; and regular testing to assess student performance. Traditionalists are skeptical that children naturally discover knowledge or will come to know much at all if left to their own devices. Traditionalists are confident that evidence, analysis, and rational thought are greater assets in the quest for knowledge and virtue than human intuition and emotions.

The romantic tradition reveres nature and natural learning. Instead of establishing explicit academic goals for children, educational progressives value a multitude of learning outcomes. They are more likely to insist on particular instructional approaches for teachers and particular character-istics of the learning environment than on the exact learning to occur, largely because of faith that, in the right setting, the proper learning for each child will unfold. These beliefs are religious, that is, they are based on faith rather than empirical tests of what is true. As Hirsch puts it, "We know in advance, in our bones, that what is natural must be better than what is artificial" and "our natural impulses work providentially for good in ways beyond our comprehending." Standards, rules, hierarchies of skill, rote practice and memorization, and the curriculum are all artificial con-structions of culture and society.

Gail Burrill begins the book's math chapters with a call for overhauling an outmoded curriculum. The curriculum reflects its historical time. Burrill argues that progressive reform is essential in mathematics because of the rapid changes in today's society and the future demands that students will face from technological innovations. She points out that the math curricu-lum is largely an invention of the early twentieth century, when most stu-dents completed only eighth grade and advanced courses such as algebra, geometry, and calculus were reserved for the few students who went to college. The NCTM's landmark 1989 document, *Curriculum and Evalu-ation Standards for School Mathematics*, offers an agenda for reform that Burrill enthusiastically supports. Three critical aspects of math instruction are altered: a shift in content from learning skills and procedures to using math for problem solving, a shift in teaching from disseminating informa-tion to stimulating student thinking and inquiry, and a shift in assessment from serving as end-of-the-unit tests to assisting teachers in diagnosing and addressing students' strengths and weaknesses.

Much of the NCTM blueprint is grounded on a progressive theory of teaching and learning known as constructivism. Michael T. Battista ar-gues that scientific research supports constructivist approaches over tradi-tional ways of teaching math. A narrow focus on computation may produce students who are able to come up with the right answers but are unable to explain why the answers are correct or to discern the appropriate calcula-tions to arrive at them. Stressing memorization and imitation over under-standing, thinking, and reasoning renders students' knowledge of mathematics impersonal and shallow. Battista quotes students defending incorrect answers. They possess a blind confidence in the results of procedure, even if the procedures are incorrect and the answers inconsistent with intuition, logic, or concrete reality.

Battista draws a distinction between a simplistic view of constructivism as "discovery" learning, teaching with manipulatives or other nonrigorous forms of teaching that allow students to do whatever they want, and the sophisticated theory and empirical evidence supporting what he calls "scientific constructivism." Math learning occurs as students cycle through phases of action, reflection, and abstraction that allow them to build ever more sophisticated mental models of mathematics. These models are tied to real-world quantities and rooted in interactions with, and the need to explain, one's environment. Battista cites several studies, including one of his own, in which students in constructivist-oriented classrooms improved on achievement tests measuring conceptual understanding or problem-solving skills without a loss in computational ability. Failed math reform programs, Battista concludes, are due to flawed mechanisms for converting theory into practice—teacher training, textbook creation, and teaching—not flaws in the theory of constructivism or the body of research supporting it.

David C. Geary argues that constructivism is theoretically suspect in light of the evolutionary history of the brain. Are human beings hardwired to learn math? Children almost certainly have an inherent sense of numbers, counting, and simple addition and subtraction, competencies that are found in preindustrial cultures and even in limited form among chimpanzees and other primates. Like language, these competencies seem to develop from an innate capacity that is elaborated through a child's natural activities, especially social play. This evolved capacity lays the foundation for children grasping simple arithmetic.

But innate mechanisms are not sufficient to lead children to most of the mathematics taught through formal schooling. Learning how the base-10 system operates, for example, is more difficult than learning rudimentary number-counting skills, just as learning how to read and write is more difficult than learning the language of one's parents. Children are not inherently motivated to study math, Geary argues, which makes the value that the larger society and culture place on academic pursuits, along with a teacher's ability to organize and guide instruction, all the more crucial. Instructional practices that are predicated on children's natural instincts, such as constructivism, are doomed to fail a large proportion of children, Geary concludes.

Do we know anything about how these theories play out in classrooms? Roger Shouse examines data from the National Education Longitudinal Study (NELS:88) and explores whether practices similar to math reformers' recommendations succeed in raising student achievement. He reports several surprising findings. The first is that, in 1990, 62 percent of tenth graders said that their math teachers asked them to "really understand the material, rather than just give an answer" and 77 percent said they were "really challenged" in the subject. Both figures are higher than those from any other academic subject, contradicting the notion that in 1990, about the time of the release of the NCTM standards, rote learning and "drill and kill" methods dominated math instruction.

Does math reform work? In eighth grade the effect of practices usually endorsed by math reformers is a mixed bag. Many practices have a different effect on achievement in schools serving advantaged and disadvantaged populations. Reformers frequently recommend grouping students heterogeneously by ability, for example. But students in detracked, mixed-ability classes evidence lower math achievement, and the negative effect is especially pronounced for students in disadvantaged schools. The effect of calculator use is significantly negative in disadvantaged schools but slightly positive elsewhere. An emphasis on algebra and problem solving boosts achievement in all types of schools.

Shouse also looks at the tenth grade, where some traditional practices are shown to be effective. Achievement gains are associated with learning facts, rules, and problem-solving skills but not from the use of hands-on activities. Textbooks and daily review are helpful, but student discussions are not. Achievement falls when teachers stress "the importance of math in everyday life." Other findings favor reform. Calculators seem to raise achievement, even though computers do not. Negative effects were detected for an emphasis on "speedy computations," a finding any reformer would applaud, and an emphasis on "students' questions about math" and "math concepts" produced positive results.

Adam Gamoran argues that the conflict over the math curriculum poses a false dichotomy between rigorous content and in-depth understanding. Taking the position that they are both desirable, he reviews several studies to show that they are both present in successful math classes. He first details studies by James Stigler of UCLA comparing Japanese and American teachers' instructional styles. The studies suggest that Japanese students' superior math achievement may be due to instructional practice. Japanese math teachers typically present a problem, discuss alternative solutions generated by students, present a general formula, and then provide time for students to apply the formula while working on problems on their own. American teachers, on the other hand, typically demonstrate how a formula works, then assign practice problems for students to complete. Gamoran argues that the Japanese approach demands content mastery from students while encouraging deeper exploration of the material and allowing students the time to think.

Gamoran describes an American program, Modeling in Mathematics and Science Collaborative, which exhibits many of the Japanese education traits and shows promising results on achievement tests. He reviews the favorable findings of a study by Fred Newmann and colleagues of authentic pedagogy—instructional techniques that combine constructivist principles with the mastery of disciplinary content. He also describes a study of transition courses, where math classes featuring a hands-on, problem-solving curriculum are offered as an alternative to general math classes for students not yet ready for advanced mathematics. These studies suggest that progressive instructional strategies can be effective if directed toward the learning of serious content.

Richard Askey declares his stand in his chapter title: good intentions are not enough. Askey agrees that NCTM reformers are seeking to improve mathematics in schools, but he identifies several flaws in their approach. The NCTM standards do not address the problem that Askey considers the most critical in math reform: the lack of classroom teachers' firm content knowledge. The NCTM also did not examine the math curriculum of other countries or include mathematicians in the writing of the standards.

Askey points out that teaching mathematics well using indirect strategies, methods favored by the NCTM, means that teachers must possess a deeper understanding of the subject than has been expected in the past. Today's elementary grade math texts are written with the awareness that teachers using the books may know little math. Not only do the new reform-oriented texts, which were financed by the National Science Foundation, lack sufficient guidance for teachers, Askey cites several instances where the books also are misleading or promulgate bad mathematics. Including professional mathematicians on editorial boards, not to mention in standards-writing efforts, would help catch such errors. Moreover, the NCTM's stated goal that conceptual understanding should be emphasized over skill development leads texts to spend an unwarranted amount of time on shallow concepts. Only math teachers with a profound understanding of their subject, with the kind of proficiency depicted in Liping Ma's *Knowing and Teaching Elementary Mathematics,* will be able to overcome these flaws in the NCTM standards and serve students well.

I am the author of the final math chapter. In it I compare the politics of the NCTM reforms with the politics of the "New Math" in the 1950s and 1960s. Both movements sprang from policy subsystems—influential networks of experts on a particular subject. The math subsystems were powerful enough to convert a reform agenda into adopted policy. Both reforms benefited from focusing events, defining moments that moved public opinion to support changes in school mathematics. For both reforms, after changes in the math curriculum had been implemented in classrooms, strong opposition arose to the new content of mathematics. In the case of the New Math, the criticism proved to be fatal, as it was routed from classrooms in the late 1960s and early 1970s. Although the fate of the NCTM reforms must still unfold, the analysis sheds light on how their popularity changed in the 1990s, from being the universally recognized model for curriculum standards at the beginning of the decade to the subject of ferocious debate at decade's end.

Diane Ravitch begins the book's reading chapters by showing that the debate on how to teach reading extends back to the nineteenth century. The methods of instruction that have dominated are the alphabet method, in which students memorize the letters of the alphabet; phonics, which makes students learn the sounds of letters and combinations of letters; and the holistic methods, in which students learn entire words and sentences, preferably as naturally as possible and without extensive skill instruction.

Three themes run through Ravitch's account. One is that reading instruction premised on some form of phonetic analysis stubbornly resists reformers' efforts to quash it. Another involves children's happiness. As early as the mid-1800s, critics complained of children being taught how to read through laborious drills that focused on memorizing the relationship of sounds and letters—that all students were really learning was to associate reading with drudgery rather than joy. By the Progressive Era of the early twentieth century, John Dewey and other reformers argued that reading instruction should be delayed until age eight to prevent damage to children's nervous systems. In the 1980s "whole language" advocates lodged similar charges against phonics, claiming that it handicaps reading comprehension and produces a lifelong aversion to reading

The third theme pertains to meaning. Supporters of phonics believe that reading for meaning must be temporarily subordinated to the analysis of abstract symbols, specifically, learning how printed letters and words can be converted into audible sounds and words. Once beginning readers acquire these skills, they are able to decode unfamiliar words and then to understand complete words, sentences, paragraphs, and stories. The opposing, progressive view is evident in the "whole word" method of the 1930s, also known as "look-say" because students were trained to look at a word and then say it. Progressives recognized that text is immediately recognizable to fluent readers, but they saw words—not letters or clusters of letters—as the smallest possible unit of learning for nonreaders. Words have meaning; parts of words do not. They thought once an extensive list of words had been learned and were recognizable on sight, beginning readers could then figure out unknown words by their context.

Ravitch shows how phonetic-based instruction has persevered, despite progressives' insistence that it makes children dislike reading, that learning how to read should be anchored in the search for meaning, and that instruction on "the whole" excels over instruction on "the part." She argues that the best elements of both approaches are supported by research and that the two sides should compromise, "declare victory and go home."

Important efforts at compromise occurred in the 1990s. Catherine E. Snow writes about the *Report on Preventing Reading Difficulties in Young Children,* issued by the National Research Council (NRC). Snow chaired the committee that issued this influential 1998 report, heralded by many as staking out common ground on which phonics and whole language supporters could agree. Snow points out that reading research had converged on several points, making the time ripe for compromise, and the committee's charge to focus on preventing reading difficulties also heightened its chances for gaining consensus.

Snow believes the English language's bidirectional complexity—in converting printed spelling to sounds and sounds to spelling—fueled the reading wars. Phonics supporters stress systematic, sequential instruction in how to make these conversions. Successfully converting letters (or graphemes) into sounds (or phonemes) is the defining task of phonemic awareness. Whole language supporters emphasize that decoding text is merely a means to an end and that reading is about constructing meaning from text. The NRC report embraced the principles supporting both positions.

It drew criticism from both sides. Some phonics supporters felt the report did not go far enough in identifying the most reliable research on the topic. They also disagreed with the report's endorsement of invented spelling and its wading into the debate over bilingual education by insisting that reading instruction first occur in a learner's primary language. Some whole language supporters felt the report neglected the social inequities that hinder literacy, adopted an alarmist tone by focusing on reading difficulties, and subordinated research based on classroom experiences to positivist, quantitative studies. Snow's chapter illustrates the difficulty of resolving these issues within the context of long-standing curriculum disputes.

Margaret Moustafa is sympathetic to the whole language position. She observes that the phonics–whole language debate is often misconstrued as a debate about *whether* letter-sound relationships should be taught. In fact, Moustafa argues, it is about *how* they should be taught. Phonics-based approaches, which she calls "traditional" reading instruction, teaches letter-sound correspondences and print words out of context, then provides children with materials featuring the words that have been taught. In the reading instruction that she favors, referred to as "contemporary" instruction, children are taught letter-sound relationships and new words while encountering them in text. One key difference is that reading skills are not acquired in isolation. Another is that decodable text takes a back seat to content in selecting children's reading materials. The parts-to-whole orientation of traditional instruction is reversed, as children are taught to read text with familiar language via shared reading, followed by letter-sound correspondences in the context of stories with predictable text. Thus reading is presented as a meaningful act even in the initial stages of learning.

Moustafa reviews several studies supporting contemporary reading instruction, focusing primarily on the superiority of teaching reading for meaning. She also argues that those who emphasize phonemic awareness as a prerequisite for reading probably have the direction of causality wrong. Good readers are phonemically aware, Moustafa agrees, but this skill can be acquired after—not necessarily before—one learns to read. She concludes that recent policy swings toward traditional reading instruction are not supported by research but have been propelled instead by misinterpretations of trends in National Assessment of Educational Progress (NAEP) reading scores and the misuse of several studies' findings.

Richard Allington writes about the effect of literacy policy on classroom practice. Like Moustafa, he traces the impetus for policies targeting reading instruction to the establishment of NAEP performance levels, which began in 1990, and to several research reports in the early 1990s. The NAEP scores indicated that large numbers of students were reading below a "basic" level, which alarmed the public. The research reports were on a variety of topics in reading but were alike in suggesting that certain approaches to instruction had been "proven" effective. As the belief spread that curriculum developers were ignoring scientific findings even as reading proficiency languished, the regulation of reading became a top priority of policymakers. In the 1990s more than 100 bills regulating aspects of reading instruction were introduced in state legislatures.

Allington argues that all this policymaking will have little effect on teaching. He points to past efforts at regulating instruction and the consistent finding of research that teachers are impervious to policy mandates. He also points out the inherent difficulties of implementing curricular reform—the time lag, for instance, between when policy is adopted and new materials actually appear in classrooms—and recommends high-quality longitudinal studies that examine the fidelity of implementation as part of program evaluation.

William Boyd and Douglas Mitchell start by acknowledging that the fight over reading is yet another skirmish in the philosophical dispute between progressive and traditional education. But they also think the 1990s debate was exacerbated by macroeconomic trends, especially public anxiety concerning globalization. This drove utilitarian concerns about U.S. competitiveness and school performance and ultimately spurred the centralization of power in social institutions during the decade. Control over the curriculum was no exception, with state and federal officials assuming greater say over reading instruction. The decade's "reading wars" featured three groups of important actors—education professionals, politicians and policymakers, and public and private interest groups (including parents)—and Boyd and Mitchell describe several "battlefronts" along which the reading wars were fought.

Boyd and Mitchell use this conceptual scheme to explain the rise and fall of whole language in California. Whole language reached its zenith in the state's 1987 English-language arts framework. Although the term *whole language* was never mentioned, several of the framework's key ideas were inspired by whole language—literature-based texts, student-centered instruction, multiculturalism, cooperative learning, and open-ended assessments soliciting student-constructed responses. These themes were placed on the defensive by stresses from globalization, Boyd and Mitchell argue, as the authority of professional educators was diminished by scientists, government officials, and public demand.

As a conclusion to this introduction, I offer five generalizations on the math and reading controversies of the 1990s.

1. The disagreement in math was largely about *what* math should be taught. In reading, it was primarily about *how* reading should be taught. Consequently, the math chapters deal primarily with content and the reading chapters with pedagogy.

2. In terms of policies, opposite philosophies were ascendant in mathematics and reading during the decade. The progressive-oriented NCTM reforms served as the model for most states as they wrote curriculum standards in mathematics. The federal Reading Excellence Act, on the other hand, embraced phonics-based instruction as the only scientifically valid form of teaching reading; this conclusion was backed by studies of the National Institute of Child Health and Human Development, a branch of the National Institutes of Health.

3. The stakes of the debate were ratcheting higher in the 1990s. States and local districts adopted standards defining what students should learn and tied the standards to periodic assessments and accountability plans. Consequently, progressive and traditional educators hauled their disagreements out of the cloistered halls of academia and thrust them before the public, into the hearing rooms of Congress and state legislatures, and onto television and other mass media.

4. Educational ideologies and conventional political ideologies are not a perfect match. The stereotypes are basically correct. Political conservatives tend to favor the traditionalist positions and liberals the progressive views. But not always. E. D. Hirsch Jr. and David Klein, for example, lean toward the left politically but back the traditionalist cause on curriculum. Conservative business groups often trumpet the virtues of cooperative learning; education's "soft skills," such as teamwork; and math reform in line with the NCTM standards—stock tenets of progressive reform.

5. Calls for compromise and a balanced approach are attractive but frequently break down when implemented in classrooms. Teachers are constrained by limited time and resources. When something has to give—and the sacrifice involves phonics or arithmetic or problem solving—those who favor the abandoned content are invariably offended. In addition, the side in political ascendancy is prone to declare that a balanced approach has been achieved. Thus critics of NCTM and the advocates of whole language were less likely to be enthralled with the balanced approaches touted by policymakers at the end of the decade.

The passion with which the following chapters argue, analyze, indict, and defend, and their willingness to describe how things are and how they should be, underscores an important point. Reading and mathematics are the two most important school subjects. Debating how they should be taught reveals our deepest convictions on what constitutes a good education.

CHAPTER TWO

The Roots of the
Education Wars

E. D. HIRSCH JR.

It is an honor to begin this volume's discussion of the great curriculum debate. At the conference I was listed as an English professor, which is a correct description of my former life and a reminder that I was being asked to discuss technical subjects to specialists in those subjects. While it is no secret that I have taken sides in this argument, my focus here is on the intellectual roots of the education wars. I started my professional life as an intellectual historian. I wrote two books about Romanticism, which was the movement that started these wars. Here I present one intellectual historian's take on those origins and proffer an explanation of the remarkable durability of Romantic educational ideas even in the face of practical failures.

An intellectual historian is an attenuated sort of historian. To get substantive educational history you go to scholars like Diane Ravitch. An intellectual historian focuses on the connections of ideas in order to understand why people hold them—often with the purpose of enabling people to liberate themselves. The great progenitor of intellectual history in the United States was A. O. Lovejoy of the Johns Hopkins University, who followed German scholars in subordinating historical influence to what the Germans called *Seelenlogik,* the logic of the soul. Ideas that may not fit together with logical consistency may nonetheless cohere emotionally. Intellectual history is a way of understanding how ideas hang together. It is an especially valuable discipline for escaping the prison house of ideology.

What does intellectual history have to say about the reading and math wars? The two sides, viewed broadly, are expressions of Romantic versus Classic orientations to education. (I will use the adjectives "Romantic" and "progressive" interchangeably for reasons that will become clear.) The whole-language approach to reading is Romantic in impulse. It makes an analogy or equivalence between the natural process of learning an oral first-language and the unnatural process of learning alphabetic writing. The emotive weight in progressivist ideas is on the value of naturalness. The natural is spiritually nourishing, and the artificial is spiritually deadening. Back in the 1920s the progressivist William Kilpatrick of Teachers College, Columbia University, and others were already advocating the whole language method of teaching reading for many of the reasons advanced today. The task of intellectual history is to explain why a method with small support in mainstream science and little success with many children should hold sway for so long.

As with reading, so with math and science. The progressivist believes that it is better to study these subjects through real-world, hands-on, natural methods than through the deadening modes of conceptual and verbal learnings or the repetitive practice of math algorithms. But the artificial symbols systems and algorithms of mathematics are the sources of its power. Natural, real-world intuitions are helpful in math, but there should be no facile opposition between terms like *understanding, hands-on,* and *real-world applications* and terms like *rote learning* and *drill and kill.* What is being killed in memorizing the multiplication table? The progressivist says: children's joy in learning, their intrinsic interest, and their deep understanding.

Artificial modes of learning are said to inhibit understanding and kill the soul, whereas natural methods are said to nourish it. There may be a practical value in applying the traditions of intellectual history to the origins and unspoken assumptions of this progressive faith. If enough people start questioning these unspoken assumptions, which, when spoken, are open to serious challenge from science and common sense, a shadow of doubt may begin to fall. Whenever I am asked which education reform program is likely to be the most effective—better teacher training, more charter schools, or various governance reforms—my reply is that there is less need for change in the structure of governance than for change in the structure of ruling ideas. The dominance of progressive ideas, not the incompetence of education professors, has induced our teacher-training institutions to deemphasize subject matter and thus produce teachers who know too little about the topics they should teach. Some education professors took personally my critique of progressivism in *The Schools We Need* (1996) as another example of education school bashing. But my thesis was not that poor teacher training is caused by ineptitude but, on the contrary, by an all-too-ept advocacy of Romantic ideas; not by incompetence but by an all-too-competent rhetoric in the service of the notion that specific subject-matter knowledge has only secondary importance. In the face of continuing practical failures, it would be hard to explain the more than nine lives of progressivism, except on the premise that its unspoken assumptions work a hidden sway not just over education schools but over the minds of Americans generally. If progressivism were not consonant with received ideas in the larger public about children and schools, the ideas would not maintain their sway. The public would not otherwise be so receptive, for example, to the disparagement of objective tests. Test bashing continues to be a successful rhetoric. One can understand that progressives should want to bash tests, when their methods consistently fail to improve test scores. But why should other citizens accept the disparagement of, say, reading tests, which are among the most valid and reliable instruments that exist? Wide public acceptance of test bashing suggests that it is tapping into powerful subterranean sentiments about children and learning.

Here are a few quick examples of the consistent practical failures of progressive ideas.

Example one. Recently the Sunday *New York Times* published an article about an ideal school that was created with unlimited funds in an ideal Florida town by the Disney Corporation. The school follows the "most advanced" progressive theories. The article, entitled "Trouble at the Happiest School on Earth," began by noting that:

> The start of the school year is just a few days away, so it was no surprise that there was a line of parents at the Celebration School office the other day. But the reason for the line was: they were queuing up to withdraw their children.

It turned out from this report that the "brand new" theories of the Disney school are rebottled versions of the theories Kilpatrick used to create his ideal progressive school in the 1920s—multiage groupings, where each child can go at his or her own pace; individualized assessments rather than objective tests; teachers as coaches rather than sages; projects instead of textbooks; and so on. As the reporter correctly remarked, "Most of these concepts have been tried in one form or another at progressive schools." But he forgot to note that the methods rarely worked well in the earlier schools either. So why haven't these failures induced more skepticism among teachers, administrators, and distinguished professors?

Example two. Some days before I read the Disney school article, I read two pieces from the *San Jose Mercury News* about two inner-city schools in Los Angeles. The disadvantaged students at one school were achieving exceptional academic results and were closing the test-score gap between groups. The other school was a progressive school with a highly similar population of students who were achieving at an abysmally low level.[1] They are valuable documents for intellectual history because of the concrete way in which the reporters examine the rhetoric that animates the successful Classical school and the unsuccessful progressive one.

Example three. The contrast between Classical and progressive public schools in Los Angeles duplicates the contrast found by distinguished sociologist James S. Coleman in the 1980s when he showed that Catholic schools achieved equity better than public schools because they follow a rich and demanding curriculum, require a lot of drill and practice, and expect every child to reach minimal goals in each subject during the year. As a result disadvantaged children prosper academically (as do their advantaged peers), and the Catholic schools narrow the gap between races and social classes. When he was criticized for condemning public schools, Coleman, chief author of the famous "Coleman Report" of 1966, pointed out that the same democratic results were being achieved by the handful of public schools that were also defying progressivist doctrine.

I have used Coleman's work of the 1980s as an example because it is a carefully controlled, large-sample work that has never been rebutted. Along with large-scale international comparisons, it is the most reliable observational data that we have regarding the validity of progressive ideas. The evidence mounts still higher if you combine Coleman's data with so-called effective-schools research, which has shown that school effectiveness is enhanced by explicit, agreed-upon academic goals for all children; a strong focus on academics, order, and discipline in the classroom; maximum time on learning tasks; and frequent evaluations of student performance—all principles followed by Classical schools but repudiated by the Disney school and also by many of the "whole school" designs for which so much fed-

---

1. The articles are too detailed to quote here, but they can be viewed at the website of the *San Jose Mercury News*, www.mercurycenter.com.

eral money is being misspent. In fact, one could take each of the principles of effective-schools research (such as uniform and explicit learning goals), negate them, and you would usually have a description of progressivist principles.

If these observational data were not enough to suggest a lack of correspondence between progressive ideas and reality, then consider as well their unfortunate lack of congruence with consensus theoretical principles that have been developed in cognitive science (such as the principle that explicit, step-by-step learning is more often effective than indirect learning). None of this has mattered. These unempirical progressive theories—dressed up with empirical claims—have held both education professors and a large portion of the American public in thrall. Why? This is a question for the intellectual historian rather than the puzzled scientist.

So to my task. The fundamental beliefs of progressivism are impervious to unfavorable data because progressivism is an expression of Romanticism, and Romanticism is a religious outlook that, like all religions, is inherently resistant to data. A religious believer is scornful of mere "evidences." Of course, most of our nonreligious ideas are also resistant to change. Even science tries to preserve its old theories against new findings, as when it held to the idea that the earth is the center of the solar system, arguing that the planets move in complicated epicycles rather than simple orbits. But religious beliefs are the most resistant to change of all.

Progressivism has all the characteristics of religious belief, including the sense of a direct connection with the holy, which it invokes by the word *nature*. We know in advance, in our bones, that what is natural must be better than what is artificial. This revelation is the absolute truth against which experience itself must be measured, and any failure of educational practice must be due to faulty implementation of progressive principles or faulty interpretation of the results. Reading tests must not be taken at face value, because such blunt instruments cannot measure the true effects of education.

The religious character of progressivism is rarely noted because it is not an overtly religious system of belief. Romanticism is a *secularized* expression of religious faith. In a justly famous essay, "Classicism and Romanticism," T. E. Hulme defined Romanticism as "spilt religion." Romanticism, he said, redirects religious emotions from a transcendent God to the natural divinity of this world. Transcendent feelings are transferred to everyday experience—as Hulme put it, like "treacle spilt all over the table." A more sympathetic definition of this tendency was offered by M. H. Abrams of Cornell University, who entitled his fine book on Romanticism *Natural Supernaturalism*. That phrase accurately describes the Romantic's fusion of the secular and the religious. The natural is supernatural. Logically speaking, that is a contradiction, but emotionally it catches the Romantic's faith that a divine breath infuses natural human beings and the natural world.

In emotional terms, Romanticism is an affirmation of this world—a refusal to deprecate this life in favor of pie in the sky. In theological terms, this sentiment is called "pantheism"—the faith that holiness inhabits all reality. Transcendent religions like Christianity, Islam, and Hinduism see this world as defective, and consider the Romantic divinizing of nature to be a heresy. For the Romantic, the words *nature* and *natural* take the place of the word *God* and give nature the emotional ultimacy that attaches to divinity. That is the source of Abrams's paradox: "natural supernaturalism."

> One impulse from the vernal woods [William Wordsworth said]
> Can teach us more of man
> Of moral evil and of good
> Than all the sages can.

Although Romantics have complete confidence that our natural impulses work providentially for good in ways beyond our comprehending, they have no such confidence in social custom and human reason. On the contrary, these are the sources of evil and the infection of the soul. This naturalism explains the no-fault complacency with which a progressivist teacher reassures the concerned parent not to worry if Johnny or Jane is not reading at grade level. All will come right when the child is developmentally ready. One must not interfere with the child's natural course of development.

The Romantic conceives education as a natural growth. Botanical metaphors are so pervasive in the educational literature that they are taken for granted. The teacher, like a gardener, should be a watchful guide on the side, not a sage on the stage. (The word *kindergarten*—literally "children-garden"—was invented by the Romantics.) Romantics began translating the Latin word *ee-duck'co* as meaning "leading out" or "unfolding," confusing it with *e-dook'co,* meaning "to lead out." It was a convenient mistake that fits in nicely with the theme of natural development, since the word *development* itself means "unfolding." But the actual Latin root word for education is *ee-duck'co,* which means "to bring up" and "instruct." It implies deliberate training according to social and cultural norms, in contrast to words like *growth* and *development*, which imply that education is the unfolding of human nature, analogous with a seed growing into a plant.

The regular textbook description of the Romantic movement is that it substituted the organic fecundity of nature for civilized constraints and rules. In education, the artificial constraints of the ordinary school were to be replaced by methods that permitted natural development. Chairs should be scattered around the room to accommodate children of various ages going at their own paces, rather than forcing children of the same age to do the same thing while sitting in neat Classical rows.

Just as Wordsworth said, "We murder to dissect," the progressivist says that phonemics in reading lessons and place value in math should not be dissected in isolation from their natural use nor imposed before the child is naturally ready. Instead of dissection, the Romantic wants integration and natural development, as happens naturally in the real world. Thus the Romantic prefers "whole language," "integrated learning," and "developmental appropriateness" to more effective analytical approaches. The Romantic holds that education that places subject matter in its natural setting is superior to the abstractions of language. Hands-on learning is superior to verbal learning. Real-world applications of mathematics provide a truer understanding of math than empty mastery of formal relationships. None of this is actually true.

The same religious sentiment underlies the Romantic celebration of individuality and diversity. The individual soul is holy because its spark is from God. Praise for diversity as superior to uniformity originates in the pantheist's sense of the plenitude of God's creation. This religious origin for the aesthetics of diversity, which we now take so much for granted, was the main theme of Lovejoy's famous book, *The Great Chain of Being*. "Nature's holy plan," as Wordsworth put it, unfolds itself with the greatest possible variety. To impose uniform standards on the individuality of children is to thwart their fulfillment and pervert the Design of Providence. The aesthetics of diversity is thus powerfully reinforced by the religious certainty that imposing any norm that is uncongenial to the child's nature is evil. Motivation to learn should be stimulated through the child's inherent interest in a subject, not through artificial rewards and punishments. Contrived inducements to learn, being unnatural, do not work permanently to the benefit of education. What others might view as complacent neglect is viewed by the progressivist as "wise passiveness" (Wordsworth's phrase again). Education should be child-centered. It should fit the child, not vice versa. As William Blake put it in *The Marriage of Heaven and Hell,* "One law for lion and ox is oppression," which is an early statement of the theme of "individual differences" and "multiple intelligences."

Whether these educational tenets can withstand empirical examination is irrelevant. Their validation comes from knowing in advance, with certainty, the overarching principle of Romantic theology: the natural is good, the artificial is bad. It is a principle that persists even when all consciousness of its original religious underpinnings has disappeared. I still remember my own astonishment, as an American bred in American Romanticism, to discover that the Elizabethans frequently used the word *artificial* to express approval. Since most of us still share the Romantic identification of the nonnatural with the nongood, it is worth pausing to contrast Romantic and Classical views on this precise point.

Plato and Aristotle based their ideas about education, ethics, and politics on the concept of nature, just as the Romantics did. A Classicist knows that any attempt to thwart human nature is bound to fail. But the Classicist does not assume that a providential design assures the ultimate rightness of relying on our individual natural impulses. On the contrary, Aristotle argued that human nature is a battleground of contradictory impulses and appetites. Selfishness is in conflict with altruism; the fulfillment of one appetite is in conflict with the fulfillment of others. Follow nature, yes, but which nature and in what degree?

Aristotle's famous solution to this problem was to optimize human fulfillment by balancing the satisfactions of all the human appetites—from food and sex to the disinterested contemplation of truth, also keeping in mind society's need for civility and security. This optimizing of conflicting impulses required the principle of moderation—the Golden Mean—not because moderation was in itself a good, but because, in a secular view of conflicted human nature, this was the most likely route to social peace and individual happiness. Against the Golden Mean, the Romantic Blake countered, "The Road of Excess leads to the Palace of Wisdom." But that would be true only if a providential nature guaranteed this happy outcome. Absent such faith in the hidden design of natural providence, the mode of human life most in accord with nature must be, according to Aristotle, through media that are artificially constructed. By this Classical logic, the optimally natural has to be self-consciously artificial.

This Classic-Romantic debate has a new currency because of recent interest in evolutionary psychology. The Darwinian moral philosophers from T. H. Huxley to E. O. Wilson reject the notion that evolution should be a direct guide to ethics or to education. On the contrary, evolutionary psychology reintroduces in its own way the Classical idea that there are inherent conflicts in human nature, both selfishness and altruism, both a desire to possess one's neighbor's spouse and a desire to get along with one's neighbor. The adjudication of these contradictory impulses requires an artificial construct like the Ten Commandments. Similarly, most of the learning required by modern schooling is not natural from the standpoint of evolution. Industrial and post-industrial life, which have arrived very recently in evolutionary terms, require kinds of learning that are constructed artificially and sometimes arduously upon the natural learning capacities of the mind.

Shakespeare was a Classicist on this score. He depicts the early ages of human life as:

> first the infant
> Mewling and puking in the nurse's arms.
> And then the whining school-boy, with his satchel
> And shining morning face, creeping like snail
> Unwillingly to school.

Shakespeare clearly had a less joyful view of schooling than Jean-Jacques Rousseau, Wordsworth, and John Dewey. The idea that skills as artificial and difficult as reading, writing, and arithmetic can be made natural for everyone is an illusion that has been able to flourish in the peaceful, prosperous United States. John Keats once observed that Romantic pantheism could only thrive in places like the English Lake District, but not in Tierra del Fuego. When John Dewey was writing during the optimistic decades of the early twentieth century, he had been influenced by the Romantic philosopher G.W. Hegel, who believed that the forward-moving processes of culture were extensions of the processes of nature. The more skeptical Classical view was memorably enunciated by the "old codger" Max Rafferty, former California superintendent of education, in speaking about the Progressive school in *Summerhill: For and Against*:

> Rousseau spawned a frenetic theory of education which after two centuries of spasmodic laboring brought forth ... Summerhill.... The child is a Noble Savage, needing only to be let alone in order to insure his intellectual salvation. Don't inhibit him. Never cross him, lest he develop horrible neuroses in later life. . . . just leave the kids alone.

They'll educate themselves. Twaddle. Schooling is not a natural process at all. It's highly artificial. No boy in his right mind ever wanted to study multiplication tables and historical dates when he could be out hunting rabbits or climbing trees. In the days when hunting and climbing contributed to the survival of homo sapiens there was some sense in letting the kids do what comes naturally, but when man's future began to hang upon the systematic mastery of orderly subject matter, the primordial, happy-go-lucky, laissez faire kind of learning had to go. . . . The story of mankind is the rise of specialization with its highly artificial concomitants. . . . When writing was invented, "natural" education went down the drain of history. From then on, children were destined to learn artificially. . . . This is civilization—the name of the game. . . . All civilization is artificial.

The Romantic versus Classic debate extends beyond the reading and math wars to the domain of moral education, and it would be myopic not to mention that aspect of the debate, since for most of human history ethical education has been considered more important than numeracy and literacy. The Romantic tradition holds that morality (like everything else) comes naturally. The child, by being immersed in real-life situations and exposed to good role models, comes to understand the need for sharing, kindness, honesty, diligence, loyalty, courage, and other virtues. Wordsworth's account of his own education, in *The Prelude,* which he subtitled "The Growth (n.b) of a Poet's Mind," contained a section entitled the "Love of Nature Leading to Love of Man." Ethical understanding is gained by an inevitable natural progress, such as Hegel portrayed.

The Romantic wishes to encourage the basic goodness of the natural soul, unspoiled by habit, custom, and convention. The principal means for such encouragement is to develop the child's creativity and imagination—two words that gained currency in the Romantic movement. Before the Romantics, it was considered impious to use the term *creativity* for human productions, but that ceased to be the case when the human soul was conceived as inherently godly. Moral education and the development of creativity and imagination were felt to go hand in hand. The gradual dominance of this new vision of moral education can be traced in the history of American language arts curriculum. In the nineteenth and early twentieth century, schoolbooks like the McGuffey Readers strongly emphasized moral instruction and factual knowledge. Gradually, the subject matter of language arts in the early grades began to focus on fairy tales and poetry. The imparting of explicit moral instruction gave way to the development of creativity and imagination. Imagination, Samuel Coleridge said in his *Biographia Literaria*, "brings the whole soul of man into activity." When we exercise our imaginations, we connect with our divine nature, develop our moral sensibilities.

It must be obvious from the tenor of my brief account of progressive education, as being based on religious faith in nature, that I believe it to be a thoroughly misplaced faith. We will begin to see widespread improvement in our public education only when we see widespread doubt cast on its endemic Romanticism. Everyone grants that schooling must start off from what is natural. But schooling cannot effectively stay mired there. A new educational era will dawn only when the word *natural*, as applied to schooling, is viewed with greater skepticism, and when the word *artificial* ceases to imply only disapproval. One does not have to be a confirmed Classicist to perform this transvaluation of values; one need only be a confirmed pragmatist, devoted to what works. With as great a certainty as these things can be known, we know that analytical and explicit instruction works better for most learning than inductive, implicit instruction. To be analytical and explicit in instruction is to be artificial. Also, it is to be skeptical that children will naturally construct for themselves either knowledge or goodness.

To conclude, one cannot hope to argue against a religious faith that is impervious to refutation. But there can be hope for change when that religious faith is secular and pertains to the world itself. When the early Romantics lived long enough to experience the disappointments of life, they abandoned their Romanticism. This happened to Blake, Wordsworth, and Coleridge.

One of Wordsworth's most moving works was the late poem, "Elegiac Stanzas," which bade farewell to his faith in nature. The other Romantics penned similar farewells to illusion. There is a potential instability in natural supernaturalism. Romantic religion is vulnerable because it is a religion of this world. If one's hopes and faith are pinned on the here and now—on the faith that reading, arithmetic, and morals will develop naturally out of human nature—then that faith may gradually decline when this world continually drips its disappointments.

Moreover, Romantic faith in the providence of nature is inconsistent with our modern understanding of the contingency of all things. Modern evolutionary theory is a hymn to contingency. So is much modern poetry. Robert Frost gives us this little post-Romantic poem called "Design."

I found a dimpled spider, fat and white,
On a white heal-all, holding up a moth
Like a white piece of satin cloth—
Assorted characters of death and blight
Mixed ready to begin the morning right,
Like the ingredients of a witch's broth—
A snow-drop spider, a flower like a froth,
And dead wings carried like a paper kite.

What had that flower to do with being white,
The wayside blue and innocent heal-all?
What brought the kindred spider to that height,
Then steered the white moth thither in the night?
What but design of darkness to appall?
If design govern in a thing so small.

The Romantic thinks nature has a holy plan. The Classicist, the modernist, and the pragmatist do not, and neither does the scientist. In the end, the most pressing questions in the education wars are not for me just empirical, scientific questions, but also ethical ones regarding the unfortunate social consequences of the progressive faith, especially the perpetuation of the test-score gap between groups. Are we to value the aesthetics of diversity and the theology of spilt religion above economic justice and political justice? That is the unasked question that needs to be asked ever more insistently. Economic and political justice are strenuous goals. They cannot be achieved by doing what comes naturally.

CHAPTER THREE

Mathematics Education: The Future and the Past Create a Context for Today's Issues

GAIL BURRILL

Recently a young lady—a third grader who was learn-ing how to multiply in her math class at school—was sitting next to me on an airplane trip. As the stewardess began to serve beverages, she leaned over and asked me, "Is it okay to use technology now?" I assured her it was; she reached down for her backpack and pulled out a small computer, which she booted up and proceeded to use. Careful checking on my part revealed that she was playing a game that had to do with fractions—fitting things together and taking them apart. She was totally engrossed, solving one puzzle after another, moving numbers and figures around with total confidence.

Early this fall I was walking down the hall in a high school and passed the school engineer, who was standing on a ladder that had a computer perched on the stand where I have always put a can of paint. A ceiling tile had been removed, and he had attached the computer to an object in the ceiling. He was checking something that was registering on the screen, inputting data, and interpreting the results. When questioned, he explained that the school's heating and air conditioning systems were computerized, and he was making adjustments—and he referred to the mathematics he needed to understand to carry out the task.

To make sense of the issues surrounding standards and mathematics education today, it seems important to set a context for reflection, a context that is shaped by the nature of mathematics education in the past and its role in the future.

The Future

These two stories point toward a future that is significantly different from the past. The technical demands of the workplace will call for an increasingly sophisticated knowledge of mathematics. The jobs of the next century will involve discrete mathematics, operations research, statistics and data analysis, information processing, and coding. The environment in which students will live will require them to be sophisticated consumers of technology, understanding what it can do. Data indicate that a post-secondary education will be as necessary in the future as a high school education is today. The continued escalation of ways to collect information about nearly everything from shopping habits to medical information to weather patterns will require an understanding of how to organize and interpret such information. For example, according to one market survey, people are more apt to buy on impulse if those items are placed in certain proximity to other items—usually unrelated in any obvious way. Scientists, on the other hand, are collecting data to help them understand how flies can walk on ceilings and why lobsters are not swept off rocks by heavy waves. The ability to simulate complex situations and relationships will yield increasingly more advanced medical treatments, more sophisticated means of travel, and more efficient ways to carry out business and industrial operations. The future will be different. Our students will be shaped by an environment and by experiences we cannot yet imagine, and their way of thinking about mathematics will not be limited by the basic content we learned and the rote fashion in which most of us learned it.

The Past

Although we cannot predict the future, we can reflect on the past and what it might contribute to this future. Over the last hundred years, mathematics education in the United States has been a reflection of the society of the time (Coxford 1970). Who was taught, what was taught, and by whom are by-products of the conditions in which people lived. In the early 1900s the economy was primarily built around farming. Schools were relatively independent local institutions, attended by most students only through the eighth grade, and teachers often had little formal education. Only a few students continued through high school, and fewer yet went on to a university. The curriculum for "all" was only for the primary grades and was shaped by what was considered necessary to be a good citizen and to function as a member of the work force. This meant primarily reading, writing, and arithmetic—skills necessary to carry out correspondence; to sign purchase agreements or legal papers; and to buy and sell produce, groceries, or land. For those who continued their schooling, algebra and geometry were courses with content much like that in many texts today. Trigonometry, analysis, and precalculus were reserved for university study. The advent of the industrial era, with machines and manufacturing, shifted the base of the economy and had a corresponding impact on education. World Wars I and II opened the doors to greater independence for women, who began to push for more education. By the mid-1950s it was a common expectation that most students would finish high school. During that time, high school mathematics consisted of algebra, geometry, and perhaps a second year of algebra and trigonometry. The civil rights movement led to an increased emphasis on the need to offer equal educational opportunities for all students. The advent of technology, the shifting nature of the work force, and changes in society continued to push the need for more education for more people. These changes also signaled the increasing importance of mathematics and science.

Throughout the century there have been continual cries of alarm about the dismal mathematics preparation of students. E. H. Moore, the retiring president of the American Mathematics Society, "called for integrated mathematics and cooperative learning in his 1902 address 'On the Foundations of Mathematics'" (Moore 1967). In 1927 the National Association of Manufacturers claimed that 40 percent of high school graduates were not able to do basic arithmetic.[1] Throughout most of the century, however, the essence of what transpired in mathematics classrooms did not change substantially. In the last thirty years there has been a barrage of approaches to reforming mathematics classrooms. Each was in response to a perceived need, and each was viewed as the magic bullet that made things better.

The School Mathematics Study Group (SMSG) and "new math" came about because a group of mathematicians raised concerns over existing mathematics programs and because the public demanded that we educate

1. Patrick Welsh, "Our Teachers' Ed: Another Week of Hot Air," *Washington Post,* September 5, 1999.

students who could put a man on the moon. We did—and for some students (many of whom are teachers today) the new math of the 1960s worked well. But for others, it did not. As a consequence, we were faced with a "back to the basics" period during which most words were stripped from mathematics texts, and pages of manipulation problems were introduced. We had mastery learning and outcomes-based education and the Madeline Hunter method—all based on someone's good idea. But we saw little positive impact on improving the quality of mathematics education or on students' performance.

In 1989 the National Council of Teachers of Mathematics (NCTM), responding to a series of national reports on the inadequate mathematics preparation of students, released the *Curriculum and Evaluation Standards for School Mathematics*. This document was followed by the *Professional Teaching Standards* in 1991 and the *Assessment Standards for School Mathematics* in 1995.[2] These documents, produced by NCTM and intended for the mathematics community to provide guidance for teachers and educators in their efforts to improve the teaching and learning of mathematics, formed a foundation for change in mathematics curriculum, teaching, and assessment. The standards called for a shift in content from learning only skills and procedures to being able to use mathematical knowledge to solve problems, a shift in teaching from disseminating information to enabling students to learn using student thinking as the platform, and a shift in assessment from an end-of-unit test to using the results of assessment to inform the teaching and learning process. They are characterized by their emphasis on improving mathematics education for *all* students, building on student thinking to inform instruction, and utilizing assessments that measure what students know—not what they do not. In support of the standards, new curricular materials were developed that attempted to reconcile developing conceptual understanding with building skills; used concrete materials and contextual situations to motivate students, as well as provide scaffolding for understanding; integrated content strands as is done in other countries; and configured the curricu-

2. It is perhaps important to note that the NCTM is a professional organization whose work is conceived and carried out by committees and task forces consisting of volunteers from the ranks of classroom teachers, mathematics educators, mathematics supervisors, and mathematics education researchers, as well as some mathematicians and administrators. The NCTM headquarters facilitates the work of the volunteers and is primarily staffed by those not from the field.

lum in different ways with different emphases at different points in the educational sequence.

Mathematics Education Today

The current status of mathematics education has many faces. Classes across the United States are more diverse than at any other time during this century, with students from multiple cultural and economic backgrounds. More students than ever before are enrolled in mathematics programs at the high school level. More than 70 percent of all students continue on to higher education. One consequence is that far too many students are in remedial education courses at the college level, although this number has actually been decreasing in university mathematics in recent years (Loftsgaarden, Rung, and Watkins 1997). University mathematics classes, once reserved only for those who were interested in studying mathematics and science, are now filled with students who, in the past, would not have been in school at all. Others, who would once have avoided mathematics in favor of social science or the humanities, now need a mathematics or statistics course as a prerequisite for their preferred field. Technology is in education as well as in the world—in the form of distance learning, computer-assisted instruction, computer labs for word processing, and computers and calculators in mathematics classrooms.

Current achievement data indicate that students are improving. The National Assessment of Educational Progress (NAEP) trend scores show that students are significantly better in computation than they were in 1971 (Reese et al. 1997). The data also show, however, that student knowledge is fragile; when asked to use mathematical skills in performance tasks, to solve multistep problems, or to explain their reasoning, U.S. students do not do well. For example, only 8 percent of eighth graders correctly solved a multistep problem involving distance, miles per gallon, and fractional parts (Wearne and Kouba 1999).

Today we are clearly at the point where a high-quality mathematics education is recognized as the right of all students (NCTM 1998). Most high schools require three years of mathematics, and nearly 10 percent of eligible students take advanced placement calculus in high school. The curriculum has changed; modeling, statistics and probability, and discrete mathematics are part of the mathematics program, although in many instances these programs are given little more than lip service.

The relics of the past are still with us. The curricular materials most commonly used have become large volumes that contain nearly everything remotely linked to the topic. Consider, for instance, that a typical first-year algebra book contains lessons (probably 200 of them) on percents, decimals, integer operations, the Pythagorean theorem, and coordinate graphing, as well as topics traditionally associated with beginning algebra. The materials have an "opener" (a Madeline Hunter technique to enable teachers to take roll and do management tasks while keeping students busy), illustrate the lesson theme with three examples that use exact technical language and notation (a legacy of modern math), provide an abundance of drill exercises on the lesson (back to the basics), contain some problems that are words around numbers (problem solving), and one or two problems at most that focus on developing the mathematical concept. Teachers are left with trying to make sense of their task. Should they cover all the text or create their own version of what the subject really is about? What will the state assess and how can they include that in their lessons? How can mathematical content that was once taught only to those who were identified as having the math gene be successfully taught to everyone?

NCTM embarked on a project to clarify and update the standards documents. Three years were spent seeking input and posing questions for the mathematics community to capture the thinking of the field for the updated *Principles and Standards for School Mathematics,* released in April 2000. Two significant differences between the *Principles and Standards for School Mathematics* and the previous NCTM standards are the addition of a set of principles that form a context for thinking about teaching and learning mathematics and the effort to identify key mathematical ideas in each content strand, with illustrations on how these should grow and develop throughout each grade band.

Mathematics education has become a public domain. The attempts to bring change, initially ignored by most outside of classrooms, have become enmeshed in criticism from a variety of areas. Part of the concern is natural in any change process, as people question assumptions that differ from those with which they are familiar. Part is due to the natural desire of some to preserve what worked for them. But some of the dissension has gone beyond any expected discomfort with change. (A note worth considering here is that the changes and issues are not unique to mathematics education but are often couched in language and outcomes that can be found across disciplines and in relation to education in general.)

Issues

Many of the issues raised are issues of value or belief. A large segment of the population, including some teachers, believes that the curriculum and instruction of the past should be continued in the future. This belief has merit for those who achieved under that system. It does not, however, recognize that the future will be vastly different, with demands for a knowledge of different mathematics—mathematics that did not even exist in the school curriculum in the past. (I recently heard an eighth grader give a clear explanation of fuzzy logic and why it made sense as a way to analyze social and economic problems that cannot be coded on, off or yes, no.) When things do not go the way they are expected to go, the tendency is to blame the students, teachers, or poor texts—blame without responsibility. This belief does not recognize that the old system, which was perhaps not inappropriate for the society in which it existed, did not serve *all* students equally well. Although some learned, a large segment of the population did not, as evidenced by the plethora of jokes at the expense of mathematics and the continuing reluctance of the majority of the public to become comfortable with mathematical ideas. Hiebert (1999, 13) claims that "presuming traditional approaches have proven to be successful is ignoring the largest database we have. The evidence indicates that the traditional curriculum and instructional methods in the United States are not serving our students well." Without changes, we will continue to disenfranchise a large portion of the population. We cannot afford to do that.

To that end, I'd like to identify some of the myths that have plagued mathematics education and to offer some background and research that support the need to change the teaching of mathematics so that more of our nation's students are offered equitable opportunities to study higher levels of mathematics.

Myth: Learning mathematics is linear, and facts and skills must be learned before problem solving.

There is little evidence supporting the belief that mathematics can only be learned in a well-ordered linear structure. Clear evidence exists, however, that some students solve challenging mathematical problems without having demonstrated highly proficient arithmetic skills. Evidence has shown that stand-alone examples and repetitious practice do little to promote understanding of mathematical concepts and that drill does little to effect learning and transfer of learning to other areas (Suydam and Dessart 1980; Resnick and Ford 1981; Farrell and Farmer 1988). The issue of basic skills and conceptual development is not whether one should come before the other and to what degree, but how to juxtapose the two so that students can learn mathematics in ways that promote understanding and enable them to use what they know to solve problems. There is also evidence that some styles of teaching do not work for all students. "Traditionally, mathematics has been taught by using an expository method in a linear, rigorous, analytical manner . . . that addresses the reasoning style of the analytic, field-independent learner" (Malloy and Malloy 1998). Although this may work well for some students, it excludes a vast majority of our student population.

Clear evidence has shown that some people learn better visually, while others do so abstractly. Evidence also indicates that students learn when they are motivated to do so—challenging problems, often applications-based, can engage students in thinking deeply about mathematics. There is evidence that concrete images of mathematical concepts provide a touchstone that grounds students' understanding as their knowledge continues to evolve. Historically, geometry came first, then algebra; now it is usually taught the other way around at the high school level. The United States is one of the few nations that does not teach integrated mathematics.

Misconceptions abound. Because we have organized a learning experience in the most efficient and obvious way for us, many believe that this same organization will make sense to others. All children do not operate intellectually in the same way. Children do not accept the fact that fire is hot, nor do they understand the consequences of their actions—they need to experience the situation for themselves to understand. In fact, mathematicians do not develop what they do and how they come to understand in a nice logical sequence—this comes after the problem has been worked out and false starts explored and discarded.

Myth: Calculators are harmful and interfere with learning basic skills.

I recently heard a mathematician proclaim that there is no evidence that calculators did not harm students or that they helped students learn mathematics. His reasoning was based on the fact that he and his peers had learned mathematics without calculators, so such aids were clearly unnecessary. Focusing on calculators misses the point. The issue is not whether calculators are dangerous but rather what are the tools we can use to help students learn the mathematics they will need to know, particularly in the context of all students and different mathematics. Calculators allow students access to understanding mathematics using new and different strategies. They allow all students to do more challenging mathematics earlier than was previously possible; they provide the opportunity for students to investigate and explore in new ways; and they are necessary to do some of the new mathematics that students will need for a different world. Calculators allow students in elementary grades to explore and investigate mathematics they could not previously do (for example, to investigate the difference between patterns where the rate of change is constant and patterns where the rate of change is not, laying the foundation for the study of linear and exponential growth). They allow elementary students to investigate operations and their relation to each other—to explore the opposite of squaring and cubing, to use spreadsheets to develop an understanding of variables and expressions, and to gain proficiencies in using formulas before they encounter them in a more formal way. Calculators allow students in high school to explore force fields, to model phenomena and investigate the consequences of their model, to relate graphic representations to algebraic ones, and to observe what each representation has to offer. They allow students to study statistics and discrete mathematics and to simulate probabilities rather than memorize definitions.

There are many red herrings in the discussion of calculator use: calculators are crutches that will prevent students from learning basic skills, students use calculators to do foolish things (as if students never did foolish things with pencil and paper!), and students use calculators to do math they should do in their head (and it is not clear who decides who can do what in whose head). The reality is that calculator and computer technology has changed the way that students carry out the arithmetic and algebraic calculations that used to dominate school mathematics. This is true even in the domain of mathematics itself. A respected mathematician recently indicated that computer and calculation technology has caused a ground shift in approaches and thinking in his field.

Myth: Standards should specify content but not process.

The word *standard* has different meanings in different contexts. The NCTM standards documents (1989, 1991, 1995, 2001) do not define performance levels, nor do they prescribe policy. They are guidelines for curriculum, teaching, and assessment and, as such, make statements about good teaching as well as high-quality mathematics content. If standards only specify content and not the process of instruction, they have not given teachers the context in which to make the content real. There is an intrinsic connection between process and product. It is possible to have good products from poor processes—but such processes have limited success.

Many are imperfect and unformed, and the cost is great. A system of education that does not address process is much like a manufacturing system that makes large quantities of toasters and throws out those that malfunction. The entire field of quality control is based on finding ways to measure and improve the system and maximize the process of generating a product or an outcome. The challenges of knowing how to reach a goal in ways that are effective and efficient in fact constitute a field of study for many areas, such as those in operations research, medicine, and system efficiency.

We know something about how students learn. If teachers are provided with this knowledge, they can design lessons that capitalize on what we know. "There is no doubt that educational practice can be strengthened by careful scientific research" (NRC 1999a, 2). *Improving Student Learning* (NRC 1999a), which is about learning in general and not specific to mathematics, makes strong statements about the importance of the process of teaching in learning. The report indicates that the new science of learning (NRC 1999b) suggests significantly different approaches to pedagogy and instruction. "Teachers need to make time to hear their students' ideas and questions. . . . They need to be prepared to assess children's thinking abilities, to decide when to make connections between existing knowledge and school learning and when to help the child overcome misconceptions or naïve understandings" (NRC 1999a, 25). The NRC report characterizes classroom teaching as not paying enough attention to critical thinking and conceptual understanding by focusing too heavily on memorization of information. It goes on to say that "students who learn to solve problems by following formulas, for example, often are unable to use their skills in new situations" (Redish 1996).

Other countries pay more attention to the process of teaching than the United States does. According to data from Third International Mathematics and Science Study (TIMSS) (NCES 1996) and other studies, Japanese lessons are carefully crafted; a large part of the teacher's day involves working with colleagues to refine lessons and thinking about how to structure the activities, what tasks to give, what questions to pose, and how to collect and use student thinking to build a community for learning (Stigler and Hiebert 1997). Realistic mathematics has become the curriculum in the Netherlands through a careful research and development process that takes into account what the developers learned about how students learn mathematics (de Lange 1990).

None of this indicates that one style of teaching is best or that all instruction should be done in cooperative groups or that all instruction should be lecture. It does suggest, however, that there is much to learn about the process of teaching and implies it is unlikely that teachers will come to this knowledge on their own.

Assessment

Another fundamental issue is how success is measured. What counts as successful mathematics teaching and learning? How do we know when we have made a difference? What do we want to have as successful outcomes—students who can do mathematics, who do not fear mathematics, who recognize its power and utility, or who understand the struggle and are willing to take risks? The answers are based on values and beliefs. If you value computation, you measure success by how well students can compute. If you value problem solving, you measure success by how well students can solve problems. As long as the public and those establishing the measures of success have different values, there will be little agreement on where we are, where we need to go, and what success we will have. The challenge is to find some common ground.

Currently, high-stakes tests of student achievement are seen as the ultimate measure of success, yet for many schools, teachers, and students, this is a recipe for disaster. The outcome is sorting, and in many cases a high-stakes assessment is not necessary to know who will be at the bottom of the list. Nowhere in the literature is there support for the practice that telling someone they are bad will make them strive to be better. High-stakes testing is problematic for many reasons, including the fact that what is high-stakes for adults may not be at all important for students. The alignment of standards and assessment is limited (Schmidt 1999); teachers shape their curriculum around the tests, often at the direction of the administration. "The evidence is clear that reliance on norm-referenced tests of basic skills encourages schools and teachers to narrow the curriculum to the material tested and to spend undue time teaching test-taking skills or low level basic skills rather than challenging content" (NRC 1999c p. 24). "Children are tested to the point of absurdity in the name of accountability. . . . The more schools commit themselves to improving performance on these [standardized tests], the more meaningful opportunities to learn are sacrificed. Thus the drive for high scores is tantamount to lowering standards—a paradox rarely appreciated by those who make, or report on, education policy."[3] Classrooms across the nation are conducted under a rubric such as, "When you see this on the test . . ." or "Remember, if you see total, it means add." If the tests contained good tasks that measured what children know, it might be different. Currently there is far too little attention paid to the nature of tests and the nature of the items to place any reliability on the results as evidence of students' mathematical understanding. In *Keeping Score,* Shannon (1999) recounts the enormous effect on success that changing the context or wording of a task can have.

The standards argue for multiple measures of what students understand. It has been stated repeatedly that one single test cannot serve all purposes—guiding instruction; monitoring student, school, and district performance; and holding schools accountable. Relying on one measure increases the opportunity for bias to be part of the judgment process and opens the door to errors that have far-reaching consequences (such as the error that occurred in scoring the tests for New York City students that resulted in incorrect scores for many students, which kept them from moving to the next grade). To be effective, assessment should involve a range of strategies appropriate for inferences relevant to each kind of assessment: individual students, classrooms, schools, districts, and states. I would submit, in addition to testing to determine what students know and can do and where schools are in helping their students achieve, that we pay attention to other measures. For example, schools might offer as evidence of successful programs answers to the following questions:

—How many students take advanced mathematics courses and why— because they enjoy math and see it as useful or because they are forced to do so to satisfy a college or graduation requirement?

—What are student attitudes toward mathematics (that, in fact, is one of the few areas in which students in the United States scored high in TIMSS—they like mathematics).

—What kind of opportunities for individual growth exist in the school system—are there provisions for helping those who are struggling and challenges for those who excel? Math clubs, teams, competitions, student tutors?

Positive answers to these questions are signs of a healthy and vibrant mathematics curriculum and should be considered as part of the measure of success as well as achievement scores on tests.

3. Alfie Kohn, "Getting Back to the Basics," *Washington Post,* October 10, 1999.

Implementation

Ferrini-Mundy and Schram (1997) portray the problems inherent in describing standards-based classrooms and attribute some of the tension to confusion between implementation and interpretation. Issues of implementation driven by interpretation have rightly caused concern. In some cases, there has been a focus on the "trappings of reform"—cooperative groups, manipulatives, hands-on activities—with little attention to mathematics as the focus of instruction. Ferrini-Mundy offers that superficial implementation may, in fact, be shallow by necessity as an initial step in changing practice (Ferrini-Mundy and Schram 1997, 9). Driving reform with slogans and mandates—such as "teacher as a guide," "textbooks are bad," "all mathematics should be driven by applications"—has unfortunate consequences if carried out literally and demonstrates the fragile link between implementation and interpretation. Unfortunately some of these misled interpretations have fueled the dissension (Wu 1998).

Teacher preparation is another implementation issue. Although there are many teachers who excel and who have the necessary knowledge of content and pedagogy, many others have not been prepared to implement change—to understand and teach new content, to manage classroom discourse, and to make connections that are meaningful. These teachers do not usually have the long-term support that is essential to figuring out what they should be doing differently, and many have no idea what change should look like in their classrooms. We are learning about successful professional development practice (Cohen and Hill 1998); we need to learn more and to use what we learn to help teachers grow as professionals.

Research

There are other issues. Research can and should be a useful tool in helping us understand what students are learning, how effective new programs are, the current state of mathematics education (Hiebert 1999), and how students learn. Research, however, is not based on anecdotes or personal stories as is often the case in today's media. In Hiebert's view, the absence of data leads to the pendulum swings that characterize mathematics education in the United States. However, research findings are not always related to practice, and, often, research has not focused on the problems of the field. Currently, research has been primarily qualitative—leaving many uncomfortable with the nature of the evidence that stems from observations, conclusions based on small samples, and the researcher's interpretation of individual student behavior. Unless both quantitative and qualitative methods are applied, the findings will be questioned. It would seem that we need three things to make research a more fundamental element in the change process. First, we need a concerted effort on the part of mathematics education researchers to identify and address critical questions that will help the field move forward and connect to practice. The current state seems to an outsider almost random, where each researcher focuses on a piece (often a very small piece) and no one is looking for a coherent whole (contrary to medical research, for example, where there is a clear commitment to look at the pieces that make up the knowledge around a given disease). Second, we should reaffirm the importance of quantitative research as a valuable first step where observations and conclusions can then be informed and enlightened by qualitative research. Third, we should find effective methods to make this knowledge available to teachers in ways that will help them understand how to use it to change what happens in their classrooms.

Some General Recommendations

We need teachers who are better prepared with the knowledge of mathematics and how to teach mathematics. But to improve the system, teacher preparation programs also have to produce teachers who understand the shifting landscape, and practicing teachers need support to understand change and to sustain it.

We need to resolve the conflicting messages we are sending to students, teachers, and the public. Some of the inconsistencies between the rhetoric and practice include:

—mandating rigorous mathematics for all students, including algebra and geometry, but tests that focus primarily on computational skills and procedures

—requiring all students to take three years of mathematics, including algebra and geometry, but giving tests that are required for high school graduation to students in the eighth grade

—devising high standards for all students, but large-scale tests that discriminate against segments of the population

—raising standards and requirements for teachers, but allowing alternative paths to teaching that ignore these requirements

—pronouncing the importance of mathematics and science as critical skills, but directing most funding resources and time to reading

—valuing problem solving and understanding, but giving multiple choice tests.

There is a real risk that uncontrolled criticism and arbitrary assessment will set us back. Fey (1999) points out that critics often suggest only two alternatives—radical reform or going back to traditional programs. They ignore the fact that the standards and subsequent curricular shifts are motivated by concern about the inadequate effects of the long-standing traditions in curriculum, teaching, and testing. Then, before any proposals can be adequately developed and tested, reaction sets in and the innovation is abandoned because the critics are in haste to make sure we have not erred. Change takes time; somehow we must make sure the system has the time it needs to ground the changes in practice, to evaluate the results, and to modify the programs accordingly.

At this point, all parties agree that mathematics education can be improved. All other fields of endeavor operate on that premise—medicine, weather forecasting, manufacturing, and even ventilating systems. The question then becomes: Who is responsible for defining change? Should it be the mathematicians who know the subject? Should it be the teachers who know how to teach the subject? Should it be the researchers who have studied the problem? Should it be those who actually use mathematics?

Relics of the past are still with us. The challenge is to sort out what students will need to be prepared for the future—a future that will make greater and different demands on all students and one that should set the context for teaching and learning mathematics today. This is an opportunity for those across the community to jointly consider the issues. But it must be done in positive and respectful ways, where the contributions of all are recognized and the discussion is grounded in more than anecdotal evidence. It is not helpful to concentrate on pointing out errors and broadcasting them across the nation. Picking on individuals or organizations as the culprit for perceived ills deflects the purpose and wastes everyone's time. The issue is about students—all students and how to get them to learn the mathematics that is important to their future and to ours. It is not the way it was, and we cannot be the way we were. Constructive criticism and serious consideration of the issues will help us make the changes that will make a difference to our students.

References

Cohen, David K., and Heather Hill. 1998. *Instructional Policy and Classroom Performance: The Mathematics Reform in California.* University of Michigan.

Coxford, Art. 1970. "A History of Mathematics Education in the United States and Canada." *Thirty Second Yearbook of the National Council of Teachers of Mathematics.* Reston, Va.: National Council of Teachers of Mathematics.

de Lange, Jan. 1990. *Insights into Learning.* Utrecht, The Netherlands: Freudenthal Institute.

Farrell, Margaret A., and Walter A. Farmer. 1988. *Secondary Mathematics Instruction: An Integrated Approach.* Providence, R.I.: Janson Publications.

Fey, James. 1999. *Standards under Fire: Issues and Options in the Math Wars.* Summary of keynote session, Show-Me Project Curriculum Showcase. St. Louis, Mo.

Ferrini-Mundy, Joan, and Thomas Schram, eds. 1997. *The Recognizing and Recording Reform in Mathematics Education Project: Insights, Issues, and Implications.* Monograph No. 8, *Journal for Research in Mathematics Education.* Reston, Va.: National Council of Teachers of Mathematics.

Hiebert, James. 1999. "Relationship between Research and the NCTM Standards." *Journal for Research in Mathematics Education* 30 (1): 3–19.

Loftsgaarden, Don O., Donald C. Rung, and Ann E. Watkins. 1997. *Statistical Abstract of Undergraduate Programs in the Mathematical Sciences in the United States.* Washington: Conference Board on Mathematical Sciences.

Malloy, Carol E., and William W. Malloy. 1998. "Issues of Culture in Mathematics Teaching and Learning." *Urban Review* 30 (3): 245–57.

Moore, Eliakim Hastings. 1967. "On the Foundations of Mathematics." *Mathematics Teacher* 60 (April): 360–74. A reprinting of the 1902 address, first published in 1902 in *Science* and later included in a "General Survey of Progress in the Last Twenty-Five Years," *First Yearbook of the National Council of Teachers of Mathematics,* 1926. Reston, Va.: National Council of Teachers of Mathematics.

National Center for Educational Statistics (NCES). 1996. *Pursuing Excellence.* Government Printing Office.

National Council of Teachers of Mathematics (NCTM). 1989. *Curriculum and Evaluation Standards for School Mathematics.*

———. 1991. *Professional Standards for Teaching Mathematics.* Reston, Va.

———. 1995. *Assessment Standards for School Mathematics.* Reston, Va.

———. 1998. *Beliefs Statement.* Reston, Va.

———. 2000. *Principles and Standards for School Mathematics.* Reston, Va.

National Research Council (NRC). 1999a. *Improving Student Learning.* Committee on a Feasibility Study for a Strategic Education Research Program, Commission on Behavioral and Social Sciences and Education. Washington: National Academy Press.

———. 1999b. *How People Learn: Brain, Mind, Experience, and School.* Committee on Developments in the Science of Learning, Commission on Behavioral and Social Sciences and Education. J. Bransford, A. Brown, and R. Cocking, eds. Washington: National Academy Press.

———. 1999c. *Testing, Teaching, and Learning. A Guide for States and School Districts.* Committee on Title I Testing and Assessment, Board on Testing and Assessment. Washington: National Academy Press.

Redish, E. F. 1996. *Discipline-Specific Science Education and Educational Research: The Case of Physics.* Paper prepared for the Committee on Developments in the Science of Learning, for The Sciences of Science Learning: An Interdisciplinary Discussion. Department of Physics and Astronomy, University of Maryland.

Reese, C. M., K. E. Miller, J. Mazzeo, and J. A. Dossey. 1997. *NAEP 1996 Mathematics Report Card for the Nation and the States.* Washington: National Center for Education Statistics.

Resnick, Lauren B., and Wendy W. Ford. 1981. *The Psychology of Mathematics for Instruction.* Hillsdale, N.J.: Lawrence Erlbaum.

Schmidt, William. 1999. "Internal Report on Alignment of State Standards and Assessment." Washington: Achieve.

Shannon, Ann. 1999. *Keeping Score.* Washington: National Academy Press.

Stiff, Lee V. 1990. "African-American Students and the Promise of the Curriculum and Evaluation Standards." In *Teaching and Learning Mathematics in 1990's: 1990 Yearbook of the National Council of Teachers of Mathematics,* edited by Thomas J. Cooney, 152–58. Reston, Va.: National Council of Teachers of Mathematics.

Stigler, J. W., and J. Hiebert. 1997. "Understanding and Improving Classroom Mathematics Instruction: An Overview of the TIMSS Video Study." *Phi Delta Kappan* 79 (1): 14–21.

Suydam, Marilyn N., and Donald J. Dessart. 1980. "Skill Learning." In *Research in Mathematics Education,* edited by Richard J. Shumway, 207–43. Reston, Va.: National Council of Teachers of Mathematics.

Wearne, D., and V. L. Kouba. 1999. "Rational Numbers." In *Results from the Seventh Mathematics Assessment of the National Assessment of Educational Progress,* edited by E. A. Silver and P. A. Kenney, pp. 163–92. Reston, Va.: National Council of Teachers of Mathematics.

Wu, H. March 2, 1998. "Some Observations on the 1997 Battle of the Two Standards in the California Math War." Expanded version of a colloquium lecture at California State University, Sacramento, February 12, 1998. Department of Mathematics, University of California.

CHAPTER FOUR

Research and Reform in Mathematics Education

MICHAEL T. BATTISTA

The movement to reform school mathematics in the United States began in the mid–1980s in response to the documented failure of traditional mathematics teaching, to curriculum changes necessitated by the widespread availability of electronic computing devices, and to substantial progress in the scientific study of mathematics learning. Guiding the reform are recommendations given in the *Curriculum and Evaluation Standards for School Mathematics* (1989) and subsequent "standards" documents developed by the National Council of Teachers of Mathematics (NCTM). These recommendations call for fundamental changes in how mathematics is taught, in the content of school mathematics, and in how mathematics learning is conceptualized.

In this chapter issues relevant to the reform of mathematics education in the United States are analyzed from the perspective of current scientific research on how students learn mathematics. Of course, research alone cannot specify mathematics curricula; much of what is taught is determined by the goals decided upon by various stakeholders in the educational system. Nevertheless, research can reveal what goals are achievable, which students are attaining goals, how various goals can be achieved, and how different factors affect goal attainment. My position is that sound educational practice must be guided by appropriate scientific research (Battista 1999a).

Traditional versus Reform Teaching

In traditional mathematics instruction—which is still overwhelmingly predominate in American schools (Hiebert 1999)—the major theme is for teachers to demonstrate, and students to practice, formal symbolic procedures. Indeed, according to the Third International Mathematics and Science Study (TIMSS), for close to 80 percent of the topics covered in eighth-grade American mathematics classes, teachers merely demonstrated or stated procedures, not explained or developed them, and 90 percent of students' seatwork involved practicing procedures that had already been demonstrated (Hiebert 1999). Furthermore, this theme is played out in an almost universal script. Every day the first thing that happens in the instructional routine is that answers are given for the previous day's homework. Next, the teacher gives a brief description of new material, then assigns exercises to be completed for homework. The remainder of the period is devoted to students working independently on these exercises while the teacher circulates around the room answering students' questions.

In contrast, the focus in the classroom environments envisioned by NCTM is on inquiry, sense making, and problem solving (1989). In such classrooms, teachers provide students with numerous opportunities to solve complex and interesting problems; to read, represent, discuss, and communicate mathematics; and to formulate and test the validity of personally constructed mathematical ideas. Students use demonstrations, drawings, and physical objects—as well as formal mathematical and logical arguments—to convince themselves and their peers of the validity of their problem solutions. In reform classrooms, students develop competency not only with appropriate computation skills but with mathematical reasoning and application.

Traditional versus Reform Mathematics Content

The mathematics covered in current traditional mathematics classrooms is almost identical to what most adults were taught when they were children (for example, Hiebert 1999). Students spend most of their time attempting to learn traditional computational procedures—things that can be done on most calculators. This is consistent with the historical goal of teaching paper-and-pencil computation to the masses (Resnick 1987), a reasonable approach given that there was no other practical way to complete such computations.

The situation has changed dramatically over the last two decades, however. Advancing technology has eliminated the need for a tight focus on paper-and-pencil computational skill. As a result, a major thrust of the reform movement is replacing the current mathematics-as-computation curriculum with a curriculum that genuinely embraces conceptual understanding, reasoning, and problem solving as fundamental goals of instruction. The reform movement calls for the abandonment of curricula that promote thinking about "mathematics as a rigid system of externally dictated rules governed by standards of accuracy, speed, and memory. . . . A mathematics curriculum that emphasizes computation and rules is like a writing curriculum that emphasizes grammar and spelling; both put the cart before the horse. There is no place in a proper curriculum for mindless mimicry mathematics" (National Research Council 1989, 44). Indeed, one of the most critical aspects of reform is seeing mathematics differently than it has been viewed in the past. As the chairperson of the commission that wrote the NCTM standards has stated, "The single most compelling issue in improving school mathematics is to change the epistemology of mathematics in schools, the sense on the part of teachers and students of what the mathematical enterprise is all about" (Romberg 1992, 433).

To illustrate the difference between traditional and reform goals for school mathematics, consider the problem: "What is $2\frac{1}{2}$ divided by $\frac{1}{4}$?" Traditionally taught students are trained to solve such problems by using the "invert and multiply" method (which students memorize, quickly forget, and almost never understand): $2\frac{1}{2} \div \frac{1}{4} = \frac{5}{2} \times \frac{4}{1}$. The focus on computation skill is so narrow that those students who are lucky enough to be able to compute an answer rarely can explain or demonstrate why the answer is correct (other than saying something like, "My teacher said we are supposed to invert and multiply"). Even worse, students rarely know when the computation should be applied (for example, Kouba, Zawojewski, and Strutchens 1997; Ma 1999).

In contrast, students who have made sense of fractions and the operation of division do not need a symbolic algorithm to compute an answer to this problem. Because they interpret the symbolic statement in terms of appropriate mental models of quantities, they are quickly able to reason that, since there are 4 fourths in each unit and 2 fourths in a half, there are 10 fourths in $2\frac{1}{2}$. Younger students might draw a picture to support such reasoning. (See figure 4-1.)

Figure 4-1. *Drawing for 2¹/₂ divided by ¹/₄*

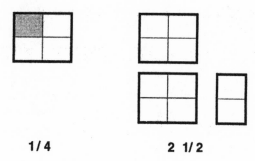

1 / 4   **2 1/ 2**

Students who truly make sense of this situation are not manipulating symbols, oblivious to what they represent; they are purposefully and meaningfully reasoning about quantities. They are not blindly following rules invented by others; they are making personal sense of ideas. These students have developed powerful conceptual structures and reasoning patterns that enable them to apply their mathematical knowledge to numerous real-world situations, giving them intellectual autonomy in their mathematical reasoning.

The picture of mathematics that traditionally taught students develop is a mere caricature of genuine mathematical activity. Mathematics is first and foremost a form of reasoning. In the context of analytically reasoning about particular types of quantitative and spatial phenomena, mathematics consists of thinking in a logical manner; formulating and testing conjectures; making sense of things; and forming as well as justifying propositions, inferences, and conclusions. We do mathematics when we recognize and describe patterns; construct conceptual models of phenomena; create and use symbol systems to help us represent, manipulate, and reflect on ideas; and invent procedures to solve problems.

The view of mathematics that emerges in reform classrooms is similar to how many mathematicians describe the process of *doing* mathematics, as opposed to how the results of mathematical activity are formally recorded in books and journals. For instance, mathematician Saunders MacLane states: "Mathematics starts from a variety of human activities, disentangles from them a number of notions which are generic and not arbitrary, then formalizes these notions and their manifold interrelations" (as quoted in Pinker 1997, 340). George Polya observes: "Finished mathematics presented in a finished form appears as purely demonstrative. . . .

Yet mathematics in the making resembles any other human knowledge in the making. You have to guess a mathematical theorem before you prove it; you have to have the idea of the proof before you carry through the details. You have to combine observations and follow analogies; you have to try and try again" (as quoted in Hersh 1997, 36). Finally, Reuben Hersh says, "In developing and understanding a [mathematical] subject, axioms come late. Then in the formal presentations, they come early. . . . The view that mathematics is in essence derivations from axioms is backward. In fact, it is wrong. . . . The standard exposition purges mathematics of the personal, the controversial, the tentative, leaving little trace of humanity in the creator or consumer" (1997, 6).

There Is Still a Need for Fluency

Even though reform mathematics curricula have shifted the focus from computation to understanding and personal sense making, it is clearly insufficient to involve students only in sense making, reasoning, and the construction of mathematical knowledge. Sound curricula must have clear long-range goals for assuring that students become *fluent* in utilizing those mathematical concepts, ways of reasoning, and procedures that our culture has found most useful. Students should be able to readily and correctly apply important mathematical strategies, procedures, and lines of reasoning in numerous situations. They should possess knowledge that supports mathematical reasoning. For instance, students should know the "basic number facts" because such knowledge is essential for mental computation, estimation, performance of computational procedures, and problem solving.

Because not all problems can be easily solved using informal or pictorial strategies as in the fraction example described earlier, students must also develop facility in using symbolism to support and extend their mathematical reasoning. For instance, to see how students can be guided from thinking about quantities to symbolic manipulations, consider again division of fractions. A student might produce an answer to the problem $1^3/_4 \div 1/_2$ using the reasoning described earlier by asking, "How many halves in $1^3/_4$?" Alternatively, the student might convert the problem to a form that is easier to think about, $7/_4 \div 2/_4$, asking, "How many pieces of size $2/_4$ are there in a piece of size $7/_4$?" Because each of these "pieces" is now easily seen to be composed of a whole number of parts of the same size (fourths), the student can think in terms of whole numbers—"How many groups of

2 are in 7: $7 \div 2 = 3^{1}/_{2}$?" Even more, this thinking can be encapsulated in a general symbolic algorithm for division of fractions: $^{7}/_{4} \div ^{1}/_{2} = ^{7}/_{4} \div ^{2}/_{4} = 7 \div 2 = 3^{1}/_{2}$.

Thus in addition to conceptual knowledge and reasoning, sound mathematics curricula must develop in students understanding of and facility with symbolic representations and manipulations, and even an appreciation for the workings of axiomatic systems that describe how to deal formally with mathematical symbols. But students' learning of symbolic manipulations must never become disconnected from their reasoning about quantities in contexts that are genuinely meaningful to them. For example, if students believe that dealing with fractions consists of following formal rules that have no quantitative referential meaning, they will use only what they know of these rules to guide and constrain their fraction work (compare with Resnick, Cauzinille-Marmeche, and Mathieu 1987). In contrast, if students see dealing with fractions in terms of manipulations of palpable quantities, they will be able to use the powerful cognitive processes they have developed for reasoning about physical quantities to guide their reasoning about symbolic manipulations of fractions.

When learning is disconnected from personal sense making, most students are overwhelmed in their attempts to memorize countless rules for manipulating symbols by rote. Even more, when students lose sight of what symbol manipulations imply about real-world quantities, doing mathematics becomes an academic ritual that has no real-world usefulness. In fact, to be able to use mathematics to make sense of the world, students must first make sense of mathematics.

Research on How Students Learn Mathematics

Research across the world indicates that mathematics students are not acquiring the necessary knowledge, skills, beliefs, and motivation to successfully deal with new problems and learning tasks (De Corte, Greer, and Verschaffel 1996). The problem is particularly acute in the United States.

Traditional U.S. Mathematics Instruction as Ineffective

Numerous studies have shown that U.S. students' mathematics learning is deficient, especially in the area of problem solving (Mullis et al. 1993; National Center for Education Statistics [NCES] 1996; Hiebert 1999). For instance, results published by the National Assessment of Edu-

cational Progress indicate that only about 13–18 percent of students in
twelfth grade are proficient in mathematics (Mullis et al. 1993; Reese et
al. 1997). Moreover, according to the National Research Council (1989),
60 percent of college mathematics enrollments are in courses ordinarily
taught in high school, 75 percent of Americans stop studying mathematics
before they complete career or job prerequisites, and the business sector
spends as much on remedial mathematics education for employees as is
spent on mathematics education in schools, colleges, and universities combined.

Although most people acknowledge that many students have difficulty
with mathematics, they take solace in the belief that bright students are
doing just fine. This belief is unfounded. A closer look reveals that even
the brightest American students are being dramatically affected by the
mathematics miseducation of traditional curricula. For instance, a bright
eighth grader who was three weeks from completing a standard course in
high school geometry—so she was two years ahead of schedule for college
prep students—responded as follows on the problem shown in figure 4-2
(Battista 1998).

> Student: It's 45 packages. And the way I found it is I multiplied how
> many packages could fit in the height by the number in the width,
> which is 3 times 3 equals 9. Then I took that and multiplied it by
> the length, which is 5, and came up with 9 times 5, which is 45.
> Observer: How do you know that is the right answer?
> Student: Because the equation for the volume of a box is length times
> width times height.
> Observer: Do you know why that equation works?
> Student: Because you are covering all three dimensions, I think. I'm
> not really sure. I just know the equation.

This student did not understand that the mathematical formula she
applied assumed a particularly structured mathematical model of a real-
world situation, one that was inappropriate for the problem at hand. Indeed, research shows that despite its simplicity, genuinely understanding
why the volume formula ($V = l \times w \times h$) works is surprisingly difficult for
students. Although this bright student had learned an impressive amount
of routine mathematical procedures, the above example illustrates that
much of the learning she accomplished in her accelerated mathematics
program was only at the surface level, a finding that is all too common
among bright students. Indeed, only 38 percent of the students in her ge-

Figure 4-2. *Packaging Problem for Bright Eighth Graders*

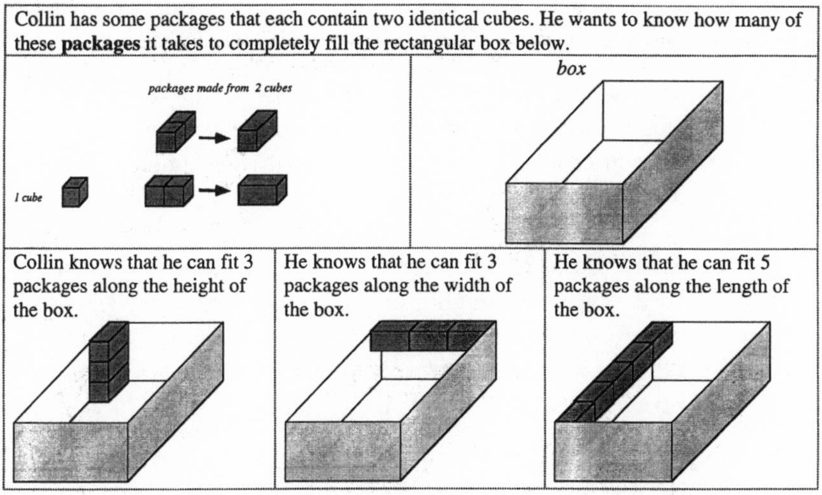

Collin has some packages that each contain two identical cubes. He wants to know how many of these **packages** it takes to completely fill the rectangular box below.

ometry class answered the item correctly, despite the fact that all of them had scored at or above the ninety-fifth percentile in mathematics on a widely used standardized mathematics test in fifth grade, all had already passed the state's ninth-grade proficiency test in mathematics, and the class was taught by a highly regarded teacher. Because such students obviously have the capability to make sense of mathematics if given the chance, the case could be made that these students, more than any others, are being terribly shortchanged by traditional mathematics instruction.

What's Wrong with Traditional Mathematics Instruction?

More important than showing deficiencies in traditional mathematics instruction, research also indicates why traditional teaching is so ineffective. For instance, despite research denoting that learning with understanding produces better "transfer" than learning by memorization (Bransford, Brown, and Cocking 1999; Mayer and Wittrock 1996), traditional instruction places more emphasis on memorization and imitation than on understanding, thinking, and reasoning (De Corte, Greer, and Verschaffel 1996; Greeno, Collins, and Resnick 1996; Silver and Stein 1996). Furthermore, even when traditional instruction attempts to promote understanding, it does so using derivations and justifications that are too formal and abstract for most students to make personal sense of (Battista and Larson 1994; Bransford, Brown, and Cocking 1999). In fact, the National Research Council concluded:

> Research on learning shows that most students cannot learn mathematics effectively by only listening and imitating; yet most teachers teach mathematics just this way. Research in learning shows that students actually construct their own understanding based on new experiences that enlarge the intellectual framework in which ideas can be created. Mathematics becomes useful to a student only when it has been developed through a personal intellectual engagement that creates new understanding. *Much of the failure in school mathematics is due to a tradition of teaching that is inappropriate to the way most students learn.* (1989, 6, italics added)

Research also makes clear that what students learn in mathematics instruction is not restricted to knowledge but extends to beliefs about mathematics and learning mathematics, which, in turn, affect the quality of future learning (De Corte, Greer, and Verschaffel 1996; Hiebert and Carpenter 1992; Nickson 1992). Because traditional instruction focuses so much on fixed symbolic computation procedures, many students come to believe that mathematics is mainly a matter of following rules, that it consists mostly of symbol manipulation, and that the rules and symbols have no connection to their own intuitive ideas about dealing with mathematical situations (De Corte, Greer, and Verschaffel 1996; Hiebert and Carpenter 1992). In fact, students in traditional classrooms have been found to believe that the "mathematical" tasks they engage in have no "real-world" value, but rather are simply what they have to *do* to meet their obligations in the social situation of the classroom (Nickson 1992). Instead of seeing mathematics as a worthwhile intellectual endeavor involving exploration, reflection, and discussion, students see it as a set of procedures to be learned through imitation.

In sum, traditional instruction unintentionally encourages students to believe that doing mathematics consists of following procedures that have little or no relation to personal sense making. This belief, in turn, causes students to focus on imitation rather than sense making and conceptual understanding. An example from Paul Cobb of Vanderbilt University poignantly illustrates this point.

Second-grader Auburn was asked to solve the horizontal sentences $16 + 9 = \_\_$, $28 + 13 = \_\_$, $37 + 24 = \_\_$, and $39 + 53 = \_\_$. For each problem, she counted-on by ones as she sequentially put up fingers. (So, for example, for 16 + 9, she counted 16—17, 18, 19, 20, 21, 22, 23, 24, 25.) Two days later, Auburn was asked to complete a worksheet that presented these same problems in standard vertical form:

$$
\begin{array}{cccc}
16 & 28 & 37 & 39 \\
\underline{+9} & \underline{+13} & \underline{+24} & \underline{+53}
\end{array}
$$

For each of these tasks, Auburn first added the ones column, then the tens. However, she failed to "carry" and produced answers of 15, 31, 51, and 82. As soon as she completed the worksheet, the interviewer presented the horizontal sentence 16 + 9 = ___ and Auburn counted-on and gave 25 as her answer.

> Interviewer: So when we count we get 25 and when we do it this way (points to worksheet) we get 15. Is that OK to get two answers or do you think there should be only one?
> Auburn: (Shrugs shoulders.)
> Interviewer: Which one do you think is the best answer?
> Auburn: Twenty-five.
> Interviewer: Why?
> Auburn: I don't know.
> Interviewer: If we had 16 cookies and 9 more, would we have 15 altogether?
> Auburn: No.
> Interviewer: Why not?
> Auburn: Because if you counted them up together, you would get 25.
> Interviewer: But is this (points to answer of 15 on the worksheet) right sometimes or is it always wrong?
> Auburn: It's always right. (Cobb 1988, 98)

As Cobb comments, "The contrast between Auburn's behavior in the two parts of the interview and her final comment indicate that the arithmetic she was currently studying in school had nothing to do with the world of physical objects and real-life problems or her self-generated methods. For her, school arithmetic seemed to be an isolated, self-contained context in which the possibility of doing anything other than attempting to recall prescribed methods did not arise" (1988, 98). Auburn's loss of intellectual autonomy in the worksheet setting was almost complete. Authority had indicated that this was the correct method; it did not matter that the answer made no sense to her or that it was inconsistent with her self-generated methods for thinking about this type of situation.

Other Deficiencies in Traditional Mathematics Instruction: Myths

The methods of traditional mathematics teaching are based, for the most part, on folk and outdated psychological theories. Typical of such theories are their inclusion of myths.

COVERAGE. One of the major components of traditional mathematics teaching is the almost universal belief among mathematics teachers in what I call the "myth of coverage." According to this myth, "If mathematics is 'covered,' students will learn it." This myth is so deeply imbedded in traditional mathematics instruction that, at each grade level, teachers feel tremendous pressure to teach huge amounts of material at breakneck speeds. It has encouraged a curriculum that is a "mile wide and an inch deep." It has encouraged acceleration rather than depth of understanding, even for the brightest students. Belief in this myth causes teachers to criticize reform curricula as inefficient because students in such curricula study far fewer topics at each grade level.

Basing his conclusions on scientific research, Alan Bell of the Shell Centre for Mathematical Education at the University of Nottingham turns this myth-based reasoning on its head: "It may be felt that there is no time for a method which involves intensive discussion of particular points. But on the evidence presented . . . we have to ask whether we can afford to waste pupils' time on [traditional] methods which have such little long term effect when . . . we could be doing so much better."[1] That is, because students in traditional curricula learn ideas and procedures rotely rather than meaningfully, they quickly forget them, so the ideas must be retaught year after year. In contrast, in sense-making curricula, because students retain learned ideas for long periods of time and because a natural part of sense making is to interrelate ideas, rather than repeatedly forgetting the same ideas, students accumulate an ever-increasing store of well-integrated knowledge.

Consistent with Bell's claim, TIMSS data suggest that Japanese teachers, whose students significantly outperform U.S. students in mathemat-

1. Adam Bell, "Teaching for the Test," *Times Educational Supplement, London,* October 27, 1989.

ics, spend much more time than U.S. teachers having students delve deeply into mathematical ideas (NCES 1996). Bransford, Brown, and Cocking suggest why focusing on coverage does not work: "Attempts to cover too many topics too quickly may hinder learning and subsequent transfer because students (a) learn only isolated sets of facts that are not organized and connected or (b) are introduced to organizing principles that they cannot grasp because they lack enough specific knowledge to make them meaningful" (1999, 46).

SKILL BEFORE UNDERSTANDING. Many people, including many teachers, believe that students, especially those in lower level classes, should "master" mathematical procedures first, then later try to understand them. However, research indicates that if students have already memorized procedures through much practice, it is difficult for them to later return to understand them (Hiebert 1999; Mack 1993). For example, Wearne and Hiebert found that fifth and sixth graders who had practiced rules for adding and subtracting decimals by lining up the decimal points were less likely than fourth graders with no such experience to acquire conceptual knowledge from meaning-based instruction (Hiebert and Carpenter 1992).

Changing Paradigms: From Behaviorism to Constructivism[2]

Mathematics education is struggling mightily to escape the stranglehold of the outdated and inadequate behaviorist learning theory that has dictated the course of mathematics teaching for more than forty years. In its place, all current major scientific theories describing students' mathematics learning agree that mathematical ideas must be personally constructed by students as they intentionally try to make sense of situations (Bransford, Brown, and Cocking 1999; De Corte, Greer, and Verschaffel 1996; Greeno, Collins, and Resnick 1996; NRC 1989; Lester 1994; Hiebert and Carpenter 1992; Prawat 1999; Schoenfeld 1996; Steffe and Kieren,1994; Romberg 1992).

2. There are various "brands" of constructivism. They vary in the degree to which they emphasize psychological versus sociocultural factors in learning, philosophical versus empirical foundations, and explicitness in describing learning mechanisms. In this chapter a version of constructivism is explicated that is scientifically based, includes detailed descriptions of actual learning mechanisms (both psychological and sociocultural), and can be reasonably used to undergird powerful approaches to mathematics instruction that may not explicitly claim constructivism as a foundation.

Support for the basic tenets of this "constructivist" view come from the noted psychologist Jean Piaget and, more recently, scientists attempting to connect brain function to psychology (Anderson 1997). For instance, according to Nobel Prize winner Francis Crick, "Seeing is a constructive process, meaning that the brain does not passively record the incoming visual information. It actively seeks to interpret it" (1994, 30–31). "The structure and properties in the image we end up seeing are brain constructions prompted by an object. There is no picture of the object being transferred from the object to the retina and from the retina to the brain. There is, rather, a set of correspondences between physical characteristics of the object and the modes of reaction of the organism according to which an internally generated image is constructed" (Damasio 1999, 321).

Similarly, Robert Ornstein asserts, "Our experiences, percepts, memories are not of the world directly but are our own creation, a dream of the world, one that evolved to produce just enough information for us to adapt to local circumstances" (1991, 160). Indeed, the brain operates on and abstracts its own operation—not the "world" directly. "The brain is more in touch with itself than with anything else" (Restak 1995, 93).

To illustrate the constructive nature of perception, consider figure 4-3. Most people see an equilateral triangle partially obscured by a right triangle. However, the right triangle is not really there; it is not part of the visual stimulus. Instead, individual minds construct it. (Mental constructions in mathematics will be illustrated in a later section.)

Although scientists examining the operation of the mind at both the perceptual and conceptual levels see the mind as constructing meaning, not receiving it, the difference between the two levels is that at the higher, conceptual level, much of the construction is conscious. But we should not think that the mental processes involved in perception and conception are fundamentally different. "The same neural and cognitive mechanisms that allow us to perceive and move around also create our conceptual systems and modes of reason" (Lakoff and Johnson 1999, 4).

The evidence for the constructivist view of mind is so strong that Alan Schoenfeld, a mathematics educator and recent past president of the American Educational Research Association, has said, "The 'constructivist perspective' is better grounded in empirical and experimental evidence than the theory of evolution; we should just assume it and get on with our business (while working . . . to flesh it out and understand it more fully)" (1994, 78). More than two decades of scientific research in mathematics education have refined the constructivist view of mathematics learning to provide detailed explanations of how students construct increasingly so-

Figure 4-3. *Seeing a Triangle That "Isn't There"*

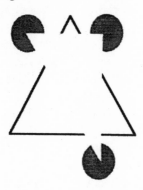

phisticated ideas about particular mathematical topics, what students' mathematical experiences are like, what mental operations give rise to those experiences, and the sociocultural factors that affect students' construction of mathematical meaning. To distinguish this empirical research-based theory from the broad philosophical constructivist stance taken by educators specializing in other disciplines, I will refer to it as *scientific constructivism.*

Unfortunately, most educators and laypersons have no substantive understanding of the research-based constructivist theory. Many of them conceive of constructivism as a pedagogical paradigm entailing a type of nonrigorous, intellectual anarchy that lets students pursue whatever interests them and invent and use any mathematical methods they wish, whether these methods are correct or not. Others take constructivism to be synonymous with "discovery" learning from the "new math" era, or even as a way of teaching that focuses on using manipulatives or cooperative learning. None of these conceptions is consistent with the view taken by researchers in mathematics education. Scientific constructivism is a well-developed scientific theory that has proved invaluable in understanding empirical research on students' learning of mathematics. To illustrate the depth of scientific constructivism, in the following sections some of its fundamental learning mechanisms are discussed and an example is given of the insights that can result from constructivist research.

Constructivist Mechanisms for Learning

From a constructivist perspective, an individual's mathematical "reality" is determined by the set of mental structures that the individual's mind has constructed and is currently using to deal with mathematical problems and situations. It is through these established structures, sometimes called frames, that the individual interprets and builds subsequent mathematical experiences. In fact, these structures determine the very nature of those experiences: "Framing provides a means of 'constructing' a world, of characterizing its flow, of segmenting events within this world . . . . After becoming accustomed to a certain kind of framing, the strip of reality interpreted accordingly appears for the individual as natural, evident, somehow logical" (Krummheuer 1995, 250; compare with Bruner 1990). Indeed, arguing from what Cleeremans calls a "constructivist" view of cognition, Schyns, Goldstone, and Thibaut (1998) provide evidence that not only are new features of the environment conceptually *created* during learning, but substantial changes occur to perceptual systems as a result of this feature creation. Similarly, research in mathematics education has demonstrated repeatedly that students build new mathematics understandings out of their current relevant mental structures (for example, Battista and Larson 1994; Bransford, Brown, and Cocking 1999; Hiebert and Carpenter 1992; Mack 1990; McCombs 1993; Cognition and Technology Group at Vanderbilt 1993).

How are these mental structures "constructed"? According to scientific constructivism, abstraction is the fundamental mental mechanism by which new mathematical mental structures are generated (Steffe 1988). *Abstraction* is the process by which the mind selects, coordinates, combines, and registers in memory a collection of *mental* items or acts that appear in the attentional field. There are different degrees of abstraction, ranging from isolating an item in the experiential flow and grasping it as a unit, to disembedding it from its original perceptual context so that it can be freely operated on in imagination, including "projecting" it into other perceptual material and utilizing it in novel situations. Although the process of abstraction has been discussed for centuries, current scientific constructivist research is elaborating its exact role in mathematics learning while neuroscience contemplates its implementation by the brain (Battista 1999a; Battista et al. 1998; Steffe 1992; von Glasersfeld 1995).

For example, to perceptually abstract a physical object, neuroscientists explain that the brain must record "the neural activity that takes place in the sensory and motor cortices during interaction with [the] given object. The records are patterns of synaptic connections that can re-create the separate sets of activity that define an object or event. . . . When these records are reactivated, they can re-create the varied sensations and actions associated with a particular entity or category of entities" (Damasio and Damasio 1993, 58, 60). According to Crick (1994), experiencing a perceptual unit—that is, abstracting an object—might occur as the brain binds together all neurons actively responding to the different aspects of the object. This binding would take place as a relatively small portion of special cortical neurons fire simultaneously and activate other neurons that somehow correspond to the meaning of the perceived object. The brain's ability to attend to and record not merely the neural activity activated by sensory input, but also the pattern of neural activity that arises out of processing this input (including sequences of binding operations), enables the mind to *construct* the mental objects it uses to conceptualize the physical world. Thus abstraction is the critical mechanism that enables the mind to construct the mental entities that individuals use to conceptualize and reason about their "mathematical realities."

Meaningful learning and understanding of mathematics require more than abstraction. They require *reflection*, the conscious process of mentally replaying experiences, actions, or mental processes and considering their results or how they are composed. As acts of reflection are themselves abstracted, they can become the content—what is acted upon—in future acts of reflection and abstraction. Meaningful learning also occurs as a result of accommodation, which is the adaptation of one's current cognitive structures in response to new experiences. Accommodations are triggered by perturbations—disturbances in mental equilibrium caused by things such as an unexpected happening, a realization that something is amiss, or a dissatisfaction with one's understanding of a state of affairs (von Glasersfeld 1995). Perturbations arise as individuals interact and attempt to make sense of their physical and social environments.

Two additional mechanisms that are fundamental to understanding meaningful mathematics learning are mental models and schemes (Battista 1999b). Mental models are nonverbal recall-of-experience-like mental versions of situations that have structures isomorphic to the perceived structures of the situations they represent (Battista 1994; Johnson-Laird 1983). Mental models consist of integrated sets of abstractions that are activated to interpret and reason about situations that one is dealing with in action or thought. They are derived from experiences and reflection on those experiences, and most often have an image-like quality. When using a mental model to reason about a situation, a person can mentally move around, manipulate, combine, and transform objects, as well as mentally perform other operations like those that can be performed on objects in the physical world. We make sense of a situation when we have constructed a mental model for it. Similar to frames, mental models determine how we imagine, visualize, and reason about situations.

Mental models also determine use of schemes, which are organized sequences of actions or mental operations that have been abstracted from experience and can be applied in response to similar circumstances. Schemes consist of a mechanism for recognizing a situation, a mental model that is activated to interpret actions within the situation, and a set of expectations (usually embedded in the behavior of the model) about the possible results of those actions.

What emerges from this theory is a picture of meaningful mathematics learning coming about as individuals recursively cycle through phases of action (physical and mental), reflection, and abstraction in a way that enables them to develop ever more sophisticated mental models and action schemes. In fact, students' ability to understand and effectively use our culture's formal mathematical systems to make sense of their quantitative and spatial surroundings depends critically on their construction of elaborated sequences of mental models. Initial models in these sequences arise as students learn to reason about physical manipulations of real-world objects. Later models permit them to reason with mental images of real-world objects. Finally, symbolic models enable them to reason about real-world quantities by meaningfully manipulating mathematical symbols. Without this recursively developed sequence of mental models, students' learning about mathematical symbol systems is strictly syntactic, and their use of symbolic procedures is totally disconnected from real-world situations. As noted earlier, research has shown repeatedly that rote learning of syntactic rules for manipulating symbols is exactly what results for most students in traditional mathematics curricula.

Sense Making, Understanding, and Connections

The central goal in the reform of mathematics education is for students to make sense of mathematics, to understand it. But *understanding* is a difficult concept to characterize precisely. Hiebert and colleagues (1997) state that we understand something when we see how it is related or connected to other things, and that understanding comes about as we reflect and communicate. Johnson-Laird extends the description and posits mental models as the fundamental mental mechanism that enables understanding: "If you know what causes a phenomenon, what results from it, how to influence, control, initiate, or prevent it, how it relates to other states of affairs or how it resembles them, how to predict its onset and course, what its internal or underlying 'structure' is, then to some extent you understand it. The psychological core of understanding . . . consists in having a 'working [mental] model' of the phenomenon in your mind" (Johnson-Laird 1983). Knowledge is understood and "usable" not when it consists of a mere list of disconnected facts, but when it is connected and organized around important concepts (Bransford, Brown, and Cocking 1999).

Scientific constructivism provides genuine insight into the notion of understanding. For instance, as students reflect on their mathematical ideas and reasoning, either in isolation or in communication with others, the course of their reflective thought is often abstracted. So, in thinking about problems such as finding 3/4 of 12 objects, a student might partition the set of 12 into 4 sets of 3, then enumerate the objects in 3 of these sets, getting 9. If the student's reflective reasoning moves from partitioning and enumerating to the related whole-number operations of multiplication and division, then abstraction of this reasoning sequence at a sufficiently high level interconnects the fraction concept to the operations—to find 3/4 of a number, divide the number by 4, then multiply the quotient by 3. This is an essential mathematical idea that many ostensibly successful middle school students do not understand (Battista 1999c). (Note that such reflection and abstraction must be performed by students. Neither textbook nor teacher can perform these processes for students—although teachers can attempt to engender such processing by students.)

Sense Making, Inquiry, and Survival

According to constructivists, the function of cognition is adaptive and serves to organize and make sense of our interactions with our environments (von Glasersfeld 1987; Kilpatrick 1987). This view is consistent with that of many neuroscientists who claim that the brain exists in order to construct internal representations that enable us to understand and manage the world (Gazzaniga 1998; Ornstein 1991; Restak 1995). We "possess a brain that is pre-wired to come up with explanations that provide us with a sense of meaningfulness" (Restak 1994, 93). "We build mental models that represent significant aspects of our physical and social world, and we manipulate elements of those models when we think, plan, and try to explain events of that world. The ability to construct and manipulate valid models of reality provides humans with our distinctive adaptive advantage; it must be considered one of the crowning achievements of the human intellect" (Bower and Morrow 1990, as quoted in Calvin 1996, 112). The ability to form mental models of the world and to distinguish these models from ongoing perceptual experience "frees the individual from the bondage of an immediate time frame or ongoing events occurring in real time" (Edelman 1992, 133). This is a hallmark of the higher-order consciousness that separates humans from other species (Edelman 1992). The capability to form and use mental models—guided by our values and felt needs—allows us to consider and mentally "try out" possible actions to contemplate which is best, to consider future situations before they occur, and to effectively utilize knowledge of past events in dealing with the future; indeed, it "permits our hypotheses to die in our stead" (Popper as quoted in Calvin 1996, 103; see also Johnson-Laird 1983). Thus sense making via mental models enables us to consider possible actions and events as well as their consequences, greatly improving our chances of making good decisions in our quest to manage the world. It is therefore a primary function of cognition and, indeed, a basic survival mechanism (Damasio 1999).

Sense making is intentional and involves an active process of inquiry, both at the conscious level and deeper: "Consciousness . . . never results passively from stimulation by incoming sensory signals. Consciousness is the result of a motivated searching operation" (Ellis 1995, 55; compare with Strike and Posner 1985). Our brains must actively inquire about information in the environment before we can consciously see that information (Ellis 1995). "Each time any one of us encounters an object, the visual system begins a constant questioning process. Fragmentary evidence comes in and the higher centers . . . then pose a series of visual questions. . . . In this manner, the impoverished image is progressively worked on and refined (with bits 'filled in,' when appropriate)" (Ramachandran and Blakeslee 1998, 112).

Because an inquiry disposition seems to be a natural characteristic of the mind's overall sense-making function, individuals learn more effectively when they adopt an active, questioning frame of mind that satisfies this disposition. For instance, research cited by Ellis (1995) and Feldman and Kalmar (1996) indicates that having students attempt to formulate questions for which information given in written paragraphs constitutes the answers engages students in constructing theories that coherently interrelate and integrate the information given in the text, thus enabling them to understand, make sense of, and have greater recall of the information.

Sociocultural Factors in Constructivist Learning

Students' construction of mathematics is enabled and constrained not only by internal cognitive factors but by cultural artifacts such as language and symbol-representation systems; by the social norms, interaction patterns, and mathematical practices of the various communities in which students participate; and by direct interactions with other people (Bruner 1990; Cobb and Yackel 1995; De Corte et al. 1996). For instance, consider the previous comments about how classroom practices in mathematics instruction can influence students' beliefs about mathematics and learning, which then mediate students' learning. Also consider ways that students' small and large group work can affect learning (compare with Cobb et al. 1997; Forman and Cazden 1985; von Glasersfeld 1995; Yackel, Cobb, and Wood 1991). Students might change their current thinking (a) when they attempt to resolve perturbations that arise from comparing their views with discrepant views of others; (b) when elements of the communicated reasoning of others prompt them to personally construct, alter, or extend related components of their own reasoning; (c) when they elaborate personally developed ideas so that they can be communicated to others; and (d) when they change their attentional foci or the direction of their conceptual analysis as they discuss ideas with others.

Power in Particulars

Despite the power of the general scientific constructivist theory of learning described above, a careful reading of constructivist literature in mathematics education reveals that the power and usefulness of the theory does not reside in the simple notion that students actively construct their own knowledge (the extent of most constructivist approaches in education). Rather, the power of this theory comes from its delineation of specific learning mechanisms and its application to particular mathematical topics and learning situations. Contemporary researchers in mathematics education have gone beyond general constructivist tenets to develop specific models of students' ways of thinking and operating as they construct increasingly sophisticated mathematical knowledge in particular mathematical situations (Steffe and Kieren 1994). This elaboration and particularization of the general theory makes it possible to study students' knowledge construction in ways that are genuinely relevant to teaching mathematics (Cobb, Wood, and Yackel 1990; Steffe and Kieren 1994).

Attending to Students' Mathematical Constructions

An example from elementary school geometry illustrates the insights that can be gained by carefully examining students' construction of particular mathematical ideas (Battista et al. 1998). CS, a second grader, was shown a plastic, one-inch square and the 7-inch by 3-inch rectangle shown in figure 4-4a. She was also shown that the plastic square was the same size as one of the squares suggested by the tick marks on the rectangle. She was then asked to predict how many of the plastic squares it would take to completely cover the rectangle. CS drew squares where she thought they would go and counted 30, as shown in figure 4-4b.

On a similar problem, CS was asked to predict how many squares would cover the rectangle shown in figure 4-4c (this time, however, she was asked to make a prediction without drawing). CS pointed and counted as shown in figure 4-4d, predicting 30. When checking her answer with plastic squares, she pointed to and counted squares as shown in figure 4-4e, getting 30. But she got confused, so she counted again, getting 24, then 27.

Clearly CS was not imagining the row-by-column organization that most people "see" in these rectangular arrays of squares. Although, as educated adults, we easily "see" how rows and columns of squares cover rectangles A and C, CS had not yet mentally constructed this organization. *For CS, this row-by-column organization was not there.* To construct a proper row-by-column structuring of such arrays, CS would have to spatially coordinate the elements in the orthogonal dimensions of rows and columns, something that is quite difficult for many students (Battista et al. 1998).

CS's thinking is not unusual. My research indicates that only 19 percent of second graders, 31 percent of third graders, 54 percent of fourth graders, and 78 percent of fifth graders make correct predictions for problem C. These are sobering findings, given that for students in these grades, traditional instruction uses rectangular arrays as a model to give meaning to multiplication, *assuming* that students see such arrays as sets of equivalent columns and rows. Row-by-column structuring is also assumed in traditional treatments of area.

Other examples of students' personal constructions abound in mathematics education research. For instance, a number of researchers have found that for solving simple addition and subtraction problems many primary-grade children invent solution strategies—some correct and some incorrect—that were not taught to them (Carpenter and Moser 1984; De

Figure 4-4. *Work of CS, a Second Grader*

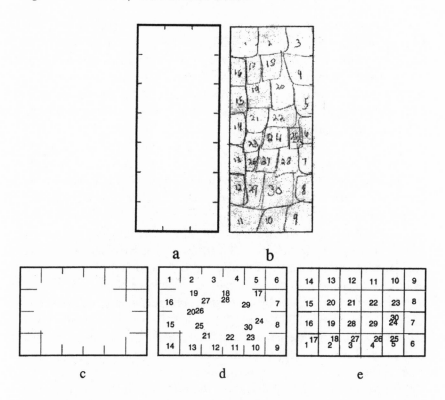

a   b

c   d   e

Corte et al. 1996; Lamon 1993). For an example of a correct student construction, consider the many students who move from counting-all to counting-on, without having been taught this new method.[3] This milestone in student enumeration comes about as a result of appropriate experience and students' construction of a new conceptualization of the relationship between counting acts and numerosity (Cobb and Wheatley 1988). For an example of an incorrect construction, recall second-grader Auburn. She constructed her own personal conceptualization of how to manipulate symbols in two-digit addition problems. She was not taught this conceptualization; instead, she constructed it based on related conceptions and experiences.

3. For example, to determine the sum of 8 and 5, a student might count-all by reciting all the counting numbers from 1 to 13. A student counting-on might say 8–9, 10, 11, 12, 13.

The Constructivist View of Teaching

To develop powerful mathematical thinking in students, constructivist instruction attempts to carefully guide and support their personal construction of ideas.[4] It pushes students to build mathematical meanings that are more complex, abstract, and powerful than they currently possess. In the spirit of inquiry, problem solving, and sense making, constructivist instruction encourages students to invent, test, and refine their own ideas rather than unquestioningly follow procedures given to them by others. Because constructivists see learning as resulting from accommodations students make to their current mental structures, constructivist teaching attempts to promote such accommodations by using carefully selected sequences of problematic tasks to provoke appropriate perturbations in students' thinking.

Unlike instruction that focuses only on classroom inquiry, in the constructivist paradigm selection of instructional tasks is based on knowledge of *students'* mathematics (Steffe and D'Ambrosia 1995); the choice of tasks is "grounded in detailed analyses of children's mathematical experiences and the processes by which they construct mathematical knowledge" (Cobb, Wood, and Yackel 1990, 130). Thus to be consistent with scientific constructivism, mathematics teaching must use scientific research on how students construct meanings for specific mathematical topics, including the conceptual advances that students can make for those topics.

Without appropriate attention to and knowledge of student meanings and cognitive constructions—knowledge generated by modern research in mathematics education—teachers and curriculum developers implementing inquiry instruction in the name of either constructivism or the reform movement will be less than maximally effective. In fact, they will be no different than teachers who used discovery-inquiry teaching three decades ago in the "new math" era. Like their predecessors, they will teach in ways that fail to account for the nature of students' mathematical ideas (Steffe and Kieren 1994). The present reform will, in many ways, reinvent the last, sadly ignoring all the progress that has been made by modern mathematics education research and inevitably leading to the same disappointments. To teach in a way that is consistent with current scientific theories of learning mathematics, teachers must acquire a much greater

---

4. Because traditional instruction ignores students' personal construction of mathematical meaning, the development of their mathematical thought is not properly nurtured, resulting in stunted growth.

store of knowledge than they have heretofore possessed; they must thoroughly learn the vast field of what has been called "the mathematics of children"—the mathematical ideas children construct in response to the tasks they face.

Different Paradigms, Same Recommendations

Knowledge of how students learn particular topics in mathematics is also critical in paradigms on mathematics teaching and learning that do not explicitly label themselves as constructivist. Arguing from psychological and cognitive science views, McCombs (1993) as well as Baroody and Ginsburg (1990) claim that to promote meaningful learning of mathematics, instruction must be built on students' existing knowledge. Battista and Larson (1994), in reviewing twenty-five years of research on elementary school mathematics, concluded "Students' informal mathematical ideas cannot be ignored. These informal ideas, along with previously learned formal ideas, form the current experiential mathematical reality of students. This reality must serve as the starting point for the construction of more sophisticated mathematical structures" (181). Similarly, in describing one of the major alternate paradigms to constructivism, Koehler and Grouws state, "The underlying philosophy of Cognitively Guided Instruction (CGI) is that teachers need to make instructional decisions based on knowledge from cognitive science about how students learn particular content" (1992, 119). According to the CGI paradigm, teachers must "have an understanding of the general stages that students pass through in acquiring the concepts and procedures in the domain, the processes that are used to solve different problems at each stage, and the nature of the knowledge that underlies these processes" (Carpenter and Fennema 1991, 11).

Research Support for Constructivist-Consistent Instruction

An abundance of research has shown that mathematics instruction that focuses on inquiry, problem solving, and personal sense making produces powerful mathematical thinkers who not only can compute but have strong conceptions of mathematics and problem-solving skills (Hiebert 1999). For example, in a year-long project conducted by Cobb et al. (1991), ten second-grade classes that participated in mathematics instruction that was compatible with constructivism and recommendations of the NCTM standards were compared to eight traditional classes. At the end of the study

the levels of computational performance of the two groups were comparable, but constructivist instruction students had higher levels of conceptual understanding in mathematics; held stronger beliefs about the
importance of understanding and collaborating; and attributed less importance to conforming to the solution methods of others. Wood and Sellers (1996, 1997) compared classes receiving problem-centered mathematics
instruction for two years (in second and third grade) with students in traditional classes for two years. Results indicated that students in reform-
based classes scored significantly higher on standardized measures of
computational proficiency as well as on conceptual understanding.
Muthukrishna and Borkowski (1996) found that the meaningful math-
ematics-learning performance of third graders in constructivist instruction not only was superior to that of students in direct instruction and
traditional instruction, but that the constructivist students evidenced greater
use of "deep processing strategies."

   Similar positive results for conceptual, sense-making instruction were
obtained by Fennema et al. (1996) and Carpenter et al. (1998) at the primary grade level; Ben-Chaim, Fey, and Fitzgerald (1998) and Silver et al.
(1996) at the junior high level, with the latter in urban districts; and Quinn
at the university level (Quinn 1997). At the senior high level in England,
Boaler found that "students who followed a traditional approach developed a procedural knowledge that was of limited use to them in unfamiliar situations. Students who learned mathematics in an open, project-based
environment developed a conceptual understanding that provided them
with advantages in a range of assessments and situations" (1998, 41).

An Example of Constructive Learning

   To illustrate the nature and power of the constructivist approach, an
example from my own research is summarized here (full details are given
in Battista 1999b). A teacher who was highly skilled in creating a classroom culture of inquiry, problem solving, and sense making taught the
fifth-grade students observed in this study. Students worked collaboratively
in pairs on the activity shown in figure 4-5, predicting how many cubes
would fit in graphically represented boxes, then checking their answers by
making the boxes from grid paper and filling them with cubes.

EPISODE 1, DAY 1.   For Box A (see figure 4-5), students P and N (two
boys) silently analyze the pictures, then explain their thinking to one

Figure 4-5. *"How Many Cubes" Activity Sheet*

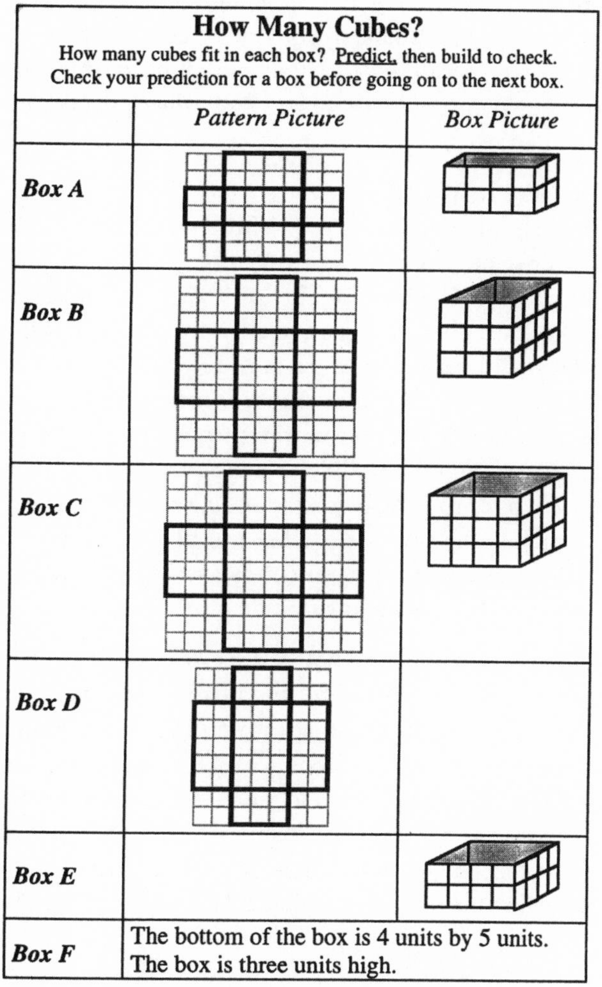

How Many Cubes?
How many cubes fit in each box? Predict, then build to check.
Check your prediction for a box before going on to the next box.
Pattern Picture
Box Picture
Box A
Box B
Box C
Box D
Box E
Box F
The bottom of the box is 4 units by 5 units.
The box is three units high.

Figure 4-6. *Work of N and P, Fifth Graders*

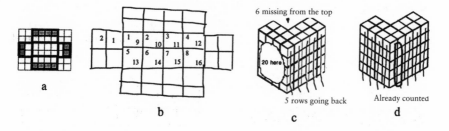

a
2
1
1
9
2
10
3
11
4
12
5
13
6
14
7
15
8
16
b
6 missing from the top
20 here
5 rows going back
c
Already counted
d

another. N counts the 12 outermost squares on the 4 side flaps of the pattern picture (see figure 4-6a), then multiplies by 2: "There's 2 little squares going up on each side, so you times them." P counts the 12 visible cube faces on box picture A, then doubles that for the hidden lateral faces of the box. The two students agree on 24 as their prediction.

P: [After putting 4 rows of 4 cubes into the box] We're wrong. It's 4 sets of 4 equals 16.

N: What are we doing wrong? [Neither student has an answer, so they move on to Box B.]

P: What do you think we should do? [Pause.] [Pointing at 2 visible faces of the cube at the bottom right front corner of box picture B] This is 1 box [cube], those 2.

N: Oh, I know what we did wrong! We counted this [pointing to the front face of the bottom right front cube] and then the side over there [pointing to the right face of that cube].

P: So we'll have to take away 4 [pointing to the 4 vertical edges of box picture A], no wait, we have to take away 8. [P then subtracts 8 from their prediction of 24 and tells N that this subtraction would have made their prediction correct.]

[In their prediction for Box B, P counts 21 visible cube faces on the box picture, then doubles it for the box's hidden lateral faces. He subtracts 8 for double-counting (not taking into account that this box is 3 cubes high, not 2, like Box A), predicting 42 − 8 = 34. N adds 12 and 12 for the right and left lateral sides of box picture B, then 3 and 3 for the middle column of both the front and back, explaining that the outer columns of 3 on the front and back were counted when he enumerated the right and left faces. He predicts 30.]

For Box A, N and P made predictions based on different mental models for the cube array. N looked at the pattern picture and multiplied by 2 for the "two squares going up." P looked at the box picture and multiplied by 2 for the two lateral sides that could not be seen in the box picture. Although the boys agreed on a prediction of 24, the discrepancy between their predicted and actual answers initiated a perturbation that caused them to reflect on and reevaluate their enumeration schemes.

As P applied his enumeration scheme to box picture B, he focused on the cube faces, particularly on the two adjacent lateral faces of the bottom right corner cube. By coordinating the positions of these faces in three-dimensional (3D) space, he was able to realize that they were, in fact, the front and right faces of the same cube. As N and P extended this new interpretation of the adjacent faces to other vertical-edge cubes, they recognized that P's current enumeration scheme double-counted such cubes. The accommodations of enumeration schemes that resulted dealt with the double-counting error in different ways. P compensated for the error by subtracting the number of cubes he thought he had double-counted. N, in contrast, attempted to imagine the cubes so he would not double-count them, deriving a complete restructuring of the array.

EPISODE 2. After Box B is constructed, the boys find that 36 cubes fit (an answer inconsistent with their predictions).

P: What are you thinking we should do?
N: Well, I was thinking I forgot some in the middle, 3 in the middle.
P: I got it! We were doing minus 8 [pointing to box picture A] but really there are 1, 2, 3—4, 5, 6—7, 8, 9—10, 11, 12 [pointing successively to the 4 vertical edges of box picture B]. [He looks at box picture B and does some recounting, but seems puzzled, possibly because subtracting 12 instead of 8 from 42 still does not give the correct answer.] If there's 21 here and 21 there [referring first to the front and right sides, then to the back and left sides], there's still some left in the middle. I got it. We missed 2 in the middle. There's 2 more blocks in the middle, and that would make 36.

The discrepancy between the two students' predicted and actual answers for Box B again initiated a perturbation, leading them to reflect further on the situation. Although neither P nor N had yet developed a spatial structuring of 3D arrays that led to correct enumeration of cubes, they were making progress. As they reflected on, analyzed, discussed, and revised their work, they abstracted important aspects of the spatial organization of the arrays that would help them make the needed restructuring.

EPISODE 3. N and P jointly count 21 outside cube faces for Box C, not double-counting cubes on the right front vertical edge. They then multiply by 2 for the hidden lateral sides and add 2 for the middle cubes (which is how many cubes they concluded they had missed in the middle of Box B).

They predict 44 cubes. Not confident in this prediction, P counts 24 visible cubes on box picture C, then multiplies by 2 to get 48. He subtracts 12 for double-counting the vertical edge cubes, getting a total of 36. This is the same number of cubes they found for Box B, and because they decide that Box C is bigger than Box B, N does not think this is right and P agrees. So P decides that they need to add 2 for the middle, getting 38, but cannot convince N that this prediction is correct. The boys make and fill the box and find that it contains 48 cubes. They are puzzled, but class ends before they have any time to discuss the problem further.

N and P begin Day 2 by reflecting on their incorrect predictions for Box C. P concludes that they failed to count some of the "middle" cubes. However, as in his previous adjustments, he derives the number to be added to compensate for these omitted cubes by comparing the predicted and actual answers.

EPISODE 4.

N: I think I know Box D; I think it's going to be 30. Here, it goes 2 up [pointing to a column in the upper flap of pattern picture D]. So 5 plus 5 plus 5 [pointing to the columns in the pattern's middle] is 15. Then you need to do 3 more rows of that because you need to do the top; 20, 25, 30 [pointing to middle columns again].

P: I don't know—that'd probably work, I guess.

[After the students make a box and find that it contains 30 cubes as N predicted, both smile. P then asks N to explain his strategy again, which N does.]

P: So there's 15 right here [pointing to the bottom of the box].

N: Yeah, on the bottom. And in the top part here [motioning] there'd be another 15.

P: All this top here [motioning along the top rows of the sides of the box]?

In Episode 4, N made a correct prediction by structuring the array into 2 layers of 3 columns of 5 cubes. Because he had suspected that there was a better way to solve the problem, he had reflected on and analyzed the situation, coming up with a new strategy. Only after P saw that N's strategy gave the correct answer did he become interested in really listening to and making sense of N's description of his strategy.

EPISODE 5. On the next problem [box picture E], because neither boy is able to employ their new layering scheme in this different graphic context, both return to variants of their old schemes. After the boys complete the pattern for Box E, N is able to apply his layering scheme to it, but he is not yet confident in its validity. When the boys find that 32 cubes actually fit in the box, N comments, "It is 32," seemingly realizing that his new layering strategy is, in fact, valid in this situation.

EPISODE 6. For Box F, the boys are unwilling to make a prediction until after they draw the pattern. Once the pattern is drawn on grid paper, N silently points to and counts the squares in the middle section of the pattern, 1–20 for the first layer, 21–40 for the second, and 41–60 for the third. The boys build the box, fill it with rows of 5 cubes, and then count the cubes by fives to 60. They do not seem relieved that their count matches their prediction but expect their answer to be correct. In fact, the boys readily apply their layering strategy to subsequent problems.

Once the boys drew the pattern for Box F, N returned to his layering strategy, quite confident not only that he understood the location of the cubes but that his newly developed strategy was correct. Although N performed the enumeration, P seemed to follow what N was saying, enough, at least, to think that the prediction of 60 was valid, so he did not have to make his own prediction. By the end of Episode 6 both boys had abstracted their newly developed layering strategy to a level sufficient to apply it in other problems.

Throughout their work on this instructional activity, N and P each tried to develop strategies for making correct predictions. Their focus of attention seemed to cycle through predictions, to what actually happened in counting, to attempts to integrate what they abstracted from predicting, counting, and discussing. Discrepancies between their predicted and actual answers resulted in perturbations that caused them to reflect on both their enumeration strategies and their structuring of the cube arrays. Initially their enumeration strategies were based on more primitive spatial structurings of 3D arrays—seeing them in terms of the faces of the prism formed. P, especially, seemed to focus more on numerical strategies than on a deep analysis of the spatial organization of the cubes. However, because their initial spatial structuring lead to incorrect predictions, the boys refocused their attention on structuring the arrays, with N taking the lead in this restructuring. Finally, while working on Box D, N and P developed the layer-based enumeration strategy that they verified, refined, and became confident in on subsequent problems.

EPISODE 7, DAY 3. N and P explain what they wrote for their enumeration strategy: "You find the number of cubes that fit on the bottom [by looking at the pattern] then multiply by the number of cubes going up." The researcher then asks the boys how many cubes would be in a box that has the same bottom as Box A but is 3 cubes high.

P: Eight times 3 equals 24.
N: Yeah, 8, 16, 24. I'm not too good at my multiplication facts.

[The boys then describe their solutions for a problem very different from the ones they had been solving.]

P: [See figure 4-6c.] There's 20 on the left side, times 5 rows going back, equals 100. There's 6 cubes missing from the top, and it's 5 down, so we have to subtract 6 five times. 100 minus 6 equals 94, 94 minus 6 equals 88, 88 minus 6 equals 82, 82 minus 6 equals 76, 76 minus 6 equals 70; 70 is the answer.
N: [Referring to the cube faces in the columns of the left side, as in figure 4-6d] I counted each of these twice because there's 2 back. I didn't count these [first 2 columns on the right side] because they've already been counted. I then counted each of these twice [referring to the cube faces in the remaining columns of the right side] because they go 2 back this way. [N counted by ones from 1 through 70.]

On this problem, both boys successfully adapted their layer-based enumeration strategies to apply them in a new situation. They had developed a powerful and general way of reasoning about an important class of problems. In fact, by the end of the instructional unit, almost all the 47 students in this instructional unit were capable of properly structuring and enumerating 3D cube arrays, a very difficult concept for middle-school and junior high students (Battista 1999b).

From Theory to Practice

Through a broad spectrum of studies, the constructivist view of learning and teaching described in earlier sections has been scientifically established—"constructivism" has become the dominant theoretical position among mathematics education researchers (Lester 1994). Although, as with all scientific theories, this theory requires further elaboration, testing, and refinement, it is far and away the best analysis of students' mathematics learning. Thus mathematics teaching that implements scientific constructivism with high fidelity is scientifically sound both theoretically and empirically.

Dilutions and Distortions

The critical question is: To what extent is scientific constructivism implemented in current mathematics curricula and in schools? At this time, no mathematics curricula systematically and completely based on scientific constructivism are commercially available. Even the NCTM standards are not completely consistent with scientific constructivism, embracing the general tenets but not fully accounting for some of the particulars.

Nevertheless, the U.S. curricula that come closest to implementing scientific constructivism are those that were developed specifically, with support from the National Science Foundation, to implement the NCTM standards. To the extent that the standards are based on the basic tenets of constructivism, and because these curricula were tested in a wide variety of classrooms, these curricula are scientifically sound. In fact, research conducted during development shows these curricula to be more effective than traditional curricula (National Science Foundation 1995). However, these curricula represent the first point at which dilution of scientific constructivism may have occurred. When it comes to instructional units to teach particular mathematical topics, even the most accomplished curriculum developers may pay inadequate attention to research on how students learn the topics. Worse yet, even with these reform-consistent curricula, teachers with incorrect conceptions of and beliefs about mathematics or about how mathematics is learned can greatly distort the original ideas of the curricula's creators (Battista 1994; Spillane and Zeuli 1999).

Next we move to curricula produced by publishing companies. Because such companies are for-profit organizations, for the most part, they publish what will sell—regardless of scientific research on students' mathematics learning. Because most teachers do not have a firm understanding of scientific constructivism or standards-based teaching but are familiar with highlights of the standards (NCES 1996; Spillane and Zeuli 1999), they are easily sold on commercially available mathematics textbooks that consist of traditional curricula with enough superficial changes tacked on so that publishing companies can market them as "new" and consistent with the NCTM standards (American Association for the Advancement of Science 1999). These curricula represent a severe distortion of the principles of scientific constructivism.

Thus, although many school districts claim to be implementing standards-based mathematics curricula, their implementations usually have misconstrued the tenets of the standards and scientific constructivism and are far removed from scientific research on mathematics learning (Hiebert 1999; NCES 1996; Spillane and Zeuli 1999). As a consequence, great care must be taken in evaluating school districts' implementations of such curricula. Just because a particular implementation fails, one cannot reasonably conclude that the theory and research are wrong, only that there are flawed mechanisms for putting the theory into practice—teacher training and inservice, textbook creation, and teaching.

Other Issues

There are several other issues that should be considered in reflecting on what research says about high quality mathematics teaching.

To Inquire or Not to Inquire

Inquiry is the preferred method of instruction for constructivists because inquiry-based classrooms tend to elicit classroom cultures that support students' natural inquisition-based sense making and because such classrooms focus on the development of students' reasoning, not the disconnected rote acquisition of formal, ready-made ideas contained in textbooks. Inquiry is also the mainstay of reform-recommended instruction. However, the critical ingredient in constructivist teaching is the focus on the development of students' personal mathematical meaning making. This focus suggests that inquiry-based teaching that does not focus on students' construction of personally meaningful ideas is not completely consistent with scientific constructivism. It also suggests the possibility that demonstrations and even lectures might create meaningful learning if students are capable of and intentionally focus on personal sense making and understanding (Bransford, Brown, and Cocking 1999). For instance, everyone can probably think of examples of individuals who have made personal sense out of a mathematical idea they encountered in a book or lecture (although they may have done a considerable amount of personal reflection to accomplish this sense making).

Many constructivists are uncomfortable with such direct approaches. For instance, Steffe and Tzur state, "This method of teaching—demonstrating, explaining, and discussing—does not respect the mathematics of children nor does it contribute to our concept of children with mathematical knowledge of their own" (1994, 24). This discomfort is quite understandable, given that research has repeatedly shown that lecture-demonstration, *as it is implemented in most traditional mathematics instruction*, does not produce meaningful learning (Cobb et al. 1992; DeCorte et al. 1996). There is even evidence that people remember more of what they generate for themselves than what others explain to them (Keegan 1995). The question of whether and when lecture-demonstration—the most common mode of teaching found in American schools—*can* produce meaningful mathematics learning has not received much attention in the constructivist era. Research is needed that thoroughly investigates the role that this cherished traditional instructional tool *might* play in meaningful mathematics learning.

Fluency

In the effort to focus on understanding and concept formation instead of computation, some reform curricula deemphasize various forms of mathematical fluency. Often, what there is of practice is embedded in problem-solving contexts rather than being separate and explicit. However, there seems to be nothing in the constructivist framework that prohibits practice—as long as students' engagement in it does not change their beliefs about the nature of mathematics and mathematics learning, and as long as practice does not become the major activity in mathematics classes. If students come to believe that mathematics is simply rule following rather than sense making, they will not learn it meaningfully.

Teacher Preparation

As has already been mentioned, the fidelity of mathematics teaching to the principles of scientific constructivism depends on many factors, one of the most important of which is teacher beliefs and knowledge. Research has shown that teachers' beliefs and knowledge about mathematics, math-

ematics learning, and students' mathematical thinking can heavily influence the ways they teach (Bransford, Brown, and Cocking 1999; Fennema
and Franke 1992; Thompson 1992), and can cause them to grossly distort
the intent of reform-consistent instruction (Battista 1994; Spillane and
Zeuli 1999). Even though most teachers claim to understand the NCTM
standards and to be teaching consistent with them, the majority still ad-
heres to teaching that is traditional at its core (Battista 1999c; Beaton et
al. 1996; Spillane and Zeuli 1999). Also important in teachers' implementation of mathematics curricula that focus on student sense making are
teachers' knowledge of mathematics, their knowledge of how students
think about mathematical content and how they construct it, and their
skill in creating instructional classroom environments in which students
can inquire and make sense of mathematics (Bransford, Brown, and Cocking 1999; Carpenter and Fennema 1991; Hammond and Ball 1997; Ma
1999). Thus teachers' knowledge and beliefs are an absolutely critical component in properly applying the modern science of mathematics learning
in U.S. classrooms.

General versus Mathematics-Specific Factors

Debates about the effectiveness of mathematics education often fail to
distinguish general from mathematics instruction–specific factors, thereby
clouding analyses of the issues. For instance, there is little doubt that students' beliefs about the value of school—which develop via students' interaction with family, peers, schools, and community—affect their overall
motivation to learn all subjects, including mathematics (Macleod 1992).
This value system may be extremely weak in certain communities or in
dysfunctional schools (Hart and Allexsaht-Snider 1996; Hewson and Davies
1999). Consequently, discrepancies in values and motivation may be a
major cause for the mathematics achievement gap between low- and high-
socioeconomic status students—often appearing as racial differences. More
well-to-do and highly educated parents may not only value schooling more,
they may articulate, model, and inculcate that value system more effectively than less educated parents, thereby promoting higher academic
motivation in their children (for example, Hart and Allexsaht-Snider 1996).
This higher motivation may produce greater student effort in all mathematics curricula, but especially in those, like traditional curricula, that
are less intrinsically motivating.

Thus for many students, especially older ones, a critical issue in their mathematics education is whether they care about education in general, that is, whether they are willing to engage in the intellectual life of the school—including mathematics instruction. Many factors that are traditionally examined by research in mathematics education may be less relevant for students who are disengaged from school in general than for students who come to school already believing and acting as if academic education is important.

Conversely, the quality of instruction can affect student beliefs about whether and how they should participate in mathematics instruction. For instance, when mathematics instruction emphasizes understanding in facilitative classroom environments, students are more receptive and less anxious than when authoritarian teachers stress rote activities (Middleton and Spanias 1999). Also, students' willingness to attempt mathematics learning depends on their belief and appreciation that what they are being asked to learn is worth learning, both immediately and in the long run (Middleton and Spanias 1999).

Finally, success in mathematics learning is a powerful influence on students' motivation to achieve, as are attributions of success to effort rather than fixed ability (Middleton and Spanias 1999). However, students' conceptions about what "success" in mathematics learning means are strongly influenced by their instruction-engendered beliefs about the nature of mathematics and mathematics learning. For instance, traditional mathematics instruction causes students to value (and see success in terms of) speedy computation, imitating the teacher's mathematical actions, and getting answers judged by authorities as correct (Middleton and Spanias 1999), whereas students exposed to constructivist instruction place greater value on understanding, personal sense making, explaining, and collaborating (Muthukrishna and Borkowski 1996).

Conclusion

One of the major reasons that American educational practice in general, and mathematics education in particular, make so little progress is because they ignore scientific research. Too often the educational programs and methods used in schools are formulated with a total disregard for such research. Because educational practice is not properly grounded scientifically and is not subject to the critical scrutiny of scientific analysis and review, educators continually "reinvent the wheel." They follow one bandwagon after another.

Compounding the problem, misconceptions about mathematics and mathematics learning are so deeply ingrained in our society that most people—including most who make decisions about mathematics instruction—do not truly comprehend the improvements recommended by research, so they fear and resist them. Consequently, American mathematics instruction remains inconsistent with professional standards and scientific research and continues to take its toll on students and the nation.

To rectify this unfortunate state of affairs, the practice of mathematics education must be made more scientific. Scientific research in mathematics education has made great progress in the last two decades, progress that can drastically improve the effectiveness of mathematics instruction. It has documented the ineffectiveness of traditional mathematics instruction and uncovered causes for this ineffectiveness. It has developed new and improved theories of mathematics learning and teaching and documented the beneficial effects of their application in instructional programs. American mathematics education must respond to these research findings and change accordingly.

However, we should not develop unrealistic expectations for moving to research-based mathematics instruction. Even authentic reform curricula that are totally consistent with scientific constructivism will not be perfect. Although such curricula have been tested in actual classrooms, because funding agencies did not support the projects that developed them long enough for long-term assessment and revision, and because the curricula were first attempts at substantive reform, their extended use is bound to reveal needed alterations and refinements. Instead of reacting to perceived snags or failures in new curricula by rejecting them—and returning to traditional methods that research has shown do not work—we should work together to find better ways of implementing them. We must accept the challenge of finding effective ways to incorporate the science of mathematics learning and teaching into the educational system.

References

American Association for the Advancement of Science. 1999. *Middle Grades Mathematics Textbooks: A Benchmarks-Based Evaluation.* Washington. Available at www.project2061.org/matheval/index.htm.

Anderson, O. R. 1997. "A Neurocognitive Perspective on Current Learning Theory and Science Instructional Strategies." *Science Education* 81: 67–89.

Baroody, A. J., and H. P. Ginsburg. 1990. "Children's Learning: A Cognitive View." In *Constructivist Views on the Teaching and Learning of Mathematics*, Journal for Research in Mathematics Education Monograph Number 4, edited by R. B. Davis, C. A. Maher, and N. Noddings, 51–64. Reston, Va.: National Council of Teachers of Mathematics.

Battista, M. T. 1994. "Teacher Beliefs and the Reform Movement in Mathematics Education." *Phi Delta Kappan* 75, 6 (February): 462–70.

———. 1998. "How Many Blocks?" *Mathematics Teaching in the Middle Grades* 3, 6 (March–April): 404–11.

———. 1999a. "The Mathematical Miseducation of America's Youth: Ignoring Research and Scientific Study in Education." *Phi Delta Kappan* 80, 6 (February): 424–33.

———. July 1999b. "Fifth Graders' Enumeration of Cubes in 3D Arrays: Conceptual Progress in an Inquiry-Based Classroom." *Journal for Research in Mathematics Education* 30 (4): 417–48.

———. 1999c. "Mathematics Education Reform at Lafayette Middle School." Paper presented at the annual meeting of the American Educational Research Association, Montreal, Canada.

Battista, M. T., D. H. Clements, J. Arnoff, K. Battista, and C. V. A. Borrow. 1998. "Students' Spatial Structuring and Enumeration of 2D Arrays of Squares." *Journal for Research in Mathematics Education* 29 (5): 503–32.

Battista, M. T., and C. L Larson. 1994. "The Role of JRME in Advancing the Learning and Teaching of Elementary School Mathematics." *Teaching Children Mathematics* 1, 3 (November): 178–82.

Beaton, A. E., I. V. S. Mullis, M.O. Martin, E. J. Gonzalez, D. L. Kelly, and T. A. Smith. 1996. *Mathematics Achievement in the Middle School Years: IEA's Third International Mathematics and Science Study (TIMSS)*. Chestnut Hill, Mass.: Boston College Press.

Ben-Chaim, D., J. T. Fey, and W. M. Fitzgerald. 1998. "Proportional Reasoning among 7th Grade Students with Different Curricular Experiences." *Educational Studies in Mathematics* 36 (3): 247–73.

Boaler, J. 1998. "Open and Closed Mathematics: Student Experiences and Understandings." *Journal for Research in Mathematics Education* 29 (1): 41–62.

Bransford, J. D., A. L. Brown, and R. R. Cocking. 1999. *How People Learn: Brain, Mind, Experience, and School*. Washington: National Research Council.

Bruner, J. 1990. *Acts of Meaning*. Harvard University Press.

Calvin, W. H. 1996. *How Brains Think*. Basic Books.

Carpenter, T. P., and E. Fennema. 1991. "Research and Cognitively Guided Instruction." In *Integrating Research on Teaching and Learning Mathematics*, edited by E. Fennema, T. P. Carpenter, and S. J. Lamon, 1–16. State University of New York Press.

Carpenter, T. P., M. L. Franke, V. R. Jacobs, E. Fennema, and S. B. Empson. 1998. "A Longitudinal Study of Invention and Understanding in Children's Multidigit Addition and Subtraction." *Journal for Research in Mathematics Education* 29 (1): 3–20.

Carpenter, T. P., and J. M. Moser. 1984. "The Acquisition of Addition and Subtraction Concepts in Grades One through Three." *Journal for Research in Mathematics Education* 15 (May): 179–202.

Cobb, P. 1988. "The Tension between Theories of Learning and Instruction in Mathematics Education." *Educational Psychologist* 23 (May): 87–103.

Cobb, P., A. Boufi, K. McClain, and J. Whitenack. 1997. "Reflective Discourse and Collective Reflection." *Journal for Research in Mathematics Education* 28: 258–77.

Cobb, P., and G. Wheatley. 1988. "Children's Initial Understanding of Ten." *Focus on Learning Problems in Mathematics* 10 (3): 1–28.

Cobb, P., T. Wood, and E. Yackel. 1990. "Classrooms as Learning Environments for Teachers and Researchers." In *Constructivist Views on the Teaching and Learning of Mathematics*, Journal for Research in Mathematics Education Monograph Number 4, edited by R. B. Davis, C. A. Maher, and N. Noddings, 125–146. Reston, Va.: National Council of Teachers of Mathematics.

Cobb, P., T. Wood, E. Yackel, and B. McNeal. 1992. "Characteristics of Classroom Mathematics Traditions: An Interactional Analysis." *American Educational Research Journal* 29 (3): 573–604.

Cobb, P., T. Wood, E. Yackel, J. Nicholls, G. Wheatley, B. Trigatti, and M. Perlwitz. 1991. Assessment of a Problem-Centered Second-Grade Mathematics Project. *Journal for Research in Mathematics Education* 22 (1): 3–29.

Cobb, P., and E. Yackel. 1995. "Constructivist, Emergent, and Sociocultural Perspectives in the Context of Developmental Research." In *Proceedings of the Seventeenth Annual Meeting of the North American Chapter of the International Group for the Psychology of Mathematics Education*, Vol. 1, edited by D. T. Owens, M. K. Reed, and G. M. Millsaps, 3–29. Columbus, Ohio: ERIC Clearinghouse for Science, Mathematics, and Environmental Education.

Cognition and Technology Group at Vanderbilt. 1993. "The Jasper Series: Theoretical Foundations and Data on Problem Solving and Transfer." In *The Challenge in Mathematics and Science Education: Psychology's Response*, edited by L. A. Penner, G. M. Batsche, H. M. Knoff, and D. L. Nelson, 113–52. Washington: American Psychological Association.

Crick, F. 1994. *The Astonishing Hypothesis*. New York: Touchstone.

Damasio, A. R. 1999. *The Feeling of What Happens*. Harcourt Brace.

Damasio, A. R., and H. Damasio. 1993. "Brain and Language." In *Mind and Brain: Readings from Scientific American Magazine*, 54–65. W. H. Freeman.

De Corte, E., B. Greer, and L. Verschaffel. 1996. "Mathematics Teaching and Learning." In *Handbook of Educational Psychology*, edited by D. C. Berliner and R. C. Calfee, 491–549. Simon and Schuster Macmillan.

Edelman, G. M. 1992. *Bright Air, Brilliant Fire*. Basic Books.

Ellis, R. D. 1995. *Questioning Consciousness: The Interplay of Imagery, Cognition, and Emotion in the Human Brain*. Amsterdam/Philadelphia: John Benjamins.

Feldman, C. F., and D. A. Kalmar. 1996. "Some Educational Implications of Genre-Based Mental Models: The Interpretive Cognition of Text Understanding." In *The Handbook of Education and Human Development,* edited by D. R. Olson and N. Torrance, 434–60. Oxford, U.K.: Blackwell.

Fennema, E., and M. L. Franke. 1992. "Teachers' Knowledge and Its Impact." In *Handbook of Research on Mathematics Teaching,* edited by D. A. Grouws, 127–64. Reston, Va.: National Council of Teachers of Mathematics/Macmillan.

Fennema, E., T. P. Carpenter, M. L. Franke, L. Levi, V. R. Jacobs, and S. B. Empson. 1996. "A Longitudinal Study of Learning to Use Children's Thinking in Mathematics Instruction." *Journal for Research in Mathematics Education* 27 (4): 403–34.

Forman, E. A., and C. B. Cazden. 1985. "Exploring Vygotskian Perspectives in Education: The Cognitive Value of Peer Interaction." In *Culture, Communication, and Cognition: Vygotskian Perspectives,* edited by J. V. Wertsch, 323–47. Cambridge, U.K.: Cambridge University Press.

Gazzaniga, M. S. 1998. *The Mind's Past.* University of California Press.

Greeno, J. G., A. M. Collins, and L. Resnick. 1996. "Cognition and Learning." In *Handbook of Educational Psychology,* edited by D. C. Berliner and R. C. Calfee, 15–46. Simon and Schuster Macmillan.

Hammond, L. D., and D. L. Ball. 1997. *Teaching for High Standards: What Policymakers Need to Know and Be Able to Do.* National Education Goals Panel. Available at www.negp.gov/reports/highstds.htm.

Hart, L. E., and M. Allexsaht-Snider. 1996. "Sociocultural and Motivational Contexts of Mathematics Learning for Diverse Students." In *Motivation in Mathematics,* edited by M. Carr, 1–24. Cresskill, N.J.: Hampton Press.

Hersh, R. 1997. *What Is Mathematics, Really?* Oxford University Press.

Hewson, P., and D. Davies. 1999. "Urban Middle School: How Much Is Too Much?" Paper presented at the annual meeting of the American Educational Research Association, Montreal, Canada.

Hiebert, J. 1999. "Relationships between Research and the NCTM Standards." *Journal for Research in Mathematics Education* 30 (1): 3–19.

Hiebert, J., and T. P. Carpenter. 1992. "Learning and Teaching with Understanding." In *Handbook of Research on Mathematics Teaching,* edited by D. A. Grouws, 65–97. Reston, Va.: National Council of Teachers of Mathematics/Macmillan.

Hiebert, J., T. P. Carpenter, E. Fennema, K. C. Fuson, D. Wearne, H. Murray, A. Olivier, and P. Human. 1997. *Making Sense: Teaching and Learning Mathematics with Understanding.* Portsmouth, N.H.: Heinemann.

Johnson-Laird, N. 1983. *Mental Models: Towards a Cognitive Science of Language, Inference, and Consciousness.* Harvard University Press.

Keegan, M. 1995. "Psychological and Physiological Mechanisms by Which Discovery and Didactic Methods Work." *School Science and Mathematics* 95 (1): 3–10.

Koehler, M., and D. A. Grouws. 1992. "Mathematics Teaching Practices and Their Effects." In *Handbook of Research on Mathematics Teaching,* edited by D. A. Grouws, 115–126. Reston, Va.: National Council of Teachers of Mathematics/Macmillan.

Kouba, V. L., J. S. Zawojewski, and M. E. Strutchens. 1997. "What Do Students Know about Numbers and Operations." In *Results from the Sixth Mathematics Assessment of the National Assessment of Educational Progress,* edited by P. A. Kenney and E. A. Silver, 87–140. Reston, Va.: National Council of Teachers of Mathematics.

Krummheuer, G. 1995. "The Ethnography of Argumentation." In *The Emergence of Mathematical Meaning: Interaction in Classroom Cultures,* edited by P. Cobb and H. Bauersfeld, 229–69. Hillsdale, N.J.: Lawrence Erlbaum.

Lakoff, G., and M. Johnson. 1999. *Philosophy in the Flesh: The Embodied Mind and Its Challenge to Western Thought.* Basic Books.

Lamon, S. J. 1993. "Ratio and Proportion: Connecting Content and Children's Thinking." *Journal for Research in Mathematics Education* 24 (January): 41–61.

Lester, F. K. 1994. "Musing about Mathematical Problem-Solving Research: 1970–1994." *Journal for Research in Mathematics Education* 25 (6): 660–75.

Ma, Liping. 1999. *Knowing and Teaching Elementary Mathematics.* Mahwah, N.J.: Lawrence Erlbaum.

Mack, N. K. 1990. "Learning Fractions with Understanding: Building on Informal Knowledge." *Journal for Research in Mathematics Education* 21 (1): 16–32.

———. 1993. "Learning Rational Numbers with Understanding: The Case of Informal Knowledge." In *Rational Numbers: An Integration of Research,* edited by T. P. Carpenter, E. Fennema, and T. A. Romberg. Hillsdale, N.J.: Lawrence Erlbaum.

Macleod, Douglas B. 1992. "Research on Affect in Mathematics Education: A Reconceptualization." In D. A. Grouws, ed. *Handbook of Research on Mathematics Teaching,* edited by T. P. Carpenter, E. Fennema, and T. A. Romberg, 575–96. Reston, Va.: National Council of Teachers of Mathematics/Macmillan.

Mayer, R. E., and M. C. Wittrock. 1996. "Problem-Solving Transfer." In *Handbook of Educational Psychology,* edited by D. C. Berliner and R. C. Calfee, 47–62. Simon and Schuster Macmillan.

McCombs, B. L. 1993. "Learner-Centered Psychological Principles for Enhancing Education: Applications in School Settings." In *The Challenge in Mathematics and Science Education: Psychology's Response,* edited by L. A. Penner, G. M. Batsche, H. M. Knoff, and D. L. Nelson, 287–313. Washington: American Psychological Association.

Middleton, J. A., and A. Spanias. 1999. "Motivation for Achievement in Mathematics: Findings, Generalizations, and Criticisms of the Research." *Journal for Research in Mathematics Education* 30 (1): 65–88.

Mullis, I. V. S., J. A. Dossey, E. H. Owen, and G. W. Phillips. 1993. *NAEP 1992 Mathematics Report Card for the Nation and States.* Report No. 23–ST02. Washington: National Center for Education Statistics.

Muthukrishna, N., and J. G. Borkowski. 1996. "Constructivism and the Motivated Transfer of Skills." In *Motivation in Mathematics,* edited by M. Carr, 40–63. Cresskill, N.J.: Hampton Press.

National Center for Education Statistics (NCES). 1996. *Pursuing Excellence: A Study of U.S. Eighth-Grade Mathematics and Science Teaching, Learning,*

Curriculum, and Achievement in International Context. U.S. Department of Education.

National Council of Teachers of Mathematics. 1989. *Curriculum and Evaluation Standards for School Mathematics.* Reston, Va.

National Research Council. 1989. *Everybody Counts.* Washington: National Academy Press.

National Science Foundation. 1995. *The Success of Standards-Based Mathematics Curricula for All Students: A Preliminary Report.* University of Chicago School Mathematics Project.

Nickson, M. 1992. "The Culture of the Mathematics Classroom: An Unknown Quantity?" In *Handbook of Research on Mathematics Teaching,* edited by D. A. Grouws, 101–14. Reston, Va.: National Council of Teachers of Mathematics/Macmillan.

Ornstein, R. 1991. *Evolution of Consciousness.* New York: Touchstone.

Pinker, S. 1997. *How the Mind Works.* W. W. Norton.

Prawat, R. S. 1999. "Dewey, Peirce, and the Learning Paradox." *American Educational Research Journal* 36 (1): 47–76.

Quinn, A. L. 1997. "Justifications, Argumentations, and Sense Making of Preservice Elementary Education Teachers in a Constructivist Mathematics Classroom." Ph.D. dissertation, Kent State University.

Ramachandran, V. S., and S. Blakeslee. 1998. *Phantoms in the Brain.* William Morrow.

Reese, C. M., K. E. Miller, J. Mazzeo, and J. A. Dossey. 1997. *NAEP 1996 Mathematics Report Card for the Nation and the States.* Washington: National Center for Education Statistics.

Resnick, L. B. 1987. *Education and Learning to Think.* Washington: National Academy Press.

Resnick, L. B., E. Cauzinille-Marmeche, and J. Mathieu. 1987. "Understanding Algebra." In *Cognitive Processes in Mathematics,* edited by J. Sloboda and D. Roger, 169–203. Oxford University Press.

Restak, Richard M. 1994. *The Modular Brain.* Simon and Schuster.

———. 1995. *Brainscapes.* New York: Hyperion.

Romberg, T. A. 1992. "Further Thoughts on the Standards: A Reaction to Apple." *Journal for Research in Mathematics Education* 23(5): 432–37.

Schoenfeld, A. C. 1994. "What Do We Know about Mathematics Curricula." *Journal of Mathematical Behavior* 13: 55–80.

Schyns, G., R. L. Goldstone, and J.-P. Thibaut. 1998. "The Development of Features in Object Concepts." *Behavioral and Brain Sciences* 21 (1): 1–54.

Silver, E. A., and M. K. Stein. 1996. "The QUASAR Project: The 'Revolution of the Possible' in Mathematics Instructional Reform in Urban Middle Schools." *Urban Education* 30: 476–521.

Spillane, J. P., and J. S. Zeuli. 1999. "Reform and Teaching: Exploring Patterns of Practice and Context of National and State Mathematics Reforms." *Educational Evaluation and Policy Analysis* 21 (1): 1–27.

Steffe, L. P. 1988. "Children's Construction of Number Sequences and Multiplying Schemes." In *Number Concepts and Operations in the Middle Grades,* edited by J. Hiebert and M. Behr, 119–40. Reston, Va.: National Council of Teachers of Mathematics.

———. 1992. "Schemes of Action and Operation Involving Composite Units." *Learning and Individual Differences* 4(3): 259–309.

Steffe, L. P., and B. S. D'Ambrosio. 1995. "Toward a Working Model of Constructivist Teaching: A Reaction to Simon." *Journal for Research in Mathematics Education* 26 (2): 146–59.

Steffe, L. P., and T. Kieren. 1994. "Radical Constructivism and Mathematics Education." *Journal for Research in Mathematics Education* 25 (6): 711–33.

Steffe, L. P., and R. Tzur. 1994. "Interaction and Children's Mathematics." In *Constructing Mathematical Knowledge: Epistemology and Mathematics Education*, edited by Paul Ernst, 8–32. London: Falmer Press.

Strike, K. A., and G. J. Posner. 1985. "A Conceptual Change View of Learning and Understanding." In *Cognitive Structure and Conceptual Change*, edited by L. H. T. West and A. L. Pines, 211–31. Orlando: Academic Press.

Thompson, A. 1992. "Teachers' Beliefs and Conceptions: A Synthesis of the Research." In *Handbook of Research on Mathematics Teaching*, edited by D. A. Grouws, 127–46. Reston, Va.: National Council of Teachers of Mathematics/ Macmillan.

von Glasersfeld, Ernst. 1987. "Learning as a Constructive Activity." In *Problems of Representation in the Teaching and Learning of Mathematics*, edited by C. Janvier, 3–17. Hillsdale, N.J.: Lawrence Erlbaum.

———. 1995. *Radical Constructivism: A Way of Knowing and Learning*. Washington: Falmer Press.

Wood, T., and P. Sellers. 1996. "Assessment of a Problem-Centered Mathematics Program: Third Grade." *Journal for Research in Mathematics Education* 27 (3): 337–53.

———. 1997. "Deepening the Analysis: Longitudinal Assessment of a Problem-Centered Mathematics Program." *Journal for Research in Mathematics Education* 28 (2): 163–86.

Yackel, E., P. Cobb, and T. Wood. 1991. "Small-Group Interactions as a Source of Learning Opportunities in Second-Grade Mathematics." *Journal for Research in Mathematics Education* 22: 390–408.

CHAPTER FIVE

A Darwinian Perspective on Mathematics and Instruction

DAVID C. GEARY

Educational practices in the United States are faddish, fluctuating from one instructional approach to another and depending more on ideology and the influence of a few educational leaders than on scientific studies of human learning (Hirsch 1996). This chapter provides a scientific framework for grounding educational practices and illustrates the usefulness of this approach for the domain of mathematics (Geary 1995). The theoretical grounding of educational practices requires consideration of the evolutionary function of mind and brain. As an analogy, nearly all the scientific advances in human anatomy, physiology, and medicine have been predicated on the question: What is the function of this organ? (Mayr 1983). There is every reason to believe that understanding the function of the mind and brain will provide a solid foundation for the development of instructional techniques, just as understanding the function of other organs provides the foundation for modern medicine. In other words, to fully appreciate the importance of schooling and effective instructional practices for the development of academic competencies one must understand how different these academic competencies are from the evolved cognitive competencies that the human mind and brain are designed to develop.

The preparation of this chapter was supported, in part, by a summer research fellowship provided by the Research Council of the University of Missouri at Columbia.

This discussion of how evolution informs instructional practices is broken into two sections. The first provides an overview of the evolved functions of the human mind and brain, including a discussion of the architecture of the mind and the developmental experiences that foster the elaboration of the associated cognitive competencies. The second provides a contrast of these evolved competencies and the competencies that children are expected to learn in school, with an emphasis on mathematics. A discussion of associated motivational and instructional issues is also provided.

Evolution and Function of Mind and Brain

Two approaches have been used to make inferences about the evolutionary function of mind and brain. The first involves reverse engineering, whereby the current capabilities of the mind—such as language—are taken as a starting point and from there models of the selection pressures that likely contributed to the evolution of these capabilities are constructed (Pinker 1997). Although reverse engineering helps to understand the functioning of any organ, the resulting evolutionary explanations for adaptations associated with mind and brain are often depicted as a collection of "just so" stories—that is, unverifiable *post hoc* explanations of the phenomenon in question (for example, Eagly and Wood 1999; Halpern 1997). In some, but not all, cases, this appears to be the case. The second approach, especially when judiciously combined with the first, provides a scientifically more defensible method for making inferences about the evolutionary function of mind and brain. With this approach, the behavior, body structure (for example, beak size), or physiology of evolutionarily related species—those with a recent common ancestor—that occupy different social or ecological niches are compared (Foley and Lee 1989; Weiner 1995). If there is a systematic relation between differences in social and ecological condition and differences in the behavior, body structure, or physiology of related species, then a plausible conclusion is that the former influenced the evolution of the latter.

Studies of the relationships among the size of primate species' neocortex (the evolutionarily most recent part of the brain), the length of the developmental period, and the species' social system provide an example of the utility of this approach. The results indicate a systematic relation among the size of the neocortex, the length of the developmental period, and the complexity of the social systems (for example, average group size) within which primate species live, develop, and presumably evolved (Barton

1996; Dunbar 1993; Joffe 1997; Sawaguchi 1997). Neocortex size—after controlling for body size—is largest in those species that live in the most complex social systems, and these same species have the longest developmental periods. These comparative patterns suggest that social factors, such as social competition, contributed to the evolution of the mind and brain and that a long developmental period is needed to practice and refine the associated social skills (Geary and Flinn 2001).

The former interpretation is supported by brain-imaging studies that indicate that portions of the prefrontal cortex—the most recently evolved portion of the neocortex—support several social competencies, such as aspects of language and theory of mind (for example, the ability to infer the feelings of other people; Baron-Cohen et al. 1994; Pugh et al. 1997). For humans, the latter interpretation is supported by the early social competencies of infants and the large proportion of time children spend in social discourse with peers, combined with the finding that these social relations promote social and psychological competencies (Harris 1995).

Functional Organization of the Human Mind

On the basis of this approach and results from more traditional research in anthropology and psychology, Geary (1998) proposed a functional taxonomy for the human mind. As shown in figure 5-1, this taxonomy includes cognitive systems designed to attend to and process social, biological (for example, prey species), and physical features of the world, although there are other evolved domains as well, such as number (described below) and music (which appears to serve a social-emotional function). The gist is that the evolution of the human mind was centered on those competencies involved in securing the social, biological (for example, food), and physical (for example, territory) resources that supported the survival and reproduction of our ancestors. Stated somewhat differently, Darwin's (1859) conceptualization of natural selection as resulting from a "struggle for life" is more precisely defined as a struggle for control of the resources that support life and that allow one to reproduce. The mind and brain, and its evolution, are thus conceptualized as supporting attempts to secure or control social, biological, and physical resources by selectively attending to and processing the associated features of the environment (for example, facial expression). These cognitive systems are complemented by parallel behavioral strategies (for example, social persuasion) that are directed at these features of the world and that

Figure 5-1. *Evolved Domains of Mind*

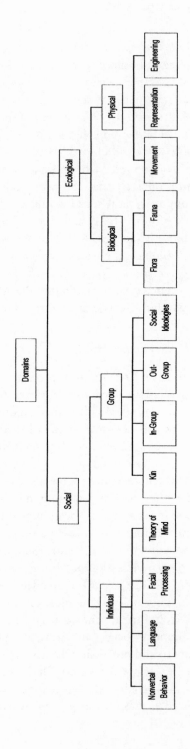

support actual attempts to gain social influence, secure food, and so forth. Brief discussion of the cognitive skills associated with these social, biological, and physical domains, as well as those associated with what appears to be an evolved number system, is provided below.

SOCIAL DOMAINS. Comparative studies (Foley 1996), psychological research (Harris 1995), as well as common sense support the position that a significant portion of the human mind and brain is devoted to social endeavors. The position here is that the associate cognitive skills can be subdivided into those that allow one to develop individual relationships and interact in dyads, as well as other skills that parse the social universe into groups, as shown in figure 5-1 (Geary 1998). The individual-level social skills would include the ability to "read" the nonverbal behaviors, such as gestures and facial expressions of other people, as well as language and theory of mind. Theory of mind involves the use of information provided by people's gestures, speech, and facial expressions to construct a mental model, or basic psychological representation, of their emotional state, intention, likely future behavior, and so forth. The ability to construct these mental models would greatly aid in the development and maintenance of friendships, and aid in social competition, which, in turn, would provide the survival and reproductive advantages that would be needed for any such cognitive system to evolve.

Individual humans, and the individuals of many other species, are selective in terms of whom they affiliate with and whom they do not. In many, theoretically all, species this parsing of the social universe is related, in part, to kinship; individuals form social groups with kin much more readily than with nonkin (Altmann et al. 1996). The preferential treatment of kin is readily understood in terms of inclusive fitness. Behaviors that promote the survival and reproduction of kin will necessarily promote the evolution of the altruists' genes, to the degree that the donor and receiver of this preferential treatment are genetically related (Hamilton 1964). Perhaps more important is the finding that humans, as well as individuals in many other species, form and maintain cooperative relationships with nonkin, termed *friendship* by psychologists and *reciprocal altruism* by evolutionary biologists (Hartup and Stevens 1997; Trivers 1971). These relationships are mutually beneficial to all those involved, in the form of "you scratch my back and I'll scratch yours."

These friends, and political allies, define one's in-group, who, in turn, are evaluated and treated more favorably than are other people (Stephan

1985). The out-group is composed of other individuals, especially groups that are competing with one's in-group for scarce resources. This type of parsing of the social universe is not limited to humans. It is also found in other species, including one of our closest relatives, the chimpanzee (*Pan troglodytes*; Goodall 1986). However, the ability to form in-groups on the basis of social ideologies, such as religion or nationality, appears to be unique to humans and allows the formation of large social groups (that is, groups in which all members do not personally know one another). The selection pressure for the evolution of ideology-based in-groups and out-groups was probably intergroup competition, given the competitive advantage associated with a larger group size (Alexander 1979). In any case, it is clear that humans have inherent cognitive systems for regulating dyadic interactions and relationships and for forming favored and disfavored social groupings.

BIOLOGICAL DOMAINS.   It is clear, although not always appreciated or often studied by cognitive psychologists, that people in preindustrial societies develop elaborate knowledge systems of local flora and fauna and develop mental models of the behavior (for example, growth patterns) of these plants and animals (Atran 1998; Malt 1995). Through ethnobiological studies, "it has become apparent that, while individual societies may differ considerably in their conceptualization of plants and animals, there are a number of strikingly regular structural principles of folk biological classification which are quite general" (Berlin, Breedlove, and Raven 1973, 214). Moreover, these preindustrial classification systems are similar to the scientific classification of the same organisms (Atran 1994), although the system within a particular culture is more or less elaborated contingent on the social and biological significance of the plants or animals to the people in the culture (Atran 1998; Malt 1995).

In preindustrial societies, the classification of flora and fauna is based on morphology, behavior, growth patterns, and ecological niche, which, in combination, represent the basic "essence" of the species (Atran 1994). In effect, the essence is a mental model of the salient characteristics of the species. These mental models allow people to predict the likely behavior of organisms and make reasonably accurate inferences about the essence of unfamiliar species. So, knowledge of one species of frog allows inferences to be drawn about the likely essence of other species of frog but tells little about the essence of birds. In short, survival in preindustrial contexts perforce required the exploitation of biological resources (for example, hunted species and harvested crops), which, in turn, almost certainly created strong selection pressures for the evolution of cognitive systems for categorizing and learning the essence of these species.

PHYSICAL DOMAINS. It is necessarily true that any species that moves about in the physical world must have some cognitive systems that support this movement. Some species also have cognitive systems that can generate mental representations of the environment and enable the use of tools to manipulate objects in the environment (Geary 1998; Pinker 1997; Shepard 1994). The cognitive and perceptual systems that support movement in the physical world are almost certainly the oldest of these systems, with respect to evolutionary time. These systems not only allow organisms to move around, or navigate, in the environment, they also support prey location and capture, predator avoidance, location of food sources, and so forth. In many species the ability to form mental representations of the environment appears to be less developed than the ability to simply navigate in the environment (Dyer 1998). When they are evident, the associated skills would include the ability to visualize familiar environments and to develop mental maps to facilitate navigating in these environments (Matthews 1992). It is clear that tool use has a long evolutionary history in humans, and a few other species, including chimpanzees, although little is currently known about the cognitive skills that enable the construction of primitive tools (Gowlett 1992; Trinkaus 1992).

MATHEMATICAL DOMAINS. Although not emphasized in the taxonomy presented in figure 5-1, it is almost certain that humans, and many other species, have an inherent sense of number, counting, and simple arithmetic (Boysen and Berntson 1989; Boysen and Capaldi 1993; Geary 1995). In the first few days of life, human infants can distinguish, for instance, sets of two objects from sets of three objects and appear to make this discrimination based on an intuitive understanding of quantity (Antell and Keating 1983; Starkey and R. Cooper 1980). By five to six months of age, infants are aware that the addition of one object to another increases set size and that the subtraction of one object from a set of two objects decreases set size (Wynn 1992). By about eighteen months of age, infants begin to show an understanding of ordinal relationships, at least for small quantities—for example, that a set of two objects is more than a set of one object but less than a set of three objects (Strauss and Curtis 1984). Soon thereafter toddlers begin to use a form of nonverbal counting for adding and subtracting small quantities of objects (Starkey 1992). Between two and three years of age children begin to show an intuitive understanding of counting principles and begin to use language during the counting process (Gelman and Gallistel 1978).

During the preschool years, children's knowledge of numbers, counting, and arithmetic grows, although the extent to which this development reflects the elaboration of inherent knowledge or informal teaching by parents is not currently known. In any case, by four to five years of age children use counting to solve simple addition and subtraction problems, such as 5 + 3, and, depending on how it is worded, can use this knowledge to solve simple arithmetical word problems (Geary 1994). It is likely that certain aspects of geometry also have an inherent basis to them, as described later, but these appear to be largely distinct from the inherent number-counting-arithmetic system. These basic mathematical competencies appear to emerge without formal instruction and are found in preindustrial cultures and to some degree in the chimpanzee and some other primates (Boysen and Berntson 1989; Saxe 1982). Nonetheless, these competencies are rudimentary in comparison to the competencies that define the modern field of mathematics and the competencies that are necessary for gainful employment in a technologically advanced society such as our own (Geary 1995).

Development of Evolved Cognitive Systems

A long period of development, as is found in humans, has a clear risk—death before the age of reproduction—and thus would only evolve if there were benefits that outweighed this risk. Comparative studies suggest that one purpose, and an important adaptive benefit, of delayed maturation is the accompanying ability to refine the physical, social, and cognitive competencies that supported the survival and reproduction of the species' ancestors. As an example, a long developmental period is found in all highly social primates, and the length of this period increases with expansions in the complexity of the species' social system, as noted above (Joffe 1997). These patterns suggest that one purpose of childhood is to practice and refine the social-cognitive, such as language, and other competencies shown in figure 5-1. In short, one function of a long childhood is to engage in the activities that allow children to practice and refine the physical, social, and cognitive skills associated with the survival (for example, hunting) and reproduction (for example, parenting skills) of our ancestors (Geary and Bjorklund 2000).

Play, social interactions, and exploration of the environment and objects appear to be the mechanisms through which these emerging competencies are practiced and refined during childhood. In theory, child-initiated social play, exploration, and so forth are intimately linked to cognitive and neural development, in that these activities provide experiences with the social, biological, and physical world. These experiences, in turn, interact with the inherent but skeletal structure of the cognitive systems outlined in figure 5-1 and ensure their normal development and adaptation to local conditions (Geary 1998; Gelman 1990; for an alternative view see Elman et al. 1996). In other words, evolution has resulted in the human mind and brain being composed of the cognitive systems described above, but these systems are only skeletal in nature and must be fleshed out and adapted to local conditions through experience (Greenough 1991; Greenough, Black, and Wallace 1987). Children are biologically prepared and motivated to engage in the activities that result in these experiences and, as a result, they learn about people, local flora and fauna, and the surrounding physical world and automatically flesh out the supporting cognitive and neural systems.

The Training of Mind and Brain in Modern Society

Now that a basic introduction to the evolutionary function of mind and brain has been provided, attention shifts to the relation between mind and brain and schooling in modern society. The basic issues concern differences between evolved cognitive competencies and the academic competencies that children are expected to learn in these societies and differences in the experiences and motivation needed to develop these two different types of cognitive skill. The former is addressed in the first section below, and the latter in the second.

Schooling and Academic Domains

The cognitive competencies described above, such as language, have been found to develop in all human societies in which these skills have been studied. As noted above, the development of these competencies appears to be guided by an innate skeletal structure and an inherent bias for children to engage in the types of activities that will ensure the fleshing out of this skeletal structure. The result is that the basic structure for evolved competencies is molded to the local social group and ecology. As an example, language appears to have an inherent but skeletal structure and becomes elaborated without formal instruction and during the course of children's natural activities, such as social play. The result of these experiences is that the inherent ability to learn any natural human language becomes fine-tuned, such that the language to which the child is exposed gradually becomes the language the child understands and uses (Kuhl 1994; Kuhl et al. 1997).

In contrast, many, perhaps most, of the academic competencies, such as reading and writing, that American children are expected to learn in school are not found across human societies and, in fact, do not emerge in modern society without formal schooling (Geary 1995). If the mind and brain were biologically prepared to learn how to read and write, and if children's natural activities were sufficient for the learning of these competencies, then children in all cultures would learn to read and write just as easily as they learn their culture's language. That they do not is prima facie evidence that evolution has not provided the mind and brain with the skeletal structure that will automatically and effortlessly result in children learning how to, for instance, read. Nor has evolution provided children with an inherent bias to engage in the activities that result in the automatic and effortless acquisition of reading skills (Geary 1995).

The same argument is applicable to mathematics and, in fact, all other academic domains. As noted earlier, the rudimentary but inherent number-counting-arithmetic skills are very different from the mathematics that children are expected to learn in school and the mathematics that will influence their later employability, productivity, and wages in modern society (Rivera-Batiz 1992). To be sure, these basic competencies provide a stepping-stone for learning some aspects of formal arithmetic, such as adding and subtracting more complex numbers than described above (for example, 45 + 97), but they appear to be more distantly related or unrelated to other areas of arithmetic. Although people in preindustrial societies and children in modern societies do not appear to naturally understand the basic concepts of formal multiplication and division, their inherent understanding of addition and subtraction provides a foundation for learning these aspects of arithmetic.

On the other hand, there appears to be little relation between children's intuitive understanding of number-counting-arithmetic and the base-10 structure of the Arabic number system (that is, that the number series repeats in sequences of 10, as in 1, 2, 3 . . . 10, 10 + 1, 10 + 2, that is, 11, 12 . . .). The base-10 structure is an essential feature of modern arithmetic and there is no indication that children, or many educated adults for that matter, have an intuitive understanding of this structure. In other words, the base-10 system emerged from the focused activities of early mathematicians as they struggled to develop increasingly effective means of representing quantities and performing arithmetical operations (Al-Uqlidisi 1978) and is in no way related to the evolution of the number-counting-arithmetic system. In this view, it is expected—and is in fact the case—that the learning of the base-10 system and associated procedures (for example, borrowing, as in 45 – 29) will be much more difficult for children than the acquisition of basic number-counting-arithmetic skills and concepts (Geary 1994), just as learning to read is more difficult for children than learning their parents' language.

In some cases, the evolution of systems that appear to be unrelated to the evolution of the number-counting-arithmetic system can provide a foundation for some aspects of mathematics. In particular, a relation between spatial abilities and mathematics has been posited for thousands of years (Dehaene et al. 1999); in fact, geometry can be defined as the study of space and shape. Using both behavioral and brain-imaging methods, Dehaene and his colleagues recently demonstrated that some arithmetic skills, such as the ability to estimate quantities, are based on spatial abilities, whereas other skills, such as the ability to remember basic facts, are not. The estimation skills appeared to involve the construction of a mental number line. The use of this number line to estimate quantity was, in turn, associated with activation of parts of the brain that typically support spatial abilities. It is not likely that these brain regions evolved to support a mental number line, but, with schooling and experience, can be used for this purpose.

Spatial abilities, especially those associated with navigating in the world, may also provide an intuitive understanding of certain features of geometry (Gallistel 1990; Geary 1995). Basically, there is order and structure to the physical universe, and many of the spatial abilities of humans, and other species, reflect the evolution of mind and brain systems that are sensitive to this order (Shepard 1994). The associated competencies, as described above, include the ability to navigate in the world and generate a mental map of this world, as well as more basic skills (such as the ability to visually track moving objects). Nearly all of this knowledge of the physical world is implicit, or unconscious; that is, the systems that support moving about in the world work more or less automatically, in the same way that breathing occurs automatically (Geary 1998). Some aspects of this intuitive knowledge appear to form the foundation for some aspects of Euclidean geometry. As an example, Euclid's first principle—a line can be drawn from any point to any point, that is, a line is a straight line— reflects the intuitive understanding that the fastest way to get from one place to another is to "go as the crow flies," that is, go in a straight line (if possible, of course). At the same time, there is little reason to believe that other aspects of formal geometry, such as theorems, are as intimately related to spatial knowledge.

There are other aspects of mathematics that may be difficult to learn because people's intuitive (and apparently evolved) knowledge interferes with formal learning, or at least the use of formal mathematics. For instance, people often make judgments about the relative risk of various activities (for example, flying in an airplane) based on how easily they can remember examples of mishaps associated with those activities (plane crashes). This memory-based method, or heuristic, for determining risk often leads to poor probability and risk judgments in modern societies. This is because mass media coverage of rare events produces an inaccurate picture of the actual risk associated with various activities. Most people greatly overestimate the risk associated with flying because they can remember many disturbing plane crashes. Most people have not personally experienced these crashes, but they were exposed to them through television (Lichtenstein et al. 1978). The use of this memory-based heuristic probably worked rather well in natural environments—those in which our ancestors evolved—but it leads to poor risk assessment in modern societies and appears to interfere with the learning and use of formal statistics to make risk assessments (Brace, Cosmides, and Tooby 1998).

In sum, economic and technological changes continue to increase the gap between the types of environments within which our mind and brain evolved and the types of environments within which we currently live and work. The associated cumulative advances in the field of mathematics and the demands of math-intensive occupations have resulted in an increasing gap between the competencies that define the evolved number-counting-arithmetic system and other systems (for example, spatial) that are related to mathematics and the quantitative skills needed to work in math-intensive occupations. In other words, there is a substantive gap between the evolved quantitative and spatial competencies that provide a rudimentary foundation for aspects of arithmetic and mathematics and the much more diverse and complex quantitative skills that children are expected to learn in modern society (Geary 1995).

Motivation and Instructional Practices

The issue of motivation and school learning is addressed in the first section below. The second section provides a contrast of the activities that appear to be necessary for the mastery of school-based competencies and the activities necessary for the refinement of evolved competencies.

MOTIVATION AND SCHOOL LEARNING. Whereas children appear to be biologically motivated to engage in the activities that lead to the refinement of the evolved cognitive skills described earlier, there is no a priori reason to believe that they are similarly motivated to engage in the activities that foster the acquisition of nonevolved, school-based competencies. In fact, there is reason to believe that children are *not* inherently motivated to engage in the activities that facilitate school-based learning.

When viewed from an evolutionary perspective, children's basic motivational systems—those that guide goal-directed activities—are designed to orient children to other people and to prompt children to explore the biological and physical world in which they live. These activities often involve an element of fun, which, in turn, further motivates engagement in these activities. As described earlier, the associated experiences appear to flesh out the neural, cognitive, and behavioral skills associated with evolved competencies (Geary 1995, 1998; Greenough et al. 1987). However, many academic competencies, such as reading, writing, and higher mathematics, are very different from the evolved competencies to which inherent motivational systems appear to be geared. Whereas nearly all children will be inherently interested in learning about people and the wider ecology—although there will be individual differences in these interests—there is no reason to believe that children have an inherent interest in academic domains or an inherent motivation to master these domains. This perspective does not mean that no one will be motivated to pursue school-based learning (Geary 1995). Rather, the motivation to pursue evolved goals, such as being part of a social group, will be more or less universal but the motivation to pursue nonevolved goals, such as mastery of algebra, will not.

Two important implications follow from this view. First, universal education will be dependent to a large degree on the social valuation of school-based competencies (Stevenson and Stigler 1992). In other words, the need to learn many academic competencies comes from the demands of the wider society and not the inherent interests of children. Social and cultural supports, such as spelling bees, social and parental valuation of school achievement, and so forth, are thus likely to be needed to support children's investment in school learning. Second, most children will prefer to engage in evolved instead of nonevolved activities, such as interacting with their friends rather than sitting in a classroom. Because of this, one essential function of schools is to organize the behavior of children such that they engage in activities—preferably effective instructional activities—that they otherwise would not engage in. Stated somewhat differently, teachers must organize and guide children's academic development because it cannot be assumed that children's "natural curiosity" will result in an interest in all academic domains or the motivation needed to engage in the activities that will foster the mastery of these domains.

This is not to say that some people will not voluntarily engage in nonevolved activities, such as reading. The motivation to read is probably driven by the content of what is being read rather than by the process itself. In fact, the content of many stories and other nonevolved activities, such as video games and television, might reflect evolutionarily relevant themes that motivate engagement in these activities, such as social relationships and competition (Geary 1998). Furthermore, the finding that intellectual curiosity is a basic dimension of human personality, and the personality of some other species it seems, suggests that, in any given society, there will be a number of intellectually curious individuals who will pursue nonevolved activities (Goldberg 1993; Gosling and John 1999). Euclid's investment in formalizing and proving the principles of geometry is one example. However, this type of discovery reflects the activities and insights of only a few individuals and the associated advances spread through the larger society largely by means of formal instruction. In sum, the motivation to engage in the activities that will promote the acquisition of academic competencies is not likely to be universal. Thus one important function of schooling is to organize the activities of children to ensure that they engage in instructional activities that they would not otherwise choose.

INSTRUCTION AND SCHOOL LEARNING. Just as it cannot be assumed that all children are inherently motivated to learn academic competencies, it cannot be assumed that the activities that promote the refinement of evolved cognitive competencies are sufficient for the learning of these academic competencies. Theoretically, the activities (such as play and social discourse) that are necessary and sufficient for the refinement of evolved cognitive competencies are *not* expected to be sufficient for the development of academic competencies (Geary 1995). If they were, then all that would be needed is for children to be exposed to books, numbers, and so forth for them to learn to read, write, do complex arithmetic, and so forth. This is, of course, the basic assumption of some current educational practices, specifically constructivism. However, empirical research indicates that, in many academic domains, most children need direct, explicit, and teacher-directed instruction to master the associated competencies (Bradley and Bryant 1983; Geary 1994). The failure of constructivists and others to make the distinction between what is necessary for the elaboration of evolved cognitive competencies and nonevolved academic competencies has resulted in the wide-scale adoption of instructional practices, such as whole language, that will fail with a large proportion of children.

This is a crucial and, in a sense, educationally fatal conceptual error. Whereas evolution has provided structure to the mind and brain and the associated childhood activities such that evolved competencies are automatically practiced and refined, evolution has provided no such structure for the learning of nonevolved competencies. This is where schooling is critical; instructional practices must provide the structure and organization needed for the acquisition of nonevolved competencies, just as evolution has provided the structure and organization needed for the refinement of evolved competencies. In this view, school learning is uncharted territory, something that is a recent cultural innovation, especially the goal of universal education. At no point in human evolution has there been the social goal of having all, or nearly all, children learn a vast array of academic competencies that their mind and brain were not designed to learn.

Because of this and the insight that children's natural activities are not likely to be sufficient for the learning of academic competencies, instructional practices *must* be based on empirical research. People may have intuitions about how children learn and what children prefer to do, but these intuitions are almost certainly related to the refinement of evolved competencies, such as language, and not nonevolved competencies, such as reading. Instructional practices based on intuition and children's preferences are not likely to be successful, in terms of fostering the mastery of the wide array of academic competencies children are now expected to learn. Although there is much to be learned, especially how evolved biases interact with instructional practices, much is known about effective instructional techniques, in reading and in mathematics.

For many academic domains, direct and explicit instruction—instruction focused on the acquisition of well-defined academic skills (for example, word decoding)—appears to be the most effective strategy for teaching the largest number of children (Bradley and Bryant 1983; Geary 1994). However, somewhat different instructional strategies appear to be needed to foster different types of academic competencies. In mathematics, academic competencies can be roughly subdivided into procedural skills, such as the rules for manipulating algebraic equations, and conceptual knowledge, that is, the underlying principles of the domain. Although it is becoming increasingly clear that the acquisition of procedural skills influences children's conceptual knowledge and that conceptual knowledge influences which procedures are used and which are not (Sophian 1997), from an instructional perspective they should probably be considered distinct.

Indeed, research in cognitive and educational psychology suggests that the acquisition of procedural skills and conceptual knowledge require, to some degree, different forms of instruction (Cooper and Sweller 1987). Briefly, procedural learning requires extensive practice on the whole range of problems on which the procedure might eventually be used. Practice should not involve the use of the same procedure on the same type of problem for an extended period of time. Wenger (1987) argued that this form of practice results in the development of procedural bugs, that is, procedures that are correct for some problems but incorrectly extended to other problems. Rather, practice should involve the use of a mixture of procedures that are practiced on a variety of different types of problems. Practice should also occur in small doses (for example, 20 minutes a day) and over an extended period of time (Cooper 1989). For example, Bahrick and Hall (1991) showed that the retention of basic algebraic skills over a fifty-year period was related to repeated exposure to algebra in high school and college. A procedure that is practiced on one or two worksheets for a day or two will likely be forgotten rather quickly (Bahrick 1993).

Basically, the procedure should be practiced until the child can automatically execute the procedure with the different types of problems that the procedure is normally used to solve. Once automatized, procedures require little conscious effort to use, which, in turn, frees attentional and working memory resources for use on other, more important features of the problem. The practice of basic procedures, especially when mixed with other problems that require the use of different procedures, should also provide the child with an opportunity to come to understand how the procedure works. In other words, practice provides a context within which children can elaborate their understanding of the procedure and any associated conceptual knowledge. Recent studies also suggest that movement from the use of less sophisticated procedures to the more sophisticated procedures can occur in the context of drill-and-practice (Siegler and Stern 1998), although these changes also appear to be related to children's conceptual understanding of the domain (Geary, Bow-Thomas, and Yao 1992).

Research suggests that a deep conceptual understanding of a mathematical domain requires a lot of experience but does not appear to require drill-and-practice per se (Cooper and Sweller 1987). Conceptual knowledge reflects the child's understanding of the basic principles of the domain and allows the child to see similarities across problems that have different superficial features (Morales, Shute, and Pellegrino 1985). A child might demonstrate a good conceptual understanding of counting, for instance, when she knows that counting can occur from left to right, right to left, or haphazardly, and, as long as all the items are counted, still yield the same answer (Briars and Siegler 1984). One useful way to promote the learning of concepts is to ask students to generate as many ways as possible to solve a particular problem or class of problems (Sweller, Mawer, and Ward 1983). For this example, instruction might involve having the children count in as many different ways as they can (for example, left to right, right to left). Another important instructional feature that might facilitate children's development of conceptual knowledge involves presenting problems in familiar contexts, those that the child can relate to personal experiences (Perry, VanderStoep, and Yu 1993).

Other research suggests that children's more natural activities, such as working in groups and trying to understand how other children are solving problems, also facilitate the learning of some procedures and concepts. As an example, Siegler (1995) demonstrated that asking children to explain why another person solved a particular problem one way and not another helped these children to better understand the associated concept. This particular manipulation was tapping into children's theory of mind, that is, their tendency to try to understand what other people are thinking. Explaining their own problem-solving strategies to others can also foster the development of more effective problem-solving approaches and conceptual knowledge, apparently by making the goal of problem solving more explicit (Crowley and Siegler 1999). In other words, some features of children's more natural ways of learning and understanding the world can be used to foster the acquisition of some nonevolved academic competencies, although these more natural activities are not, in and of themselves, sufficient for much of this learning. The real issue is to find the best mix of natural and instructional activities needed to foster the mastery of crucial academic competencies. It is almost certainly the case that this mix will vary from one domain, such as arithmetic, to the next, such as geometric theorems. The only way to determine the best mix is through empirical research.

Conclusion

Educational practices will continue to swing from one fad to another, to the educational detriment of millions of American children and potentially the U.S. economy (Bishop 1989), until these practices are firmly grounded in scientific research and theory. The position here is that the fundamental principles of education must be informed by both an understanding of the evolved functions of mind and brain and by empirical research on children's learning (Geary 1995). The former is needed to appreciate what we are asking of children: in modern society, children are expected to learn a vast array of academic competencies that their mind and brain were not designed to learn. In this view, it is not surprising—it is expected—that most children will find learning how to read, learning the base-10 structure of the Arabic number system, and learning a host of other skills and concepts difficult and time-consuming endeavors. Moreover, it is expected that this learning will not occur for most children without explicit and informed guidance from teachers.

In short, evolution has provided children with the mind and brain systems, as well as the motivation, to seek out associated experiences that will automatically and effortlessly result in their learning language, how to navigate in the world, and some aspects of number, counting, and arithmetic, among other skills. Evolution has not resulted in a similar preparation to learn how to read, learn the base-10 system, geometric theorems, and so on. In a sense, schooling and instruction must provide children with the organization and structure needed to learn these academic competencies, in a way that is analogous to the structure evolution has provided for the elaboration of evolved competencies. It is almost certain that children's preferences and educators' intuitions are not enough to know how to best organize children's academic development. Given the evolutionary novelty of academic competencies and the recent goal of universal education, only empirical research based on accepted scientific methods will tell us which instructional practices will and will not work (Geary 1995; Hirsch 1996).

References

Alexander, R. D. 1979. *Darwinism and Human Affairs*. University of Washington Press.

Al-Uqlidisi, A. 1978. *The Arithmetic of Al-Uqlidisi*. S. A. Saidan, trans. Boston: D. Reidel Publishing.

Altmann, J., S. C. Alberts, S. A. Haines, J. Dubach, P. Muruthi, T. Coote, E. Geffen, D. J. Chessman, R. S. Mututua, S. N. Saiyalel, R. K. Wayne, R. C. Lacy, and M. W. Bruford. 1996. "Behavior Predicts Genetic Structure in a Wild Primate Group." *Proceedings of the National Academy of Sciences USA* 93: 5797–801.

Antell, S. E., and D. P. Keating. 1983. "Perception of Numerical Invariance in Neonates." *Child Development* 54: 695–701.

Atran, S. 1994. "Core Domains versus Scientific Theories: Evidence from Systematics and Itza-Maya Folkbiology." In *Mapping the Mind: Domain Specificity in Cognition and Culture,* edited by L. A. Hirschfeld and S. A. Gelman, 316–40. Cambridge University Press.

———. 1998. "Folk Biology and the Anthropology of Science: Cognitive Universals and Cultural Particulars." *Behavioral and Brain Sciences* 21: 547–609.

Bahrick, H. P. 1993. "Extending the Life-Span of Knowledge." In *The Challenge in Mathematics and Science Education: Psychology's Response,* edited by L. A. Penner, G. M. Batsche, H. M. Knoff, and D. L. Nelson, 61–82. Washington: American Psychological Association.

Bahrick, H. P., and L. K. Hall, 1991. "Lifetime Maintenance of High School Mathematics Content." *Journal of Experimental Psychology: General* 120: 22–33.

Baron-Cohen, S., H. Ring, J. Moriarty, B. Schmitz, D. Costa, and P. Ell. 1994. "Recognition of Mental State Terms: Clinical Findings in Children with Autism and a Functional Neuroimaging Study of Normal Adults." *British Journal of Psychiatry* 165: 640–49.

Barton, R. A. 1996. "Neocortex Size and Behavioural Ecology in Primates." *Proceedings of the Royal Society of London B* 263: 173–77.

Berlin, B., D. E. Breedlove, and P. H. Raven. 1973. "General Principles of Classification and Nomenclature in Folk Biology." *American Anthropologist* 75: 214–42.

Bishop, J. H. 1989. "Is the Test Score Decline Responsible for the Productivity Growth Decline?" *American Economic Review* 79: 178–97.

Boysen, S. T., and G. G. Berntson. 1989. "Numerical Competence in a Chimpanzee (*Pan troglodytes*)." *Journal of Comparative Psychology* 103: 23–31.

Boysen, S. T., and E. J. Capaldi, eds. 1993. *The Development of Numerical Competence: Animal and Human Models*. Hillsdale, N.J.: Lawrence Erlbaum.

Brace, G. L., L. Cosmides, and J. Tooby. 1998. "Individuation, Counting, and Statistical Inference: The Frequency and Whole-Object Representations in Judgment under Uncertainty." *Journal of Experimental Psychology: General* 127: 3–21.

Bradley, L., and P. E. Bryant. 1983. "Categorizing Sounds and Learning to Read—A Causal Connection." *Nature* 301: 419–21.

Briars, D., and R. S. Siegler. 1984. "A Featural Analysis of Preschoolers' Counting Knowledge." *Developmental Psychology* 20: 607–18.

Cooper, G., and J. Sweller. 1987. "Effects of Schema Acquisition and Rule Automation on Mathematical Problem-Solving Transfer." *Journal of Educational Psychology* 79: 347–62.

Cooper, H. 1989. "Synthesis of Research on Homework." *Educational Leadership* 47: 85–91.

Crowley, K., and R. S. Siegler. 1999. "Explanation and Generalization in Young Children's Strategy Learning." *Child Development* 70: 304–16.

Darwin, C. 1859. *On the Origin of Species by Means of Natural Selection*. London: John Murray.

Dehaene, S., E. Spelke, P. Pinel, R. Stanescu, and S. Tsivkin. 1999. "Sources of Mathematical Thinking: Behavioral and Brain-Imaging Evidence." *Science* 284: 970–74.

Dunbar, R. I. M. 1993. "Coevolution of Neocortical Size, Group Size and Language in Humans." *Behavioral and Brain Sciences* 16: 681–735.

Dyer, F. C. 1998. "Cognitive Ecology of Navigation." In *Cognitive Ecology: The Evolutionary Ecology of Information Processing and Decision Making*, edited by R. Dukas, 201–60. University of Chicago Press.

Eagly, A. H., and W. Wood. 1999. "The Origins of Sex Differences in Human Behavior: Evolved Dispositions versus Social Roles." *American Psychologist* 54: 408–23.

Elman, J. L., E. A. Bates, M. H. Johnson, A. Karmiloff-Smith, D. Parisi, and K. Plunkett. 1996. *Rethinking Innateness: A Connectionist Perspective on Development*. MIT Press/Bradford Books.

Foley, R. A. 1996. "An Evolutionary and Chronological Framework for Human Social Behavior." *Proceedings of the British Academy* 88: 95–117.

Foley, R. A., and P. C. Lee. 1989. "Finite Social Space, Evolutionary Pathways, and Reconstructing Hominid Behavior." *Science* 243: 901–06.

Gallistel, C. R. 1990. *The Organization of Learning*. MIT Press/Bradford Books.

Geary, D. C. 1994. *Children's Mathematical Development: Research and Practical Applications*. Washington: American Psychological Association.

———. 1995. "Reflections of Evolution and Culture in Children's Cognition: Implications for Mathematical Development and Instruction." *American Psychologist* 50: 24–37.

———. 1998. *Male, Female: The Evolution of Human Sex Differences*. Washington: American Psychological Association.

Geary, D. C., and D. F. Bjorklund. 2000. "Evolutionary Developmental Psychology." *Child Developmen* 71: 57–65.

Geary, D. C., C. C. Bow-Thomas, and Y. Yao. 1992. "Counting Knowledge and Skill in Cognitive Addition: A Comparison of Normal and Mathematically Disabled Children." *Journal of Experimental Child Psychology* 54: 372–91.

Geary, D. C., and M. V. Flinn. 2001. "Evolution of Human Parental Behavior and the Human Family." *Parenting: Science and Practice* 1: 5–61.

Gelman, R. 1990. "First Principles Organize Attention to and Learning about Relevant Data: Number and Animate-Inanimate Distinction as Examples." *Cognitive Science* 14: 79–106.

Gelman, R., and C. R. Gallistel. 1978. *The Child's Understanding of Number.* Harvard University Press.

Gosling, S. D., and O. P. John. 1999. "Personality Dimensions in Nonhuman Animals: A Cross-Species Review." *Current Directions in Psychological Science* 8: 69–75.

Greenough, W. T. 1991. "Experience as a Component of Normal Development: Evolutionary Considerations." *Developmental Psychology* 27: 14–17.

Greenough, W. T., J. E. Black, and C. S. Wallace. 1987. "Experience and Brain Development." *Child Development* 58: 539–59.

Goldberg, L. R. 1993. "The Structure of Phenotypic Personality Traits." *American Psychologist* 48: 26–34.

Goodall, J. 1986. *The Chimpanzees of Gombe: Patterns of Behavior.* Cambridge, Mass.: Belknap Press.

Gowlett, J. A. J. 1992. "Tools—The Paleolithic Record." In *The Cambridge Encyclopedia of Human Evolution,* edited by S. Jones, R. Martin, and D. Pilbeam, 350–60. Cambridge University Press.

Halpern, D. F. 1997. "Sex Differences in Intelligence and Their Implications for Education." *American Psychologist* 52: 1091–102.

Hamilton, W. D. 1964. "The Genetical Evolution of Social Behavior. II." *Journal of Theoretical Biology* 7: 17–52.

Harris, J. R. 1995. "Where Is the Child's Environment? A Group Socialization Theory of Development." *Psychological Review* 102: 458–89.

Hartup, W. W., and N. Stevens. 1997. "Friendships and Adaptation in the Life Course." *Psychological Bulletin* 121: 355–70.

Hirsch, E. D., Jr. 1996. *The Schools We Need: Why We Don't Have Them.* Doubleday.

Joffe, T. H. 1997. "Social Pressures Have Selected for an Extended Juvenile Period in Primates." *Journal of Human Evolution* 32: 593–605.

Kuhl, P. K. 1994. "Learning and Representation in Speech and Language." *Current Opinion in Neurobiology* 4: 812–22.

Kuhl, P. K., J. E. Andruski, I. A. Chistovich, L. A. Chistovich, E. V. Kozhevnikova, V. L. Ryskina, E. I. Stolyarova, U. Sundberg, and F. Lacerda. 1997. "Cross-Language Analysis of Phonetic Units in Language Addressed to Infants." *Science* 277: 684–86.

Lichtenstein, S., P. Slovic, B. Fischhoff, M. Layman, and B. Combs. 1978. "Judged Frequency of Lethal Events." *Journal of Experimental Psychology: Human Learning and Memory* 4: 551–78.

Malt, B. C. 1995. "Category Coherence in Cross-Cultural Perspective." *Cognitive Psychology* 29: 85–148.

Matthews, M. H. 1992. *Making Sense of Place: Children's Understanding of Large-Scale Environments.* Savage, Md.: Barnes and Noble Books.

Mayr, E. 1983. "How to Carry out the Adaptationist Program?" *American Naturalist* 121: 324–34.

Morales, R. V., V. J. Shute, and J. W. Pellegrino. 1985. "Developmental Differences in Understanding and Solving Simple Mathematics Word Problems." *Cognition and Instruction* 2: 41–57.

Perry, M., S. W. VanderStoep, and S. L. Yu. 1993. "Asking Questions in First-Grade Mathematics Classes: Potential Influences on Mathematical Thought." *Journal of Educational Psychology* 85: 31–40.

Pinker, S. 1997. *How the Mind Works.* W. W. Norton and Co.

Pugh, K. R., B. A. Shaywitz, S. E. Shaywitz, D. P. Shankweiler, L. Katz, J. M. Fletcher, P. Skudlarski, R. K. Fulbright, R. T. Constable, R. A. Bronen, C. Lacadie, and J. C. Gore. 1997. "Predicting Reading Performance from Neuroimaging Profiles: The Cerebral Basis of Phonological Effects in Printed Word Identification." *Journal of Experimental Psychology: Human Perception and Performance* 23: 299–318.

Rivera-Batiz, F. L. 1992. "Quantitative Literacy and the Likelihood of Employment among Young Adults in the United States." *Journal of Human Resources* 27: 313–28.

Sawaguchi, T. 1997. "Possible Involvement of Sexual Selection in Neocortical Evolution of Monkeys and Apes." *Folia Primatologica* 68: 95–99.

Saxe, G. B. 1982. "Developing Forms of Arithmetical Thought among the Oksapmin of Papua New Guinea." *Developmental Psychology* 18: 583–94.

Shepard, R. N. 1994. "Perceptual-Cognitive Universals as Reflections of the World." *Psychonomic Bulletin and Review* 1: 2–28.

Siegler, R. S. 1995. "How Does Change Occur: A Microgenetic Study of Number Conservation." *Cognitive Psychology* 28: 225–73.

Siegler, R. S., and E. Stern. 1998. "Conscious and Unconscious Strategy Discoveries: A Microgenetic Analysis." *Journal of Experimental Psychology: General* 127: 377–97.

Sophian, C. 1997. "Beyond Competence: The Significance of Performance for Conceptual Development." *Cognitive Development* 12: 281–303.

Starkey, P. 1992. "The Early Development of Numerical Reasoning." *Cognition* 43: 93–126.

Starkey, P., and R. G. Cooper Jr. 1980. "Perception of Numbers by Human Infants." *Science* 210: 1033–35.

Strauss, M. S., and L. E. Curtis. 1984. "Development of Numerical Concepts in Infancy." In *Origins of Cognitive Skills: The Eighteenth Annual Carnegie Symposium on Cognition,* edited by C. Sophian, 131–55. Hillsdale, N.J.: Lawrence Erlbaum.

Stephan, W. G. 1985. "Intergroup Relations." In *Handbook of Social Psychology: Volume II: Special Fields and Applications,* edited by G. Lindzey and E. Aronson, 599–658. Random House.

Stevenson, H. W., and J. W. Stigler. 1992. *"The Learning Gap: Why Our Schools Are Failing and What We Can Learn from Japanese and Chinese Education.* New York: Summit Books.

Sweller, J., R. F. Mawer, and M. R. Ward. 1983. "Development of Expertise in Mathematical Problem Solving." *Journal of Experimental Psychology: General* 112: 639–61.

Trinkaus, E. 1992. "Evolution of Human Manipulation." In *The Cambridge Encyclopedia of Human Evolution,* edited by S. Jones, R. Martin, and D. Pilbeam, 346–49. Cambridge University Press.

Trivers, R. L. 1971. "The Evolution of Reciprocal Altruism." *Quarterly Review of Biology* 46: 35–57.

Weiner, J. 1995. *The Beak of the Finch.* New York: Vintage Books.

Wenger, R. H. 1987. "Cognitive Science and Algebra Learning." In *Cognitive Science and Mathematics Education,* edited by A. H. Schoenfeld, 217–51. Hillsdale, N.J.: Lawrence Erlbaum.

Wynn, K. 1992. "Addition and Subtraction by Human Infants." *Nature* 358: 749–50.

CHAPTER SIX

The Impact of Traditional and Reform-Style Practices on Student Mathematics Achievement

ROGER SHOUSE

In 1989 the National Council of Teachers of Mathematics (NCTM) issued the final version of its *Curriculum and Evaluation Standards for School Mathematics* (NCTM 1989). Among its recommendations for change, the following have attracted the most controversy: (1) deemphasize pencil-and-paper computation in favor of the use of calculators, computers, and estimation; (2) move from separate year-long courses in algebra, geometry, and trigonometry to a more seamless integrated course format; (3) increase focus on using math to solve "real life" problems; (4) reduce the time devoted to teacher-led instruction in exchange for more cooperative and student-focused inquiry, analysis, and communication of mathematical ideas; and (5) expand the availability of higher value mathematical knowledge and instruction (algebra, geometry) to students traditionally shuttled into courses of lower value (arithmetic, general math).

Critics of the standards have drawn beads on these and other recommendations, finding them sharply at odds with what they believe are valid traditional understandings of mathematics teaching and learning. In addition, they charge that many of the new ideas contained in the standards represent watered-down and ineffective curricular and instructional practices. Finally, they argue that the standards represent a philosophically driven "solution," totally independent of the problems plaguing American math education (for example, poor teacher quality, achievement gaps between poor and affluent American students and between America and other nations).

It is sadly inadequate to say that the debate over NCTM's recommendations has been heated. In fact, it has taken on the trappings of myth and metaphor as few other educational issues have in recent history ("busing" and sex education come to mind as comparable). On both sides can be found those who take the debate quite personally, as if it touched on their most deeply held beliefs about schooling, society, and equality.

Also sad is the lack of reliable empirical evidence with which to weigh each side's assertions. The dearth of any research base for the standards was notable at the time of their release and remains evident today (Research Advisory Committee 1988). While some surveys and experimental studies have been attempted, criticisms of their methodologies (and, occasionally, of their authors' motives) tend to render them inconclusive, unreliable, or impotent. In short, effective large-scale analysis of what impact NCTM curricular reforms have had or might have on student math learning remains unrealized.

This chapter seeks to fill this void by performing something of an "end run" around the lack of current data. In fact, large-scale national data from which to draw inferences about the achievement effects of practices similar to those recommended in NCTM standards have been available since the early 1990s. Specifically, the National Education Longitudinal Study (NELS:88) contains data from principals, students, and math teachers regarding the types of practices and emphases found in American eighth-, tenth-, and twelfth-grade math classrooms in the years 1988, 1990, and 1992, respectively. In addition, NELS:88 contains student-level math achievement scores that can be used to evaluate their impact on student learning. This chapter highlights those areas of contention between reform advocates and their critics on which NELS:88 evidence either focuses directly or sheds substantial light.

Source of Data

The National Education Longitudinal Study of 1988 (NELS:88) serves as the primary source of data in this study. Of particular interest are its student and teacher reports of school and classroom organizational, curricular, and instructional practices and emphases related to mathematics education. Conducted by the National Center for Education Statistics (NCES), NELS:88 began its data collection phase in 1988, surveying a national sample of eighth-grade students, their parents, teachers, and principals. These students (along with their teachers and principals) were surveyed again in the tenth and twelfth grade. This study focuses on data from the eighth and tenth grade, years when nearly all students are required to take mathematics.

To obtain a representative sample of students and schools, NELS:88 employed a two-stage design. The first stage involved identifying a stratified representative sample of American schools serving eighth-grade students. In the second stage a representative sample of eighth graders was selected within each school. On average, 26 students were sampled in each school, resulting in a total base year sample of more than 24,000 students clustered across approximately 800 public and 200 private schools. At the tenth grade, the overall student sample dropped to approximately 20,000 students across approximately 1,300 high schools.[1]

In both the eighth- and tenth-grade samples, NELS:88 gathered information on a wide range of student, school, and teacher characteristics. For students, this included family background, school attitudes, social and academic experiences, and future aspirations. NELS students also completed cognitive tests in math, science, English, and history. For each student in the sample, two teachers (one from either math or science, the other from either English or history) provided specific information about the student, as well as about their own classroom instructional practices, course emphases, teaching experience, and opinions concerning general school operations. At the school level, principals provided information about a range of school social, organizational, and academic features. (Methodological details are presented in a later section.)

Issues of Contention

Before outlining the areas of disagreement between reformers and critics, an important area of agreement should be pointed out. Specifically, several critics praise the standards' emphasis on practical application and demand for more challenging content for all types of students regardless of background or future career path (Finn and Ravitch 1996). Both sides of the reform debate recognize the stubborn tendency over the years for students of lesser demonstrated ability to be shunted off the path of main-

1. For a number of reasons (such as students dropping out, missing responses, students not taking math) the number of student cases used in this study falls below these levels.

stream mathematics learning onto dead-end curricular sidetracks (to "basic math," "consumer math," "business math," or to "low" or "general" ability courses offering similarly weak content). Both sides also recognize the tendency for more experienced and talented teachers to be assigned to higher ability classes. Critics of the reform movement point out, however, that these problems result from poor resource distribution rather than from anything fundamental about traditional mathematics.

This issue aside, the standards' agenda—and that of math reform advocates in general—seems open to vigorous challenge in at least three key areas. One of these concerns whether "traditional" curricular and instructional practices have been fairly characterized and criticized. A second area concerns reformers' assertions about the kinds of mathematics students ought to learn. The third involves their assertions as to what types of instructional practices and processes are best suited to developing students' mathematical knowledge and understanding. These last two areas are fundamentally connected, as is evident in the view of many reformers that what one learns is a function of how one learns it.

Each of these areas can be addressed by NELS:88 data. The issue of the nature and value of traditional math practices will be examined via descriptive analysis of student perceptions of their mathematics courses. The latter two issues will be examined jointly and inferentially using regression analysis of the effects of traditional and reform practices on student achievement.

Characterizations of Traditional Math Instruction

Reformers argue that "traditional" math instruction is ill suited for preparing students for the massive waves of social and economic change they perceive to be headed for our educational shores. Early on in the standards readers are told that the "information society . . . has become an economic reality" spawning "new social goals for education . . . mathematically literate workers . . . lifelong learning . . . opportunity for all . . . an informed electorate" (NCTM 1989, 3). Since compelling evidence or examples are not provided, the reader is largely left to assume that such goals are inherently unreachable in traditional settings and would more likely be attained via the use of standards-type curricular and instructional practices.

In the years since the standards were released, their supporters have become more strident in their criticisms of traditional math instruction.

Sometimes their fervor seems excessive, however, as, for example, when they attempt to portray traditional instruction as at best little more than rote learning, and at worst something akin to the galley scene from the film *Ben Hur*. Traditional math is portrayed as "an endless sequence of memorizing and forgetting facts and procedures that make little sense . . ." (Battista 1999, 426); a process of "forcing young children to blindly memorize scores of standard algorithms" (Cossey 1999, 443); or "mindless mimicry" (National Research Council 1989). Such mischaracterizations are often accompanied by similarly bitter attacks on reform critics themselves, casting them as unscientific, intolerant, backward, or ignorant of "what the research says" (O'Brien 1999, for example).

In fact, while traditional math curricula emphasize the importance of memorization and practice in the use of facts, formulas, and algorithms, the goal of such endeavor has always been the development of mathematical understanding, intuition, and application. For example, interesting practical word problems can be found in elementary and secondary school textbooks at least as far back as the 1800s.[2] I suspect that most adults over age forty can point to at least one teacher who, working in a traditional framework, made math seem meaningful, useful, and perhaps even fun.

Evidence from the NELS:88 tenth-grade student sample also suggests that reformers have overstated their complaints about traditional math instruction. Students were asked to report on the quality of their mathematics class across a number of key variables. Recall that these data were collected in 1990, a time for which it is fair to say that few schools had widely implemented the 1989 NCTM standards. Student responses (see table 6-1) reveal a portrait of "pre-standards" mathematics instruction quite different than the one described by many reformers. For example, one notes from table 6-1 that majorities of students report being asked to "show they understand the material" and being "really challenged" to use their minds. On the whole, students judge their math courses to be more intellectually challenging than their other academic courses. Other descriptive evidence from NELS:88 (not tabulated in table 6-1) also belies the reformers' attack on traditional math. Specifically, majorities of tenth-

---

2. The following problem, circa 1867, was found among the notes of a female high school student: "Three men undertook to saw a log 3 feet in diameter. What part of the length of the diameter must each pass over in order that they may perform equal parts of the labor?" (from author's collection).

Table 6-1. *Tenth-Grade Student Perceptions of Intellectual Demand, by Subject Area*[a]

Subject	Seldom/never	Often/almost every day
"In each of your current classes, how often are you asked to show that you really understand the material, rather than just give an answer?"[b]		
Math	22	62
English	30	52
History	34	47
Science	27	54
"In each of your current classes, how often do you feel really challenged to use your mind?"[b]		
Math	13	77
English	23	60
History	23	60
Science	15	73

Source: Author's calculations based on NELS:88 data.

a. Number of responses for each subject: math = 17,158; English = 17,441; history = 12,131; science = 16,004.

b. A third category—"about once a week"—has been omitted.

grade students across high school programs report that their teachers place moderate or major emphasis on learning ways to solve problems, further study in math, and the importance of math in life. In addition, a majority of students in average and high-ability classes have math teachers who report placing their greatest emphasis on "problem solving" or "helping students understand concepts."

In many instances, reformers' attacks on traditional practices appear to reflect a failure to distinguish between "traditional math" and "traditional math taught badly." The figures cited above, of course, reflect high school experiences, where teachers tend to have stronger mathematics backgrounds than those in elementary schools and where math instruction is more frequent. According to the 1991 Schools and Staffing Survey, in fact, nearly one-fifth of American elementary teachers offer no more than three hours of math instruction per week, and in some urban districts the percentage rises to nearly one-third (Huinker 1996).

High school math instruction is not trouble-free, however. For example, among those NELS tenth-grade students whose math teachers were asked, 22 percent had math teachers who could not identify the correct answer to a basic algebra problem;[3] 31 percent of these students' teachers either

3. NELS:88 teacher questionnaire item F1T2M29 poses the following to math teachers: "Your students have been learning how to write math statements expressing proportions. Last night you assigned the following: A one pound bag contains 50 percent more tan

believed it impossible or unnecessary to explain why the product of two negative numbers is always positive (see NCES 1992). Such statistics reflect weaknesses of teachers—and perhaps math education programs—but not problems inherent to traditional teaching methods.

In their zeal, however, reformers overlook these weaknesses in teachers' content knowledge, preferring to focus blame on instructional methodology. At times, their attacks reflect something approaching hubris, as revealed in the following excerpt:

> How would you react if your doctor treated you or your children with methods that were 10 to 15 years out-of-date, ignored current scientific findings about diseases and medical treatments, and contradicted all professional recommendations for practice? (Battista 1999, 425–26)

Since many of the "out-of-date" teaching methods referred to here have been used for centuries, is it not somewhat arrogant to suggest that we—math education experts, that is—have "wised up" so much in the past two decades? Do reformers really believe that young students' math education would be harmed by, say, learning geometry from Euclid? Unfortunately, the reasonable criticisms made by many reform advocates are often crushed beneath such brute force rhetoric.

What Students Should Learn/How Teachers Should Teach It

Many of the questions related to curricular content and instructional processes that can be examined using NELS:88 data seem to overlap. For example, is "problem solving" an area of content or an instructional approach? The same question applies to proficiency in using calculators. For this reason, and because the evidence to be presented for both issues comes from the same regression models, content and process questions are addressed jointly here.

M&Ms than green ones. Write a mathematical statement that represents the relationship between the tan (t) and green (g) M&Ms, using t and g to stand for the number of tan and green M&Ms. Here are some responses you get from students:

Kelly: $1.5t = g$
Lee: $.50t = g$
Pat: $.5g = t$
Sandy: g plus $1/2g = t$

Which of the students has represented the relationship best?"

Before detailing these analyses, it is best to first discuss the basic arguments offered by reformers regarding curricular content and process. As touched on earlier, reformers have argued that traditional mathematics instruction has tended to place too much emphasis on facts, algorithms, and isolated problem solution. The argument is typically targeted not just at low-level math courses (where students may be asked to memorize basic formulas for things like area, volume, and so on) but also to higher level courses as well (such as geometry, where students have traditionally been asked to memorize principles and prove basic theorems). Indeed, some reform advocates have actually dismissed the value of having students memorize basic number facts.[4]

Not entirely eschewing the value of facts and rules, reformers suggest that mathematical understanding is largely independent of memorization and that students are more likely to develop understanding when their teachers present problems that allow them to discover or construct knowledge for themselves. Put more simply, one might say that traditionalists offer tools with which students can solve problems; reformers offer problems that prompt students to develop tools.

Put yet another way, traditional math unfolds in a linear logical fashion—it is a "course of study" in the fundamental sense of that phrase. Rules and procedures are introduced, practiced to the point of reasonable skill, then applied to problems designed to show the practical aspects of math and to help reinforce prior learning. This process is then applied to other increasingly complex sets of rules, procedures, and problems that tap into and build upon those that came before. In the reform vision, the learning process is conceived as much more open ended and nonlinear. A problem spurs students to ask questions, test ideas, and offer reasoned (although not always correct) procedures for solving it. Ostensibly, this approach aims at overcoming what reformers see as a major problem of traditional math instruction: that while students can learn rules and algo-

---

4. In 1990, as a graduate student, I attended a meeting where students and faculty engaged in a freewheeling discussion regarding a grant application targeting the improvement of urban schooling. After remarking with some dismay how an elementary school math specialist in my former district had stated that young students "really didn't need to memorize their times tables," a math education faculty member commented that "current research" supported the specialist's view. While many reform advocates now back away from such views, a second grade teacher in the district in which I now live recently told parents that she does not teach the memorization of multiplication tables and suggested that parents desiring such instruction should do it themselves.

rithms, they often fail to understand why they work or when it is appropriate to use them.

At this point, content and process issues converge, and reformers make a number of key assertions about how students learn best. For one, they argue that the type of constructivist problem-centered learning they advocate cannot occur when teachers rely on direct whole-class instruction. Instead, students need to work in small cooperative settings with the teacher serving more as a guide than a leader. The learning process is enhanced further, they claim, as students engage in "hands-on" or "manipulative" activities, become experienced in the use of calculators and computers, and focus on "real life" problems, especially those highlighting students' interests. Finally, reformers argue, teachers need to provide opportunities for students to demonstrate evidence of learning, such as class discussions, written assignments, or concrete projects that require them to explain their thinking and display their skill.

Used judiciously and at appropriate age or skill levels, few traditionalists would deny that such activities are potentially valuable. Indeed, in various forms they constitute what are often referred to as the supplemental, enrichment, or support elements of the traditional math curriculum. Traditionalists object, however, to the extent that such elements assume the predominant share of daily instructional activity, taking the place of a rigorous and more focused emphasis on learning, practicing, and applying facts, concepts, rules, and procedures.

A widely cited (and contested) example of a reform problem-solving activity illustrates their reason for concern (see Gardner 1998; O'Brien 1999). Students in a fifth-grade class were asked, "What if everybody here had to shake hands with everybody else? How many handshakes would that be?" A classroom observer described how students worked on the problem for much of the math period using a trial-and-error approach. Defending the activity, the teacher later claimed that it took just twenty minutes, although she admitted that it continued the following day. From a traditional perspective, the activity seems poorly structured, weakly directed, and inefficient in terms of the amount of time it requires. Even if after, say, forty-five minutes students reason a guess as to the total number of possible handshakes, an inductive basis for generalizing a solution to other similar kinds of problems might still not have been established. In a more traditional approach teachers might use a series of diagrams or a smaller, more structured hand-shaking exercise to help students discover a pattern. This would lead to the presentation of a general formula for solving this type of problem.[5]

Reformers are quick to contend, however, that such an approach will likely produce students who lack the skill to solve problems requiring some extension or modification of a formula. The evidence for this assertion tends to be weak, typically consisting of illustrative cases of errors made by students presumably taught in traditional fashion. Often, the cases are stretched much too far. One reform advocate, in a rather spirited denouncement of traditional math, made a great deal out of the fact that a talented eighth-grade student came up with an incorrect answer to an abstract problem involving the number of rectangular prism-shaped packages that would fit in a box (Battista 1999; and chapter 4 in this volume). In essence, because the student had confused single units of measure with the double-unit sized packages, she had misapplied the familiar "length × width × height" formula for finding the volume of a box. Based on this one error, and because the student cannot explain her answer to the author's satisfaction,[6] he infers that all the student's prior math learning has been "only superficial." But it is much more reasonable to conclude that the student simply made a mistake—the likes of which are more likely to be corrected via thoughtful reflection, practice, or instruction than by devoting an additional class period to, say, filling boxes with blocks. The "dual interpretation" many reformers apply to student errors is puzzling. On the one hand, errors committed in reform settings are viewed as part of the natural process of learning. On the other hand, those committed in traditional settings are seen as evidence that little or no learning has occurred.

"One-Size Reform" Might Not Fit All

The discussion to this point highlights a number of curricular and instructional practices the value of which can be explored using NELS:88 data. Before turning to this analysis, however, one additional issue deserves

5. Romesh Ratnesar, "This Is Math? Suddenly, Math Becomes Fun and Games," *Time*, August 25, 1997, pp. 66–67.

6. When questioned by the observer as to why the "l × w × h" formula "works," the student responds: "Because you are covering all three dimensions, I think. I'm not really sure. I just know the formula." While one might claim her response as evidence of superficiality, many would view it as typical of how even a knowledgeable eighth grader might reply in an oral testing situation.

mention; that is, whether standards-type reforms might have different, perhaps even negative academic consequences in socioeconomically disadvantaged schools. The basis for this suspicion follows from studies reporting math achievement in such schools to be negatively associated with certain reform-style practices. One study of urban eighth-grade schools found, for example, that while homogeneous grouping had significant positive effects on math achievement, the effects of cooperative learning were significantly negative (Shouse 1998). Results like these may stem from a tendency for disadvantaged students to respond better academically to more structured, teacher-directed instruction (Pogrow 1997). It may also stem from the fact that reform-style instructional practices tend to be highly complex (if done well), often overstressing the human, social, and fiscal resources of disadvantaged schools. As such, they also pose greater risks to students who may lack the social and academic supports necessary to overcome their schools' instructional deficiencies (Shouse and Mussoline 1999). Although technical issues related to the NELS:88 data set constrain researchers' ability to examine these kinds of differential effects at the tenth-grade level, such analyses are more readily conducted at the eighth-grade level and are included in a following section.[7]

Methods

The analytic strategy employed in this study consisted of conducting ordinary least squares (OLS) regressions on NELS:88 eighth and tenth-grade student and teacher data. These analyses are presented in two parts. The first examines the extent to which eighth-grade students' math achievement scores were significantly related to teachers' instructional practices and emphases after controlling for key student background characteristics (sex, race, family socioeconomic status [SES], grades, and other indicators of prior ability). To gauge the extent to which these associations varied across categories of school affluence, separate OLS models were constructed for high- and low-SES schools (based on the principal's report of the percentage of students coming from "welfare or unemployed" families). The second portion of the analysis highlights tenth-grade achievement effects associated with math teachers' practices and emphases, as reported by

7. The tenth grade school sample contains no satisfactory measure of school affluence. The effect of school socioeconomic status can still be examined, but at the cost of using a smaller, less representative school subsample. Reasonable measures of school affluence are available at the eighth grade level.

both teachers and students. Here, too, appropriate controls were included to compensate for the influence of student characteristics.

Because of the complex structure of the NELS:88 sample, there are different sample sizes for each regression analysis. As described earlier, NELS:88 contains data based on responses from two of each student's teachers—one from either math or science, the other from either English or social studies. Thus the eighth-grade analyses are based on a sample of 10,490 students whose math teachers were included in the NELS eighth-grade teacher sample. These teachers provided information about their own instructional practices and emphases. The tenth-grade analyses are based on two different samples. One consists of 16,912 students who provided information about their math teachers' instructional practices and emphases. The other consists of 7,234 students whose math teachers were included in the NELS tenth-grade teacher sample. These teachers provided information similar (although not identical) to that provided by their eighth-grade counterparts.

In both the eighth- and tenth-grade analyses, NELS:88 mathematics standardized test scores served as the outcome variable. Aside from math achievement being the focus of this study, the NELS:88 math test has the advantage of having higher reliability and being more immune from "ceiling" and "floor" effects than the other NELS:88 cognitive tests (for psychometric details on NELS:88 standardized tests see Rock, Pollock, and Quinn 1995). The math scores used here are "Item Response Theory" (IRT) scores, which can be roughly interpreted as representing each student's number of correct responses where questions represent constant intervals of difficulty. (See Appendix 6A for descriptions of the variables used in these analyses.)

Two caveats deserve mention. Although NELS:88 is a longitudinal study of a representative sample of American secondary school students, a cross-sectional strategy was employed here. This was done to ensure the largest possible sample size at both the eighth- and tenth-grade level in view of the fact that (1) a substantial number of eighth-grade student respondents left the sample prior to tenth grade, (2) a substantial number of new student respondents were added to the tenth-grade sample, and (3) there was no assurance that the surveyed students would be paired with a math teacher at both grade levels. The second caveat concerns the fact that although the full student samples at both grade levels constitute representative samples of American students, the same cannot be guaranteed for the subsamples of student–math teacher pairings. The NELS student-teacher pairings were selected on a random basis, however, and no substantial differences were found between these subsamples and the full sample across several key student background variables.

Eighth-Grade Results

Table 6-2 presents standardized coefficients representing the association between math achievement and teacher-reported classroom practices and emphases across two categories of school affluence. These "effects" represent the difference in student achievement one would expect given a one-unit difference in a particular independent variable. The "units" here (for both dependent and independent variables) are standard deviations. For example, table 6-2 indicates that for students in low-SES schools, a one-standard-deviation difference in student SES is linked to a .16 (16 percent) difference in math achievement. As a rule, standardized effects smaller than .10 are considered "trivial," even when statistically significant. Keep in mind, however, that small effects often represent parts of a larger, more salient cluster of practices.

The first eight variables presented in table 6-2 ("Student SES" to "Student in mixed ability math class") represent controls for student background and prior ability. The last of these, however, "mixed ability in math class," represents a characteristic generally associated with the math reform movement. Although NCTM standards make no specific mention of ability grouping, heterogeneous grouping is considered by reform advocates to be congruent with the goal of providing high-quality learning for all students (Davenport 1993). Yet table 6-2 reveals a negative effect associated with this practice, especially for students attending disadvantaged schools.

The next seven variables ("Frequency of textbook use" to "Has individual instruction per week") represent effects associated with classroom practices. This is a rather mixed pattern of effects with respect to reform practices. For example, the effect of calculator use is significantly negative in disadvantaged schools but slightly positive in others. Exploratory analyses (not tabulated here) indicated that the low-SES negative effect occurred primarily in classes where teachers emphasized lower-level math topics ("common fractions," "decimal fractions," "ratio and proportion," "percent," and "measurement"). This finding suggests that calculator use can be problematic for students who have not yet acquired a foundation of basic mathematical skill.

Table 6-2. *Achievement Effects of Eighth-Grade Teachers' Instructional Practices by School Affluence*[a]

Variable	Low-SES schools	Other schools
Student SES	.16*	.20*
Female student	–.06*	–.05*
Student ability composite[b]	.27*	.31*
Hours homework completed per week	.00	.08*
Student		
Black or Hispanic	–.15*	–.11*
In low ability math class[c]	–.08*	–.06*
In high ability math class[c]	.23*	.15*
In mixed ability math class[c]	–.07*	–.02*
Frequency of		
Textbook use	–.04*	–.03*
Use of other material	–.03	–.05*
Calculator use	–.05*	.02*
Hours		
Homework assigned per week	–.01	.00
Whole class instruction per week	.06*	.02*
Small group instruction per week	–.05*	–.02*
Individual instruction per week	.05*	–.02*
Emphasis on		
Common fractions	–.19*	–.01
Decimal fractions	.04	–.08*
Ratio and proportion	.02	.04*
Percent	.00	–.07*
Measurement	–.05	–.06*
Geometry	–.02	.00
Algebra	.06*	.11*
Integers	.00	–.01
Probability and statistics	.04	–.02*
Problem solving	.06*	.05*
N	1,413	9,165
Adj. R-square	.47	.57

*p ≤ .05.

a. Standardized beta coefficients. Schools are defined as low SES if percent of "welfare or unemployed families" was at least 1 standard deviation below mean (based on HES33F from *Hopkins Enhancement Survey of NELS:88 Middle Grades Practices*; see Epstein, McPartland, and MacIver 1991).

b. Factor composite based on student grades in all subjects and self-reported ability group in math.

c. Based on teacher's report of class average ability.

A mixed pattern is also evident in the effects associated with use of textbooks, other materials, and whole-class and small-group instruction. On one hand, the results suggest that eighth graders learn more when their teachers untether themselves from textbook-driven instruction. On the other hand, contrary to the claims of much reform literature, the impact of whole-class instruction is positive while that of small-group instruction is negative—and again, the pattern is more pronounced in low-SES schools. These results lend support to an earlier point, that teacher-directed instruction can be an effective method for producing student learning.

The final ten variables in table 6-2 serve primarily as controls for variation in course content; that is, they increase our confidence that the effects discussed above are not actually driven by covariance between instructional content and instructional practices. Nevertheless, the contrast between disadvantaged and more advantaged schools deserves some mention. Although students in both types of schools benefit when their teachers emphasize higher status material such as algebra and problem solving, more affluent students experience some negative effect when their teachers emphasize such basic topics as decimals and percents.

Tenth-Grade Results

The tenth-grade analyses differ from those presented above in two ways. First, as described earlier, data on instructional practices are available from both students and teachers. Second, because of the large number of variables examined, and because of technical issues involving sample sizes, effects are not broken down by school SES here (see note 6). Exploratory regressions (results not tabulated here) revealed a number of intriguing contrasts, however, and these will be referred to where appropriate. As was the case with the eighth-grade regressions, the effects presented here are represented by standardized beta coefficients.

Table 6-3 presents math achievement effects associated with student perceptions of teachers' practices and emphases. The first eleven variables listed ("student sex" to "student won an academic honor") serve as controls for student background and prior ability.[8] The next five variables ("teacher emphasis on increasing interest in math" to "teacher emphasis on importance of math in life") represent students' perceptions of their teachers' instructional emphasis. The coefficients reported for these five variables indicate positive links between students' math achievement and their teachers' focus on "facts and rules," "further study in math," and

8. Student eighth grade math achievement score is not included as a control in order to maintain the largest possible sample sizes in the tenth grade regression models. To check for biased results, exploratory regressions were conducted using a smaller sample with the eighth grade math score as a control. The results did not differ substantially from those presented here.

Table 6-3. *Tenth-Grade Achievement Effects Associated with Student Perceptions of Math Teacher's Emphasis and Practices*

Variable	Effect
Student	
Sex	−.04*
SES	.16*
Black or Hispanic	−.14*
In academic program	.10*
In vocational program	−.09*
Time spent on math homework out of school	.03*
Math grades since ninth grade	.14*
Mathematics is one of my best subjects	.13*
Others think of me as a good student	.06*
Coursework in geometry	.26*
Student won an academic honor	.04*
Teacher emphasis on	
Increasing interest in math	−.02*
Learning math facts/rules	.07*
Further study in math	.04*
Ways to solve math problems	.04*
Importance of math in life	−.12*
Review math work from previous day often	.05*
Use books other than math text books often	−.11*
Copy teacher's notes in math class often	.01
Do problem solving in math class often	.04*
Use computers in math class often	−.03*
Use hands-on materials in math class often	−.05*
Use calculators in math class often	.06*
Participate in student discussion often	−.07*
Explain math work in class orally often	.00
N	16,912
Adjusted R^2	.53

*$p \le .05$.

"ways to solve problems." In addition, exploratory analyses by school affluence (not tabulated here) indicated that teachers' emphasis of "facts and rules" had an even stronger positive effect in low-SES schools. Student achievement appears to suffer, however, when teachers emphasize "importance of math in life" and "increasing interest in math." Interestingly, exploratory analysis indicated the former of these to be especially problematic for low-SES schools, the latter especially problematic for more affluent schools.

The final nine variables in table 6-3 ("often review math work from previous day" to "often explain math work in class orally") represent students' perceptions of teacher practices. Here, again, there is a mixed pattern of result. Reviewing work, problem solving, and use of calculators have positive effects. Negative effects, however, are linked to the use of books other than textbooks, computers, hands-on material, and student discussions. Analyses by school SES revealed overall consistency in the first four of these effects. The last (student discussions) was found to be more problematic in low-SES schools.

In general, the portrait of instructional effectiveness offered by table 6-3 provides only limited support for the types of changes advocated within the reformist vision. There are benefits associated with learning facts, rules, and problem solving, but not from the use of hands-on activities. Some benefit is seen from the use of textbooks and daily review, but not from student discussions. While calculators appear beneficial to student learning, computers do not.

The next two tables examine effects associated with teachers' reports of curricular emphases and instructional practices. Because of the large and sometimes overlapping number of math-specific items in the NELS:88 tenth-grade teacher survey, discretion was required in selecting variables for analysis. In some instances, the high number of missing responses for a particular item limited its usefulness as an independent variable. The variables examined in tables 6-4 and 6-5 are those having a manageable number of missing cases and a reasonable relationship to the math reform debate. Recall that the sample size is smaller here because only a portion of the NELS tenth-grade student sample had math teachers selected for inclusion in the teacher sample. Although not tabulated, tables 6-4 and 6-5 contain the same controls for student background and ability as table 6-3. Each table also adds two controls for teachers' academic demand and mathematical knowledge (the amount of homework they assign and whether they correctly answered the algebra problem detailed in note 3).

Table 6-4, which focuses on the impact of math teachers' instructional emphases, reflects the sort of mixed pattern of effect revealed in prior tables. Negative effects are linked to teachers stressing the "importance of math in everyday life" and "math in business and industry." A slight negative effect is also tied to teachers' emphasis on "speedy computation," while positive effects are tied to their emphasis on "students' questions about math," "math concepts," and "math in science."

Perhaps the most intriguing finding in table 6-4 is the contrast between the respective negative and positive impact of teachers' emphasis on "memorizing facts, rules, and steps" and "knowing facts, principles, and

Table 6-4. *Achievement Effects on Tenth-Grade Teachers' Instructional Emphasis*[a]

Variable	Effect
Hours homework assigned	0.04*
Teacher correctly answered algebra problem	0.06*
Emphasis on logical structure	0.02
Emphasis on nature of proof	0.06*
Emphasis on memorizing facts	−0.04*
Emphasis on interest in math	0.01
Emphasis on knowing facts	0.03*
Emphasis on importance of math	−0.10*
Emphasis on problem solution	0.02*
Emphasis on speedy computation	−0.02*
Emphasis on math in science	0.09*
Emphasis on math concepts	0.06*
Emphasis on math in business	−0.06*
Emphasis on student's questions about math	0.02*
N	7,234
Adjusted R^2	.53

*$p \leq .05$.
a. Student controls are the same as those in table 6-3.

algorithms." On its surface, this finding appears to sum up much of the major message of the math reform movement—students should understand, not simply "parrot" mathematical rules. And yet, in line with earlier arguments, memorization sans understanding has never really been a distinguishing characteristic of traditional math education. In fact, among NELS tenth-grade students whose math teachers were sampled, 47 percent had math teachers who reported "heavy emphasis" on "knowing facts," while just 28 percent reported the same for "memorizing facts." In addition, virtually none of their teachers emphasized the latter without also stressing the former.

Table 6-5 presents effects associated with instructional practices teachers report using in their classes generally, as well as in their most recent class at the time they completed the survey. On the traditional side, positive achievement effects are linked to the amount of time teachers "work with" or "instruct" the whole class, as well as with the use of textbooks and audiovisual materials. But such traditional strategies as worksheets and textbook seatwork appear to have negative impact on achievement. On the reform side, allowing students to work with calculators or in small student groups are both positively related to achievement. Yet, negative effects are tied to the use of "hands-on" materials and the use of "other reading materials."

Table 6-5. *Achievement Effects on Tenth-Grade Teachers'*
Instructional Practices[a]

Variable	Effect
Hours homework assigned	.05*
Teacher correctly answered algebra problem	.06*
Most recent class	
Lecture	.01
Discussion	.01
Calculators	.04*
Computers	−.01
Hands-on material	−.02*
Textbook seatwork	−.02*
Worksheets	−.03*
Homework assigned	.02*
Minutes allocated for most recent class	−.04*
Minutes worked with entire class	.06*
Minutes worked with small groups	−.01
Minutes students worked individually	−.01
Minutes students worked in small groups	.05*
Time spent instructing	
Whole class	.03*
Small groups	.00
Individuals	−.03*
Use of	
Text books	.04*
Other reading materials	−.03*
Audiovisual materials	.03*
Other instructional materials	−.02
N	7,234
Adjusted R^2	.52

*p ≤ .05.
a. Student controls are the same as those in table 6-3.

Discussion

Given the mixed picture of instructional effectiveness offered by these
analyses, what kinds of observations or conclusions can be drawn? First,
it is clear that nearly all the effects associated with math teachers' emphases and practices are quite small, often falling into a category of what
many researchers would consider trivial. As mentioned earlier, combinations of such small effects may lead to more potent influences on students.
But as has been shown, negative as well as positive effects are linked to
both traditional and reform practices. Thus, had this study employed an
"index" or "composite" approach to representing "reform" versus "traditional" practice, the effects would likely have been even smaller.

In contrast, effects associated with student background, ability, and math course taking tend to be much larger. In fact, among the larger overall effects at the tenth-grade level is that linked to "coursework in geometry." Similarly, eighth graders tend to do better when their teachers emphasize algebra. In other words, exposure to higher level mathematical content outweighs the impact of particular types of classroom practices.

These considerations aside, the pattern of effect revealed here suggests that while reform advocates have some valid points concerning the need for instructional change, they have overstated their case against traditional math, at least at the secondary school level. For instance, the data here provide cautious support for the use of calculators, once students have attained a reasonable level of skill without them. Modest support is evident, at the tenth-grade level, for having students work in small groups. Students also appear to perform better when allowed to regularly engage in problem-solving activities.

But reform advocates will be hard pressed to view this last finding as supporting their position. After all, it is likely that the "problem-solving" activities reported by NELS teachers and students in 1988 and 1990 represent a much more traditional than constructivist approach. That is, the problems tend to be presented after students have practiced "in isolation" the rules and skills necessary to solve them. Since many reformers, and the standards themselves, find fault with this approach (see NCTM 1989, 242), the findings here regarding problem solving actually undercut their arguments.

Also troublesome for the reform case are the findings here regarding several other of its key elements. For tenth graders, lower math achievement levels are associated with the use of hands-on activities, computers, written assignments, class discussions, and nontext materials. For eighth graders, reform advocates can find some support in the positive impact of nontext reading materials, but they will have to balance that with the negative impact of small-group instruction and calculator use in disadvantaged schools.

Overall, the findings here do not support any large-scale restructuring of mathematics instruction in American secondary schools, nor the reformist view of traditional math as consisting mainly of vapid mimicry, void of opportunity for students to solve problems and achieve understanding. But neither do they support a belief that "all is well" in American math education. In her recent book, *Knowing and Teaching Elementary Mathematics,* Liping Ma's (1999) analysis indicates that compared to their

Chinese counterparts, American elementary school teachers display weak mathematical understanding. For example, fewer than 20 percent of the American teachers surveyed (compared to 80 percent of the Chinese teachers) could explain the so-called regrouping process used in subtraction. Interestingly, Ma reports that Chinese teachers pointed to their own elementary and secondary school education as the most important source of their mathematical knowledge. Aside from the question of whether responsibility for the knowledge gap between American and Chinese teachers lies with elementary and secondary schools, departments of mathematics, or colleges of education, it indicates the vital need for improvement in the quality of our nation's teacher corps.

Reformers have simply failed to make the case that such improvement cannot occur incrementally, from a platform of traditional understandings about the way students learn. Chinese math (like Asian math, generally) looks much like traditional Western math taught well (Stigler and Hiebert 1997).[9] As an elementary student, not one of my very traditional teachers ever taught us how to "borrow" in subtraction without also explaining to us why we were borrowing or what it was we were borrowing from. As a math teacher in a large urban school district, the battery of traditional math courses I took to earn my certification gave me the knowledge and intuition I needed to explain a wide range of concepts to my students, from simple basic skills to advanced algebra and geometry.

The point here thus lies in a series of conjectures. Perhaps elementary teachers need to take more higher level math courses. Perhaps all teachers need to learn to become more thoughtful with their students. Perhaps they need to become more reflective about their craft and become more engaged in a discussion about how to improve it. But this reflection and engagement should not occur under any faction's sole purview. Reform advocates have some valid points to make within the school improvement process. But their formal recommendations have been met with a substantial number of valid arguments from an informed opposition. Reformers

9. "It is interesting to note that in some respects Japanese lessons appear consistent with reform recommendations proposed by such documents as the *Professional Standards for Teaching Mathematics* of the National Council of Teachers of Mathematics. Japanese lessons include high-level mathematics, a clear focus on thinking and problem solving, and an emphasis on students' deriving alternative solution methods and explaining their thinking. In other respects, though, Japanese lessons do not follow such reform guidelines. They include more lecturing and demonstration than even the more traditional U.S. lessons, and we never observed calculators being used in a Japanese classroom" (cited from online version: http://www.pdkintl.org/kappan/kstg9709.htm).

are not educational saboteurs, nor are reform opponents unscientific, politi-cally driven reactionaries. Yet, truth be told, the responsibility for much of this rancor must lie at the doorstep of those who have so vigorously attempted to portray traditional math instruction in the most negative terms. Perhaps when their war against traditional math ends, the process of improving math education can truly begin.

Appendix: Details Regarding Variables Used in this Study

Table 6A-1. *Descriptions of Eighth-Grade Variables from Table 6-2*

Variable	NELS item[a]	Description
Eighth-grade math achievement	BY2XMIRR	Dependent variable: number correctly answered items
Female student	BYSES	Standardized NELS composite
Student sex	BYSEX	Dichotomous: male = 1
Student academic ability	[b]	Standardized factor composite
Hours homework/week	BYS79A	7 categories: "none" to "10 or more"
Student minority status	[c]	Dichotomous: black or Hispanic = 1
Class ability level is		
Low	BYT2_2	Dichotomous: Yes = 1
High	BYT2_2	Dichotomous: Yes = 1
Mixed	BYT2_2	Dichotomous: Yes = 1
Frequency of use of		
Textbooks	BYT2_9A[d]	4 categories: "primary resource" to "not used"
Other materials	BYT2_9B[d]	4 categories: "primary resource" to "not used"
Calculators	BYT2_22[d]	3 categories: "several times a week" to "hardly ever"
Hours of		
Homework assigned/week	BYT2_7H	Discrete
Whole class instruction/week	BYT2_16A	7 categories: "none" to "five or more"
Small group instruction/week	BYT2_16B	7 categories: "none" to "five or more"
Individual instruction/week	BYT2_16C	7 categories: "none" to "five or more"
Emphasis on		
Common fractions	BYT2_20A[d]	4 categories: "major topic" to "not covered"
Decimal fractions	BYT2_20B[d]	4 categories: "major topic" to "not covered"
Ratio and proportion	BYT2_20C[d]	4 categories: "major topic" to "not covered"
Percent	BYT2_20D[d]	4 categories: "major topic" to "not covered"
Measurement	BYT2_20E[d]	4 categories: "major topic" to "not covered"
Geometry	BYT2_20F[d]	4 categories: "major topic" to "not covered"
Algebra	BYT2_20G[d]	4 categories: "major topic" to "not covered"
Integers	BYT2_20H[d]	4 categories: "major topic" to "not covered"
Probability and statistics	BYT2_20I[d]	4 categories: "major topic" to "not covered"
Problem solving	BYT2_20J[d]	4 categories: "major topic" to "not covered"

a. Item names starting with BYS come from student reports; those starting with BYT come from teacher reports.

b. Factor composite based on NELS items BYGRADS (grades composite), BYS81B (student reported math grades), and BYS60A (student reported math ability group).

c. Rescaled from NELS item, RACE.

d. Scale reversed from original NELS item so higher values indicate positive direction.

Table 6A-2. *Descriptions of Tenth-Grade Variables from Tables 6-3 through 6-5*

Variable	NELS item[a]	Description
Student controls (tables 6-3 through 6-5)		
Tenth-grade math achievement	F12XMIRR	Dependent variable: Number correctly answered items
Student		
Sex	F1SEX	Dichotomous: Male = 1
SES	F1SES	Standardized NELS composite
Minority status	[b]	Dichotomous: black or Hispanic = 1
Academic program	F1HSPROG	Dichotomous: Yes = 1
Student in vocational program	F1HSPROG	Dichotomous: Yes = 1
Time spent on math homework	F1S36B2	7 categories: "none" to "over 15 hours"
Math grades since ninth grade	F1S39A	8 categories: "mostly A" to "mostly < D"
Math "one of my best subjects"	F1S63D	6 categories: "false" to "true"
Seen as "good student"	F1S67D[c]	3 categories: "not at all" to "very"
Courses in geometry	F1S22D	5 categories: "none" to "2 years"
Won an academic honor	F1S8C[c]	Dichotomous: "yes" = 1
From table 6-3		
Emphasis on		
Interest in math	F1S31A	4 categories: "none" to "major"
Facts and rules	F1S31B	4 categories: "none" to "major"
Further math study	F1S31C	4 categories: "none" to "major"
Ways to solve problems	F1S31D	4 categories: "none" to "major"
Math in life	F1S31E	4 categories: "none" to "major"
Review previous day's work	F1S32A	3 categories: "never" to "often"
Copy teacher's notes	F1S32C	3 categories: "never" to "often"
Do problem solving	F1S32D	3 categories: "never" to "often"
Use		
Books other than math text	F1S32B	3 categories: "never" to "often"
Computers	F1S32E	3 categories: "never" to "often"
Hands-on materials	F1S32F	3 categories: "never" to "often"
Calculators	F1S32G	3 categories: "never" to "often"
Participate in student discussions	F1S32H	3 categories: "never" to "often"
Explain math work orally	F1S32I	3 categories: "never" to "often"
From table 6-4		
Hours of homework assigned per week	F1T2_9H	Discrete (used in tables 6-5)
Correct answer to algebra problem	F1T2M29	Dichotomous: correct answer = 1 (used in tables 6-4 and 6-5)
Emphasis on		
Logical structure	F1T2M19A	4 categories: "none" to "heavy"
Nature of proof	F1T2M19B	4 categories: "none" to "heavy"
Memorizing facts	F1T2M19C	4 categories: "none" to "heavy"
Knowing facts	F1T2M19E	4 categories: "none" to "heavy"

continues

Table 6-2. *continued*

Variable	NELS item[a]	Description
Interest in math	F1T2M19D	4 categories: "none" to "heavy"
Importance of math	F1T2M19F	4 categories: "none" to "heavy"
Problem solving	F1T2M19G	4 categories: "none" to "heavy"
Speedy computation	F1T2M19H	4 categories: "none" to "heavy"
Math in science	F1T2M19I	4 categories: "none" to "heavy"
Math concepts	F1T2M19J	4 categories: "none" to "heavy"
Math in business	F1T2M19K	4 categories: "none" to "heavy"
Student math questions	F1T2M19L	4 categories: "none" to "heavy"
From table 6-5		
Most recent class		
Lecture	F1T2M27A	Dichotomous: "yes" = 1
Discussion	F1T2M27B	Dichotomous: "yes" = 1
Calculators	F1T2M27D	Dichotomous: "yes" = 1
Computers	F1T2M27E	Dichotomous: "yes" = 1
Hands-on material	F1T2M27F	Dichotomous: "yes" = 1
Textbook seatwork	F1T2M27G	Dichotomous: "yes" = 1
Worksheets	F1T2M27H	Dichotomous: "yes" = 1
Homework assigned	F1T2M27I	Dichotomous: "yes" = 1
Minutes allocated for	F1TM26A	Discrete: 2–95 minutes
Minutes technical work, entire class	F1TM26B	Discrete: 0–95 min.
Minutes technical work, small groups	F1TM26C	Discrete: 0–95 min.
Minutes students work individually	F1TM26D	Discrete: 0–95 min.
Minutes student work in small groups	F1TM26E	Discrete: 0–95 min.
Time spent instructing		
Whole class	F1T2_16A	6 categories: "none" to "75-100%"
Small groups	F1T2_16B	6 categories: "none" to "75-100%"
Individuals	F1T2_16C	6 categories: "none" to "75-100%"
Use of		
Textbooks	F1T2_12A	6 categories: "not used" to "frequently"
Other reading materials	F1T2_12B	6 categories: "not used" to "frequently"
Audiovisual materials	F1T2_12C	6 categories: "not used" to "frequently"
Other instructional materials	F1T2_12D	6 categories: "not used" to "frequently"

a. Item names starting with BYS come from student reports; those starting with BYT, from teacher reports.
b. Rescaled from NELS item, RACE.
c. Scale reversed from original NELS item so higher values indicate positive direction.

References

Battista, Michael T. 1999. "The Mathematical Miseducation of America's Youth: Ignoring Research and Scientific Study in Education." *Phi Delta Kappan* 80 (6): 425–33.

Cossey, Ruth. 1999. "Are California's Math Standards up to the Challenge?" *Phi Delta Kappan* 80 (6): 441–43.

Davenport, Linda Ruiz. 1993. "The Effects of Homogeneous Groupings in Mathematics." *ERIC/CSMEE Digest* (July). ERIC document no. ED359065.

Epstein, Joyce L., James M. McPartland, and Douglas J. MacIver. 1991. *Hopkins Enhancement Survey of NELS:88 Middle Grades Practices: Codebook and Data Collection Instruments*. Baltimore: Center for Research on Effective Schooling for Disadvantaged Students, Johns Hopkins University.

Finn, Chester E., and Diane Ravitch. 1996. "Education Reform 1995–1996." Report available from the Hudson Institute, Indianapolis.

Gardner, Martin. 1998. "The New New Math." *New York Review of Books*, September 24.

Huinker, DeAnn M. 1996. "Teaching Mathematics and Science in Urban Elementary Schools." *School Science and Mathematics* 96 (7): 340–49.

National Research Council. 1989. "Everybody Counts: A Report to the Nation on the Future of Mathematics Education." Washington: National Academy Press.

National Center for Education Statistics (NCES). 1992. *National Education Longitudinal Study of 1988, First Follow-Up: Teacher Component Data File User's Manual*. U.S. Department of Education.

National Council of Teachers of Mathematics (NCTM). 1989. *Curriculum and Evaluation Standards for School Mathematics*. Reston, Va.

Ma, Liping. 1999. *Knowing and Teaching Elementary Mathematics*. Hillsdale, N.J.: Lawrence Erlbaum.

O'Brien, Thomas C. 1999. "Parrot Math." *Phi Delta Kappan* 80 (6): 434–38.

Pogrow, Stanley. 1997. "The Tyranny and Folly of Ideological Progressivism." *Education Week* (November 12). Available at www.edweek.org/ew/1997/12pogrow.h17.

Research Advisory Committee. 1988. "NCTM Curricular and Evaluation Standards for School Mathematics: Responses from the Research Community." *Journal for Research in Mathematics Education* 19 (4): 338–44.

Rock, D. A., J. M. Pollock, and P. Quinn. 1995. *Psychometric Report for the NELS:88 Base Year through Second Follow-Up* (NCES 95–382). U.S. Department of Education, Office of Educational Research and Improvement.

Shouse, Roger. 1998. "Restructuring's Impact on Student Achievement: Contrasts by School Urbanicity." *Educational Administration Quarterly* 34 (supplement): 677–99.

Shouse, Roger, and Lawrence Mussoline. 1999. "High Risk, Low Return: The Achievement Effects of Restructuring in Disadvantaged Schools." *Social Psychology of Education* 3 (4): 245–59.

Stigler, James W., and James Hiebert. 1977. "Understanding and Improving Classroom Mathematics Instruction: An Overview of the TIMSS Video Study." *Phi Delta Kappan* 79 (1): 14–21.

CHAPTER SEVEN

Beyond Curriculum Wars: Content and Understanding in Mathematics

ADAM GAMORAN

Faced with the prospects for school reform in the twenty-first century, it is imperative that educators move beyond the "curriculum wars" of the late twentieth. In mathematics the battle has been waged between those who emphasize rigorous content and those who promote in-depth understanding, as if these two approaches were mutually incompatible. In fact, precisely the opposite is true: content and understanding are mutually interdependent. Understanding is meaningless if there is no serious content to understand, and content is trivialized if understanding is superficial. The two sides in this debate tend to caricature one another instead of aiming for a synthesis that draws on the best of both approaches. In this chapter I argue that the goal of school mathematics should be to promote in-depth understanding of rigorous content and provide evidence that students whose teachers meet this goal outperform students whose teachers do not. The discussion begins with Japan, an example that is especially telling because both sides in the debate claim support from Japanese illustrations. Next, three small-scale studies in the

Support for this research was provided by the National Center for Improving Student Learning and Achievement in Mathematics and Science at the Wisconsin Center for Education Research, University of Wisconsin, Madison, with funds from the U.S. Department of Education, Office of Educational Research and Improvement (grant no. R305A60007). Tona Williams provided able research assistance for the study. Findings and conclusions are those of the author and do not necessarily reflect the views of the supporting agencies.

United States show how the combination of rigorous content with in-depth understanding promotes high achievement. Finally, a large-scale, longitudinal analysis of mathematical achievement provides more limited support for my claim.

What's Wrong with School Mathematics in the United States?

The mathematics curriculum in American schools is deficient in two areas: it covers too little rigorous content, spiraling out slowly and repeating much of the previous year's content in the subsequent year; and it is too shallow, emphasizing excessive repetition of basic operations with little attention to in-depth analysis of complex, meaningful problems. Viewed in this light, *both* sides in the math curriculum war are correct about the flaws of school mathematics in the United States. Instead of seeing both problems, however, critics tend to focus on one or the other and reject opposing solutions that are equally as one-sided as their own. In a recent *New York Times* essay, for example, Howard Gardner criticized traditional school mathematics as being trivial and inauthentic: "In real life no one presents us with four choices, the last of which reads, 'none of the above.'"[1] Similarly Richard Prawat (1997, 30) cites as an indictment of traditional math problems the following example: "'There are 26 sheep and 10 goats on a ship. How old is the captain?' Nearly 80 percent of the elementary students responding to this query in a 1986 study simply added the two numbers together." These examples caricature traditional school mathematics by taking trivial examples out of context. They ignore any possible value of solving problems that have clear solutions, and they misconstrue programs of content-oriented, skills-based learning, such as Direct Instruction and Core Knowledge, which emphasize knowledge and skills that are far more important than sheep and goats on a ship.

Caricatures are not the sole province of understanding-oriented reformers, however. Those on the knowledge and skills side of the debate are equally prone to taking trivial examples out of context as if they stood for the whole reform. Loveless (1997, 36) suggests that "parents worry when their 5th graders can't multiply single-digit numbers without pocketfuls of beans and sticks," as if this were the outcome of a focus on conceptual understanding in mathematics. When he claims there is a general outcry

---

1. H. Gardner, "Towards Good Thinking on Essential Questions," *New York Times*, September 11, 1999, pp. A15, A17.

over "a warm, fuzzy, mathematics that values student happiness over student competency" (1997, 48), he misrepresents the approach and further reinforces the caricature. Similarly, *Time* magazine quotes biologist Michael McKeown as saying, "whole math [a derisive term for teaching mathematics with emphasis on conceptual understanding] means less material covered in less depth in less rigor."[2] This statement is at most one-third true: teaching mathematics with an emphasis on understanding means less coverage, if coverage refers to the number of different topics addressed; but it also means more depth and more rigor on the topics it does address (Carpenter and Lehrer 1999). Here again, the critic caricatures the opposing view instead of addressing its merits and weaknesses systematically and dispassionately. Reform proposals such as those of the National Council of Teachers of Mathematics (NCTM) place more emphasis, not less, on depth and rigor, compared to the traditional programs they are seeking to replace.

To move beyond these curriculum battles, it must be understood that rigorous content and in-depth understanding are not in opposition; they are inextricably intertwined. Although John Dewey is often cited (or blamed) for the focus on a child-centered curriculum at the expense of subject matter, Prawat (1997, 30) gives Dewey the credit for recognizing the essential link between content and understanding:

> What Dewey proposed was a whole new way of thinking about content: subject-matter knowledge as a set of powerful ideas, developed in disciplines, available to everyone, used as a means to illuminate aspects of the world that otherwise would remain closed off to the individual forever. Subject matter, for Dewey, was literally a way to "be" in the world, at least in a perceptual sense. The concept of photosynthesis allows one to see green leafy plants in a new way. The same is true of negative number in mathematics; a person who has grasped this notion views realities like temperature or financial indebtedness with new eyes. Or additive composition, the idea that number can be taken apart and put back together in different ways; one looks at number differently having grasped this notion.

High school math teacher Betsy Smith (1997, 42) puts it more plainly: "The bottom line, as I see it, is that balance is needed—balance between

---

2. R. Ratnesar, "This Is Math?" *Time,* August 25, 1997, pp. 66–67.

the ideas put forth by the [NCTM] standards and the traditional concept of learning basic skills and working problems for practice."

Instead of focusing on extreme examples, reformers would do better to recognize that school mathematics in American schools is weak on both counts: it fails to cover enough rigorous content and it fails to address what it does cover in sufficient depth. Rather than emphasizing one short-coming and ignoring the other, reformers should seek solutions that rectify both.

Lessons from Observational Studies

Loveless (1997) is correct on one point: there is no single large-scale study that confirms that mathematics teaching for in-depth understanding, such as that advocated by the NCTM standards, promotes higher achievement than an approach that places greater emphasis on drill and practice of standard mathematical routines. However, a growing body of small- and medium-sized case studies and observational studies is accumulating data that supports the NCTM claims with increasing strength. Noticeably, in each case, the focus on understanding occurs in the context of rigorous mathematical content. These studies do *not* suggest that beans and sticks constitute essential mathematics, but, speaking metaphorically, when beans and sticks are used to apprehend an important idea, they enhance mathematical understanding and ultimately student achievement.

As an initial illustration, consider what is known about mathematics instruction in Japan. The Japanese case is particularly instructive because each side in the U.S. curriculum war has cited it as evidence to support its case. In fact, it is the combination of important content and the focus on student understanding that underlies Japan's achievement advantage. Following this are descriptions of three U.S. studies that further illustrate this point.

Knowledge and Understanding in Japan

It is well known that student achievement in mathematics, in every grade level that has been comparatively tested, is substantially higher in Japan than in the United States. This finding is as clear in the Third International Mathematics and Science Study (TIMSS) of the 1990s as it was in the Second International Mathematics Study (SIMS) of the 1980s. The contrast is not merely a reflection of greater economic and ethnic diversity in the United States, as it holds throughout the achievement distribution: in one study, the top 5 percent of American students would have scored at only about the fiftieth percentile in Japan (McKnight et al. 1987, 26–27). What are the reasons for this cross-national achievement disparity? Most of the explanations have to do with more schoolwork, more homework, and a more rigorous curriculum in Japan—explanations that fit well within the "rigorous content" side of our curriculum war. American schools follow a "spiral curriculum" in mathematics; that is, they spend such a substantial proportion of time on review each year that only limited progress can be made with new material (McKnight et al. 1987). American students who perform poorly in arithmetic are subject to a special form of the spiral curriculum, which might be termed the "circular curriculum": they repeat arithmetic over and over until they stop studying math (Gamoran et al. 1997). By contrast, Japanese schools spend less time on review, expecting students to master the curriculum they have been taught (McKnight et al. 1987). They also assign a lot more homework, and they have a longer school year (Rohlen 1983). Japanese students who want to enroll in higher education must succeed on examinations upon entry to and exit from high school, and this motivates them to study hard; for many students, it also means an extensive system of "shadow education" in which they receive private tutoring outside of school (Rohlen 1983; LeTendre 1999). American eighth graders who study a curriculum as demanding as the Japanese eighth-grade curriculum tend to achieve about as well, but few students encounter demands that are as rigorous as those found in Japan (Westbury 1992, 1993; Hawkes, Kimmelman, and Kroeze 1997).

Although curriculum differences account for much of the Japanese–U.S. achievement gap, they do not account for all of it. As David Baker (1993, 19) points out, "Japanese students are learning over 60% of what they are taught in a year, while their American counterparts learn only 40%." This occurs even though Japanese teachers introduce *more* new material and move at a *faster* pace compared to American teachers. Part of the difference may reflect extra homework and tutoring in Japan, but, as Baker points out, the difference may also reflect not only *what* is taught but also *how* it is taught. More recent evidence suggests this is indeed the case.

James Stigler and his colleagues have collected extensive videotaped evidence of mathematics instruction in Japanese and American classrooms. This approach permits systematic analysis of a wide range of classrooms, making possible a cross-national analysis of representative samples. The largest study, conducted in connection with TIMSS, includes 81 American eighth-grade classrooms and 50 in Japan (along with 100 in Germany). At one level, the videotaped evidence confirms what is already known: compared to Japanese teachers, American teachers spend more time on review and less on presenting new material, and they place more emphasis on elementary concepts, such as number, and less on advanced topics, such as elements of algebra and geometry (Stigler et al. 1999).

The videotaped evidence also reveals a difference in emphasis, between skills in the United States and thinking in Japan. In the United States teachers state concepts and move directly to applications—that is, repeated practice exercises using the technique the teacher has demonstrated. Japanese teachers develop concepts over the course of the lesson instead of simply stating the concept at the outset. In Japan 42 percent of the eighth-grade lessons included alternative solutions proposed by *students*; only 8 percent of U.S. lessons had this character.

In a smaller videotape study of fifth-grade classrooms, Stigler, Fernandez, and Yoshida (1996) compared twenty Japanese and twenty American lessons in which the subject matter was how to find the area of a triangle. In effect, they controlled for content and explored differences in classroom activities. A typical American lesson unfolds as follows: there is a bit of review of previous concepts, which may or may not relate to the topic of the day; the teacher explains the concept of base times height divided by two, and demonstrates a few problems, and then students spend substantial time practicing problems using this formulation. In Japan the lesson unfolds differently: first the teacher presents the problem; students then attempt to solve the problem on their own; next there is a class discussion of solutions the students derived, leading to the general formula; and, finally, students work on problems on their own. About the same amount of time is spent on seatwork in the two cases, but in American classes most of the seatwork occurs *after* the teacher has explained the formula, whereas in Japan most of the seatwork consists of students trying to figure out how to solve the problem. More time in discussion occurs in Japan, whereas more lecture time occurs in the United States, a finding that is confirmed in the larger eighth-grade study (Stigler et al. 1999). According to Stigler, Fernandez, and Yoshida, "the key difference between the Japanese and American classroom traditions is in the emphasis placed on students' thinking and problem solving during instruction. . . . Our major conclusion is that American students have very few opportunities to think during classroom instruction, whereas Japanese students have many such opportunities" (1996, 150).

When American teachers prepare for lessons, they focus on their own actions—the concepts they plan to explain and the methods of explanation—and they note the classwork and homework assignments. When Japanese teachers plan instruction, they focus on the responses they anticipate from their students, who will be trying to solve a novel problem. Anticipating student responses allows teachers to devise approaches to help students understand where their solutions may fall short and how their solutions may fit into a more general conclusion. This is considered an essential element of good teaching in Japan, and it is made possible by a storehouse of knowledge available to Japanese teachers. As Stigler, Fernandez, and Yoshida explained: "There are reference books and publications available to Japanese teachers that detail students' thinking about all of the topics in the mathematics curriculum" (1996, 173). American teachers have no such lore of student responses.

The conclusions of Stigler and his colleagues sound more like the claims of math reformers who emphasize conceptual understanding than like those of their opponents in the content-oriented camp. The key point is to notice that Japanese instruction typically emphasizes both rigorous content and time for students to think. In the comparative study of fifth-grade classrooms, one does not observe the content difference because that is controlled; the content difference is more evident in the cross-nationally representative study of eighth-grade classrooms. The rigorous content is necessary because it gives the Japanese students something important to think about. In American classrooms, students have little chance to think even when the content is important. Frequently, the content is overly repetitive and trivial (for example, goats and sheep on a boat), and giving time to think about such trivia cannot be expected to result in serious learning. If students had more opportunity to think about the core ideas of mathematics, the evidence from Japan suggests U.S. students would score better on international tests.

The Japanese evidence is not conclusive, because it is missing a key link: no analysis has demonstrated that the emphasis on mathematical content and thinking accounts statistically for achievement differences between the United States and Japan. The videotaping studies lack achievement data, and the international achievement studies lack observational evidence. Hence, although the evidence is highly suggestive, research that combines classroom observations with data on student achievement is essential for a definitive finding. Although no nationally representative study provides such evidence in the United States, several studies with more limited samples offer evidence consistent with this conclusion.

Modeling in Mathematics and Science

The "Modeling in Mathematics and Science Collaborative" is a group of elementary-school teachers and researchers in a Wisconsin school district whose members have engaged in an ongoing seminar over the past several years aimed at fostering children's in-depth understanding of the central ideas of mathematics and science. The seminar was built on the foundation of an earlier collaborative project that involved a smaller group of researchers and teachers (Lehrer et al. 1998). The collaborative work has expanded over time, and by the late 1990s some teachers had spent five years or more in this effort, and close to half the elementary teachers in the district had participated at some time or another. Teachers who participate in the seminar focus on children's thinking as a means of guiding their instructional practices. In classrooms, students develop models to represent increasingly complex ideas and they communicate their thinking to teachers and other students verbally or in writing. Evidence from classrooms reveals instructional activities that are significantly different than those of the typical American classroom, and assessment of student learning documents achievement levels that are much higher than that of the typical American student.

One source of evidence about instruction comes from teachers' written accounts of their classroom activities. These accounts, complete with samples of student work, have been collected in a book for teachers entitled *Children's Work with Data* (Modeling in Mathematics and Science Collaborative 1997). In preparing this book and others that may follow, these teachers and researchers are taking a step toward accumulating the body of knowledge that is necessary for teachers to anticipate students' thinking so they can prepare activities that enable students to deepen their understanding. Mathematical concepts featured in the book include data, number, classification, and space. For example, in a chapter on graphing based on work that occurred leading up to the creation of the collaborative, second-grade teacher Jennie Clement (1997, 107) explains that "graphing lies at the intersection of spatial visualization, number, and data." The goal of her chapter is to describe some of the major landmarks in children's thinking that she identified as her students worked with graphs.

A conventional approach to teaching graphing would follow the outline observed in the typical classrooms of the videotape studies: explain what a graph is and what it is used for, show how to mark a graph, give children a set of numbers that refers to some hypothetical data (or have children collect data if it is a science lesson), pass out graph paper, and have them fill in the graph. This sort of mechanical approach is an efficient way to get the homework done, but it is unlikely to generalize to unfamiliar situations (Hiebert 1999).

Teachers in the Modeling in Mathematics and Science Collaborative often take a different approach. For example, Clement (1997, 116) describes a lesson on graphing:

> After reading the book, *Tall City, Wide Country* (Chwast 1983) I asked the kids to *think* about where each of them would prefer to live, in the "tall city" or in the "wide country." On the board I had two small pieces of tag board, one labeled Tall City and the other labeled Wide Country. Using links I asked each child to place a link on the card showing where they would prefer to live. . . . Most kids preferred the country over the city. . . . We found that there were 17 links [representing the country] . . . and counted 4 links [representing the city]. I asked the kids to tell me how many more kids felt at home in the country than in the city. Counting up and using [subtraction] facts, the kids determined the answer to be 13. . . . I gave each child a piece of graph paper and asked then if they could take the information on the board and make a graph. . . . Some children just copied the drawing of the links. . . . Others substituted bars for links, but did not pay any attention to the size of each of the units constituting the bars. Some children did pay attention to the size of each of the units making up the bar, but thought that the orientation needed to be the same as the drawing. Other children worried less about the orientation of the links and decided either horizontal or vertical depictions would work better.

During several class sessions, the children worked on constructing graphs, comparing and discussing their graphs with one another, and offering observations about the strengths and weaknesses of graphing approaches they had taken. The teacher-author concludes her account of this exercise with comments (1997, 117):

> *Reflections: Children's ideas about visual representation seem to begin with literal depictions, like their art work. Over time, they seem to*

be able to create greater "distance" between the items being depicted and the graph. Over time, children learn to reason about which parts of graphs serve which functions, and they learn the value of certain conventions, like equal-sized intervals and orientations where greater height means greater quantity, and so on. [italics in the original]

Four points about this case are noteworthy. First, the content of this lesson addresses some of the core disciplinary ideas of mathematics. As the teacher argues, issues of number, data, and space are fundamental concepts, and graphing is a topic that brings them together. Second, although the teacher is focusing on conceptual understanding rather than on repeated practice of a skill, it is through repeated experience with graphs that students are able to move from literal to abstract understanding in creating and interpreting their graphs. Third, the lesson allows time for students to *think*, not just listen and follow directions. The opportunity to examine and discuss one another's graphs helps lead students to greater understanding of the uses of graphs and the concepts that underlie them (Lehrer et al. 1999). Fourth, the conceptual understanding students acquire ought to pay off in a greater ability to use and interpret graphs in an unfamiliar situation (Lehrer et al. 1998). This point has been confirmed by analyses of student performance on items drawn from the National Assessment of Educational Progress (NAEP), for which national norms have been established. On items involving graphs, *second-grade* students of teachers who participated in the collaborative performed at or above the level of *seventh-grade* students in the NAEP national sample (Lehrer and Schauble, forthcoming). For example, students were shown a bar graph portraying different numbers of boxes of apples and pears picked at a fruit farm on five successive days. About 90 percent of second graders whose teachers participated in the collaborative provided correct answers to questions about these graphs ("How many boxes of pears and apples were picked on Tuesday?" "On which day did workers pick more boxes of apples than boxes of pears?"). By comparison, success rates among seventh graders nationally who answered similar NAEP questions ranged from 64 to 87 percent. The NAEP item was more challenging in one sense because it included three types of fruit instead of two, but it was easier in another sense because it presented the data in a table as well as in a graph. In any case the comparison shows remarkably high levels of facility with graphs among students of collaborative teachers (Lehrer and Schauble, forthcoming).

Evidence from this collaborative venture strongly suggests that when teachers focus on student understanding of core mathematical concepts, their students perform well on complex mathematical problems. It is not only the focus on core ideas, and not only the focus on student thinking, but the combination of rigorous content and an emphasis on understanding that is responsible for success in this context.

Authentic Pedagogy and Authentic Student Performance

A second example of the benefits of combining rigorous content with a focus on in-depth understanding comes from a study by Fred Newmann and his colleagues (1996) of twenty-four highly restructured schools. Although the researchers began with a "constructivist" orientation to apprehending teaching, they soon realized that students were unable to construct meaningful knowledge when the content they had to deal with was trivial. As Newmann, Marks, and Gamoran (1996, 281) explained,

> [E]ven highly active students can produce work that is intellectually shallow and weak. We have observed situations like the following: students working in small groups to complete routine mathematics or vocabulary assignments, but one student gives the answers for others to copy; students completing interviews of community residents, with all questions prespecified by the teacher and the students merely recording respondents' short answers, without trying to interpret their cumulative meaning; and students using the card catalogue, computers, and mathematics manipulatives to gain superficial exposure to fragments of knowledge without gaining in-depth understanding of an idea.

In response to these weaknesses of "active learning," Newmann and his colleagues (1996) devised standards for high-quality teaching, which they term *authentic pedagogy*, that include not only construction of knowledge and relevance to the world outside school, but also "disciplined inquiry"—that is, in-depth understanding and elaborated communication that builds on the prior knowledge accumulated in a field. In this approach, authentic pedagogy incorporates both rigorous content drawn from a specific body of knowledge and in-depth analysis that allows students to uncover ideas and construct meaning without having all conclusions prespecified by the teacher or textbook. Authentic pedagogy gives students something important to learn and think about.

To assess authentic pedagogy, Newmann and associates (1996) examined both classroom instruction and the tasks that teachers assigned to students. In rating instruction for authentic pedagogy, the researchers considered the following standards: higher-order thinking, substantive conversation, connections to the world outside the classroom (all elements of a constructivist approach), and deep knowledge, which they defined as instruction that "addresses central ideas of a topic or discipline with enough thoroughness to explore connections and relationships and to produce relatively complex understandings" (1996, 33). Similar elements were used to judge the quality of assigned tasks. The focus on deep knowledge is especially noteworthy in this formulation because it reflects the view that in-depth understanding is only meaningful when it occurs in the context of rigorous content. This principle could equally well be articulated by such content-oriented educational approaches as Core Knowledge and Direct Instruction.

Newmann and associates also rated the quality of student performance on tasks that teachers had assigned, using a similar rubric as the standard. They carried out a statistical analysis using a three-level model of students within classrooms within schools. Controlling for gender, socioeconomic status, race-ethnicity, and performance on a standardized test with items drawn from NAEP, students who encountered higher levels of authentic pedagogy produced work that met higher standards of authentic performance. In short, authentic pedagogy was associated with more authentic student performance. The main study reports results that combine mathematics and social studies classes, but a technical appendix also shows that the results hold up for mathematics classes considered alone (Marks, Gamoran, and Newmann 1995). Table 7-1 presents the results for mathematics. According to these findings, instruction that combines rigorous, discipline-based content with active learning and construction of meaning yields high levels of student learning.

Standards-Based Teaching as an Upgrading Strategy

Whereas the evidence of higher student performance in the first example is limited to comparisons with national norms, the second example considers student achievement as a response to higher and lower levels of authentic pedagogy. The third example is similar in that researchers created a scale for assessing instruction that reflects both content areas and instructional processes and examined variation in student achievement as

Table 7-1. *Authentic Pedagogy and Authentic Student Performance in Twenty-Four Restructured Schools*[a]

Independent variable	Dependent variable: authentic academic performance in		
	Elementary (N = 386)	Middle (N = 353)	High (N = 254)
Student level			
Intercept	-.07 (.12)	-.09 (.10)	.05 (.11)
Female	-.01 (.07)	.24** (.08)	.16** (.08)
African American	-.21 (.11)	-.28 (.16)	-.25* (.10)
Hispanic	-.10 (.11)	-.36* (.17)	.00 (.13)
Socioeconomic status	.02 (.05)	.13* (.05)	-.03 (.05)
NAEP achievement	.26*** (.04)	.33*** (.06)	.16** (.04)
Class level			
Class authentic pedagogy	.38** (.10)	.20* (.08)	.62*** (.09)
Percentage of between-class variance explained	16.3	59.0	36.4

Source: Marks, Gamoran, and Newmann (1995, table A6A, 9).
*p < .05
**p < .01
***p < .001
a. Estimates are from a three-level model of students within classrooms within schools. Level 3 (school level) has no predictors. Dependent variable is standardized to a mean of 0, standard deviation of 1. Standard errors are in parentheses.

a response to differences in instructional quality. Unlike the restructuring study, however, this case does not rely on highly restructured schools but instead focuses on ordinary schools in four school districts in which teachers attempted to upgrade their mathematics curricula in an effort to improve mathematics performance among low-income, low-achieving high school students.

In the four districts—San Francisco and San Diego, California, and Buffalo and Rochester, New York—teachers implemented a course that was intended to serve as a transition between elementary and advanced mathematics. Instead of enrolling in general math, a dead-end course that typically diverts students from more advanced mathematics study, students enrolled in the transition courses in the expectation of moving on to a college-preparatory sequence. The transition courses emphasized a hands-on, problem-oriented approach with far more rigorous curricular content than appeared in general math. This was particularly true for "Math A" and "Math B," the courses implemented in both California districts, and the University of Chicago School Mathematics Program (UCSMP) Transition Math, which was used in Buffalo. The Rochester schools in the study used "Stretch Regents," a course that followed the college-preparatory Regents curriculum but stretched out each year's instruction over two years. All three transition courses incorporated elements of algebra and geometry, instead of being limited to arithmetic as ordinarily occurs in general math.

To assess the impact of the transition courses, a team of researchers led by Andrew Porter examined student achievement at three points during the school year and devised a scale for assessing instructional quality as a likely mediator of achievement differences (Gamoran et al. 1997). The achievement test was drawn from NAEP items and emphasized complex problems, such as those advocated by the NCTM standards. The test also served as a measuring rod for assessing classroom instruction, as the researchers examined the extent to which tested content and cognitive demands were present in the classrooms of the study, which included college-preparatory and general math classes in addition to the transition courses. Test items were classified according to a taxonomy of topic areas (for example, linear equations, functions, triangles, and solid geometry) and cognitive demands (for example, memorize facts, understand concepts, and solve novel problems). Building on these classifications, the researchers used detailed teacher reports of instructional topics and activities to identify the extent to which tested content was covered in class using the types of cognitive demands found on the test. Analyses of class-level data indicated that student performance was weakly predicted when instruction was measured by either topic area or cognitive demand alone; student performance was much more sensitive to the intersection of topic area and cognitive demand (Porter 1998). This finding supports the claim that rigorous content and in-depth analysis must be combined to enhance student achievement.

In the next step of the analysis, the researchers examined achievement growth over the course of the school year with a three-level model that included achievement tested at three points in time (fall, winter, and spring) for each student in each classroom (Gamoran et al. 1997). Controlling for students' prior grades and race-ethnicity at the student level and socioeconomic status at the class level, the researchers found, not surprisingly, that achievement was highest in the college-preparatory classes and lowest in the general math classes. Student performance in the transition courses fell in between the two extremes. Most interestingly for our purposes, instructional quality (measured as the intersection of topic areas and cognitive demands) accounted for much of the achievement gaps between the different types of courses. In figure 7-1 the upper panel displays average

Figure 7-1. *Estimated Learning Gains*[a]

a. By course type
Achievement score

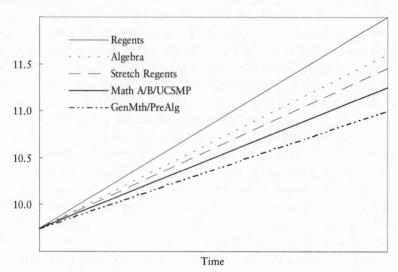

b. Controlling for content
Achievement score

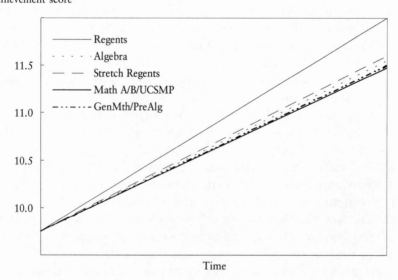

Source: Gamoran et al., 1997.

a. Regents and Algebra are college preparatory courses. GenMth/PreAlg refers to general math and prealgebra, which are not college preparatory. Math A, B, and UCSMP are combined in one category of transition course, and Stretch Regents is the other transition course.

achievement in the different types of classes; the lower panel simulates the levels of achievement that would occur if all classes had the same instruction as the Regents classes (the most rigorous classes according to the scale used). It appears that the benefits of the transition courses (Math A and B, UCSMP Transition, and Stretch Regents) over general math are largely a reflection of better instruction, and the advantage of algebra classes over the transition courses also reflects instructional differences. Only the Regents courses—which have the added element of a high-stakes test at their culmination—stand out after instructional quality has been statistically controlled. These findings further support the conclusion that instruction that incorporates serious content and complex conceptual demands promotes greater student learning.

Content and Understanding in a Large-Scale Survey Analysis

Although the three studies described above come from different and somewhat special contexts (especially the first two examples), taken together they provide strong support for the central claim of this chapter. However, one may question their generalizability: To what extent can these claims be verified in nationally representative studies? Analysis of available national survey data can help address this question, although the national survey analysis has other drawbacks alongside the benefits of representativeness.

Generally, research with national data reveals stronger effects on achievement of content indicators (for example, courses taken and coverage of material) than process indicators (for example, class discussion, inquiry methods, and active learning). This may indicate that the content emphasis is correct, and the emphasis on understanding-oriented methods is misplaced. Alternatively, it may be that instructional processes aimed at fostering deep understanding matter only when content is rigorous, so it is necessary to examine the interaction of content and instructional activities.

There are also methodological reasons that may account for why content effects appear more salient than process effects. It is relatively straightforward to obtain an "objective" assessment of content, particularly in mathematics, where course titles typically provide at least a rough guide to course content. Students who enroll in algebra and geometry are invariably exposed to more rigorous mathematical content than students enrolled in lower-level math courses. In addition, course enrollment can be assessed with transcripts and teacher reports in addition to student self-reports. By contrast, a classroom emphasis on understanding is difficult to measure well with surveys. Porter's (1998) fine-grained account of identifying cognitive demands for each topic area appeared successful, as did a similar approach taken by Mayer (1998, 1999) in a study of a single district, but completing the questionnaire is a laborious task and national studies have not adopted this method. Instead, surveys rely on cruder, subjective indicators of classroom processes, which are error-laden. As Stigler et al. (1999, 2–3) explained, identifying teacher behavior such as "problem solving" by asking teachers raises ambiguities:

> the words researchers use to describe the complexities of classroom instruction may not be understood in the same way by teachers or in a consistent way across teachers. The phrase "problem solving" is a good example ... different teachers interpret this phrase in different ways. One teacher may believe that working on word problems is synonymous with problem solving, even if the problems are so simple that students can solve one in 15 seconds. Another teacher may believe that a problem that can be solved in less than a full class period is not a real problem but only an exercise.

Yet another methodological reason for greater predictive power of content than process indicators has to do with the timing of national data collections. Whereas one can tally all the courses students have taken to obtain a complete picture of content exposure, studies that survey teachers in some years but not others yield a fragmentary picture of classroom activities. For example, the National Educational Longitudinal Survey surveyed tenth- and twelfth-grade teachers but not ninth- and eleventh-grade teachers, so that although one can count students' courses for the whole high school period, evidence on classroom experiences is at best partial. In response to this problem Lee, Smith, and Croninger (1997) aggregated teacher reports of instruction to the school level. They could not find a relation between "authentic pedagogy" and achievement when pedagogy was measured for each student's own tenth- and twelfth-grade teachers, but they discovered a positive relation when pedagogy was aggregated to the school level. By averaging over multiple teachers, the researchers have probably improved the reliability of the measure. At the same time, this approach ignores important instructional differences within schools, particularly those related to tracking and course taking. In examining a different national survey, this discussion builds on these findings by aggregating the reports of a student's teachers over time, separately for each student, so that the aggregation is over time for each student but not over students for each school. This approach captures the improved reliability of aggregation, without eliminating instructional differences among students in the same schools.

Data and Methods

Data for this analysis come from the younger cohort of the Longitudinal Study of American Youth (LSAY), a study that began with seventh graders in 1987 who were followed up in eighth, ninth, and tenth grades during 1988–91. Achievement was measured in the fall of each year, so the time period encompassed by the achievement tests consists of seventh, eighth, and ninth grades, and those grades are the focus of this analysis. The survey began with 3,116 students and, in addition to achievement tests, it included surveys of students, parents, teachers, and principals. There were no classroom observations. Missing data on 226 students (mainly missing test data) reduced the sample to 2,890, and another 323 students had insufficient course taking or teacher data to be included in the analysis, so the sample for analysis was 2,567 students, which is 82 percent of the original sample.

ACHIEVEMENT AND BACKGROUND VARIABLES. Mathematics achievement was assessed in the fall of grades seven, eight, nine, and ten with a multiple-choice test that included items on mathematical routines, skills and knowledge, and problem solving. Item response theory scaling was used to place the scores from all four waves of testing on a common metric. Socioeconomic status (SES) was measured with an unweighted linear composite variable drawn from parent responses to questions about mother's and father's education, mother's and father's occupation, and family income. (If parent data were missing, student responses to these questions were used to construct the SES composite.) Race and ethnic background were taken from student questionnaires, and the analyses include dummy variables for African American, Asian American, and Hispanic students, compared to whites. Students for whom data were missing on these variables were taken into account by including dummy variables to indicate that race or ethnicity was unreported. Students' grades in sixth grade were used as an additional control for prior knowledge. Grades were reported by students, and missing values were set at the mean with a dummy variable included in the analyses to indicate that data were missing on grades. Dummy variables were also included to note the region of the country and the urban status (urban, suburban, or rural) in which the school was located. Means and standard deviations of all variables included in the analyses are listed in the appendix.

CONTENT VARIABLES. Four variables were constructed to indicate the rigor and quantity of instructional content. Course topics were coded from students' reported course schedules and the number of years each student enrolled in *advanced course content* (that is, algebra, geometry) was tallied. Because three grades were included (seventh, eighth, and ninth), this variable ranges from 0 to 3. A second variable, which also ranges from 0 to 3, indicates the number of years a student was enrolled in any course at the *honors level*. These items are meant to index the rigor of course content. Quantity is indicated by student reports of time spent on homework (hours per week) and by teacher reports of the percentage of the textbook they covered.

INSTRUCTIONAL PROCESS VARIABLES. Three variables were constructed to reflect instructional processes that emphasize conceptual understanding of mathematical ideas, as opposed to memorization and repeated practice of routines. All three were taken from teacher responses. The responses of teachers in the spring of seventh, eighth, and ninth grades were averaged for each student. If a student's teacher failed to respond in one or two of the years, responses from the teacher or teachers who did respond were used. If none of a student's teachers responded, the student was omitted from the analyses. The three items were:
—How much emphasis did each of the following objectives receive: Develop problem solving/inquiry skills (None, minor emphasis, moderate emphasis, heavy emphasis).
—About how much time did you spend on each of the following with this class during a typical week: Leading discussions (None, 30 min., 1 hr., 2 hrs., More than 3 hrs.).
—About how much time did you spend on each of the following with this class during a typical week: Student work in small groups or laboratory (None, 30 min., 1 hr., 2 hrs., More than 3 hrs.).
The reliability of these items is open to question, but these are the best indicators available in the LSAY data. For each student, the responses of the seventh-, eighth-, and ninth-grade teachers were averaged. This aggregation may improve the reliability of the indicators. Teacher reports were

not highly correlated across years, however. Alpha reliabilities over the three years for problem solving, discussion, and small-group time were .35, .12, and .22, respectively. The low correlations do not merely reflect measurement error, but also the fact that students may encounter different instructional emphases from one year to the next.

METHODS. The data were analyzed in a three-level growth model of the four time points nested within students clustered within schools (Bryk and Raudenbush 1992).[3] One advantage of this approach is that students who are missing test scores at one or two of the time points can still be included in the analysis. As long as the large majority of students have test scores at three or four time points, the growth curve can be identified, and that information can be used to fit the curve for students whose test scores are present for two or three time points. A second advantage is that growth in student achievement can be assessed more reliably in a growth model with test scores at four points in time than in an analysis of covariance that rests on achievement tests at only two points.

The main results reported here draw on a linear model of achievement growth. That is, achievement is assumed to increase in a linear fashion over time. The robustness of findings from this model was tested with two nonlinear specifications: one in which achievement is linear during grades seven and eight but has a different slope during grade nine, and a second in which achievement follows a curvilinear pattern over the whole time period.

Studies of this sort are always vulnerable to unmeasured selection bias: effects that appear to result from course content or instructional practice may actually reflect differences among the students who enroll in different courses or who have access to different teachers. I address this problem in two ways. First, the background variables adjust for preexisting differences among students. Second, the enhanced reliability of growth models helps reduce the vulnerability to selection bias. Achievement differences due to unmeasured conditions should be incorporated into the intercept (that is, seventh-grade achievement), so that effects of instructional content and process reflect differences in students' experiences, not prior conditions. Still, selection bias cannot be ruled out completely, because new unmeasured conditions may be introduced beyond seventh grade and be-

---

3. More precisely, the students were clustered within school *districts*, since many students changed schools between grades eight and nine but remained in the same districts.

cause unmeasured conditions that previously existed may exert different effects as children enter adolescence.

For the analysis, all the background variables have been centered around (that is, deviated from) their overall means, so that the intercept indicates achievement for a student of average background characteristics in a typical school. The content and process indicators are also centered, except for advanced content and honors courses that are assessed on scales from 0 for no courses to 3 for three years of such coursework. Thus, when all the instructional variables are included in the model, the intercept for achievement growth indicates growth for the average student in a typical school who took no advanced content or honors courses.

Results

Table 7-2 presents four sets of coefficients from the linear growth models (content, process, content and process, and interactions). All the models control for the background and school variables and for the missing value dummies noted above. The first column (content) displays effects of the content variables on growth in student achievement. The benefits of rigorous content are evident in the significant positive coefficients for advanced course content and textbook coverage. For each year of advanced content, student achievement rose by an additional 1.61 points, and a teacher who covered 100 percent of the textbook would increase achievement growth by 4 points per year, compared to a teacher who covered none of the textbook (100 × .04 = 4 points). These are substantial associations on a test for which the average growth per year was about 2.75 points (as indicated in an unconditional growth model, not shown). Coefficients for honors-level classes and homework time are positive but not statistically significant. The nonsignificant coefficient for the honors ranking with course content controlled is consistent with past research at the high school level, which noted that course content accounts for most of tracking's impact on achievement in mathematics (Gamoran 1987).

In the second column of table 7-2 are the coefficients for instructional processes that reflect an emphasis on understanding. The effects of discussion and problem solving are positive, but the coefficient for small-group time is unexpectedly negative. This may reflect differences among teachers in what they mean when they report small group time. Nystrand, Gamoran, and Heck (1993) reported that much of what at first appears to be small-group time is actually "collaborative seatwork," that is, seatwork

Table 7-2. *Effects of Instructional Content and Process on Growth in Student Achievement in Mathematics during Grades Seven through Nine*[a]

	Content (1)	Process (2)	Content and and process (3)	Interactions (4)
Effects on initial achievement				
Intercept	50.43*	50.42*	50.43*	50.43*
	(.42)	(.42)	(.42)	(.42)
Effects on achievement growth				
Intercept	1.39*	2.77*	1.44*	1.47*
	(.17)	(.14)	(.18)	(.19)
Content				
Advanced content	1.61*		1.55*	2.06*
	(.12)		(.13)	(.57)
Honors level	.24		.23	.32
	(.18)		(.18)	(.18)
Text coverage	.04*		.04*	.03
	(.01)		(.01)	(.03)
Homework time	.09		.09	.09
	(.05)		(.05)	(.05)
Process				
Problem solving		1.04*	.47*	−.14
		(.18)	(.19)	(1.02)
Discussion time		.42*	.37*	2.21*
		(.16)	(.16)	(1.12)
Small-group time		−.36*	−.22	−.58
		(.16)	(.16)	(.85)
Interactions				
Advanced content X problem solving				−.35
				(.22)
Advanced content X discussion				.12
				(.20)
Advanced content X small group				.43*
				(.18)
Text coverage X problem solving				.01
				(.01)
Text coverage X discussion				−.02
				(.01)
Text coverage X small group				.00
				(.01)
Variance explained in achievement growth[b]	.08	.16	.10	.11

*p < .05

a. Parameters are from a three-level model of time points ($N = 9,282$) within students ($N = 2,567$) within schools ($N = 51$). Estimates control for region and urbanicity at the school level, and gender, race, ethnicity, socioeconomic status, grades, and missing data on race, ethnicity, and grades at the student level.

b. Reduction in residual parameter variance of achievement growth within schools, compared to unconditional model.

done with students' desks pushed together. That study referred to English classes, but, if the same holds for mathematics, that may account for the negative association.

The third column of table 7-2 includes both the content and process variables. All the effects that were positive and significant in the first two columns (advanced content, text coverage, problem solving, and discussion time) remain so in the third. In the combined model, the coefficient for problem solving (.47) is only about half as large as it appeared when the process variables were entered without the content indicators. Thus about half of the association of problem solving with achievement reflects a link between problem solving and content emphasis: classes with advanced content also place more emphasis on problem solving. The remaining effect of problem solving is independent of content, as is almost all the impact of discussion time. Similarly, the effects of advanced content and text coverage are largely independent of classroom processes, as evident in the trivial changes in the coefficients for those variables between the first and third columns. Overall, these results suggest that rigorous content and processes that favor conceptual understanding have distinct benefits for student achievement in mathematics.

In the fourth column, interactions between content and process variables are added to the model. Most of the coefficients are insignificant and close to zero. Only the coefficient for the interaction of advanced content by small-group time exhibits the expected positive significant value (.43). This coefficient suggests that small-group time in classes of advanced content may benefit student achievement, in contrast to the usual effects of small-group time that tend to be negative. On the whole, however, the data fail to support the hypothesis that the combination of rigorous content and processes that emphasize understanding is essential for high achievement. Instead, it appears that rigorous and extensive content is important, and spending time on discussion and problem solving also enhances achievement, holding constant content coverage.

Figure 7-2 provides simulations to illustrate the results implied by the linear, additive growth model. Results in table 7-2 imply that initial (seventh-grade) achievement for an average student was 50.43 points. How much such a student gains over the next three years depends on the instructional conditions that student encounters. Consider a student who takes no advanced content or honors classes during grades 7–9 and whose teachers cover only two-thirds of their textbooks on average. Having failed to reach algebra by ninth grade, such a student is on a "low track." Based

Figure 7-2. *Simulated Achievement Growth for Students Exposed to Different Levels of Instructional Content and Process*

Percent

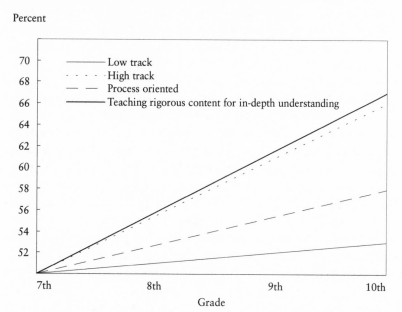

on the results in column 3 of table 7-2, achievement for this student in tenth grade would rise only to 52.83 points.[4] By contrast, achievement for a "high-track" student, defined as one who enrolled in two courses with advanced content and whose teachers completed the entire textbook each year, would rise to 66.13 points by tenth grade—an advantage of a full 1.0 standard deviation over the low-track student. A student in a "process-oriented" class, that is, one with average text coverage and no advanced content but an extra two hours of discussion per week above the average and a "heavy emphasis" on problem solving, would exhibit achievement growth to 57.71 points over the same time period—an advantage over the low track of about 0.4 of a standard deviation. Finally, a student who encounters instruction that might be termed *rigorous content for in-*

4. The projected total of 52.83 points after three years is derived as follows: a baseline of 50.43, plus a yearly gain of 1.44 points for each of three years, reduced by (.04 × −16) = −.64 points for each of three years reflecting two-thirds text coverage (−16 percent is the difference between two-thirds coverage and the average mark of about 83 percent, and .04 is the coefficient for the effects of text coverage). This works out as follows: 50.43 + (3 × 1.44) + (3 × (-16 × .04)) = 52.83.

depth understanding—defined as two years of advanced content with average coverage, two hours above the weekly average of discussion and a heavy emphasis on problem-solving—would reach 67.04 points on the LSAY math test by the beginning of tenth grade. Such a student would be almost 1.2 standard deviations above the low-track student after only three years, even though both had the same achievement in the fall of seventh grade.

Although both content and process variables yield statistically significant effects on achievement, inspection of figure 7-2 suggests that the content effects are considerably more powerful in substantive terms. The hypothetical "process-oriented" class is more productive than the low track, but the high-track class outstrips both of them. The class that emphasizes both rigorous content and in-depth understanding is only slightly better than the high-track class with its heavy content focus and average emphasis on discussion and problem solving in this simulation.

The robustness of these findings to the assumption of linear growth was tested by estimating two alternative models. In one, growth was held to be linear during grades seven and eight, but the slope was allowed to be steeper or shallower during ninth grade. In the other growth was allowed to be nonlinear over the entire period. In both cases, the term for nonlinear achievement growth failed to reach statistical significance, so one can conclude that the linear growth model is appropriate. Consequently, the linear growth model is presented in table 7-2, and because the interactions were largely insignificant, the results in column 3 (the additive model including content and process variables) have been emphasized and figure 7-2 is based on these results.

Conclusion

This chapter set out to advance a particular claim: considered alone, neither rigorous content nor the pursuit of in-depth understanding is sufficient; instead, both are necessary at the same time. According to this argument, the U.S. mathematics curriculum is weak in two areas: it emphasizes neither rigorous content nor conceptual understanding. Evidence consistent with this claim appeared in studies of mathematics instruction in Japan, as well as in three studies of instruction and achievement in the United States, each of which focused on schools that were attempting to improve mathematics teaching and learning.

The attempt here to make the same point more conclusively with national survey data from the United States met with moderate success. Indicators of both instructional content and processes that emphasize conceptual understanding emerged as predictors of achievement growth in mathematics during grades 7–9. However, contrary to expectations, the effects of content and process variables were largely independent of one another, and the interaction of content and process variables was for the most part unrelated to learning. Also, whereas both content and process measures had statistically significant effects, the content indicators appeared more important substantively. This conclusion may indicate that content is the most important element of high-quality instruction, or it may reflect the weakness of survey indicators of instructional activities.

The reliance on teacher reports for evidence of classroom instruction is an important limitation of this analysis. A far better way to assess the quality of teaching, particularly the extent to which teachers focus on in-depth understanding, would be through classroom observation. In light of the latest technological advances in the recording, storage, and analysis of videotape data, it seems feasible now to carry out a large-scale study that would use videotaping instead of surveys to gather data on classroom process. Stigler's three-nation study involved more than 200 classrooms, each observed once. This design yielded good measures of differences between countries, but it would not be satisfactory for linking instruction and achievement, because one observation per classroom was not enough to obtain reliable classroom-level data. However, if the same 200 observations were distributed among 50 classrooms within the same country, instruction would likely be measured with enough precision at the class level for a videotape-based analysis of classroom instruction and student achievement. Such a study could indicate on a broader basis whether an emphasis on thinking, a focus on problem solving, and substantial time devoted to discussing students' solutions to problems—all elements noted in the Japanese videos—were associated with higher achievement, argued here.

Instead of battling over content versus process, education reformers must recognize that both areas need improvement in American schools. Prominent reform packages tend to emphasize one over the other, but many recognize both needs implicitly if not explicitly. It is time to move beyond the "curriculum wars" to reform programs that call for rigorous content and conceptual understanding. Even the limited support garnered from this survey analysis is consistent with this view, and the cases presented offer strong support for this position.

Appendix: Means and Standard Deviations of Variables in LSAY Analysis

Standard	Mean	Deviation
Within-student variables (N = 9,282)		
Time (0–3 for grades 7–10)	1.41	1.11
Test score	54.83	12.33
Student-level variables (N = 2,567)		
Background		
Socioeconomic status	.01	.76
Race (dummy; 1 = yes)		
Black	.11	.32
Asian American	.03	.18
No data for race	.11	.31
Ethnicity (dummy; 1 = yes)		
Hispanic	.08	.28
No data for ethnicity	.29	.45
Grades in sixth grade (0–4)	3.10	.77
Content		
Advanced content (years)	.85	.72
Honors level (years)	.14	.45
Text coverage (percent)	82.70	10.72
Homework time (hours/week)	2.51	1.42
Process		
Emphasis on problem solving (0–3)	2.46	.46
Discussion time (hours/week)	.89	.51
Small-group time (hours/week)	.55	.48
School-level variables (N = 51)		
Urbanicity (dummy; 1 = yes)		
Rural	.33	.48
Urban	.25	.44
Surburban	.41	.50
Region (dummy; 1 = yes)		
Northeast	.18	.39
Northcentral	.33	.48
South	.33	.48
West	.16	.37

References

Baker, D. 1993. "Compared to Japan, the U.S. Is a Low Achiever . . . Really." *Educational Researcher* 22 (3): 18–20.

Bryk, A. S., and S. W. Raudenbush. 1992. *Hierarchical Linear Models.* Sage.

Carpenter, T., and R. Lehrer. 1999. "Teaching and Learning Mathematics with Understanding." In *Mathematics Classrooms That Promote Understanding,* edited by E. Fennema and T. A. Romberg, 19–32. Mahwah, N.J.: Lawrence Erlbaum.

Chwast, S. 1983. *Tall City, Wide Country.* Viking

Clement, J. 1997. "Graphing." In *Children's Work with Data,* Modeling in Mathematics and Science Collaborative, 107–26. Madison: Wisconsin Center for Education Research.

Gamoran, A. 1987. "The Stratification of High School Learning Opportunities." *Sociology of Education* 60: 135–55.

Gamoran, A., A. C. Porter, J. Smithson, and P. A. White. 1997. "Upgrading High School Math Instruction: Improving Learning Opportunities for Low-Achieving, Low-Income Youth." *Educational Evaluation and Policy Analysis* 19: 325–38.

Hawkes, M., P. Kimmelman, and D. Kroeze. 1997. "Becoming 'First in the World' in Math and Science: Moving High Expectations and Promising Practices to Scale." *Phi Delta Kappan* 79 (1): 30–33.

Hiebert, J. 1999. "Relationships between Research and the NCTM Standards." *Journal for Research in Mathematics Education* 30: 3–19.

Lee, V. E., J. B. Smith, and R. C. Croninger. 1997. "How High School Organization Influences the Equitable Distribution of Learning in Mathematics and Science." *Sociology of Education* 70: 128–50.

Lehrer, R., C. Jacobson, V. Kemeny, and D. Strom. 1999. "Building on Children's Intuitions to Develop Mathematical Understanding of Space." In *Mathematics Classrooms That Promote Understanding,* edited by E. Fennema and T. A. Romberg, 63–87. Mahwah, N.J.: Lawrence Erlbaum.

Lehrer, R., C. Jacobson, G. Thoyre, V. Kemeny, D. Strom, J. Horvath, S. Gance, and M. Koehler. 1998. "Developing Understanding of Geometry and Space in the Primary Grades." In *Designing Learning Environments for Developing Understanding of Geometry and Space,* edited by R. Lehrer and D. Chazan, 169–200. Mahwah, N.J.: Lawrence Erlbaum.

Lehrer, R., and L. Schauble. Forthcoming. *Modeling in Mathematics and Science.*

LeTendre, G. 1999. "Introduction." In *The Educational System of Japan: Case Study Findings,* 1–22. U.S. Department of Education.

Loveless, T. 1997. "The Second Great Math Rebellion." *Education Week* (October 15): 48.

Marks, H. M., A. Gamoran, and F. M. Newmann. 1995. *Technical Appendix to: Authentic Pedagogy and Student Performance.* Madison, Wis.: Center on Organization and Restructuring of Schools.

Mayer, D. P. 1998. "Do New Teaching Standards Undermine Performance on Old Tests?" *Educational Evaluation and Policy Analysis* 20: 53–73.

————. 1999. "Measuring Instructional Practice: Can Policymakers Trust Survey Data?" *Educational Evaluation and Policy Analysis* 21: 29–45.

McKnight, C. C., F. J. Crosswhite, J. Dossey, E. Kifer, J. Swafford, K. J. Travers, and T. J. Cooney. 1987. *The Underachieving Curriculum.* Champaign, Ill.: Stipes Publishing.

Modeling in Mathematics and Science Collaborative. 1997. *Children's Work with Data.* Madison: Wisconsin Center for Education Research.

Newmann, F. M., and associates. 1996. *Authentic Achievement: Restructuring Schools for Intellectual Quality.* Jossey-Bass.

Newmann, F. M., H. M. Marks, and A. Gamoran. 1996. "Authentic Pedagogy and Student Performance." *American Journal of Education* 104: 280–312.

Nystrand, M., A. Gamoran, and M. J. Heck. 1993. "Using Small Groups for Response to and Thinking about Literature." *English Journal* 82 (1): 12–22.

Porter, A. 1998. "The Effects of Upgrading Policies on High School Mathematics and Science." In *Brookings Papers on Educational Policy, 1998,* edited by Diane Ravitch, 123–64. Brookings.

Prawat, R. S. 1997. "Fuzzy Math, Old Math, and Dewey." *Education Week* (December 10): 30, 34.

Rohlen, T. P. 1983. *Japan's High Schools.* University of California Press.

Smith, B. 1997. "Math Reform Redux: Balance Is Needed." *Education Week* (November 19): 42.

Stigler, J., C. Fernandez, and M. Yoshida. 1996. "Traditions of School Mathematics in Japanese and American Elementary Schools." In *Theories of Mathematical Learning,* edited by L. P. Steffe, P. Nesher, P. Cobb, G. Goldin, and B. Greer, 149–75. Mahwah, N.J.: Lawrence Erlbaum.

Stigler, J., P. Gonzales, T. Kawanaka, S. Knoll, and A. Serrano. 1999. *The TIMSS Videotape Classroom Study.* U.S. Department of Education.

Westbury, I. 1992. "Comparing American and Japanese Achievement: Is the United States Really a Low Achiever?" *Educational Researcher* 21 (5): 18–24.

————. 1993. "American and Japanese Achievement . . . Again: A Response to Baker." *Educational Researcher* 22 (3): 21–25.

CHAPTER EIGHT

Good Intentions
Are Not Enough

RICHARD ASKEY

If you want a good piece of apple pie, you either have to learn to bake well or else buy it from someone who can.

In 1980, in response to a mathematics education system that did not work well, the National Council of Teachers of Mathematics (NCTM) proposed doing something and came up with *An Agenda for Action.* There was little reaction to this proposal, and no serious objections were raised, so NCTM took this as a first step toward the standards that followed.

Less than ten years later NCTM published their *Curriculum and Evaluation Standards for School Mathematics,* the first of three volumes that defined NCTM's view of what school mathematics should be and how it should be taught (see NCTM 1991, 1995, for the other two volumes).

While there was a need to do something to improve school mathematics education, NCTM did not face up to the most critical problem—the lack of firm content knowledge of far too many teachers. There were other deficiencies in their program. NCTM did not look seriously at mathematics education in other countries. Mathematicians were not involved in the

Harold Stevenson has helped educate me in more ways than he knows. Ralph Raimi is a useful person to know when one wants the help of a good editor, and David Roberts pointed out an error in a draft of this chapter. Each has my thanks, as do many others who have made useful suggestions or comments through the years.

development of the standards. The authors of the NCTM standards had the strange notion that it is possible to teach conceptual understanding without developing technical skill at the same time. Instances of all these failures and what came from them will be given below.

The 1923 report of the National Committee on Mathematical Requirements (NCMR) of the Mathematical Association of America (MAA) is contrasted here with the NCTM standards from the late 1980s and early 1990s to illustrate how the errors committed by NCTM could have been avoided (NCMR 1923; NCTM 1989, 1991).

The Mathematical Knowledge of Teachers

Six or seven years ago I spoke with a former high school teacher who was then working on developing a school program. I had been to a library and looked at the teacher's editions of two books. The topic was poorly presented in each, so I wondered whether many school teachers were able to understand what was in the teacher's editions. I said that NCTM's biggest failure in the standards was not stating that far too many teachers lacked sufficient mathematical knowledge and following this up with a proposal on how to correct this. The reply was that it would have been hard for NCTM to say this. I offered two suggestions. First, state that NCTM has proposed that teachers teach in a much more indirect fashion than they have; to do this adequately requires a much firmer knowledge of mathematics. Second, look at what U.S. teachers know and compare this with what teachers in other countries know. If it turns out that U.S. teachers do not know as much, then we should admit that we underestimated what is needed to teach well and do something about it.

The first reason seems clear and hardly needs comment. However, it can be illustrated easily by looking at textbooks from ten to fifteen years ago and pointing out why they looked like they did. Many elementary school texts were printed with each lesson on two adjacent pages, which could be opened at the start of a lesson. When I first noticed this, I asked a mathematics educator who is also a textbook author why. He said that teachers want this, so that the full lesson for the day can be open on their desk. Publishers had been told that teachers were more comfortable with having the full lesson available for them to look at easily. To go from that to a system where students are expected to develop algorithms for arithmetic computation themselves is asking for trouble. When knowledge is restricted to what is in the text and little more, a teacher will frequently be at a loss when students come up with an answer that is not obviously either right or wrong to the teacher. This can happen in a structured setting, and did when I observed an elementary school classroom in the early 1970s. A student gave a correct answer to a question, but it was not phrased in the same way as in the book, so the teacher said the answer was wrong. Other children answered until one used the language of the book. The first child got a poor message from this experience, learning that mathematics does not make sense. To their credit, NCTM does not want this to happen in classes. However, this will happen when teachers do not have adequate knowledge, and it will happen more frequently in the type of setting NCTM favors, where the teaching is indirect. Lest anyone get the idea that the only alternative to what has been proposed by NCTM is to have the teacher give procedures and have students work on low-level problems using procedures they do not understand, that is not the case. There are other options.

The new series of mathematics programs funded by the National Science Foundation (NSF) in the wake of the NCTM standards should be looked at to see if this inadequate knowledge of teachers is compensated for by the quality of the texts and the information given in the teacher's manuals. These series were developed in response to an explicit call for programs that would be modeled on the NCTM standards.

Project 2061 is an education project of the American Association for the Advancement of Science. This group developed an outline of what they think all students should learn in science and mathematics (Project 2061 1989, 1993). The second of these books contains benchmarks. Some of these benchmarks were used to evaluate twelve sets of middle-school mathematics texts and programs. The criteria based on those benchmarks were compared with those given in the NCTM *Curriculum and Evaluation Standards* (NCTM 1989) and with those in the draft of the second version of what NCTM thinks school mathematics should be (NCTM 1998).

The results of this evaluation have been summarized in electronic form and a more detailed version will be published, partly in book form and partly on a CD (Project 2061 1999). The results were that four programs were said to be satisfactory, all of them ones funded by the NSF from the call for programs mentioned above. The other eight were judged not to be satisfactory.

While this evaluation did not look at each part of all the books, teachers and students will use all of them, so it is natural to look at the highest rated program—the *Connected Mathematics Project*, a series of twenty-four books for middle school mathematics—to see whether this program provides the necessary amount of information for teachers and if all the important topics in middle-school mathematics are treated adequately (Lappan et al. 1998).

The following is an example of a question from a unit quiz and the answer given for teachers. This is taken from "Moving Straight Ahead," the fifth of eight units in the seventh-grade program (Lappan et al. 1998, 101). Problems 6 through 9 are linear equations such as $10 = x - 2.5$. Problem 12 is:

> Each equation in questions 6–9 is a specific case of a linear equation of the form $y = mx + b$. Find the slope and the y-intercept for the equation $10 = x - 2.5$.

The answer given in the teacher's guide is: "The equation $10 = x - 2.5$ is a specific case of the equation $y = x - 2.5$, which has a slope of 1 and a y-intercept of -2.5."

In addition to an answer, this guide contains two student papers and teacher's comments on them. First, the work of two pairs of students:

Kim and Beth's work

$$y = x - 2.5$$

$$X \mid 1 \mid 2$$
$$\overline{}$$
$$Y \mid -15 \mid -5 \qquad Y \text{ intercept} = -2.5$$

$$\frac{\text{Rise}}{\text{Run}} = \frac{1}{1} = 1 \text{ slope}$$

$$y = mX + b$$
$$10 = X - 2.5$$
$$X - 2.5 = 10$$
$$10 + 2.5 = 12.5$$
$$12.5 = X$$

Susy and Jeff's work
Slope 12.5
y-intercept -2.5

Next, what a teacher wrote about the two groups' work:

Beth and Kim's work for question 12 makes it clear how they found the slope for the given equation. Their work even suggests that they may have learned something from doing this problem. By constructing and finding a couple of values for a table related to the equation, they found the rise and run between two points and thus the slope. It appears that they could not just use the equation to give slope. The question I have as a teacher is, after finding slope as they did, do the students now see how they could have found the slope for the given equation?

Susy and Jeff received 1 point for the correct y-intercept.

What is wrong with this? Everything, since the question asked is not correct. The equation $10 = x - 2.5$ is not a special case of the equation $y = mx + b$. What the authors and the teacher did was to take one point on the graph of $y = x - 2.5$, $y = 10$. This is just a point, and x is then 12.5. The graph of the equation $10 = x - 2.5$ is the vertical line $x = 12.5$. This line does not intersect the y-axis, so it has no y-intercept and is vertical, so its slope is infinite. If the students have learned anything they have learned that pattern matching of a simple type will give you a good grade in a math quiz. They will also have learned some incorrect mathematics. The first pair of students did a correct calculation for a different problem. NCTM has repeatedly said that they want students to understand why the calculation being done should be done. That part of NCTM's message was not followed here. I was told about this problem by a parent whose child took this quiz. The marking was exactly as in the text.

This is far from the only error in these books. One expects some errors in texts, such as the following. This is from the same book:

In 1980, the town of Rio Rancho, located on a mesa outside Santa Fe, New Mexico, was destined for obscurity. But as a result of hard work by its city officials, it began adding manufacturing jobs at a fast rate. As a result, the city's population grew 239% from 1980 to 1990, making Rio Rancho the fastest-growing "small city" in the United States. The population of Rio Rancho in 1990 was 37,000.

a. What was the population of Rio Rancho in 1980?
b. If the same rate of population increase continues, what will the population be in the year 2000? (Lappan et al. 1998, 75)

In the teacher's guide, question "a" is solved by $2.39P = 37,000$, so $P = 15,481$ people in 1980. The authors stress number sense, but do not use it here. Growth from 15,000 to 37,000 is less than 200 percent, so the answer given cannot be correct. They forgot to use the original population in 1980, so the correct equation to solve is $P + 2.39P = 37,000$, or $3.39P = 37,000$. They made the same mistake in solving question "b."

One assumes this is carelessness and hopes that teachers know enough to catch the error. I am well aware of this type of error, since a seventh-grade teacher of mine used to make such errors frequently. These errors annoyed me greatly. However, one can understand how they arise, and I am a bit more tolerant of such errors now than as a student. With the field testing that was done, this error should have been caught. The texts list about 160 teachers who field tested the books.

There is a second problem with the answer. To give the population as 15,481 is to state the answer more precisely than is warranted by the given data. By seventh grade students should be learning about how accurately results should be stated.

The second point mentioned above—of looking at other countries— has now been done, but not by NCTM.

The Third International Mathematics and Science Study (TIMSS) did more than just ask students to take an exam to see how well they did. Background information on texts, teachers, structure of the school system, amount of homework, and many other things were studied. In *A Splintered Vision*, which was written about how U.S. students did and what might have caused this, the authors wrote: "Unfortunately, there are indications that U.S. teachers are weaker in subject matter preparation and knowledge than teachers in other countries" (Schmidt, McKnight, and Raisen 1997, 79).

There is new work by Liping Ma developing on work done by Deborah Ball in the United States. Ball (1988) asked mathematics questions of elementary school teachers. One was to divide $1^{3}/4$ by $^{1}/2$ and make up a story problem that leads to this calculation. Liping Ma was involved in a follow-up project run by Ball to ask these questions of a larger group of teachers. Ma had recently come from China and was shocked by the low level of knowledge of most U.S. teachers. She felt that the teachers she had had in Shanghai, and those she had taught with in China, had a deeper understanding of the mathematics.

Ma's book, *Knowing and Teaching Elementary Mathematics* (1999), contains a summary of answers to this and three other questions, both from Chinese teachers and from a subset of the U.S. teachers who had been interviewed. The difference in the depth of knowledge is striking and cannot be attributed to the higher mathematics courses the teachers have taken, since most of the Chinese teachers have only had an introductory course in algebra and geometry. They started normal school after grade nine and spent two or three years in this training program, during which time they did not specialize in mathematics. What they had was a good school program in mathematics taught by teachers who knew mathematics well.

The figures of how well the U.S. and Chinese teachers did on the division of fractions problem tells only part of the story. A number of U.S. teachers could not do the calculation correctly, and only one of twenty-three in the sample made up a correct story problem—and even this story was flawed since the answer was $3\frac{1}{2}$ children. The teacher was aware of the problematic nature of the question she made up, but instead of changing the story said that the students could figure out what the fractional child meant. This was hoping for a lot, since the teacher herself was unable to change the problem into another one that did not have this drawback.

Of the seventy-two Chinese teachers interviewed, all did the calculation correctly and sixty-five of them made up correct story problems. As striking as these figures are, a more important difference is the deeper knowledge—and common sense—shown by the Chinese teachers. The deeper knowledge can be illustrated by the following. One said that she did not think that division by $\frac{1}{2}$ was a good problem to give to see if children understood division of fractions, so she made up one with $1\frac{3}{4}$ divided by $\frac{4}{5}$. Another made up three different problems dealing with sugar and said she would put them on the board, have a general class discussion of them, their similarities and differences, and then have the students make up their own problems.

Ma presents another example involving the use of manipulatives to aid in learning subtraction (1999, 20–21). The students and teacher discovered that the method they used with manipulatives and the standard algorithm were different, and the one using manipulatives mirrored what one would do in everyday life when making change. The students said that the standard way was more complicated, and they did not see a reason for learning it. After further discussion, which brought out the differences, the students were still not convinced they needed to learn the standard method. The teacher suggested they save the puzzle and return to it later in the year. By the end of the year, they were doing problems with larger numbers, and the students saw a reason for learning the standard way.

This should be contrasted with some of the newer programs, where standard methods of doing arithmetic computations are not only not taught, but parents are told that they should not show their children standard methods. One such program is Investigations in Number, Data and Space, another of the NSF-funded projects that were written to conform to the NCTM standards. In *Beyond Arithmetic: Changing Mathematics in the Elementary Classroom*, Mokros, Russell, and Economopoulos (1995, 79) describe the philosophy behind this program by stating that "research studies from this country and from international comparisons have shown that students who use their own procedures do quite a bit better than students who use standard ones."

One reference Mokros and colleagues cited was a paper by Stevenson, Lee, and Stigler (1986). I wrote Harold Stevenson and asked what in this paper or other work of his could lead to its use in *Beyond Arithmetic*. He responded: "I have no idea where the Mokros et al. comments come from. They certainly don't have any bearing on anything we have written. Nor can I think of other sources that would be a basis for their opinions."

Liping Ma's work supports Stevenson's comment. When Ma found that the Chinese teachers had a much deeper understanding of elementary mathematics than the U.S. teachers did, she tried to find out how this knowledge was learned. She asked the same questions of twenty-six Chinese students in normal school and all of them did the division of fractions correctly; twenty-two of the twenty-six made up a correct story problem. This is 85 percent, not much below the 90 percent of the teachers who made up a correct story problem. Ma then asked these questions of twenty Chinese ninth-grade students in what she said was a mediocre school in Shanghai where at most half of the students were able to pass college entrance examinations. All these students did the calculation correctly, and eight of twenty made up a correct story problem. (Ma 1999, 125–26).

Is it possible to teach standard algorithms so that students learn how to do the calculations correctly and also build a foundation for later study of mathematics? Of course it is, and it should be done. In the United States mathematics educators looked at a system that did not work and tried to build one that they thought would. However, this problem was too hard and they failed to build such a system. As one small example, consider that the division of fractions is completely missing in the *Connected Mathematics Project*.

Now let us compare this recent history with recommendations made in 1923 by a committee that studied secondary school mathematics. The NCMR stated that the "United States is far behind Europe in the scientific and professional training required of its secondary teachers" (1923, 16).

A full chapter is devoted to the education of teachers, with summaries of reports about this in many countries, as well as in numerous U.S. states and cities. This chapter was written by R. C. Archibald, who was responsible for the magnificent mathematics library at Brown University. He was a compulsive gatherer of information, and the chapter reflects this tendency of his. On the topic of the level of U.S. teachers' mathematical knowledge he stated that "it will be apparent from the study of this report that a successful teacher of mathematics must not only be highly trained in his subject and have a genuine enthusiasm for it but must have also peculiar attributes of personality and above all insight of a high order into the psychology of the learning process as related to the higher mental activities" (NCMR 1923, 16). On the previous page he maintained:

> While the greater part of this report concerns itself with the content of courses in mathematics . . . the National Committee must emphasize strongly its conviction that even more fundamental is the problem of the teacher—his qualifications and training, his personality, skill, and enthusiasm. The greater part of the failure of mathematics is due to poor teaching. Good teachers have in the past succeeded, and will continue to succeed, in achieving highly satisfactory results with the traditional material; poor teachers will not succeed even with the newer and better material.

Mathematics Education in Other Countries

In addition to the example above about the mathematical knowledge of teachers in other countries, there are other things that could have been learned by looking at practice elsewhere. One important topic is the amount of aid given to teachers.

Harold Stevenson once told me the following story. He learned Japanese during World War II, so when he is in Japanese classrooms he can follow what is being said. Stevenson was observing a lesson in Saporo, and whenever a student made a statement that showed lack of knowledge or understanding, the teacher asked a question that forced thought about the answer, and someone, either the student or another student, would say something that would clarify the situation. After the class was over, Stevenson asked the teacher how it was that he was able to ask the right question immediately to help clarify what was being learned. The teacher showed him a large sheet of paper that had an outline of the lesson, the problem the students would be asked to do, suggestions for questions to ask to get the lesson started, examples of errors that frequently occur when teaching this lesson, and suggestions of questions to ask when these errors occur.

How Japanese teachers develop this type of material is briefly described in *The Teaching Gap* (Stigler and Hiebert 1999). However, not nearly enough information is provided to allow a similar system to be developed here. Explicit examples of such lessons and details of how they were developed would be needed. This program has existed in Japan for a moderately long time, and U.S. mathematics educators need to learn from it or they will spend decades developing something similar. It is foolish not to take advantage of what is available. In this direction, Stevenson has approximately 160 Japanese lessons, and only one mathematics educator has looked at them. I learned of these lessons by asking Stevenson what he had, after reading a description of one of the lessons (Sawada 1996). Another of these lessons was described in an article published in an NCTM journal (Sawada 1997).

One practice in U.S. school systems that must be corrected is allowing frequent interruptions in school classes by announcements from the office. This does not happen in Japan, where a class lesson is only interrupted for an emergency. The pace of a coherent lesson is broken by interruptions. That there have not been protests about this practice from teachers and organizations of teachers such as NCTM is an indication that they do not know that such interruptions are not common in all counties. In the university where I teach there are no intercoms in the classrooms, and if they were installed and used as often as in our elementary and secondary schools, there would be a revolt from the faculty. We know this is inappropriate and interferes with learning. NCTM should say so and work to have this practice stopped.

In addition to structural aid, it is possible to learn about interesting ways to approach mathematical topics. A lot has been written about how to teach school mathematics to prepare students for algebra. However, little has been written here about a method that has been used in Asia for at least forty-five years. When in Singapore in the summer of 1999, I described this as pictorial algebra to a mathematics educator. He said that was the name they used informally to describe their method of solving ratio, fraction, and proportion problems before algebra is started.

The following is an illustrated problem in a Singapore textbook used in the first half of the sixth grade:

Consider the following problem. Peter has two-thirds as many marbles as Henry. If Peter gets eight more marbles, he will have five-sixths as many marbles as Henry. How many marbles do Peter and Henry have? (Primary Mathematics Project Team 1995, 35)

The following picture is drawn to illustrate the original situation:

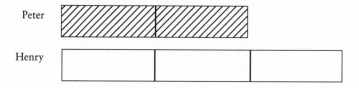

This is changed to the following when eight marbles have been added:

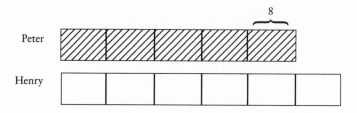

The answer is then clear: Peter had four small boxes with 8 marbles in each, and Henry had six, so Peter had 32 marbles and Henry had 48. This method is introduced in fourth grade and used for simple problems. In fifth grade it is developed more and used on slightly more complicated problems. As noted, the problem above is from a sixth-grade book. Algebra is begun in the first half of the sixth grade and is developed seriously in seventh grade. After algebra has been developed more, the pictorial approach is dropped, since the explicit use of letters is more flexible and powerful. However, the pictorial approach mirrors what is done later with letters. Hung-Hsi Wu told me that he learned this method of solving word problems when he was in Hong Kong, so it is at least forty-five years old, and probably older. It is not in U.S. texts. I had hoped that the draft of the new version of standards would contain this, and I even lent NCTM a complete set of Singapore texts for the writing team to use. Unfortunately, they did not include this. The final version of the NCTM standards appeared after the previous sentences were written. It contains one illustration of this method.

In *The Underachieving Curriculum* (McKnight et al. 1987), written about the results from the Second International Mathematics Study, the claim was that our eighth-grade mathematics students did so poorly on the SIMS test because of the middle school curriculum. Lack of appropriate education of teachers was dismissed as a cause. In reporting on TIMSS William Schmidt used the phrase "a mile wide and an inch deep" to describe the U.S. curriculum. In his first press conference on the TIMSS results (Schmidt 1996), he said that a gap in course taking by U.S. teachers did not exist. U.S. teachers have had as many college math courses as teachers in other countries, but their poor preparation in school mathematics makes this irrelevant.

While there is a gap in knowledge of teachers, the curriculum in U.S. schools is also a problem. This was pointed out explicitly in the 1923 report of the MAA, which stated: "Everywhere algebra is introduced earlier than in the United States. In certain of the German schools some work in algebra is introduced during the sixth school year and in no country except the United States, is this introductory work postponed later than the seventh school year" (NCMR 1923, 172).

This was written in 1923, and some will say that these other countries were not educating as large a fraction of their students as the United States was. That was true then, but it is no longer true. In a recent report by the Organization for Economic Cooperation and Development on high school graduation rates in almost thirty countries, only Mexico had a lower high school graduation rate than the United States. The TIMSS results showed that only 25 percent of U.S. eighth-grade students had studied algebra, while in most of the other countries all or almost all of their students had studied algebra by the time they took the eighth-grade TIMSS test.

The Role of Mathematicians

In the 1923 report mathematicians played a large, but not exclusive role. The committee that wrote this report was appointed by the MAA, which was then a relatively new group interested primarily in teaching mathematics in colleges and universities. This committee was chaired by J. W. Young, a mathematics professor at Dartmouth. Committee members included E. H. Moore, who had developed the Mathematics Department at the University of Chicago from its start in 1892, and in a short time it was the best mathematics department in the United States. Moore had also given his retiring presidential address to the American Mathematical Society on questions of education. One of Moore's Ph.D. students, Oswald

Veblen, was also on this committee. Veblen was then at Princeton and later would be the main force behind developing the School of Mathematics at the Institute for Advanced Study. Veblen wrote an article on geometry (see Young 1911), and he and Young wrote a successful pair of books on projective geometry. D. E. Smith, a distinguished historian of mathematics who had coauthored a number of school texts, was another member of this committee. The NCTM was not formed until 1920, four years after the appointment of this MAA committee. Three regional groups of school math teachers, from the middle states and Maryland, New England, and the Central States, were asked to appoint representatives. Later four others were appointed, including the commissioner of secondary education from Sacramento, California, and three more teachers.

This distinguished committee had help from others not on the committee. The chapter on mathematics curricula in other countries was written by J. C. Brown, who had written a much more detailed report on this in 1915 (Brown 1915).

To keep up with developments in their area of expertise, mathematicians regularly read papers written by authorities who live in other countries. This international perspective was probably the reason that the report contained an extensive summary of what happens in other countries (NCMR 1923).

Mathematicians were not included on the writing teams for the NCTM standards. While mathematicians of the stature of Veblen and Moore probably could not have been found to help, there were mathematicians with interest and knowledge who could have been used. NCTM added some mathematicians to the writing team for their new version of standards (NCTM 1998, 18). This is a step in the right direction.

There were probably two related reasons why mathematicians were not asked to be involved in writing the NCTM standards. Both come from the New Math, where mathematicians were heavily involved. Serious errors were made in developing the New Math, and this is not the place, nor is there time, to go into this in detail. Some mathematicians felt they had tried to develop a good program, and when it was rejected they turned away from school mathematics. With the failure of the New Math, many mathematics educators blamed mathematicians for the failure of something they helped support, but had not developed.

While mathematicians played a major role in the development of the New Math, other mathematicians pointed out some of the errors at a fairly early stage (Ahlfors 1962). William Duren (1989) feels that corrections would have been made but the reaction to some of the failures brought down the whole project before this could be done. I am not as certain that corrections were possible.

Mathematicians were not the only people who made serious errors in the New Math period. Here is an example. I was a young mathematician during the development of the New Math, so I was not directly involved except for a minor incident in Madison, Wisconsin, when I was a young faculty member in the Mathematics Department of the University of Wisconsin. The local school system proposed adoption of a math series, and I was one of a few people in the Mathematics Department who looked at this series of books. One of the books contained the following definition of the addition of rational numbers, which were denoted by the ordered pair (a, b) (see Van Engen et al. 1963, 119):

$$(a, b) + (c, d) = (a + c, b + d).$$

This type of formalism has no place in school mathematics, but beyond that, it made no sense to me, since I assumed that (a, b) meant a/b. It did not. What the book was doing was not getting fractions, that had been done earlier, but was getting the negative fractions, so (a, b) meant $a - b$ where a and b were positive rational numbers. I appeared at a local school board meeting and suggested that something was wrong with the process of textbook adoption if a book for eighth-grade mathematics students could not be read by a professional mathematician. This book was coauthored by five people: three university mathematics educators and two mathematics supervisors in school districts.

Mathematicians need to be involved in the actual development and writing of standards, not just in being asked if they support the "vision of the standards," as happened for the NCTM standards. NCTM asked the MAA to endorse their vision. Minutes of the meeting when this happened note that John Dossey, president of NCTM when the committee that wrote their standards was appointed, appeared at a MAA board meeting on January 15, 1989, and asked for endorsement and support of the vision for school mathematics embodied in the NCTM *Curriculum and Evaluation Standards for School Mathematics*. These standards were not available at the time, but an abbreviated form was provided, as was an article on these standards that had appeared in the *Virginia Mathematics Teacher*. Randall Heckmann asked about proofs, especially in Euclidean geometry. Dossey explained that there was little decrease in the theory except in two column proofs in deference to paragraph proof writing skills and convincing arguments.

How has this played out in practice? Has geometry continued to have proofs or convincing arguments, or has this slipped through the cracks? Consider something that is pushed a lot in the current reform—graphs of linear equations. One would like an argument using similar triangles that the graph of $y = mx + b$ is really a straight line, but it can be argued that this is obvious and one wastes time trying to convince students that something that is obvious needs a proof. The same can be said about the criteria for two lines to be parallel when they are given by equations of the form $y = mx + b$. However, when it comes to perpendicular lines, it is not obvious that the condition that $y = mx + b$ and $y = nx + c$ are perpendicular is $mn = -1$. In a series of books that John Dossey helped write—*Focus on Algebra* (Charles and Thompson 1998), *Focus on Geometry* (Hoffer and Koss 1998), and *Focus on Advanced Algebra* (Dossey and Vonder Embse 1998)—the definition of perpendicular lines in the two algebra books is $mn = -1$. In the geometry book, there is a geometric definition of perpendicular near the start of the book: "two lines are perpendicular if the angle between them is 90 degrees." A bit later, there is the following definition: "Two nonvertical lines are parallel if and only if their slopes are equal. Two nonvertical lines are perpendicular if and only if the product of their slopes is -1."

No connection is given between these two definitions of perpendicular. The second one should be a theorem, not a definition. It might be possible that in this book of almost 900 pages there is a proof that the two definitions give the same lines as perpendicular, but I was not able to find it. I wrote the two main authors asking if there is such a proof, but have not received a reply.

This series is only singled out because of Dossey's role in both the development of the 1989 standards and this series. Many other books treat perpendicular lines in the same way.

In the NCTM *Curriculum and Evaluation Standards* there is a downplaying of technical skills, which is unfortunate. Most mathematicians I have consulted think that skills are a vital part of mathematics, and that without them one cannot develop the understanding that we want students to have. The following is one of a number of instances where the NCTM standards not only did not say that a skill was necessary but specifically said not to develop it. The topic is work with fractions. Here is what NCTM proposed:

The mastery of a small number of basic facts with common fractions (for example, $1/4 + 1/4 = 1/2$; $3/4 + 1/2 = 1\ 1/4$; and $1/2 \times 1/2 = 1/4$) and with decimals (for example, $0.1 + 0.1 = 0.2$ and $0.1 \times 0.1 = 0.01$) contributes to students' readiness to learn estimation and for concept development and problem solving. This proficiency in the addition, subtraction, and multiplication of fractions and mixed numbers should be limited to those with simple denominators that can be visualized concretely or pictorially and are apt to occur in real-world settings; such computation promotes conceptual understanding of the operations. This is not to suggest, however, that valuable instruction time should be devoted to exercises like $17/24 + 5/18$ or $5^3/4 \times 4^1/4$, which are much harder to visualize and unlikely to occur in real-life situations. Division of fractions should be approached conceptually. An understanding of what happens when one divides by a fractional number (less than or greater than 1) is essential.

I asked Liping Ma to comment on this. She replied:

I would like to claim some interesting and important relationship between 'basic facts with common fractions (for example, $1/4 + 1/4 = 1/2$; $3/4 + 1/2 = 1\ 1/4$; and $1/2 \times 1/2 = 1/4$) and with decimals' 'that can be visualized concretely' and those "much harder to visualize and unlikely to occur in real-life situations." In fact, without the conceptual understanding of the former, it will be unlikely for one to understand the latter. However, unless one's understanding of the former is deepened and solidified by the latter (which is not as hard as people imagine), the primary conceptual understanding is still very limited and superficial and therefore too fragile to make connections to other concepts of the subject. So, students' mathematical power will be generated from a connection of the "basic facts" and "abstract concepts," rather than emphasizing or ignoring either of them.

Ma's comment reflects what I have felt all along, and what most mathematicians feel about technical skills: They need to be developed along with reasons why things work. There are times when the reasons come first, and other times when the skills are introduced and reasons developed as students become proficient. The idea that one can teach conceptual understanding without being able to do something really means that the level of the concept one asks students to learn is far too weak. A colleague of mine, Phil Miles, said a few years ago that he was happy that reformers speak about "conceptual" understanding since it is a sign that the topic in question is being watered down. He went on to say that "conceptual understanding of an exponential function is that they increase." At the time, I thought that his example was a good joke, but recently I have decided that this is a "bad joke."

The following problem appeared in a chapter in a book published by NCTM in 1998, so it was read by at least one referee and probably the editor. As background, the deer population in some counties in Wisconsin has been increasing.

Students from Boomer High recently studied a herd of 100 deer living in a nearby forest. Based on the number of female deer they were able to count, they hypothesized that the total deer population could be described by one of the following two functions:

#1: $P(t) = t^2 - t + 100$ or   #2: $D(t) = 5t + 100$

t = the number of years after the study.

1. Draw a table or graph of the deer populations represented by each function for every year over a ten year period.
2. Compare and contrast the two functions to describe what they predict will happen to the deer population over an extended period of time.

Here is a quote written by the authors.

In addition, the task is structured around significant mathematics. In particular, the task focuses on "functions that are constructed as models of real-world problems" and emphasizes "the connections among a problem situation, its model as a function in symbolic form, and the graph of that function" (NCTM 1989, 126). The teachers who developed this task chose the two functions in order to model a population that was growing linearly and one that was growing exponentially.

The use of the word *exponential* is incorrect. The function in question does not grow exponentially, it grows quadratically. Elsewhere in this chapter, student answers are given. One of the students referred to this function as a nearly exponential curve, so this student has not been taught the difference between exponential and polynomial growth, just the difference between linear and nonlinear growth, so she modified the only word she knew for nonlinear growth.

One of the students did not understand the notation D (t) and P (t), and treated both as multiplication of a letter by t, so she divided by t to get data and a graph. She referred to the nonlinear expression as having a squared term rather than one multiplied by 5. Even with this correct statement, the authors wrote that this student "recognized that symbolically, function 1 changes exponentially and function 2 changes linearly."

This is not the only error in the chapter. The last student actually wrote a nice solution to a different problem, had correct calculations (one tiny slip in one of twenty calculations) to this other problem, and found where the two graphs she drew intersected. Since each function was divided by t, the point she found is the correct intersection point for the real problem. The authors did not seem to realize this, for they wrote: "It is interesting that even though Kathy has calculated incorrect values, the point of intersection of the two functions determined by her procedure is the same as that determined by using the correct values of the functions: $t = 6$."

After a private conversation with one of the authors, I have become convinced that they were aware that the incorrect graphs had to intersect at the correct point, and they phrased their comment in a poor way. They also know the difference between a function that grows exponentially and one that grows quadratically. The authors would have been spared the embarrassment of having these errors published if the chapter had been read by a mathematician.

The fact that one student described a quadratic function as "almost exponential" is symptomatic of the vagueness that frequently accompanies an emphasis on "conceptual understanding," although this should not be the case with real understanding. One person I corresponded with about this chapter tried to explain the use of *exponential* as an informal use of the word to describe a situation where something grows faster as it gets larger. To their credit, the authors did not use this flimsy excuse to explain an error.

There are other problematic features. The functions P (t) and D (t) should be found by some sort of modeling based on past data. They clearly were not, since P (t) decreases until $t = \frac{1}{2}$, while D (t) is always increasing. The authors did not make up the problem, but they used it without commenting on this artificial aspect of it.

The next NCTM yearbook had Peter Lax on the editorial panel, and I did not see any glaring errors as in the example mentioned above. Having mathematicians involved can make a difference.

Publishers need to have mathematicians read textbooks. There are many examples of incorrect mathematics in our school texts. While reading books for California, I was shocked to read in a book dealing with number sense that there might be 1 million books in an elementary school. The author had no number sense.

There is a need to have scientists read school math books when science is treated. This final example is from the *Connected Mathematics Project*, in "Moving Straight Ahead" (Lappan et al. 1998, 78):

The graph below shows the altitude of a spaceship from 10 seconds before liftoff through 7 seconds after liftoff.

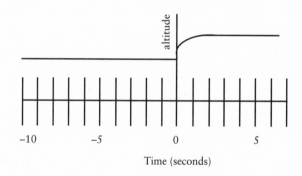

Time (seconds)

a. Describe the relationship between the altitude of the spaceship and time.
b. What is the slope for the part of the graph that is a straight line? What does this slope represent in this situation?

One hopes that at least some of the students will have watched the launch of a space ship and noticed that it rises slowly at first. There is a lot of inertia to overcome. The last sentence is a fitting conclusion to this description of a situation that needs improvement.

In the almost two years since this chapter was written, some changes have occurred. NCTM has published *Principles and Standards for School Mathematics*. About fractions, there are still problems. For division by fractions, they suggest doing this by successive subtraction and take an example where this can be made to work. However, try to divide $^1/_5$ by $^1/_3$ by successive subtraction to see that this is not adequate (NCTM 2000).

Some changes to the *Connected Mathematics Project* have been posted on the publisher's website. They now have a section dividing fractions. There is still nothing on division by decimals. In the fall of 2000 in a diagnostic test taken at the start of a course on arithmetic for prospective elementary school teachers, only one-third successfully computed 25.56 divided by 0.004.

Two of the errors mentioned in this article have been corrected. There is a new graph of the height of a space ship. The Rio Rancho problem was corrected, but now includes the following: "2.39P + P = 37,000, so P = 10,914.45428 or approximately 10,914 people in 1980." When the data are given to at most three significant figures, the answer should not be given to five, much less the ten that came from mindless recording of a calculator output. The students should have been expected to divide 37,000 by 3.39 by hand and give an answer to two or three significant figures.[1]

References

Ahlfors, L., et al. 1962. "On the Mathematics Curriculum of the High School." *American Mathematical Monthly* 69: 189–93; *Mathematics Teacher* 55: 191–95.

Ball, D. 1988. "Knowledge and Reasoning in Mathematical Pedagogy: Examining What Prospective Teachers Bring to Teacher Education." Ph.D. dissertation, Michigan State University, East Lansing.

Brown, J. C. 1915. "Curricula in Mathematics." Bulletin no. 45. U.S. Bureau of Education.

Charles, R., and A. Thompson. 1998. *Focus on Algebra*. Addison-Wesley.

Dossey, J., and Vonder Embse, C. 1998. *Focus on Advanced Algebra*. Addison-Wesley.

Duren, W. 1989. "Mathematics in American Society." In *A Century of Mathematics in America*, Part II, edited by P. Duren, 399–447. Providence, R.I.: American Mathematical Society.

Hoffer, A., and R. Koss. 1998. *Focus on Geometry*. Addison-Wesley.

Lappan, G., et al. 1998a. *Connected Mathematics Project*. Series of books for middle school mathematics. Menlo Park, Calif.: Dale Seymour.

———. 1998b. "Moving Straight Ahead: Linear Relationships," teacher's guide. In the *Connected Mathematics Project*. Menlo Park, Calif.: Dale Seymour.

Ma, L. 1999. *Knowing and Teaching Elementary Mathematics: Teachers' Understanding of Fundamental Mathematics in China and the United States*. Hillsdale, N.J.: Lawrence Erlbaum. 1999.

1. The corrections can be found at www.phschool.com/curriculum_support/openbook/math/cmp_gr7_moving_98.html. The added material on division and fractions is at www.phschool.com/math/cmp/new_student_pages.

McKnight, C., et al. 1987. *The Underachieving Curriculum: Assessing U.S. School Mathematics from an International Perspective*. Champaign, Ill.: Stipes Publishing.

Mokros, J., S. J. Russell, and K. Economopoulos. 1995. *Beyond Arithmetic: Changing Mathematics in the Elementary Classroom*. White Plains, N.Y.: Dale Seymour.

National Committee on Mathematical Requirements. 1923. *The Reorganization of Mathematics in Secondary Education*. Oberlin, Ohio: Mathematical Association of America.

National Council of Teachers of Mathematics. 1980. *An Agenda for Action: Recommendations for School Mathematics of the 1980's*. Reston, Va.

———. 1989. *Curriculum and Evaluation Standards for School Mathematics*. Reston, Va.

———. 1991. *Professional Standards for Teaching School Mathematics*. Reston, Va.

———. 1995. *Assessment Standards for School Mathematics*. Reston, Va.

———. 1998. *Principles and Standards for School Mathematics*, discussion draft. Reston, Va.

———. 2000. *Principles and Standards for School Mathematics*. Reston, Va.

Primary Mathematics Project Team. 1995. *Primary Mathematics 6A*, 2d ed. Singapore: Federal Publications.

Project 2061. 1989. *Science for All Americans*. Oxford University Press.

———. 1993. *Benchmarks for Science Literacy*. Oxford University Press.

———. 1999. *Middle Grades Mathematics Textbooks: A Benchmarks-Based Evaluation*. Available at www.project2061.org/matheval/index.html. Book with same title and companion CD-ROM forthcoming.

Sawada, D. 1996. "Mathematics as Problem Solving: A Japanese Way." *Wisconsin Teacher of Mathematics* 47 (3): 9–12.

———. 1997. "Mathematics as Reasoning: Episodes from Japan." *Mathematics Teaching in the Middle School* (May): 416–21.

Schmidt, W. 1996. Statement by William H. Schmidt, November 11. Available at http://ustimss.msu.edu/pressre.htm.

Schmidt, W., C. McKnight, and S. Raizen. 1997. *A Splintered Vision: An Investigation of U.S. Science and Mathematics Education*. Dordrecht, The Netherlands: Kluwer.

Stevenson, H., S-Y Lee, and J. Stigler. 1986. "Mathematics Achievement of Chinese, Japanese and American Children." *Science* 231: 693–99.

Stigler, J., and J. Hiebert. 1999. *The Teaching Gap*. Free Press.

Van Engen, H., et al. 1963. *Seeing through Mathematics*, Part 2. Chicago: Scott, Foresman.

Young, J. W. A., ed. 1911. *Monographs on Topics of Modern Mathematics, Relevant to the Elementary Field*. New York: Longmans, Green and Co.

CHAPTER NINE

A Tale of Two Math Reforms: The Politics of the New Math and the NCTM Standards

TOM LOVELESS

A ttendees of a joint meeting of the American Mathematical Society (AMS) and the Mathematical Association
of America (MAA) in January 1998 heard Secretary of Education Richard
Riley deliver an extraordinary address. Riley called for an end to the math
wars—the growing, often bitter controversy that, by the middle of the
1990s, had embroiled parents, math educators, mathematicians, education reformers, local school boards, federal and state policymakers, and
political pundits in a struggle over the content and teaching of mathematics. The meeting was a fitting venue for the speech. The AMS and the
MAA are made up primarily of research mathematicians and college math
instructors. Members of both organizations had publicly criticized the
document widely recognized as the nation's educational standards in K–
12 mathematics, the *Curriculum and Evaluation Standards for School
Mathematics*, released in 1989 by the National Council of Teachers of
Mathematics (NCTM), a third organization consisting mainly of high
school math teachers and math educators from schools of education (Riley
1997).

The NCTM standards are ground zero in the math wars, the guiding
document of the 1990s movement to change how elementary and second-

My thanks to Ralph Raimi, Dick Askey, and Deborah Tepper Haimo for helpful suggestions.

ary students are taught mathematics. After their release, the NCTM standards won the praise of analysts across a broad spectrum of educational
philosophies and political persuasions and were viewed for several years
as a hallmark of school reform. Then the consensus collapsed. Test scores
from California, one of the earliest and most faithful followers of the standards, showed that the state's mathematical performance had fallen below almost every other state in the nation. Advocates of NCTM reform
found themselves under attack, publicly challenged to defend their recommendations, not asked simply to describe the best way of implementing
NCTM's sweeping vision of reform (NCTM 1989).[1]

Riley's speech was not exceptional for its content. He talked about the
importance of mathematics and urged the combatants in the math wars to
conduct themselves with civility and respect. What made the talk exceptional was who delivered it. The federal government usually treats curriculum disputes like family feuds, better left to experts in the disciplines
or to educators in the local jurisdictions where disagreements occur. Numerous disputes had engulfed the field of language arts—over high school
reading lists and their dominance by "dead white males"; whether fluency, creativity, and "the process" of writing are as important as the formal rules of written composition; the benefits of using a phonics or whole
language approach in reading instruction—but, for the most part, the federal government steered clear.

Riley's speech signaled that math is different. The last time the federal
government became heavily involved with a curriculum dispute was in the
1960s, and, then as now, the subject was math. Reforms known as "the
New Math" emerged with great promise in the 1950s, dominated the
elementary math curriculum in the 1960s, and fell into disrepute in the
early 1970s.

This chapter analyzes the politics of math reform. First the New Math
and the NCTM standards are examined along three dimensions: the influence of a policy subsystem that shapes the K–12 math curriculum, the
focusing events that attracted public attention to math reform in the 1950s

---

1. All references to the "NCTM standards" in this chapter refer to National Council of
Teachers of Mathematics (1989). In 2000 the NCTM published a revised set of standards,
Principles and Standards for School Mathematics, several months after the original version
of this chapter was originally presented. For the sake of historical accuracy, references to
draft copies of the 2000 standards and the use of future verb tenses to describe their publication have been preserved. Information on the standards' publication history is available
on the NCTM website at http://www.nctm.org.

and 1980s, and the content of the two reforms, specifically, the changes that they recommended that were the most controversial. The New Math's downfall is a matter of history, but the story of the NCTM standards is still a work in progress. It is hard to predict whether the NCTM reforms will join the New Math on the never-ending list of school reforms that enjoyed a chorus of accolades before they crashed and burned. But the same three categories of analysis will be used to shed light on an intriguing question: How did NCTM reform go from near universal recognition as the model of curriculum standards at the beginning of the 1990s to the subject of bitter debate by the decade's end? Several factors that may influence math reform in the future will also be identified. Before beginning the analysis, it should be stated that no attempt was made to extend the chapter's conclusions to other reforms in education or even to math reform movements in other epochs. The research is limited to these two initiatives alone.

Subsystem Dominance

A policy subsystem is a coalition of groups exercising authority in a particular policy domain. Separately, the components of the subsystem function as part of larger host institutions, both public and private, but by forging links beyond local institutional boundaries they achieve a high degree of power and autonomy in shaping policy. As articulated by Ernest Griffith, David Truman, J. Leiper Freeman, and others, theories about subsystems are a species of elite theories of governance. The term *elite* is not used in opprobrium here but merely reflects the fact that a select group of actors exercises an extraordinary amount of influence on policy (Griffith 1939; Truman 1951; Freeman 1965; Freeman 1995; Fritschler and Hoefler 1996).[2]

Policy domains that rely on experts for guidance are prone to the dominance of subsystems, mainly because they encompass fields that are inherently complicated and informed by research with technically sophisticated methodologies. They may also be characterized by such ambiguity on essential questions that battles are fought between supporters of rival theories. Historically, subsystems have dominated policymaking in areas such as agricultural subsidies, trade, health care, transportation, tobacco, nuclear

---

2. Subsystems go by several names, including "subgovernments." For a discussion of issue networks, see Heclo (1978).

energy, military procurement, the environment, insurance, and auto safety (Barker and Peters 1993).

Subsystems may enter a period of destabilization if their power is threatened. As old members are pushed out, new elites gain entry, and a new subsystem evolves. The tobacco subsystem of the 1950s, for example, was composed of farmers, tobacco companies, officials of the Department of Agriculture, and the agricultural committees of Congress. After health concerns related to smoking became public in the 1960s, the tobacco subsystem expanded to include the Surgeon General's office, the Food and Drug Administration, the National Cancer Society, and several advocacy groups. Tobacco policies in the 1990s are crafted under the watchful eye of this coalition (Fritschler and Hoefler 1996; Ripley and Franklin 1987).

In the field of education, curriculum policy is almost exclusively decided at the state level, but most areas of curriculum policy are dominated by national subsystems in each of the subject areas. The math subsystem includes math authorities in state departments of education, specialists in local school districts, professors and researchers in the schools of education, mathematicians, the NCTM, the National Science Foundation (NSF), textbook companies, test publishers, independent reform groups containing state political leaders, such as the Education Commission of the States and the Council of Chief State School Officers, and professional groups with an interest in math, such as the California Math Project.

An individual member of the subsystem may affiliate with several of these groups in the course of a career. A freshly minted Ph.D. in math education, for instance, will probably join the faculty of a school of education, but he or she might also author a textbook, spend a couple of terms in office in the leadership of the NCTM, and serve a stint as a curriculum specialist at the state or federal level. The same person might also consult for test publishers in designing math assessments, receive an NSF grant to pilot a curriculum innovation, and serve on the advisory board of a math reform group.[3]

Curriculum reforms almost always spring from one of the subject area subsystems. The New Math grew out of research conducted in several curriculum projects in the 1950s. It was not a monolithic movement. The projects that began in the early part of the decade were mostly led by

3. For examples of subsystems' influence on state educational reform in the 1980s, see Mazzoni (1995, 53–73). For a general discussion of the influence of professional associations on education policy, see Iannaccone (1967). Also see the analysis of curriculum politics by Wirt and Kirst (1989, 104–07) and Boyd (1979a).

researchers in math education, but later projects were strongly influenced by mathematicians. The University of Illinois Committee on School Mathematics (UICSM) began in 1951, supported by the Carnegie Corporation. In 1955 the Commission on Mathematics, made up equally of high school teachers, math educators, and mathematicians,[4] issued its recommendations for a curriculum that would better prepare students for college. In her history of the New Math, Elisabeth Barlage reports that in the commission's report "little was said about the methods of teaching by which the recommended content should be taught to students" (Barlage 1982, 16). This description does not apply to the Madison Project, which began at Syracuse University in 1957. The project was based on promoting the "discovery method," and its basic assumptions sound strikingly similar to math reform in the 1990s.

> Unstructured tasks help the student learn to solve problems. By means of discussions and solving such problems he is able to discover mathematical structures himself. The attempt is to provide a learning atmosphere which lets the student think that he is the first one to deal with those problems and which lets him discover mathematics in an active way. This situation is best without a teacher's interference. This discovery process is supported by related experimenting materials, stories, and games. (Barlage 1982, 24)

Funding for the later New Math projects came from the NSF, as stipulated in the 1958 National Defense and Education Act (NDEA). The most important of these was the School Mathematics Study Group (SMSG). The director of SMSG, Edward G. Begle, was a professor of mathematics at Yale, and the project went with him when he moved to Stanford. When the New Math was debated in the 1960s, the arguments usually focused on SMSG materials, partly because Begle was a highly visible advocate for math reform but also because SMSG was the largest of the NSF initiatives, received the most NSF funding, and disseminated its ideas by producing textbooks that publishers could use as models. The list of prestigious individuals and organizations associated with the New Math, including the NCTM, persuaded textbook publishers to launch several new series based on the "modern" methods pouring forth from the labs. Local school

---

4. In this discussion "math educators" refers to academics who train math teachers and conduct research on math education. The second group, "mathematicians," refers to academics who teach and conduct research in mathematics.

boards and administrators rushed to adopt the new books and to train teachers in using the materials (Barlage 1982; Hayden 1983).

Seymour Sarason identifies how the seeds of New Math's later troubles were sewn in the transition from curriculum lab to classroom. Administrators are removed from the culture of classrooms. Although most administrators are former teachers, they are prone to respect the views of university researchers above those of teachers when considering the adoption of innovations. Administrators loved the New Math, and they urged their local boards to jump on the math reform bandwagon. But teachers, students, and parents were not demanding a new mathematics curriculum, and they were not consulted until it came time to implement the program in schools. Teachers were introduced to the curriculum through evening and summer workshops, but they were rarely given sufficient time to practice teaching with the new materials. No one asked teachers if they agreed with the new approach; they were simply told that they must learn how to use it (Sarason 1996).

The NCTM did not make the same mistakes when it began drafting a reform manifesto in 1986. The NCTM standards emerged from committee meetings rather than curriculum labs. Classroom teachers were included on the four working groups that crafted the standards in the summers of 1987 and 1988, and approximately 10,000 draft copies were circulated for review. This process does not guarantee a thorough vetting by potential critics from the grass roots, however. The teachers on the panels were probably already favorably disposed to the reforms, as were those teachers who took the time to review drafts.[5] The same basic subsystem that had existed in the 1950s remained in place, with two important exceptions. Math educators dominate the leadership of the NCTM. The working groups were appointed by John Dossey of the University of Illinois, president of NCTM, and drafting the standards was overseen by Thomas A. Romberg of the University of Wisconsin. Mathematicians had been an important force in creating the New Math. But their interest in K–12 education was sporadic, and they shied away from K–12 issues after the New Math's failure. Reflecting both the influence of math educators and a lesson learned from the New Math, the NCTM stressed that a long process of retraining teachers was necessary if the standards' ambitious goals were ever to be realized. Simply acquiring new skills would not be enough. The

5. This is speculation on my part, based on the experience of serving on several curriculum committees at the state and local level in California.

standards repeatedly stressed that changing how teachers actually think about mathematics was essential before lasting reform could take place. The NCTM devoted a large amount of organizational resources to developing the standards, and much more would be spent on their dissemination. But events beyond the control of the NCTM were required to propel math reform into the public spotlight.[6]

Focusing Event

A focusing event grabs the public's attention with such force that a public concern—even one that has been around awhile—becomes a major issue.[7] On October 4, 1957, the Russian launch of *Sputnik* shocked the United States into the realization that it was trailing in the race to develop satellites capable of orbiting the earth. America's technological superiority could no longer be taken for granted, and public institutions came under intense scrutiny. In two televised addresses to the nation, President Dwight Eisenhower declared the shortage of workers in highly skilled fields "the most critical problem of all" and warned that the Soviet Union was producing graduates in technical fields "at a much faster rate." All the way down to the high school and elementary level, schools were urged to take a hard look at their mathematics and science curriculum. The following year Congress passed the NDEA, which allocated millions of dollars for research to improve the teaching of mathematics, science, foreign languages, and other academic fields in the public schools. Development of the New Math, already well under way by 1958, was now a national priority.[8]

In the 1980s the NCTM standards benefited from a series of events that paved the way for math reform, capped by one focusing event at the end of the decade that put the standards, politically speaking, in the right place at the right time. Like the New Math, the standards also arrived on the heels of national insecurity over America's place in the world, but the

6. Both Barlage (1982) and Hayden (1983) describe mathematicians' interest in K–12 as intermittent. Details about the working groups come from the preface to the NCTM standards.

7. Kingdon (1984) discusses how focusing events convince people that a "condition" is a problem.

8. The 1955 Commission on Mathematics report was an important event, but the report remained out of the public eye until *Sputnik*. The quotes from Eisenhower are from Sundquist (1968, 114).

worries of the 1980s were about economic competitiveness rather than space, and, expressing an anxiety explicitly directed at schools, a series of public reports questioned U.S. international standing in academic achievement. In April 1983 the federal government issued a report, *A Nation at Risk,* which summarized data on fifteen years of declining test scores and declared: "The educational foundations of our society are presently being eroded by a rising tide of mediocrity that threatens our very future as a nation and a people." Later that year *Education Week* published a sixty-four-page special report on the shortcomings of math and science instruction, and this was followed by a report from the National Science Board's Commission on Precollege Education in Mathematics, Science, and Technology. The report warned that American school children were in danger of becoming "stragglers in a world of technology." Whereas *A Nation at Risk* recommended raising course requirements for a high school diploma, the science board's commission saw boosting student interest in mathematics as key. The report urged schools to teach students "how to use math skills in real life situations rather than as ends in themselves." At the University of Chicago researchers responded to this concern by launching a $12.5 million project in 1985 to design a new, more engaging mathematics program, with an appeal extending beyond the small percentage of the high school population pursuing mathematics through calculus. In 1987 a team of American researchers, reacting to an international assessment that showed precalculus students in the United States scoring last among advanced industrialized countries, declared that American students were victims of an "underachieving curriculum."[9]

By 1989 the time was ripe for math reform. In John Kingdon's terminology, the problem, politics, and solutions streams of public policy had converged to open a "policy window" for the NCTM. Math achievement was seen as a national problem, commission reports and a public outcry for better schools generated political support for ambitious reform efforts, and the NCTM stood ready with a solution for the crisis in K–12 math (Kingdon 1984).

As Kingdon emphasizes, policymaking is not always linear. Solutions frequently precede problems. Ideas may sit on the shelf for years until a fortuitous moment when public attention turns their way. Almost a decade before the standards' release in 1989, the NCTM launched a cam-

---

9. Culled from a chronology of reform events presented in Editorial Projects in Education (1993, 255–78).

paign for reforms that paralleled the standards' main themes. In 1980 the NCTM released a bold report that attempted to resuscitate the century-old dream of progressive education to radically alter classroom practices. Fighting against the "back to basics" movement that had driven curriculum policy in the late 1970s, the NCTM's *An Agenda for Action* called on educators to emphasize problem solving over drill and practice and to "introduce calculators and computers into the classroom at the earliest grade practicable." It urged that students work in small groups and spend a greater amount of time on problem solving. Classrooms should become more student-centered, the document recommended, with explorations designed by students taking the place of worksheets assigned by teachers. The implication that inexpensive, hand-held calculators had rendered basic skills less important than they had been in the past, a flash point in the later math wars, could not be missed. As Shirley Hill, former NCTM president, remarked, "It's very clearly the time to begin a careful transition from the concentration on traditional computation to a curriculum which takes advantage of the calculating tools. That isn't to say [computing skills] are no longer important. But I don't think we need to spend one or two years of the curriculum on multi-digit long division" (Walton 1983; National Science Board Commission on Precollege Education in Mathematics, Science, and Technology 1983).[10]

Despite the NCTM's efforts, *An Agenda for Action* went nowhere. State and local policies of the mid-1980s generally followed the advice of *A Nation at Risk*, raising graduation requirements, reducing electives, and tying educational success to higher scores on achievement tests. These efforts were compatible with the back-to-basics and minimum competency movements, which were anathema to the NCTM but popular with the public. In an adroit shift in strategy, the NCTM's 1989 standards capitalized on public opinion rather than fight it. The NCTM still endorsed several notions about teaching and learning that have always been controversial. But by calling the proposed reforms "standards" when no other subject's standards were in existence, and by claiming to define—in what became a mantra of the standards movement—"what students should know and be able to do," the NCTM offered a policy that the public was clamoring for and ready to try.

---

10. Hill headed a committee in the 1970s that recommended that the term "new math" not be used in reference to math reform because it had become a term of ridicule.

Richard Elmore and Susan Fuhrman make an additional point that nicely ties together this section of the chapter with the previous one: "In the presence of a well organized professional network, standards become, in effect, what professionals say they are" (Elmore and Fuhrman 1994). This is another way of saying that the professionally led subsystem was in firm control. It had learned from the New Math fiasco and from the national indifference to *An Agenda for Action*. Then the crucial focusing event for the standards occurred. President George H. Bush, who was in his first year of office, met with the nation's governors at a summit on education in the fall of 1989, and a bipartisan call went out for national standards. The NCTM standards had just rolled off the presses in March. They were the only game in town. By default, they became what standards should be. Chester Finn Jr., an assistant secretary of education under President Ronald Reagan, describes the moment:

NCTM was riding high as arbiter of K–12 math for the U.S., perhaps even the world. Its standards were held up as a model other subjects might aspire to. Never mind that they never included actual student performance levels or benchmarks. Nor, prior to their universal dissemination, were NCTM's standards subjected to field tests or clinical trials to ascertain whether they actually boost student performance. . . . Yet few responsible voices were heard even to challenge the NCTM view of math or to offer alternatives.[11]

The Content of Reform

What blocks so many promising educational reforms? Many things, to be sure: special interest groups, a flawed political strategy, the pitfalls of implementation, an intransigent system, and the fear of change. But reforms also run into political trouble because they are perceived to be—plain and simple—bad ideas. The content of policies affects the politics they engender. In the life of both New Math and NCTM reforms, a fierce opposition arose to attack the reforms' central claims. Policymakers initially saw the two reforms as embodying good ideas, but as they were introduced into

11. Statement by Chester E. Finn Jr., prepared for delivery to the National Assessment Governing Board's hearing on the proposed voluntary national mathematics test, Washington, D.C., January 21, 1998. Available on the Fordham Foundation website, www.edexcellence.org.

classrooms large numbers of parents and teachers, not to mention a significant number of scholars, perceived them as bad ideas. What happened? In addition to the obvious fact that policymakers and parents view schools from vastly different perspectives, there is something more. On close examination, it is evident that both reforms aspired to deepen the mathematical knowledge of American youth, a goal with broad political appeal. But it also clear that they embraced changes in teaching and learning that have always met stiff resistance in the real world of schooling. These contrasting elements commanded public attention at different times in the policymaking process.

The content of the two reforms is best appreciated by first noting a fundamental difference. They emphasize different types of learning. The two programs both favor hands-on materials, for example, but as routes to different destinations. The New Math was primarily concerned with getting students to understand the structure of mathematics. Even though the New Math employed hands-on materials in the elementary grades (Cuisenaire rods were a popular tool of the 1960s), the objective usually was for students to grasp an abstract principle—the commutative, associate, and distributive properties; factoring; the intersection of two sets; place value in a non–10-based number system. Models were offered as concrete representations of these abstractions, but after sufficient time working with them students were supposed to see beyond the models to apprehend math's underlying structure. The NCTM reforms are more emphatic that teachers allow students extensive use of hands-on materials, for the purpose of solving mathematical problems, especially those from everyday life. In the NCTM's view, this kind of instruction motivates students to perform more mundane tasks in math, reinforces skills through application, and teaches students how to attack problems strategically. The standards argue that "placing computation in a problem-solving context motivates students to learn computation skills and serves as an impetus for the mastery of paper and pencil algorithms" (NCTM 1989, 45).

By focusing on mathematics' structure, on the one hand, and its capacity for solving problems, on the other, the New Math and NCTM reforms left themselves vulnerable to the charge that they shortchanged basic skills. This was not evident to policymakers when the reforms were initially considered. Who could possibly be against students acquiring a deeper understanding of mathematical concepts or hesitate to support students learning how to solve problems? What is wrong with teaching skills through problem solving? Unfortunately for reformers, policies rarely look the same in classrooms as they do on paper. Instructional time is essentially zero sum in the classroom. Emphasizing one thing means deemphasizing something else. Activities involving memorization and practice were disdained by both reforms. They also dismissed the idea that math skills are hierarchical—that students must master arithmetic before going on to tackle algebra and other abstract topics. Sargent Shriver, who at the time was director of the Peace Corps and the late President John Kennedy's brother-in-law, was recruited to write the introduction to a pamphlet published by the NCTM in 1965, *The New Mathematics for Parents*. Attempting to soothe parents' concerns that their children were not getting the knowledge they needed for moving to higher levels of math, Shriver declared that the New Math and the Peace Corps were both designed "to help bring this enlarged universe within our comprehension," and he reassured parents that the New Math "simplifies and clarifies, yet enables students to begin not at the beginning but at a level reached after years of study, research, trial and error" (Heimer and Newman 1965, 9–10).

Math reformers believe that a dependency on worksheets, textbooks, and pencil-and-paper computations confines the math curriculum to lower level skills. In a paper delivered to the NCTM in 1960, Jerome Bruner, an eminent Harvard psychologist, wrote: "I am struck by the fact that certain ideas in teaching mathematics that take a student away from the banal manipulation of natural numbers have the effect of freshening his eye to the possibility of discovery. I interpret such trends as the use of set theory in the early grades partly in this light—so too the Cuisenaire rods, the use of modular arithmetic, and other comparable devices" (Bruner 1995, 330–35).

Advocates of the New Math called for a "meaning-centered" mathematics program. The NCTM standards support a "problem-based" mathematics, one that also emphasizes the understanding of math concepts and repeatedly casts memorization and practice in a negative light. Whole number computation is noticeably relegated to the bottom half of the standards for grades K–4, listed eighth of thirteen. In the first paragraph describing this standard, the document states, "Clearly, paper and pencil computations cannot continue to dominate the curriculum or there will be insufficient time for children to learn other, more important mathematics they need now and in the future." The standard goes on to advise, "The frequent use of calculators, mental computation, and estimation helps children develop a more realistic view of computation and enables them to be more flexible in their computing methods. Calculators should be used to solve problems that require tedious calculations." A reminder: these are recommendations for children in kindergarten through fourth grade. The standards for each grade-level cluster begin with a summary of what should receive "increased attention" and "decreased attention." The "increased attention" category includes: meaning of operations, operation sense, mental computation, use of calculators for complex computation, and thinking strategies for basic facts. The "decreased attention" category for K-4 includes: complex paper-and-pencil computations, addition and subtraction without renaming, isolated treatment of division facts, long division, paper-and-pencil fraction computation, and the use of rounding to estimate.

The standards for grades 5–8 are even more emphatic about deemphasizing computation. "Basic skills today and in the future mean far more than computational proficiency. Moreover, the calculator renders obsolete much of the complex paper-and-pencil proficiency traditionally emphasized in mathematics courses." The top three items for "decreased attention" in grades 5–8 are: "memorizing rules and algorithms, practicing tedious paper and pencil computations," and "finding exact forms of answers" (NCTM 1989, 20–21, 44–47, 66, 71).

Richard Askey has called structure, problems, and technique the three-legged stool on which mathematics sits. This metaphor illustrates, respectively, the teaching of concepts, problem solving, and skills in K–12 classrooms. The reforms of the 1960s stressed the first of these components; the reforms of the 1990s stressed the second; and they both urged schools to spend less time on the third. The deemphasis of skill development is firmly in the tradition of progressive education. Instruction in skills is equated with the nineteenth-century practice of drill and recitation, in which students mindlessly chanted lengthy repetitions and then stood under the threat of the cane and individually regurgitated what they had memorized. Throughout its history, progressive education has evoked this dreadful imagery whenever speaking of skill development. Today it is not unusual to see memorization and practice referred to as "drill and kill" in education journals.[12]

A significant number of educators believe something else: that whether one is learning how to play the piano or how to multiply fractions, there

---

12. For a discussion of the major points of contention in the California battles, see Jackson (1997a, b). For a progressive advocate's critique of "drill and kill" and "bunch o' facts" teaching, see Kohn (1999).

are no short cuts to mastery. A significant body of research supports the belief that memorization and practice are essential to developing skill, and that, notwithstanding Sargent Shriver's well-intentioned advice, novices really do have to "start at the beginning." Parents who hold these beliefs rebel when progressive practices are implemented in schools. Granted, there are also parents who strongly support progressive practices. However, whether one looks back on the project method in the 1920s; personal adjustment in the 1940s; the New Math, discovery learning, and open classrooms in the 1960s; or whole language, NCTM math, and authentic assessment in the 1990s; progressive reforms have faced stiff opposition when implemented in the schools (Anderson, Reder, and Simon 1998).

In the mid-1960s reports began to circulate that students spent time computing with abacuses but could not multiply simple whole numbers. Teachers complained that they were devoting an extraordinary amount of time to computing in base-7 when kids did not know how to compute in base-10. New Math advocates could not show, despite field testing in curriculum labs, that students emerged from the New Math with higher math achievement.[13] Students were bringing work home that had parents scratching their heads. By the early 1970s scores on the quantitative section of the Scholastic Aptitude Test were slipping, and two states with extensive testing systems—California and New York—reported declining math scores. In 1973 Morris Kline published a popular book excoriating the New Math, *Why Johnny Can't Add*. The New Math was in grave political danger.[14]

The NCTM standards would face a similar predicament in the 1990s.

The NCTM Controversy

This section will now examine the controversy surrounding the NCTM standards in the 1990s, organizing the discussion under the same three dimensions of reform politics: subsystem dominance, focusing events, and the content of reform. The politics of math reform changed in the late

---

13. According to Sarason (1996), the labs assessed whether teachers could teach with the materials, not whether students learned anything from their use.

14. "Whatever Happened to 'New Math': Protests Force Second Thoughts," *U.S. News & World Report*, October 4, 1976, p. 83; Bart Barnes, "The Minuses of New Math; Legacy of New Math: Pupils' Computational Skills Decline; Pupils Gain in Theory, Lose in Skills," *Washington Post*, February 13, 1977, p. A1.

1990s because of changes in these three dimensions. A few factors on the horizon that may affect math reform in the future will also be identified.

Subsystem Dominance

A division emerged in the math subsystem when mathematicians began questioning the NCTM standards. A schism developed between math educators, who continued to defend the standards, and a group of mathematicians, who made their criticism publicly known. The critics included Gunnar Carlson, Ralph Cohen, and James Milgram of Stanford, Henry Alder and Abigail Thompson of the University of California at Davis, H. Wu of the University of California at Berkeley, Richard Askey of the University of Wisconsin, and Ralph Raimi of the University of Rochester (Jackson 1997a, b). Moreover, business groups that had originally supported the NCTM's emphasis on mathematical applications and its endorsement of students working in teams not only failed to come to the NCTM's defense, but they also continued to complain that schools were not producing graduates proficient in basic mathematics.[15]

The subsystem was also breaking down from challenges by parent activists. Critics of the standards used the Internet as a powerful tool to mobilize the opposition. The most influential site, Mathematically Correct, was founded by a group of parents in San Diego, and dozens of sites followed its lead. Defenders of the standards accused the parents of being unscientific, afraid of change, and the stalking-horses for a right-wing political agenda. They had a difficult time making the charge stick with Mathematically Correct, however, because the founders included mathematicians and scientists who were lifelong Democrats. They were not merely complainers. Michael McKeown, a biologist at the Salk Institute, and Paul Clopton, a statistician in San Diego, are two of the site's leaders who have served on state panels examining various aspects of the math curriculum. The California case is discussed in greater detail below.[16]

The rebellion against math reform led to skirmishes across the country. An Arizona college professor organized parents in her district and wrote a scathing op-ed column in which she described her daughter's algebra class

15. Gilbert Chan, "America's Work Force Is Hitting the Books and Boning Up on the Three R's," *Sacramento Bee*, April 13, 1999. Retrieved from www.sacbee.com/news/.

16. The website is at: http://www.mathematicallycorrect.org. For examples of activists driving the politics of earlier curriculum controversies, see Wirt and Kirst (1989, 316); Boyd (1979b, 14).

as "rain forest" math.[17] In Michigan a mathematician at Wayne State University surveyed local college students and found that those who had taken a traditional math program in high school outscored students who had taken Core-Plus, a reform program. The Core-Plus students discovered that they had to take remedial math courses when they reached college, and they blamed their poor preparation on the high school program.[18] A physics professor at Michigan State University organized parents and founded a website to oppose her district's use of the Connected Mathematics Project in middle schools.[19] In Plano, Texas, parents challenged their school district's choice of a reform math text, and a May 1999 survey of Texas school districts showed that fewer than 10 percent were choosing math books with a reform bent.[20] Petition drives were also launched against reform texts in Oregon and Massachusetts. A group of parents in Jefferson County, Colorado, fought to convert their elementary schools to charter schools when their school district voted to replace Saxon math texts, a skill-centered program.[21] The three schools were the sole users of Saxon math in the district, and they scored substantially above the district average on standardized tests of math achievement. A district review committee ignored the schools' high achievement and ruled that the books did not meet the district's math standards, which had been modeled after the NCTM standards (Tsang 1999; Texas Public Policy Foundation 1999).

Dissenting parents and mathematicians fought to gain access to the official bodies' governing curriculum policy, and their voices are now being heard in deciding the future of the NCTM standards. These changes have weakened math educators' power in establishing K–12 standards in mathematics. Are the changes permanent? Is a new subsystem evolving? Should we expect to see mathematicians taking a continued interest in K–12 issues and professional organizations routinely reaching out to dissident parents when crafting reform proposals?

17. Marianne M. Jennings, "'Rain Forest' Algebra Course Teaches Everything but Algebra," *Christian Science Monitor*, April 2, 1996, 18.

18. Tamara Audi, "New Math Doesn't Compute with Students, Survey Finds," *Detroit Free Press*, March 19, 1999.

19. Tracy Van Moorlehem, "Bloomfield Parents Fight for Old Math," *Detroit Free Press*, January 19, 1998. Available at www.freep.com/newslibrary.

20. Kelli Conlan, "PISD Says 'No' to Alternative Math Program," *Plano Star Courier*, April 2, 1999. Available at www.mathematicallycorrect.com/programs.htm.

21. Janet Bingham, "Angry Parents Want Charters." *Denver Post Online*, May 9, 1998. Available at www.denverpost.com.

There are several reasons to doubt that a new subsystem is forming. Parent interest on educational issues is difficult to maintain over a long period of time. As children get older, parent activism tends to wane. Children move on to new schools, and their educational needs change. Academia also discourages too much activism by mathematicians. The research mathematician's career is enhanced the same way as those in other fields, through scholarship and publication. Involvement in elementary and secondary education falls under the category of outreach activities, and although encouraged by colleges and universities, they are rarely a significant factor in hiring or tenure decisions. Math educators' research, on the other hand, is concerned with improving the teaching and learning of mathematics, so their career incentives are aimed in the direction of continued dominance of the subsystem. They are also motivated to generate ideas for reform. Unless higher education begins to reward mathematicians for their efforts in K–12 education, this pattern will probably continue.

Focusing Events

Focusing events proved to be a double-edged sword for the NCTM standards. The same sense of urgency and crisis that pushed the standards to the forefront and allowed NCTM reform to spread also brought it under close scrutiny. Unlike the New Math, the principles of NCTM reform were widely encoded in policy, primarily in state frameworks and standards documents that did not exist in the 1960s. They granted the reforms a legitimacy that the New Math could never attain. The New Math relied on the prestige of its founders' and administrators' appetite for innovation, but the NCTM was able to mobilize the powers of state government to advance its agenda. But this also presents hazards. Public policies are accountable to the public, subject to constant review, and frequently contested in political forums. The claim that the NCTM reforms were truly "curriculum standards," for example, eventually came under fire. The NCTM standards go into great detail describing how teachers should teach, while the content that students should learn is described in vague terms. An emphasis on pedagogy is extraneous to curriculum standards. This characteristic of the NCTM standards was made evident as groups like the Fordham Foundation began publishing reviews of the standards adopted by individual states and as a few states began establishing specific, grade-by-grade expectations of the content that students should learn in each subject area (Raimi and Braden 1998).

Two focusing events of 1997 heightened the NCTM controversy. The first was President Bill Clinton's proposed voluntary tests in reading for fourth graders and math for eighth graders. While Congress considered the merits of the idea, the Department of Education moved ahead by appointing committees to compose the frameworks governing the exams. The math committee was heavily weighted toward math reformers, and critics howled. Lynne Cheney published op-eds in the *Weekly Standard* and the *Wall Street Journal* criticizing the NCTM reforms as "whole math" and "fuzzy math," detailed the reform bias of several committee members, and chided the administration's claim that a national consensus existed on K–12 mathematics.[22] After a series of missteps by the administration and eroding support for the exams in Congress, work on test development was halted in October. The possibility of a national test caused the public to notice that math reform did not enjoy unanimous support. The math wars could no longer be seen as simply a battle of ideas; this was about ideas with consequences (Lawton 1997b).

At the end of the year, a second major focusing event occurred. California's state board of education threw out the state's existing math framework, which had been heavily influenced by the NCTM standards, and replaced it with a more traditional, content-specific, pedagogy-free set of standards. This is in itself politically significant, but the spotlight was held on California for weeks by the reaction of NCTM supporters to the defeat. California superintendent Delaine Eastin declared that the board should "get out of the dark ages." William Schmidt, who consulted on a draft that was rejected by the board for remaining faithful to NCTM prescriptions, called the new standards "a 'back to basics' document that emphasizes memorization and computation." The day before the state board of education voted on the issue in December, Luther Williams, head of the National Science Foundation's education directorate, informed the board that the $50 million in NSF funds that California schools receive for innovative math programs might be placed in jeopardy if the state deviated from the NCTM path. One board member labeled the letter "a clear threat."[23] Debra Saunders, a columnist for the *San Francisco Chronicle*

22. Lynne V. Cheney, "President Clinton's Mandate for Fuzzy Math," *Wall Street Journal*, June 11, 1997, p. A–22; Lynne V. Cheney, "EXAM SCAM—The Latest Education Disaster: Whole Math," *Weekly Standard*, August 4, 1997. Available at www.mathematicallycorrect.com/cheney2.htm.

23. Deborah Anderluh, "Bitter Debate on Math Shift: State Education Board Set to Adopt New Standards," *Sacramento Bee*, December 8, 1997. Retrieved from www.sacbee.com/news/.

and a critic of math reform, quoted Williams as declaring that the NSF "cannot support individual school systems that embark on a course that substitutes computational proficiencies for a commitment to deep, balanced, mathematical learning."[24] Lynne Cheney recounted the incident in a February *Wall Street Journal* article entitled, "Whole Hog for Whole Math."[25] A dozen members of Congress protested in a letter to President Clinton "to use the hammer of possible withdrawal of federal funds to force a state into compliance with unproven practices is unconscionable." The NSF soon backtracked and made it clear that California would not lose its funding (Lawton 1997a).

While this firestorm was raging Secretary Riley delivered his speech urging an end to the math wars. If one steps back from the rancor in this controversy, it is apparent that the NCTM reforms are facing the trials faced by all reforms if they successfully make their way into policy. Once reforms are regarded as part of the status quo, they are subject to criticism and counter-reform. Ironically, it is now the reforms' defenders who seem guilty of being "afraid of change," the same charge they made against others in the past.

The focusing events that will affect math reform in the future cannot be predicted, of course, but three potential sources of conflict should be monitored closely. The first is the revised standards that NCTM will release in 2000. Through its web site, the NCTM solicited input from the general public, and the AMS and MAA also formed committees to give advice. A draft of the *Standards 2000* is now in circulation. The revised standards are certain not to get the free ride enjoyed by the original document. Second, watch test scores. It has been eleven years since the release of the standards. Math scores have been slowly rising in the 1990s, but if they turn down, fairly or unfairly, the NCTM standards will take the blame. New state exams are coming online, linked to each state's own standards. Expect a blizzard of studies using these new data to compare achievement in reform and traditional classrooms. If the scores fall in states that have abandoned NCTM reforms, such as California and Massachusetts, this could redound to the NCTM's benefit. An additional difficulty these states may face is if massive numbers of students repeatedly fail tests tied to

24. Debra J. Saunders, "Man of Science Has a Problem with Real Math," *San Francisco Chronicle*, December 19, 1997, p. A31.
25. Lynne V. Cheney, "Whole Hog for Whole Math," *Wall Street Journal*, February 2, 1998, A-22.

promotion or graduation, with the standards subsequently seen as unrealistic. The third thing to watch are textbooks. The content of reform that matters most to parents is conveyed to their children through texts.

Content

It took about twenty-five years for the New Math to run its course. Most NCTM-based programs have only been in place for three or four years, and many reform texts are just now reaching classrooms. Expect more local controversies as parents react to texts pushing reform to the limits.

The most controversial of the reform textbooks is the MathLand series, published by Creative Publications. As described previously, the NCTM reforms are the latest manifestation of progressive education. The MathLand series exemplifies a contemporary progressive doctrine known as constructivism, the idea that students learn best when they construct their own knowledge rather than acquire it from an external source. Constructivists support hands-on learning, self-directed tasks, and explorations that lead to several alternative solutions rather than one right answer. The teacher's role, as the saying goes, is to be "a guide on the side, rather than a sage on the stage." Teachers might provide direct instruction when needed, but the main idea is to allow students to pursue their own interests and to take responsibility for their own learning.

The NCTM standards contain a heavy dose of constructivist thinking, and, combined with the vague wording of its endorsements, textbook publishers are given wide latitude to interpret exactly what it is that the standards recommend. MathLand's interpretations have been sharply attacked for going too far in the constructivist direction. The textbooks provide ammunition for their critics. Consider this extended excerpt from a column in the *Stars and Stripes*, the newspaper for personnel at military bases around the world.[26] After two years' experience with MathLand in schools run by the Department of Defense Education Activity (DoDEA), the columnist's frustration is palpable:

Did you know that MathLand authors tell teachers that "their job is not to dispense knowledge," but to facilitate, and provide opportu-

---

26. Denise McArthur, "Don't Teach; Just Join Kids as Co-Learner," *Stars and Stripes*, July 31, 1997. Available at www.mathematicallycorrect.com/stars.htm.

nities for children to discover for themselves. Teachers are told that "they don't need to have all of the answers; they can roll up their sleeves and join the students in explorations." And that teachers "should view themselves as co-learners," as "students enjoy having teachers learn along with them."

The following statements were taken from the MathLand Teacher's Guides:

Question: "How should teachers approach this unit if they are uncomfortable with the number systems presented here?" (Gr. 5)

Answer: "The beauty of the constructivist philosophy is that it doesn't rely on the teacher as the dispenser of knowledge, but as a facilitator of experiences. In this case, the teacher should view herself as a co-learner."

Question: "The structure of these projects seems so open. Why is that, and what should the teacher be doing while the students work independently?" (Gr. 5)

Answer: "The MathLand teacher is a facilitator, rather than a dispenser of knowledge, whose role it is to set up the "big picture" . . . then let the students take over. The teacher is free to spend time observing, talking with, and assessing students."

". . . there is no such thing as a number fact. There are only relationships and these relationships are created inside the child's head." (Gr. 2)

As if that weren't bad enough, the MathLand authors also suggest that teachers should vary their expectations, based on students' "developmental maturity" and level of interest. The Teacher's Guide states: "For students who seem interested, show them how to use parentheses" and "if students become frustrated, [teachers should] encourage them to move on."

"Bashful students or students learning to write [may] tape record their reports. . . ." The authors believe that "children tend to challenge themselves at appropriate levels." (Not my kids!) Besides, they claim, "Even if the students are told what is right, they may hear it, but they won't really know it until they are ready." (These comments are from various sections of the third grade MathLand Teacher's Guides.)

The authors believe that "delaying the memorization of multiplication and division facts until fourth grade gives students time to develop [meaning-based] kinds of skills." Yet in fifth grade, children are still learning "tricks" to memorize the hardest-to-remember facts (6 × 6 to 9 × 9, which Japanese second graders have mastered) and using base ten blocks to multiply and divide.

Did you know that 87% of parents and 84% of faculty surveyed in 1994-95 by DoDEA stated that increasing student achievement in mathematics was a high priority? According to DoDEA, nearly all parents and faculty want DoDEA schools to strengthen their role in teaching students academic skills. According to the 1994 Public Agenda poll, 96% of Americans want tougher and more challenging courses in the basics. And what did we get? MathLand.

Denise McArthur
Camp Foster, Okinawa, Japan

This kind of testimony is devastating to the NCTM's cause. It underscores a profound political failure of the NCTM thus far, to identify a single textbook series that falls outside its vision of reform. Without letting teachers and parents know which books are *not* in accord with the standards, the NCTM allows just about any publisher to claim the mantle of "standards-based" reform. The NCTM appointed a committee to investigate the California standards, however, and it criticized the procedures the state followed in writing the benchmarks.

Looking ahead, what else pertaining to content might help or hinder math reform? In October 1999 the Department of Education gave its seal of approval to ten math programs, all adherents of NCTM reform. The department followed the advice of an expert panel convened in accord with 1994 legislation reorganizing the Office of Educational Research and Improvement. The panel reviewed sixty-one submissions and declared five programs "exemplary" and five "promising" based on several criteria, including faithfulness to the NCTM standards and evidence of program effectiveness.

The federal designations are bound to spark a new round of debate. To assess program effectiveness, the panel apparently relied only on evidence provided by the publishers themselves. The Core-Plus program was awarded "exemplary" status, the highest ranking. This is the same program that is controversial in Michigan for failing—its critics charge—to adequately prepare students for college. The controversial elementary grade program, MathLand, was rated "promising," despite widespread complaints echoing those of the *Stars and Stripes* editorial quoted above. The department's endorsements, coming on the heels of California's rejection of the NCTM standards, cannot help but instigate a new round of conflict over math curriculum, this time on a national platform, and a serious debate about whether it is appropriate for the federal government to endorse textbooks (Viadero 1999).

The NCTM would benefit from solid evidence that the programs following its prescriptions produce the deeper learning, the more motivated students, and the proficiency in problem solving that the standards promise. The New Math was never able to furnish this evidence in a convincing form, and as it fell further into political difficulty, the best its supporters could hope for was a compromise. Math journals of the late 1970s were filled with articles suggesting ways of salvaging the better parts of the New Math. That could happen with NCTM, too. The counter-reform movement will also face some challenges as books written to comply with the new California standards hit the market. If the books are perceived to be too hard or too boring, watch for a possible reaction in sympathy with NCTM. Then a whole new cycle of math reform might begin.

Conclusion

The New Math and the NCTM standards rose to prominence with the help of three factors: a subsystem that dominates curriculum policy in K–12 mathematics, focusing events that convinced the public of a need for change in the mathematics curriculum, and the promise of new content. But the politics of these three dimensions changed. Mathematicians and math educators parted ways; focusing events exposed weaknesses in the reform movements; and as innovative textbooks and teaching techniques entered the classroom, parents questioned whether the reforms were good for their children.

The New Math rose to prominence in the 1950s, stood tall over the K–12 math curriculum in the 1960s, and slipped into disrepute in the 1970s. The NCTM standards were released in 1989 to almost universal acclaim. In the 1990s protests stirred against the new ways of teaching and learning mathematics, and at the end of that decade the future of NCTM math reform remains cloudy. The last chapter of its political story remains to be written, but among many things, its fate hinges on the ability to satisfy parents and impress mathematicians, the trajectory of future test scores, the content of the revised standards that NCTM will release in 2000, and the quality of future math books.

References

Anderson, John R., Lynne M. Reder, and Herbert A. Simon. 1998. "Radical Constructivism and Cognitive Psychology." In *Brookings Papers on Education Policy,* edited by Diane Ravitch, 227–78. Brookings.

Barker, Anthony, and B. Guy Peters. 1993. "Science Policy and Government." In *The Politics of Expert Advice: Creating, Using and Manipulating Scientific Knowledge for Public Policy*, edited by Anthony Barker and B. Guy Peters, 1–16. University of Pittsburgh Press.

Barlage, Elisabeth. 1982. "The New Math: An Historical Account of the Reform of Mathematics Instruction in the United States of America." ERIC Document No. ED 224 703.

Boyd, William L. 1979a. "The Changing Politics of Curriculum Policy Making." In *Value Conflicts and Curriculum Issues*, edited by Jon Schaffarzick and Gary Sykes, 73–138. Berkeley: McCutchan.

———. 1979b. "The Politics of Curriculum Change and Stability." *Educational Researcher* 8, 2 (February): 12–18.

Bruner, Jerome S. 1995. "On Learning Mathematics." *Mathematics Teacher* 88, 4 (April): 330–35. Reprint of article originally published in *Mathematics Teacher* (December 1960): 610–19.

Editorial Projects in Education. 1993. *From Risk to Renewal.* Washington.

Elmore, Richard F., and Susan H. Fuhrman. 1994. "Education Professionals and Curriculum Governance." In *The Governance of Curriculum: 1994 Yearbook of the Association for Supervision and Curriculum Development*, edited by Richard F. Elmore and Susan H. Fuhrman. Alexandria, Va.: Association for Supervision and Curriculum Development, 210–15.

Freeman, J. Leiper. 1965. *The Political Process*, rev. ed. Random House.

———. 1995. "The Subsystem in Perspective." In *Public Policy Theories, Models, and Concepts: An Anthology*, edited by Daniel C. McCool, 256–61. Prentice-Hall.

Fritschler, A. Lee, and James M. Hoefler. 1996. *Smoking & Politics: Policy Making and the Federal Bureaucracy*, 5th ed. Prentice Hall.

Griffith, Ernest. 1939. *The Impasse of Democracy.* New York: Harrison-Hilton Books.

Hayden, Robert W. 1983. "A Historical View of the 'New Mathematics,'" ERIC Document No. ED 228 046.

Heclo, Hugh. 1978. "Issue Networks and the Executive Establishment." In *The New American Political System*, edited by A. King, 87–107, 115–124. Washington: American Enterprise Institute.

Heimer, Ralph T., and Miriam S. Newman. 1965. *The New Mathematics for Parents*. Holt, Rinehart, and Winston.

Iannaccone, L. 1967. *Politics in Education*. New York: Center for Applied Research in Education.

Jackson, Allyn. 1997a. "The Math Wars: California Battles It Out over Mathematics Education Reform (Part I)." *Notices of the AMS* 44, 6 (June/July): 695–702.

———. 1997b. "The Math Wars: California Battles It Out over Mathematics Education Reform (Part II)." *Notices of the AMS* 44, 7 (August): 817–23.

Kingdon, John W. 1984. *Agendas, Alternatives, and Public Policies*. Harper Collins.

Kohn, Alfie. 1999. *The Schools Our Children Deserve*. Houghton Mifflin.

Lawton, Millicent. 1997a. "Facing Deadline, Calif. Is Locked in Battle over How to Teach Math." *Education Week on the Web* (March 12). Available at www.edweek.com.

———. 1997b. "Riley Delays National Tests' Development." *Education Week on the Web* (October 1). Available at www.edweek.com.

Mazzoni, Tim L. 1995. "State Policy-Making and School Reform: Influences and Influentials." In *The Study of Educational Politics*, edited by J. D. Scribner and D. H. Layton, 53–73. Washington: Falmer Press.

National Council of Teachers of Mathematics (NCTM). 1989. *Curriculum and Evaluation Standards for School Mathematics*. Reston, Va.

———. 2000. *Principles and Standards for School Mathematics*. Reston, Va.

National Science Board Commission on Precollege Education in Mathematics, Science, and Technology. 1983. *Educating Americans for the 21st Century*. Excerpts reprinted in *Education Week* (September 14). Available at www.edweek.com.

Raimi, Ralph A., and Lawrence S. Braden. 1998. "State Mathematics Standards." Thomas B. Fordham Foundation. Available at www.edexcellence.net.

Riley, Richard. 1997. "The State of Mathematics Education: Building a Strong Foundation for the 21st Century." Remarks before the joint conference of American Mathematical Society and Mathematical Association of America, January 8.

Ripley, Randall B., and Grace A. Franklin. 1987. *Congress, the Bureaucracy, and Public Policy*, 4th ed. Chicago: Dorsey.

Sarason, Seymour B. 1996. *Revisiting the Culture of the School and the Problem of Change*. Teachers College Press.

Sundquist, James L. 1968. *Politics and Policy: The Eisenhower, Kennedy, and Johnson Years*. Brookings.

Texas Public Policy Foundation. 1999. "Texas School Districts Reject 'Fuzzy Math' Textbooks—Major Defeat for Statewide Systemic Initiatives." *Policy Action Update* 3, 12 (May 24): 1–2.

Truman, David. 1951. *The Governmental Process*. Knopf.

Tsang, Betty. 1999. "Watered-Down Math Gets a Failing Grade." *Lansing State Journal*, January 23. Available at www.nscl.msu.edu~tsang/cmp/lsj-jan99.htm.

Viadero, Debra. 1999. "Ed. Dept. Is Set to Release Its List of Recommended Math Programs." *Education Week* (October 6). Available at www.edweek.com.

Walton, Susan. 1983. "Add Understanding, Subtract Drill." *Education Week* (July 27). Available at www.edweek.com.

Wirt, Frederick M., and Michael W. Kirst. 1989. *Schools in Conflict*, 2d ed. Berkeley: McCutchan.

CHAPTER TEN

It Is Time
To Stop the War

DIANE RAVITCH

During the past quarter century or so, there has been a heated debate between supporters of different reading methods, some supporting phonics instruction and others supporting "whole language." The "reading war" in the United States did not start in the 1980s or 1990s. For most of the past century—and even as far back as the 1820s—teachers, school officials, and others have argued about the best way to teach reading. Nor is the search for better methods of reading instruction unique to the United States. In his history of reading instruction, Mitford M. Mathews of the University of Chicago has shown that as early as the sixteenth century European educators were trying to find alternatives to the traditional practice of memorizing the letters of the alphabet (Mathews 1966).

Over the course of American history, there have been variations on three methods of teaching reading. The earliest was the alphabet method, in which the student learned to read by memorizing the letters of the alphabet. This was succeeded by the teaching of phonics, which required students to learn the sounds of letters and combinations of letters. The third method maintained that children should learn words and sentences rather than letters and their sounds and that reading should be learned as naturally as possible, with a minimum of skill instruction.

In colonial and early America, most teachers believed that children learned to read by memorizing and reciting the letters and syllables in their reading books. This was a method that untrained teachers—those who intended to teach only for a year or two—found congenial. The two biggest selling reading textbooks in early America—the *New England Primer* and Noah Webster's blue-backed speller—relied principally on memory work and the alphabet method (Commager 1962). While the primers emphasized piety and religious content, Webster emphasized patriotic and moral lessons.

Webster's speller did not neglect the sound of spoken language; it incorporated both alphabetic and phonetics approaches. It sought to forge a common national language by including explicit instruction in the correct pronunciation of letters, syllables, and words. The Webster speller enjoyed a remarkable success; Henry Steele Commager wrote that it "established its sovereignty in the East; it went west with the Conestoga wagon, and in the knapsacks of countless pedagogues; it leaped the mountains and established its empire on the Pacific coast. . . ." At a time when few Americans owned any book other than the Bible, Webster's speller sold by the tens of millions (Commager 1962, 5). Webster's speller inspired countless imitators, all of which published their own lengthy tables of letters, syllables, and words.

Eventually, Webster's speller was replaced by the graduated reading series of William Holmes McGuffey. These became legendary; first published in 1836, the McGuffey readers sold more than 120 million copies over the next eighty years. The McGuffey readers taught a combination of phonics and good literature, while also inculcating such virtues as thrift, honesty, kindness, and truthfulness. They had a positive impact on the popular culture of their time, introducing young readers to Shakespeare, Dickens, Hawthorne, and other renowned English and American writers.

At the same time, however, a body of opinion began to emerge in opposition to the alphabetic method or phonics or any sort of linguistic analysis. In 1828 Samuel Worcester published a primer in which children first learned to read by seeing words, hearing them pronounced, understanding their meaning, and only then analyzing the letters in them.

In 1832 John Miller Keagy, a physician turned educator, recommended that children should be taught whole words first, then phrases. The child who saw the same words again and again, he wrote, would recognize them "as if the words were Chinese symbols, without paying any attention to the individual letters, but with special regard to the meaning." Only after the child had learned to read, said Keagy, should he learn spelling and letters (Mathews 1966, 65–66).

Other educators denounced the alphabetic method in the late 1830s
and early 1840s. Learning to read, they argued, should be as natural as
learning to talk. In 1837 a school board member from Vermont asserted
that children found the traditional method to be "tiresome drudgery" and
that the "method of nature" proceeded from "generals to particulars. We
know a tree, and can name it, long before we become acquainted with its
constituents, the leaves, limbs, trunk, and root. . . ." In 1843 the principal
of the Normal School at Lexington, Massachusetts, recommended that
reading instruction begin with simple familiar words and pictures; he asked,
since "children begin to *talk* with words, why should they not begin to
read with words?" Only after they could read sentences, he argued, should
they be taught the names and sounds of letters (Mathews 1966, 67–72).

There was much ferment in public education in this era, not least because Horace Mann worked as a state legislator in Massachusetts to create a state board of education and then became its secretary in 1837. He
used this post to crusade tirelessly for school reform. Mann hated the
alphabet method; he believed that it made learning to read a horrible experience for children, who were bored into stupefaction by mindless routines and repelled by having to learn the letters, which he called "the
twenty-six idiot strangers." The letters in the alphabet, he wrote, are "skeleton-shaped, bloodless, ghostly apparitions, and hence it is no wonder
that the children look and feel so deathlike, when compelled to face them.
The letters are more minute too, than any objects which ever attract the
attention of children. . . . The forms of the twenty-six letters have as little
variety as twenty-six grains of sand." Knowing the letters was useless, he
contended, because the names of the letters so often were unrelated to
their sound; for example, the child who spelled out *l–e–g* might conclude
that the three letters spelled *elegy*, not "leg" (Mathews 1966, 77–79).

Like other reformers of his time, Mann believed that children should be
taught whole words, whose meaning was familiar, accompanied by pictures. Like them, he believed that the child apprehends a new object as a
whole, not by learning its parts first. Mann's scathing critique drew a
lengthy rebuttal from a committee of thirty-one Boston schoolmasters,
who pointed out that Mann had confused the *names* of the letters with
their *sounds*. Nor could they resist noting that one of the word-method
books recommended by Mann was prepared by his wife. With her method,
children would learn hundreds of words, then learn the allegedly hateful
letters. But, the schoolmasters warned, children taught by these methods
were poor spellers. Worse, teachers were using a variety of methods, and

the resulting "want of system" was highly inefficient. One schoolmaster tweaked Mann by pointing out that words were composed of "whole clusters" of those "skeleton-shaped, bloodless, ghostly apparitions," that is, letters (Mathews 1966, 87–90; Remarks on the Seventh Annual Report 1844).

The debate between Mann and the Boston schoolmasters presaged the modern-day debate between the advocates of phonics and the advocates of whole language. The same arguments were advanced, often with language and allusions that are strikingly contemporary. It did not significantly change the course of reading instruction in the nation; there was no decided movement in one direction or another. Many teachers continued to use the alphabetic method or the word method alone, while others—especially those who taught with the popular McGuffey readers—combined phonics and words. As early as the 1850s several cities (including Cincinnati and Chicago) claimed that they were using the "word method," teaching children to recognize words by sight before they learned letters or sounds. Teachers were usually eclectic in method. No single method dominated the schools in the late nineteenth century and the early twentieth century (Mathews 1966, 99–100).

From 1875 until 1883 Francis Parker served as superintendent of schools in Quincy, Massachusetts, where he implemented methods that today would be called whole language. Parker urged that the best incentive to learning to read was children's interest. The main point of reading, Parker believed, was comprehension.

At the turn of the century, William Mowry, a prominent educator in New England, wrote in his autobiography that the alphabet method was obsolete and that schools had adopted a "modern way of teaching," which was called variously "the word method, the sentence method, the thought method and several phonetic systems. . . ." With these new approaches, the "learner today begins to recognize, at sight, words as signs of ideas. Then the alphabet takes care of itself. No time is lost learning it" (Mowry 1908, 20).

It seems clear that by the 1890s most schools had long since abandoned the alphabet method and were already using a combination of word recognition and phonics. In 1892, when Joseph Mayer Rice visited public schools in thirty-six cities, he found numerous examples of execrable teaching, emphasizing nothing but drill and memory. In New York City the teachers employed a combination of word and spelling method but in a barbarous manner. To teach the word *boat*, the teacher said, "The other

day I went down to the river and I saw something with a whole lot of
people on it floating in the water." She then wrote the word on the black-
board and asked, "What do you think this word is?" One guessed "*ship*,"
another guessed "*steamer*," and a third guessed "*boat*." The only thing
students learned was "a pure and simple process of memorizing word-
forms." In Buffalo, New York, Rice again witnessed dry, mechanical reading lessons taught according to the word method, without phonics (a
method, he said, that "does less to develop mental power and more to
waste time than any that I know of—excepting, *perhaps*, the alphabet
method"). In Indianapolis Rice found a classroom where the teaching was
lively and inspiring; the children talked, drew pictures, wrote stories and
participated joyfully in their lessons. They learned words, sentences, and
also phonics but in a spirit of happiness (Rice 1893, 40, 84, 101–09).
From Rice's investigations, it appeared that the word method was used as
often as the phonics method, and that both were equally susceptible to
corruption into dry, mechanical approaches.

The rise of the progressive education movement brought a renewed
effort to eliminate any kind of linguistic analysis, as well as to defer reading instruction until children were eight years old. In 1898 John Dewey
leveled a devastating attack on reading, writing, and books. He called
these things "the primary-education fetich." Back in olden times, he wrote,
book-learning was the "sole avenue to knowledge," but modern times
had created many other ways to get access to information and culture. "It
is hardly necessary to say that the conditions, intellectual as well as social,
have changed. . . . The advent of quick and cheap mails, of easy and
continuous travel and transportation, of the telegraph and telephone, the
establishment of libraries, art-galleries, literary clubs, the universal diffusion of cheap reading-matter, newspapers and magazines of all kinds and
grades—all these have worked a tremendous change in the immediate intellectual environment." These changes in communications, he claimed,
meant that "the significance attaching to reading and writing, as primary
and fundamental instruments of culture, has shrunk proportionately as
the immanent intellectual life of society has quickened and multiplied."

This was an odd argument: Dewey started off making a case for the
diminished importance of books, but he inexplicably turned it into a critique of learning to read and write, which he described as "more or less
arbitrary tasks which must be submitted to because one is going to that
mysterious thing called a school. . . ." Dewey described the physical harm
that a child might suffer if required to learn to read in the first two years of

school, referring to "a sad record of injured nervous systems and of mus-
cular disorders and distortions." Making children read before the age of
eight, he believed, "cripples rather than furthers later intellectual development" (Dewey 1972, 254–61).

The burgeoning progressive education movement adopted Dewey's belief
that children should not be taught to read too soon, that it might actually
harm them to learn to read in the early years of school. Edmund Burke
Huey's authoritative *The Psychology and Pedagogy of Reading* quoted
Dewey at length to support the idea that children should not be taught to
read before at least the age of eight or even later. Huey maintained that
children should be taught to read at home, not in school. When it was
necessary to teach reading in school, he thought it was best to teach it like
pictographs, without recourse to writing or phonetic analysis, and to teach
it incidentally, only when the student needed it for a purpose. The best
"method," he believed, was no method, and the best school readers were
compilations of the students' own work in class (Huey 1968, 304–06,
311–12, 338–39).

Huey's attitudes toward reading were likely influenced by G. Stanley
Hall, his mentor at Clark University where he had earned his doctorate in
psychology. Hall did not believe that learning to read was important. He
said that "it would not be a serious loss, if a child never learned to read.
Charlemagne could not read, and he had quite an influence upon the world's
history and was a fairly brainy man" (Hall 1904, 456–59).

Hall, the founder of the child-study movement, never tired of warning
that academic studies of any kind were dangerous to children's health.
What was the point of learning to read, he asked, since the great men of
the world could "neither read nor write," and "even the blessed mother of
our Lord knew nothing of letters" (Hall 1904, 116–17). Hall claimed that
"experiments have shown" that children should not learn to read, write,
spell, or do number work before the age of eight (Hall 1911, 618). Since
he thought that reading was vastly overvalued, it did not matter to him
which method was used to teach it.

The progressive education movement opposed any sort of phonetic
analysis, on grounds that it was inevitably unnatural and formalistic. In
the numerous private progressive schools that opened in the early decades
of the twentieth century, reading was taught informally, but seldom before the age of eight, to avoid undue stress on the child's nervous system.
Researchers in the new schools of pedagogy conducted experiments on
reading; they were particularly interested in eye movements and speed of

reading. Invariably, they concluded that oral reading slowed down the reader and that silent reading was preferable. This was significant for methodology, because oral reading had traditionally been associated with phonics instruction and with correct pronunciation of syllables and words.

Eugene Randolph Smith, the headmaster of a private school and president of the Progressive Education Association, advised parents to heed the advice of experts, who had "conclusive proof" that reading must not be taught by attention to the alphabet, phonics, or any other sort of linguistic analysis; he also warned parents not to read to their children, since this "makes it easier to get information through the ear than through the eye." Children who were read to over a period of years, he said, could be seriously handicapped. In the "modern" method, said Smith, the child was "taught to form a mental picture of an entire word or phrase," instead of recognizing the letters or their sounds (Smith 1924, 34–44; Gray 1925, 27).

In response to the emerging consensus among pedagogical experts, reading textbooks began to change their contents. The reading books of the early twentieth century usually contained a collection of fairy tales, poems, myths, stories, and speeches intended to improve children's taste for good literature. By the 1920s numerous studies showed that the school readers had a decreasing number of fairy tales, myths, legends, and poems and an increasing number of entries about the lives of ordinary boys and girls.

In 1930 William S. Gray of the University of Chicago introduced the Elson readers, better known as the "Dick and Jane" series. These readers used the "whole-word" or "look-say" method of reading. The Dick and Jane readers and others like them contained simple stories about children, home life, animals, toys, and other familiar themes. They reflected reformers' belief that reading methods should be as "natural" as possible and that the content of readers should be connected to the child's point of view, instead of imposing what adults thought they should read. *Natural*, in this context, meant that children should learn to recognize whole words, rather than learning phonetic analysis and sounding out unfamiliar words. The whole-word and look-say methods were considered modern by reading reformers, and any form of linguistic analysis such as phonics was viewed as artificial and out of date.

There matters stood until 1955, when Rudolf Flesch published his explosive book, *Why Johnny Can't Read*. Flesch's book appeared near the apogee of an era of intense criticism of public education. In the previous six years, Arthur Bestor Jr., Mortimer Smith, Albert Lynd, and others had complained bitterly about the domination of the schools by progressive educators and about the anti-intellectual consequences of their theories.

Just when educators thought that the storm of criticism was spent, Flesch's book reached the national best-seller lists, where it remained for more than thirty weeks. Flesch charged that the systematic neglect of phonics had caused a national crisis in literacy; that look-say readers like the widely used Dick and Jane series were based on a flawed theory that taught children to memorize words and guess unknown words instead of sounding them out; and that the look-say or whole-word method had swept the schools of education and the textbook market despite the fact that it had no basis in research (Flesch 1955).

Since the late 1920s, Flesch argued, the look-say method had become the only approach endorsed by the reading experts, despite a paucity of research to validate it. This method was unsuccessful, Flesch maintained, because it did not teach students the alphabet or the sounds of letters, leaving them unable to read unfamiliar words. The look-say primers consisted of a "sight reading vocabulary," made up of a limited number of words that children could recognize by sight. Instead of learning to read new words, children were memorizing the appearance of simple words—words that were repeated again and again.

Under this approach, Flesch wrote, "reading isn't taught at all. Books are put in front of the children and they are told to guess at the words or wait until Teacher tells them. But they are *not* taught to read. . . ." Because of their impoverished vocabulary, Flesch complained, the stories in the look-say readers were "artificial sequences of words—meaningless, stupid, totally uninteresting to a six-year-old child or anyone else. Without the pictures they are even unintelligible." The language of these readers, he observed, bore no resemblance to "normal English. It is word-method-reader idiom, a language to be found solely and exclusively in the books manufactured for use with and on American school children" (Flesch 1955, 17, 84–85).

Flesch's polemic set off a national debate about literacy. The book was warmly reviewed by the general press but almost unanimously rejected by reviewers in the educational journals, who said that Flesch was unqualified, irresponsible, and just plain wrong. Yet, because of its popularity, Flesch's book had a large effect on the teaching of reading. In direct response to his book, which unleashed a public demand for the revival of phonics, several publishers issued new reading textbooks that featured phonics. Reading professionals warned that the return to phonics was disastrous, and that it would lead to dull and dispirited classrooms dominated by rote memorization of meaningless sounds.

In 1961 the Carnegie Corporation of New York commissioned Jeanne S. Chall of the Harvard University Graduate School of Education to prepare a review of the controversy, with the intent of settling the debate about reading once and for all. Chall spent three years visiting hundreds of classrooms, analyzing research studies, and reviewing textbooks.

After interviewing textbook authors, reading specialists, and teachers, she reported that "their language was often more characteristic of religion and politics than of science and learning." She did not agree with Flesch that there was only one successful method for teaching beginning readers. No method had completely eliminated the problem of reading failures; some were better than others, but none was a panacea. Comparing the effectiveness of reading methods turned out to be extraordinarily tricky because each approach contained elements of the other, and "every school that introduces a new method still retains a good deal of the old one." Schools that had recently adopted phonics programs still used the conventional basal readers, and teachers tended to rely on the methods with which they were most familiar. She observed that in the 1930s phonics survived in a hostile environment because some teachers "got out their old phonics charts, *closed the doors*, and hoped the supervisor or principal would not enter unannounced." But teachers who had been trained since the 1930s never learned phonics and were likely to fall back on what they knew best, which was the whole-word or look-say method (Chall 1967, 3, 7, 278–85).

Chall reported that from 1930 until the early 1960s there was a pervasive professional consensus on the one best way to teach reading. This consensus deemphasized the use of phonics and concentrated on whole words, sentences, and stories closely geared to children's experiences and interests. Children were encouraged to identify words "at sight" by referring to pictures and to context clues; the sight vocabulary was supposed to be carefully controlled and repeated often in the primers. While phonics was not necessarily banned, it was relegated to a minor role in learning to read (Chall 1967, 13–15).

This orthodoxy, Chall found, was not supported by research. In reviewing reading research from 1912 to 1965 Chall identified two primary approaches: one stressed the importance of "breaking the code" of language, the other stressed the meaning of language. Phonics programs had a code emphasis, and look-say or whole-word programs had a meaning emphasis.

Chall concluded that studies of beginning reading over the decades clearly supported the use of a code emphasis and that "the first step in learning to read in one's native language is essentially learning a printed code for the speech we possess." Early stress on code learning, these studies indicated, not only produces better word recognition and spelling, but also makes it easier for the child eventually to read with understanding—"at least up to the beginning of the fourth grade, after which point there is practically no evidence." The code-emphasis method, she wrote, was especially effective for children of lower socioeconomic status, who were not likely to live in homes surrounded with books or adults who could help them learn to read. Chall also concluded that knowing the names of the letters and the sounds of letters *before learning to read* helps a child in the beginning stages of learning to read, regardless of which method is used. For a beginning reader, she found, knowledge of letters and sounds had more influence on reading achievement than the child's tested "mental ability," or IQ. Chall found that the rigid limits on vocabulary had produced dull stories about familiar experiences, so that the meaning-emphasis method led ironically to boring content (Chall 1967, 83, 131, 149–50, 311).

This was not merely an academic debate about reading methods. Most people had opinions about reading, and they disagreed with the experts. Flesch told them that they were right and the experts were wrong. Why weren't schools teaching the alphabet? Hadn't children always learned their "ABCs"? Why weren't they teaching children that letters have sounds?

A large part of the public did not understand the claim that it was "natural" to learn whole words rather than letters and sounds. Learning to talk was natural, but that did not mean that learning to read was. If reading was natural, why did anyone need to be taught? If reading was natural, why was there so much illiteracy in underdeveloped nations where teachers were scarce? Mitford Mathews, the historian of reading, observed that reading was "one of the most unnatural activities in which man has ever engaged. Nature has never taught anyone to read and never will. . . . Words are not like tadpoles or flowers or horses. Words are man-made" (Mathews 1966, 190).

The public also was not swayed by those who opposed teaching the alphabet. Chall speculated that early knowledge of the alphabet might be an important step in the child's intellectual development: "Pointing to and naming a letter, or writing a letter, at an early age is quite different from pointing to or drawing a picture of a cat, a truck, or a tree. The child who can identify or reproduce a letter engages in symbolic representation . . . while the child who is working with a picture of an actual object engages in iconic representation. When the child engages in symbolic representation, he is already practicing a higher form of intellectual behavior. Perhaps early mastery of this first step contributes to building the abstract attitude so necessary in our highly scientific and automated world" (Chall 1967, 159).

Chall concluded that most children needed to learn how to "decode," that is, to learn the relationship between letters and their sounds, and they also needed to read good children's literature in the early elementary grades. A combination of phonics—but only for beginning readers—and good children's literature was best, she recommended.

When Chall published her 1967 book about "the great debate," it appeared that the evidence was clear and the debate was settled. In the 1980s and 1990s, however, the debate flared up again with new ferocity as the whole-language approach to reading won the allegiance of many professors and teachers of reading. The new movement began with the writings of Frank Smith of the University of Victoria in British Columbia and Kenneth Goodman of the University of Arizona. Both believed that learning to read should be as easy and natural as learning to speak; both were critical of instruction that emphasized phonics or any other linguistic skills. Smith wrote that "the effort to read through decoding is largely futile and unnecessary." Most children, he maintained, learned to read "despite exposure to phonics" (Smith 1971, 2; Smith 1973).

Like the whole-word methods of the 1920s, whole language emphasized that children should read literature connected to their interests rather than textbooks and that they should read for meaning and pleasure rather than study the mechanics of language. Whole language was a rebellion against drill, workbooks, textbooks, and the other paraphernalia associated with phonics that, overdone, could deaden students' interest in reading. Goodman offered whole language as an alternative, which he defined thus: "Whole language learning builds around whole learners learning whole language in whole situations." Any practices that "chop language into bits and pieces," he wrote, were obviously not whole. Surround children with a rich environment, have lots of opportunities for them to read and write, and children will learn to read without direct instruction about the sounds of letters. Whole language learning involved student-centered activities, authentic reading experiences, integration of reading and writing, and freeing teachers from skill instruction. It was distinguished by what it opposed, which was instruction about language, time spent on phonics, and concern for accuracy of spelling and punctuation. Goodman wrote that children would read when they had a need to communicate, and "language learning is easy when it's whole, real, and relevant; when it makes sense and is functional; when it's encountered in the context of its use; when the learner chooses to use it." Whole-language teachers, he wrote, "reject negative, elitist, racist views of linguistic purity that would limit children to arbitrary 'proper' language. Instead, they view their role as helping children to expand on the marvelous language they already use" (Goodman 1986, 25–26).

Goodman described the teaching of phonics as "a flat-earth view of the world, since it rejects modern science about reading and writing and how they develop." He maintained that "if they are lucky enough not to have been taught phonics in isolation," children discover strategies to figure out what they want to know from print. Good readers, he believed, "guess or make hypotheses about what will occur in the text." They use "invented spelling" and eventually "move toward conventional spelling" without any prodding by the teacher; they read by figuring out words in their context. Reading was, he said, "a psycholinguistic guessing game." At the heart of the theory was the idea that "literacy develops in response to personal/social needs," and if children want to read, they will learn to read (Goodman 1986, 37–38; see also Goodman 1976, 497–508; Goodman and Goodman 1979; Smith 1992, 439).

Enthusiasm for whole language, with its attention to children's literature and the joys of learning, was an understandable reaction against an overemphasis on drill and workbooks in the 1970s. It had a ready appeal to those who disliked the formalistic demands of phonics instruction. In the 1980s whole language built up a large and dedicated following in schools of education and in professional organizations like the International Reading Association and the National Council of Teachers of English (NCTE). It was an attractive theory for those who had always believed that schools should teach "the whole child" and pay less attention to subject matter and the mastery of linguistic skills like syntax, grammar, and spelling. The rhetoric of whole language was reminiscent of Rousseau and the Romantic early twentieth-century progressive educators like Junius Meriam, director of the Laboratory School at the University of Missouri, who organized his curriculum around the premise that children learn only "when they need to do so," and Marietta Pierce Johnson of the Organic School at Fairhope, Alabama, who wanted children to have a completely "natural" education, free of pressure and artifice (Ravitch 2000, 175–77).

Nothing, it seemed, could slow the new movement, not even a report in 1985 from the National Academy of Education (called *Becoming a Nation of Readers*), which said that "on the average, children who are taught phonics get off to a better start in learning to read than children who are not taught phonics," and that phonics instruction should be completed by the end of second grade. Despite the fact that the academy's report represented the views of a panel of distinguished scholars, it drew a rebuttal from the Commission on Reading of the NCTE, which strongly supported child-centered, whole-language programs. In the NCTE's rebuttal, Kenneth Goodman lambasted the National Academy of Education's report as "a political document" that advanced the agenda of "the Far Right." Ever since the publication of Rudolf Flesch's best-selling *Why Johnny Can't Read*, conservative parent groups had championed phonics, and Goodman used this fact to try to discredit the findings of the National Academy's panel (National Academy of Education 1985, 43; Davidson 1988; see Goodman 1976).

Among the professionals, the battle lines were drawn, with whole language on one side and phonics-first, then-literature on the other. But the larger public remained completely ignorant of this new phenomenon called whole language. The best example of this confusion was California's guidelines for teaching English, released in 1987 as part of State Superintendent Bill Honig's efforts to establish a rigorous, traditional education for all children. This was one of the most curious episodes of the decade. The state document never used the term *whole language,* yet it was widely perceived as a great victory for the forces of whole language. Although it briefly acknowledged the use of phonics in the early grades, it said little about the value of teaching the relationship between sounds and the letters of the alphabet (the California Department of Education distributed a copy of *Becoming a Nation of Readers* to every school in the state, thinking that this clarified beginning reading instruction). The document's rhetoric rang with the phrases, methods, and ideology of whole language. It proclaimed "we are in the midst of a revolution—a quiet, intellectual revolution spinning out dramatic insights into how the brain works, how we acquire language, and how we construct meaning in our lives. Psycholinguistics, language acquisition theory, and research in composition and literacy unite to present new challenges for students and teachers. . . ." This was the rhetoric of whole language, for it was Frank Smith and Kenneth Goodman who described whole language as psycholinguistics—the conjunction of psychology and linguistics—and they were the leaders of this revolution. Among whole-language reformers, the California *English-Language Arts Framework* of 1987 was a milestone (California State Department of Education 1987, 1).

For a time it seemed that whole language would sweep the entire reading field and reduce the opposition to a footnote in the history of education. Developers of textbooks and instructional materials hastened to claim that their products were aligned with the hottest new trend in reading. Whole-language proponents could point to California's adoption of new textbooks that minimized skill instruction as evidence of their influence.

But the increasingly visible success of whole language soon led to counter-reaction; by 1990 *Education Week* reported that a "full-scale war" had broken out between adherents of whole language and phonics, with each side trading salvos. The director of the NCTE's commission on reading said that teaching the mechanics of reading would actually interfere with children's ability to read; the best way to teach reading, she insisted, was to let children read whole texts, "even if they can't read all the words." However, a congressionally mandated study of reading methods in 1990 by Marilyn Jager Adams, a cognitive psychologist, called for an end to the "fruitless debate" and attempted to bridge the differences between the different approaches; after reviewing the research Adams concluded that "phonemic awareness" and "systematic code instruction" were vital for beginning readers to succeed. Her study was rejected by whole-language advocates who insisted that test scores were unimportant so long as children were enjoying reading and learning to "think critically" (O'Neil 1989, 1, 6–7; Rothman 1990, 1, 10–11; Adams 1990, 7, 125; Weaver 1990, 32–33).

Something akin to verbal mud wrestling characterized the debate about reading in the early 1990s. Kenneth Goodman insisted that critics of whole language were allies of "the far right," who wanted only to undermine public education. Goodman criticized Jeanne Chall, by then an emeritus professor of reading at Harvard, for allowing "the far right" to use her "as a starting point in constructing their conspiracy theories." The detractors of whole language, said Goodman, were not afraid that it would fail; instead, they were "afraid it would work too well. They don't want people to be too widely literate, to have easy access to information that may empower them." Frank Smith, the other founder of whole language, ridi-

DIANE RAVITCH

culed supporters of systematic phonetic instruction, claiming that this method appealed mainly to mean-spirited people, to those who wanted to control children, believing them innately wicked and in need of "a proper climate of authority and retribution" (Goodman 1993, 8–9, 32; Smith 1992, 4; see also McKenna, Stahl, and Reinking 1994, 211–33).

Not many educators identified with the "far right" or thought of themselves as "insensitive mechanical pedagogues," so there was an understandable tendency to affiliate with an approach that favored "teacher empowerment" and respect for children. But whole language received an unexpected setback in 1996 when state-by-state reading scores on the National Assessment of Educational Progress (NAEP) showed that California's reading scores were near the bottom.[1] In 1992 California had been fourth from last (ahead of Mississippi, the District of Columbia, and Guam); in 1994 California was ahead of only Louisiana and Guam (the D.C. scores were not released and presumably were even worse than California's). In California 41 percent of white students in the fourth grade scored "below basic" (compared to 35 percent nationally), as did 69 percent of black students (compared to 70 percent nationally) and 78 percent of Hispanic students (compared to 67 percent nationally). Forty-six percent of the children of college graduates in the fourth grade (compared to 32 percent nationally) registered "below basic" (National Center for Education Statistics 1996, 56–57, 145, 153). NAEP scores do not show causal effects, and it was unfair to blame whole-language practices for the test scores (it was not clear how widely whole-language practices had been implemented in California classrooms), but the national press drew a straight line between the rise of whole language and the decline of reading scores. *Time* reviewed the controversy and concluded that the evidence supporting "explicit, systematic phonics instruction" was "so strong that if the subject under discussion were, say, the treatment of the mumps, there would be no discussion."[2]

The release of California's reading scores prompted a flurry of responses. The state legislature passed mandates in 1995 requiring phonics instruction, and the state board of education adopted a new English-Language Arts curriculum in 1997 that required both phonics and literature in the earliest grades. Given California's large share of the national textbook market, this decision resonated through other jurisdictions across the na-

---

1. State-by-state rankings of NAEP scores were an innovation that started in 1992.
2. James Collins, "How Johnny Should Read," *Time*, October 27, 1967.

tion. Bill Honig, the superintendent whose efforts had inadvertently launched whole language across the state, devoted himself after he left office to promoting "a balanced approach" to reading that included both explicit instruction in phonics and whole-language activities (Honig 1996, 7; California State Department of Education 1998).

Jeanne Chall had warned in 1967 in *Learning to Read: The Great Debate* that the schools should not go overboard in teaching phonics. She recommended phonics "only as a *beginning* reading method—a method to start the child on" in the early grades, followed by a quick transition to reading good stories. She predicted that if schools made a fetish of phonics, then "we will be confronted in ten or twenty years with another best seller: *Why Robert Can't Read*. The culprit in this angry book will be the 'prevailing' linguistic, systematic-phonics. . . . The suggested cure will be a 'natural' approach—one that teaches whole words and emphasizes reading for meaning and appreciation at the very beginning." She had, of course, described with uncanny accuracy the rise of the whole-language movement (Chall 1967, 307–08).

Cynics might well have concluded that the great debate would never end and that one cycle would soon follow another, long into the future. But Americans felt a particular urgency about literacy. As the economy was changing, it was painfully obvious that those with poor reading skills would have diminishing opportunities in modern society. A new consensus began to form in the late 1990s about beginning reading. First came a spate of studies funded by the National Institute of Child Health and Human Development (NICHD, part of the National Institutes of Health), which reconfirmed the earlier work of Chall and Adams about the importance of *both* phonemic awareness and reading comprehension. Then came a major report by the National Research Council (NRC), which surveyed the entire field of reading research and concluded yet again that beginning readers needed "explicit instruction and practice that lead to an appreciation that spoken words are made up of smaller units of sounds, familiarity with spelling-sound correspondences and common spelling conventions and their use in identifying printed words, 'sight' recognition of frequent words, and independent reading, including reading aloud" (Lyon and Moats 1997, 578–88; Lyon 1997; Snow, Burn, and Griffin 1998).[3]

In short, the NICHD and the NRC confirmed that both phonics and comprehension are necessary components of learning to read. Some chil-

3. See also "Reading by 9," *Baltimore Sun*, November 2–5, 1997, special supplement.

dren pick up the connection between letters and sounds on their own or at home and arrive in school with no need for phonetic instruction; others need explicit instruction to break the code. Most children need help learning to read; those whose parents are not educated need it most. Efforts to dedicate the schools solely to skill building are narrow and unrewarding; efforts to oust phonetic instruction, spelling, and attention to language from the classroom are misguided.

Throughout the curriculum wars of the 1990s the same message was clear: extremes are wrong. Children need both decoding skills and good literature (nonfiction as well as fiction). They need both basic skills and grand concepts, themes and facts. They need to read and enjoy good poems and stories, not just textbook pieces. There is no longer any reason for this war to continue. The research on good reading instruction is now overwhelming. Both sides should declare victory and go home.

References

Adams, Marilyn Jager. 1990. *Beginning to Read: Thinking and Learning about Print.* U.S. Department of Education.

California State Department of Education. 1987. *English-Language Arts Framework.* Sacramento.

————. 1998. *English-Language Arts Content Standards for California Public Schools.* Sacramento.

Chall, Jeanne S., 1967. *Learning to Read: The Great Debate.* McGraw-Hill.

Commager, Henry Steele. 1962. "Schoolmaster to America." In *Noah Webster's The American Spelling Book,* edited by Lawrence A. Cremin, 1–12. Teachers College Press.

Davidson, Jane L., ed. 1988. *Counterpoint and Beyond: A Response to Becoming a Nation of Readers.* Urbana, Ill.: National Council of Teachers of English.

Dewey, John. 1972. "The Primary-Education Fetich." In *John Dewey: The Early Works, 1882–1898.* Southern Illinois University Press. Originally published in *Forum* (May 1898): 315–28.

Flesch, Rudolf. 1955. *Why Johnny Can't Read—And What You Can Do about It.* Harper.

Goodman, Kenneth S. 1976. "Afterword" and "Reading: A Psycholinguistic Guessing Game. " In *Theoretical Models and Processes of Reading,* edited by H. Singer and R. B. Ruddell, 107–08, 497–508. Newark, Del.: International Reading Association.

————. 1986. *What's Whole in Whole Language?* Portsmouth, N.H.: Heinemann.

————. 1993. "Gurus, Professors, and the Politics of Phonics." *Reading Today* (December 1992/January).

Goodman, Kenneth S., and Yetta M. Goodman. 1979. "Learning to Read Is Natural." In *Theory and Practice of Early Reading*, vol. 1, edited by Lauren S. Resnick and Phyllis A. Weaver. Hillsdale, N.J.: Lawrence Erlbaum.

Gray, William Scott. 1925. *Summary of Investigations Relating to Reading*. University of Chicago Press.

Hall, G. Stanley. 1904. *Adolescence: Its Psychology, and Its Relations to Physiology, Anthropology, Sociology, Sex, Crime, Religion, and Education*, vol. 2. New York: D. Appleton.

———. 1911. *Educational Problems*, vol. 2. New York: D. Appleton.

Honig, Bill. 1996. *How Should We Teach Our Children to Read? The Role of Skills in a Comprehensive Reading Program—A Balanced Approach*. San Francisco: Far West Laboratory for Educational Research and Development.

Huey, Edmund Burke. 1968. *The Psychology and Pedagogy of Reading*. MIT Press. Originally published by Macmillan, 1908.

Lyon, G. Reid. 1997. "Why Kids Can't Read." Testimony to Committee on Education and the Workforce, U.S. House of Representatives, July 10.

Lyon, G. Reid, and Louisa C. Moats. 1997. "Critical Conceptual and Methodological Considerations in Reading Intervention Research." *Journal of Learning Disabilities* (November/December).

Mathews, Mitford M. 1966. *Teaching to Read Historically Considered*. University of Chicago.

McKenna, Michael C., Steven A. Stahl, and David Reinking. 1994. "A Critical Commentary on Research, Politics, and Whole Language." *Journal of Reading Behavior* 26 (2): 211–33.

Mowry, William A. 1908. *Recollections of a New England Educator, 1838–1908*. New York: Silver Burdett.

National Academy of Education. 1985. *Becoming a Nation of Readers*. U.S. Department of Education.

National Center for Education Statistics. 1996. *NAEP 1994 Reading Report Card for the Nation and the States: Findings from the National Assessment of Educational Progress and Trial State Assessments*. U.S. Department of Education.

O'Neil, John. 1989. "'Whole Language': New View of Literacy Gains in Influence." *ASCD Update* (January).

Ravitch, Diane. 2000. *Left Back: A Century of Failed School Reforms*. Simon and Schuster.

Remarks on the Seventh Annual Report of the Hon. Horace Mann, Secretary of the Massachusetts Board of Education. 1884. Boston.

Rice, Joseph Mayer. 1893. *The Public School System of the United States*. New York: Century.

Rothman, Robert. 1990. "From a 'Great Debate' to a Full-Scale War: Dispute over Teaching Reading Heats Up." *Education Week* (March 21).

Smith, Eugene Randolph. 1924. *Education Moves Ahead*. Boston: Atlantic Monthly Press.

Smith, Frank. 1971. *Understanding Reading: A Psycholinguistic Analysis of Reading and Learning to Read*. New York: Holt, Rinehart and Winston.

———. 1973. *Psycholinguistics and Reading.* New York: Holt, Rinehart, and Winston.

———. 1992. "Learning to Read: The Never-Ending Debate." *Phi Delta Kappan* (February): 439.

Snow, Catherine E., M. Susan Burn, and Peg Griffin, eds. 1998. *Preventing Reading Difficulties in Young Children.* National Academy Press.

Weaver, Connie. 1990. "Weighing Claims of 'Phonics First' Advocates." *Education Week* (March 28): 32–33.

CHAPTER ELEVEN

Preventing Reading Difficulties in Young Children: Precursors and Fallout

CATHERINE E. SNOW

The field of reading instruction, like that of math but for various reasons even more heatedly, has been a domain of enormous conflict and controversy in the United States at least since the beginning of universal expectations for literacy. A book by E. B. Huey first published in 1908, called *The Psychology and Pedagogy of Reading*, raises and discusses as controversial the issues of when formal reading instruction should begin, what children should know about print before formal reading instruction is introduced, and how much attention should be paid to phonics in reading instruction. Those same controversies again occasioned book-length reviews in the 1960s (Chall 1967) and the early 1990s (Adams 1990). This chapter sketches these controversies briefly, to account for their recurrence and intensity, to describe a moment (how prolonged it is still impossible to say) of truce in the conflict, and to outline some public relations and policy consequences of that truce—consequences that may foreshadow renewed conflict or at least indicate the depth of feelings and recalcitrance of opinion in this area.

The Conflict

As is no doubt known to all who read the newspapers or have sent children to first grade, the basic conflict of the last few decades in the field of reading—that known widely as the "reading wars"—is the conflict between two teaching methods: phonics and whole language. (This conflict replaced the previous one, between phonics and the "whole word" or "look-see" method of teaching, which was effectively ended with the publication of Flesch's book *Why Johnny Can't Read* in 1955). The phonics method focuses on teaching children by demonstration and guided practice, in a systematic sequential fashion, the ways in which letters (or, more properly, *graphemes*) represent sounds (more properly, *phonemes*) in English, as a preparation for independent reading of extended texts. The whole-language method focuses on teaching children to comprehend written texts by engaging them with literacy in a variety of ways (being read to, choral reading, listening to tapes while being cued to finger point to words, writing with invented spelling and then reading one's own and classmates' texts, and discussing texts read or heard), on the assumption that the system for representing grapheme-phoneme correspondences in English can be learned by induction or incidental teaching, without rigidly sequenced instruction, much as language is learned.

Each of these methods captures an important truth about reading. Phonics methods recognize that the phoneme-grapheme correspondences of English are rather complex, abstract, and potentially confusing. Whole-language methods recognize that reading is about constructing meaning from text. Each also runs the danger of focusing on its truth so narrowly that it fails to ensure children learn the whole system of reading. Children in strict phonics classrooms may spend so much time learning and practicing isolated grapheme-phoneme skills that they never learn about constructing meaning, while children in authentic whole-language classrooms may engage fully in hearing, pretend-reading, understanding, and discussing texts but never actually learn the system of grapheme-phoneme mappings that would enable them to become independent readers of English.

It is perhaps worth noting that the phonics and whole-language orientations to reading instruction connect to and draw theoretical support from much broader pedagogical and developmental commitments, that is, "basic skills" versus "progressive, constructivist" approaches to teaching. However, while the larger controversy is part of the educational debate worldwide, the specific translation of it into radically different approaches to teaching beginning reading has occurred only in the English-speaking world. This reflects the technical difficulty of learning initial reading skills in English, because of features that are referred to technically as phonotactic complexity and orthographic depth. Phonotactic complexity means, basically, that syllables in English can include sequences of lots of consonant sounds, as in *plinths* or *sprinkle*. This makes reading difficult because sorting out all the sounds in a word and their sequence is so much harder than in a language with many consonant-vowel syllables. Orthographic depth means, basically, that any particular sound can be spelt in a number of different ways (for example, the long-A sound can be spelt as in *way, weigh, whale, wail, prey, break)*, and that any particular spelling can be pronounced in a number of different ways (for example, the digraph EA can be pronounced as in *break,* as in *head,* as in *learn,* or as in *peak)*. Whereas most alphabetic orthographies allow for some degree of ambiguity in mapping, typically this is unidirectional—from spelling to sound or from sound to spelling. For example, French has many possible spellings for some sounds; this is why *dictées* are a central part of French literacy instruction. But on seeing a French word one has no trouble knowing how to pronounce it. Conversely, in Arabic one could legally pronounce (unvoweled) printed words in a number of different ways, but if one hears a word correctly there is no ambiguity about how to spell it.[1]

The bidirectional complexity of mappings in English may account for the high levels of attention to and controversy about methods for early reading instruction in the English-speaking world. In fact, cross-national comparisons of early reading suggest that English-speaking children take about three years of reading instruction to get to a level of word reading that speakers of Spanish or German accomplish within the first year. This probably reflects the simple fact that English speakers have a harder task— the transparency of the system they are learning is considerably lower. It is precisely the difficulty of the task that leads to the reading wars, with phonics defenders arguing that more and more systematic instruction is necessary because English orthography is so deep, and whole-language supporters arguing that the focus must be on meaning precisely because the technical details are too complicated for young children to learn.

A Possible Resolution

Given the long history and high intensity of the reading debates, it is notable that a generally accepted state of truce exists in the late 1990s among

1. While most non-English speaking societies have avoided serious conflicts about reading instruction, Israel has been subjected to such conflicts, in part because of the influence within Israel of Anglo-American research. In addition, though, unvoweled Hebrew orthography—the form that is used most widely—is, like English, a relatively deep orthographic system.

many former combatants. This truce was to some extent promoted by the decision of the National Research Council (NRC; the operating arm of the National Academies) to convene a committee that would write a report on reading. The NRC decision also reflected previous shifts in belief and attitude that presaged the truce.

Three major shifts in thinking that had been occurring during the 1980s made it possible for the decisionmakers within the NRC to contemplate the possibility in 1994 of convening a committee that would adequately represent the field of research on reading but also might be able to achieve consensus on the key issues. These shifts were:

1. *Recognition of the relevance of the preschool period to reading development.* In the 1980s a large body of work emerged that argued that the basis for the accomplishment of literacy was established, at least in children growing up in literate households, during involvement with parents or preschool teachers in literacy practices, such as story book reading, making lists, sending cards, leaving notes, checking recipes, paying bills, consulting newspapers for information about weather or scheduled events, noticing signs in public places, and so on. These various activities contributed to child capacities often referred to as "emergent literacy" to emphasize the move away from the traditional view that children spent their preschool years simply getting ready for reading instruction, which commenced in first grade. Interestingly, many of the activities identified within this emergent literacy framework as promoting children's literacy development were the kinds of authentic engagement in literacy practice that whole-language theory prescribes—and that E. B. Huey advocated in his 1908 volume. Yet the conflict with a phonics approach has been largely absent with reference to the preschool period, primarily because of a general commitment within the early childhood field to the notion of "developmentally appropriate practice," which proscribes the use of formal, curriculum-driven instruction with preschool-aged children.

2. *Accumulation of research evidence about the nature of reading.* At its most edifying, the phonics–whole language debate was really a debate about the nature of the reading process. Phonics advocates see reading primarily as a challenging cognitive, psycholinguistic accomplishment— knowing about letters and sounds and being able to perform in a certain way when asked to map one onto the other. Whole-language advocates see reading as a social, cultural activity—participating in communities of practice within which reading and writing are normal activities and thus are acquired as needed by all members. Whole-language classroom prac-

tice was predicated to a large extent on a theory developed by Frank Smith (1983, 1994) called, confusingly, a psycholinguistic account of reading; this theory drew explicit parallels between learning one's first language and learning literacy. It proposed that rapid and effective reading invoked background knowledge and involved considerable prediction and checking of meaning based on sampling some words from the text and filling in most others, using one's knowledge of grammar and of the topic. It also claimed that words were seen as wholes, with little information gained from individual letters, and that good readers relied on many extratextual sources of information to understand the text.

With the relatively generous research funding at least intermittently available in the period between 1970 and the end of the century, a great deal of research has been focused on basic questions about the processes involved in reading. This research has been largely carried out by cognitive psychologists and psycholinguists and thus has remained somewhat insulated from the debates about pedagogy and curriculum. This research had by the early 1990s generated a robust body of findings and had clarified some genuine dilemmas concerning the reading process. Points of consensus from this research include:

—Good readers read almost all the words on a page—they do not sample sparsely.

—Good readers process almost all the letters within words; while they may process frequently occurring sequences of letters as wholes, they do not ignore the information available from letters in general.

—Reading and recognizing words typically involves forming a phonological (sound-based) representation of the word; in other words, effectively processing letters means mapping them onto sounds. The phonological representation of a word constitutes a primary route of access to its meaning.

—Reading is closely connected to the capacity to engage in phonological analysis of spoken language—learning to read both depends on and enhances the ability to segment spoken words into phonemic units.

—Relevant background knowledge and the use of nontextual supports, such as pictures, headings, and so on, have a major impact in enhancing reading comprehension (that is, in helping children understand and remember something about the entire text). Such background and nontextual information does not have a major impact, though, on the speed or accuracy with which individual words within the text are read—though it might help determine which of two identically spelled words is intended.

—The complexities of spelling that aggravate the process of first learning to read in English simplify reading comprehension in later stages by providing orthographically distinct representations of identical sounding words (*sight, site,* and *cite,* for example), and by allowing the representation of information about morphology that is helpful to the reader encountering morphologically complex words.

Given these and other conclusions from the research literature, it was clear that some of the theoretical underpinnings of radical whole-language practice had collapsed. (By the time these findings emerged, demonstration of the value of whole-language practice was being sought by its supporters primarily in classrooms rather than in consistency with conclusions from laboratory research.) The existence of a consensus among researchers on these issues made it possible that agreed-upon facts about reading could be taken as a starting point for discussing issues of reading practice.

3. *A shift to a focus on prevention.* Perhaps the most crucial shift in thinking about reading that made it feasible for the NRC to establish a committee and anticipate a consensus report was the decision to focus the report on the issue of prevention rather than the issue of reading instruction. This decision, reflected in the report's title, *Preventing Reading Difficulties in Young Children* (Snow, Burns, and Griffin 1998), meant first of all that the report would not start with nor be dominated by the issue of first-grade reading instruction—the major site of (continuing) controversy. This decision gave full credit to the importance of the preschool period to good literacy development (see point 1) and enabled the committee to focus its initial discussions on domains where considerably less theoretical disagreement exists—the risk factors associated with poor reading outcomes, the societal conditions that need to be in place to ensure healthy development in infants and toddlers, the characteristics of care settings for older preschoolers that support development, and the relevance of support for language development and engagement in literacy practices during the preschool years to promoting reading success.

Eventually the committee had to grapple with the challenge of defining the features of good reading instruction and of discussing such topics as recommendations for school reform and teacher education. Remarkably enough, it turned out that the level of disagreement on these topics was quite low, once the conversation penetrated beyond differences in terminology and shared ways of talking about the most important phenomena could be decided upon.

Moment of Opportunity

Preventing Reading Difficulties in Young Children emerged at a moment of considerable opportunity for change within the field of reading, and may indeed have contributed in some small way to that change. The opportunity seems to have been generated by a number of convergent factors, including at least:

—a widespread weariness with the reading wars

—increasing national concern about the academic performance of certain subgroups of American children

—recognition of the increased literacy demands of even low-paying jobs

—high-profile consternation in the state of California at the precipitous fall in statewide reading indicators

—recognition that the political promises of the Goals 2000 campaign could be comprehensively undermined with insufficient attention to early reading

—growing worries about the preparation of teachers and the quality of in-service professional development offered to teachers, linked with a recognition of a growing need for new teachers

—interest within the Department of Education to reclaim territory lost to the research initiatives of the National Institute of Child Health and Human Development, which had funded much of the reading research referred to above

—demographic changes leading to increasing percentages of high-risk children in U.S. schools, in particular in large urban districts

—particular worries about the reading accomplishments of non-English speaking children, and growing dissatisfaction with the approaches taken within bilingual education programs.

Many of the specific initiatives undertaken in response to these worries required a certain level of convergence on some basic principles of action. Thus, having a statement of beliefs and commitments in the field of literacy that could be widely subscribed to turned out to be extremely convenient, by short-circuiting many tedious discussions and lengthy disagreements that might otherwise have delayed action, postponed decisions, and absorbed energy.

Public Reaction

The publication of *Preventing Reading Difficulties in Young Children* attracted a surprising amount of media attention, given that the report itself presented no novel findings. Nothing said in the report about reading instruction, for example, could not have been formulated by an experienced, thoughtful, reflective first-grade teacher with a few weeks' free time. Nonetheless, the report's release was covered by dozens of newspapers, in a lengthy report on National Public Radio, by public television with a twenty-minute segment on the *Newshour,* and it was featured on the *Today* program twice—immediately after its release and the following September as part of a "back to school" series.

Most of the public interest was focused on the recommendations for reading instruction incorporated within the report. Those recommendations can be summarized as a list of opportunities the report argued all children should have access to. These are:

—opportunities to develop rich skills in language and language analysis

—opportunities to learn about the functions of written language

—opportunities to develop positive attitudes toward literacy and motivation to learn to read

—opportunities to grasp and master the alphabetic principle

—opportunities for children in risk groups to benefit from well-designed prevention programs

—opportunities for children who are starting to show difficulties to receive well-designed intervention that is consistent with their classroom instruction.

In short, the committee recommendations came down to endorsing the value of excellent, language- and literacy-rich preschool settings for all children, as well as excellent reading instruction that incorporated attention to the functions of literacy, the language skills that form the basis for literacy, an understanding of the alphabetic principle, and opportunities to practice reading interesting and engaging texts so as to become fluent in applying the alphabetic principle.

If there was a complaint from committee members about the nature of the coverage, it was that it failed (predictably enough) to reflect the full subtlety of the report. Much of the coverage, in fact, could be summarized by the March 19, 1998, *New York Times* headline: "Experts Call for Mix of 2 Methods to Teach Reading." The first wave of coverage led us to make a stronger and more explicit statement in the foreword of the second edition of the report that good reading instruction involves rational selection of activities focused on both "the alphabetic principle" and on constructing meaning, and most importantly on the integration of both these foci into all instruction. In other words, the committee wished to be explicit and unambiguous about its message that "doing some phonics and doing some whole language" would *not* constitute good instruction; rather, attending to the principles underlying both models for instruction, and integrating these principles into every instructional activity, was, we argued, necessary.

The media coverage generated a certain amount of mail as well; much of it was admiring, but the letters of complaint revealed many of the same underlying dimensions of criticism that also emerged (sometimes covertly or indirectly, always less charmingly expressed) from the academic, practice, and policy communities. The major themes these letters addressed were:

—the perception that the report was insufficiently strong in endorsing phonics

—distress at the report's support for the use of invented spelling

—disagreement with the implications of putting reading into a larger prevention framework (that is, rejecting the notion that pediatricians, social workers, public health officials, and others should be involved in preventing reading difficulties)

—associated attacks on school practitioners for shirking their duties

—the danger of reduced demands on students to work hard, as exemplified in lowered demands to learn English characteristic of bilingual programs. Perhaps the most frequent theme of the letters received consisted of avowals from writers who knew (or knew someone who knew) how to teach reading successfully, accompanied by wonderment that no one had been listening to their recommendations, using their materials, and following their methods.

Reaction within the Research and Academic Community

In many ways the reaction of the research and academic community mirrored those of the public, although more of the public reaction came from the "right" while negative academic response was more likely to come from the "left." There were attacks on the report (some even before it emerged, from academics in the "whole language" camp, based perhaps on their unhappiness with the committee membership and on gossip about decisions reached in the supposedly confidential committee hearings) as failing to acknowledge sufficiently the social nature of literacy. The most comprehensive attack of this sort came from Jerome Harste, a scholar who has worked primarily in the domain of writing development. He was at the time president of the National Council of Teachers of English (the professional organization for language arts educators, whose practice has been richly informed by ideas formulated within the whole-language approach). At a symposium of the American Educational Research Association (AERA) in April 1998, members of the committee presented an overview of the report. Harste, as an invited discussant, condemned the report as building on an alarmist message concerning the rate of reading failure and concerning social and ethnic differences. He also rejected the value of the agreements emphasized in the preface to the report and in press coverage of it, saying that the "reading wars" had not caused the problem and thus enacting a truce would not solve the problem. He emphasized that the definition of reading in the report was misconceived as a linguistic process of "getting at meaning" rather than a psycho-sociocultural process of constructing meaning. He argued that the report failed to acknowledge the centrality of personal relationships in children's reading development—that caregiver relationships with children were as important as print. He said that children's conceptions of and motivations for reading had been ignored in the report and that authentic and vital home literacy practices had been undervalued. He also excoriated particular committee members (this writer among them) for having abandoned their intellectual commitment to relational and constructivist principles by signing on to the report. He claimed that the report privileged a limited research tradition—neglecting qualitative research and research embedded in classroom practice and participant expertise in favor of positivism. In short, he argued that the report endorsed power over pedagogy. He voiced an accusation previously expressed by Ken Goodman that the release of the report had been timed "for political effect," presumably to influence legislative action.

At the same symposium (and subsequently when he and I were guests on Diane Rehm's National Public Radio show), invited discussant Maris Vinovskis raised a set of helpful suggestions concerning how the report could have addressed itself more directly to policymakers: by dealing more specifically with issues such as retention and age-grading, by providing more information about some prevention programs, by providing harder estimates of the number of children who need prevention and intervention efforts, and by analyzing the costs of various prevention undertakings. He argued that the report should have included more explicit recommendations in a number of areas. His most explicit criticism addressed the recommendation concerning the desirability of teaching children to read first in their strongest language—which he argued was too explicit and unjustified as a general policy (citing as support his own case, as a fluent reader of English who had entered school speaking only Lithuanian and who had received an all-English education).

The third invited discussant at the AERA symposium, David Pearson, had served as a reviewer and review coordinator of the report for the NRC, so his comments were based on a particularly thorough familiarity with it, and indeed the published report reflected many of his helpful and thoughtful earlier comments. His criticisms focused on aspects of the report he thought had been underemphasized, specifically the value of methodological eclecticism, the view of reading difficulties as a continuum within which it may not be useful to distinguish categories like "dyslexic," and the recommendation that children with difficulties receive the same support and teaching as children progressing more rapidly—but more of it, more intensively provided. His comments emphasized the dangers of having a report like this available—warning that recommendations in the report could be interpreted as mandates regarding curriculum, that legislators would try to implement the recommendations, and that the professional organizations were needed to help disseminate and interpret the recommendations so as to protect against their misuse.[2]

Pearson has since expanded on and developed these worries about the report, in a lengthy essay review published in *Reading Research Quarterly*, the leading reading research journal (Pearson 1999). The review, like his comments at AERA, never expresses any disagreement with the findings, conclusions, or recommendations of the report, although it projects a sense that reaction to it had perhaps been overblown and worry concerning how it might be used and misused.

A theme in Harste's response to the report, which has also been picked up in a lengthy commentary on it by Gee (1999), is that the report some-

2. Since the National Council of Teachers of English, whose president had just condemned the report roundly, would be prominent among such professional organizations, this comment seemed a bit idealistic at the time. However, it should be noted that interest in the report has been high at other professional meetings, including the National Association for the Education of Young Children, International Reading Association, National Reading Conference, and others.

how endorses an inequitable status quo. By focusing on recommendations for prevention and the improvement of practice in reading instruction, the argument goes, the report fails to attack the roots of illiteracy, namely social inequity, poverty, and racism. Those interested in a more extended statement of this view, and in a reaction to it, should consult Gee (1999) and Snow (2000).

It should not be thought that all criticism of the report has come from the side of scholars who thought it was too positive. It has also been criticized for being too wishy-washy on issues of direct instruction and phonics. For example, in the March 19, 1998, edition of the *Baltimore Sun* Louisa Cook Moats, a reading researcher funded by the National Institute of Child Health and Human Development (NICHD), was quoted as saying that the report did not go far enough in stressing the importance of phonemic awareness and explicit phonics: "There's still this whole untouched issue of accountability in teacher preparation and classroom practice that isn't sufficiently addressed . . . it leaves a lot of wiggle room for the status quo."

Like the whole-language adherents, the direct instruction adherents anticipated (again, their information base is obscure, since the committee meetings where recommendations were discussed were supposedly confidential) inadequately strong recommendations concerning the importance of the alphabetic principle in instruction. These worries may have strengthened calls for the establishment, in a time period overlapping with the final meetings of the committee, of a federally mandated panel designed to review rigorously the research base on the effectiveness of different instructional techniques. This panel subsequently somewhat redefined its own charge in order to reduce overlap with *Preventing Reading Difficulties,* and its report was released in early 2000 (National Reading Panel 2000). Duane Alexander, director of NICHD (which provided a small amount of the funding for *Preventing Reading Difficulties*) was quoted in the *Sun* article as saying the report did not go far enough in determining what research could be trusted. "There's an enormous volume of literature out there; some of it's very good, some of it's crummy," said Alexander. Reid Lyon, whose division within NICHD has funded considerable reading research, was quoted in the same article as saying that the report, as a consensus document, remained ambiguous. "This report will . . . now allow the national reading panel to identify the types of research methods and evidence that are most useful for informing instructional and policy decisions."

Reaction within the Practice Community

Within communities of practitioners, among whom I include the state and district educational administrators responsible for professional development, the response to the report has been remarkably positive. In part, this has been fueled by the decision of the NRC to produce, for the first time in its history, a "popular version" of a committee report. *Starting Out Right* (Burns, Griffin, and Snow 1999) is a readable, graphically accessible, photo-rich, color-printed paperback in which much of the science-based information from *Preventing Reading Difficulties* is reprinted but in the context of a much less technical presentation of the general issues. *Starting Out Right* also includes, as a way of illustrating the research conclusions, suggestions for activities to engage in with children; lists of children's books and software consistent with the recommended practices; and many links to sources of information about literacy development, prevention programs, and additional activities. It was designed to be a useful resource to parents and early childhood educators, competing with various "how-to" books but based more solidly than most in research findings.

As of the end of January 2000 almost 41,000 copies of *Preventing Reading Difficulties* had been sold, and almost 75,000 copies of *Starting Out Right*. These are rather astonishing numbers for National Academy Press publications, which average initial print runs of 2,000 copies that rarely sell out. Sales have been driven in part by the use of these books in large- and small-scale professional development efforts (for example, within District 2 in New York and for statewide efforts in Texas) but also by individual sales to teachers and curriculum directors (*Preventing Reading Difficulties* ranked for a while in the top 4,000 books on the Amazon.com sales list). The existence and availability of these volumes has been publicized by the Center for the Improvement of Early Reading Achievement (CIERA), the only federally funded center for early reading, which is co-directed by David Pearson. CIERA has produced and disseminated pamphlets and webpage units drawn directly from PRD. Interest has been expressed in a translation of *Preventing Reading Difficulties* into Greek and Chinese, and *Starting Out Right* has been published in Spanish by the Secretaría de Educación Pública of the Mexican government. Incidentally, the two books have also been used as a basis for professional development activities in Australia (Christine van Kraayenoorde, personal communication), and have been received positively in Britain.

Other forms of dissemination include papers in practitioner-oriented journals that summarize key aspects of the report and draw implications for various practice-communities (for example, Snow, Scarborough, and Burns 1999, designed for speech/language pathologists, and Strucker and Snow 2000, designed for adult literacy teachers). Finally, responses to misinterpretations of the original report have also been written (Snow 2000). In addition, the requests to members of the committee to speak about the report have been far too numerous to keep track of, and even the small proportion of those requests that have been responded to affirmatively had added up to more than 150 presentations within a year of the appearance of *Preventing Reading Difficulties*.

Related Policy Consequences

As noted above, the report emerged into a world of considerable policy ferment around issues of education in general and reading in particular. Committee members testified before the House and the Senate committees on Education, Labor and the Workforce, and subcommittees on Head Start reauthorization, even before the report was finished, and again after its completion. The language of the Head Start reauthorization (S 2206) reveals that the committee staffers had read the book—new performance standards for Head Start classrooms and expectations for four-year-old Head Start graduates reflect the language of *Preventing Reading Difficulties* rather precisely, in particular in calling for knowledge of ten letters by Head Start "graduates." Unfortunately, the stated expectations for children translate information presented in *Preventing Reading Difficulties* as "what one might expect of most four-year-olds who have had rich language and literacy environments" into accomplishments to be expected of all children, perhaps confirming David Pearson's apprehensions. Furthermore, the performance standard stating that Head Start should be preparing children for English-language classrooms directly conflicts with the spirit of the recommendation to support first-language literacy whenever possible.

On the other hand, the recommendations in *Preventing Reading Difficulties* concerning the importance of the quality of preschoolers' language and literacy environments, and the difficulty of designing high-quality environments without professional preparation that provides an understanding of children's language and literacy development, are reflected in the reauthorization's demands for better professional preparation of Head

Start teachers. Head Start programs will be expected, by 2003, to have classroom personnel half of whom have associate's degrees. Furthermore, by 2006 half the Head Start personnel will be expected to have bachelor's degrees. These expectations go far beyond the current standard, since many Head Start personnel are in fact also Head Start parents. Providing the resources so that poorly paid Head Start employees, many of whom also have limited literacy skills and may have limited skills in spoken English, can achieve these higher educational levels constitutes a huge challenge, and one that will require creative redesign of higher educational opportunities.[3]

Another domain within which *Preventing Reading Difficulties* was invoked was the passage of the Reading Excellence Act, which provides funding to states that are successful in a competition, to support professional development activities for teachers and tutorial programs for children. The strict guidelines for Reading Excellence Act applications limited proposed activities to those that reflect "scientifically-based reading research," a description interpreted by many to mean consistent with the guidelines in and conclusions of *Preventing Reading Difficulties*. Information meetings (first, a national "Reading Summit," then regional meetings held under the title "Improving America's Schools") disseminated the findings of the report to state teams interested in applying for the funding. The funding was generous, with the result that almost all states and a couple of territories applied. In the first round seventeen were funded, with more funding available for additional rounds of applications. In the process, state education teams were formed and encouraged to come to grips with the need to base plans for reading reform in procedures that had been demonstrated to work and that were consistent with research findings about reading development. There was considerable sentiment among administrators of the grant program (which provided support to state teams

3. It should be noted that the calls for better qualifications of Head Start and other early childhood educators, and in particular greater focus in their preparation on issues of language and literacy development, have been powerfully supported by the National Association for the Education of Young Children (NAEYC), which together with the International Reading Association (IRA) issued in fall 1999 a statement on the place of literacy within developmentally appropriate practice (Bredekamp, Copple, and Neuman 1999). This statement was an explicit clarification that developmentally appropriate practice did not exclude attention to letters, sounds in words, and print, and was consistent with the inclusion of literacy materials and activities during play, activities, and circle time in preschool classrooms. IRA and NAEYC have also convened a number of professional development activities, attended largely by NAEYC members, around the country to promote this understanding among classroom practitioners.

preparing applications) that having a consensus statement on reading research made it possible to establish high criteria in defining "research-based" and that it provided at least a minimal specification of the information to be made available through the newly funded professional development activities.

Recurring Controversies

The issues around which controversies have recurred are the following:

—the recommendation to provide initial reading instruction in their native languages to non-English speaking children whenever possible

—the recommendation to postpone initial reading instruction until at least basic oral proficiency had been achieved in English if native language instruction could not be provided

—providing resources for preschool over primary instruction if a conflict arose

—ensuring that preschool classrooms were equipped with a curriculum that provided for attention to language and literacy learning

—providing resources for the professional preparation of preschool educators, and resources to increase their remuneration if necessary to enforce higher level preparatory standards

—"forcing the schools to teach phonics"

—ignoring the social inequities in reading performance, thus reinforcing rather than attacking the status quo.

What Still Needs to Be Done

The nature of these controversies is somewhat distressing, because significant action needs to be taken in order to implement many of the recommendations, and the more disagreement there is about the recommendations within the report, the more likely that the needed action will be undermined. In the view of the committee, the major front on which work needs to be done is that of professional preparation—upgrading the standards of preservice preparation for preschool teachers, the content of preservice education with special reference to knowledge about language and literacy development for preservice primary teachers, and the quality and content of in-service professional development for both these groups. The committee report makes a number of recommendations in this regard, but they are not specific, and considerable intellectual work needs to be done to sort out the best methods for improving the literacy knowledge base of teachers, the standards that they should be held to, and the practicalities of raising those standards in an era when many current teachers are retiring and alternate certification programs are burgeoning. As noted above, this is the priority to which federal funding is being directed under the provisions of the America Reads legislation, but the sad fact is that we are not entirely sure (a) what teachers need to know, (b) when they need to know it, and (c) how best to ensure they learn it.

Reading is, in some ways (not the ways that Frank Smith believed), rather like speaking a language, in that it is something most of us do easily, automatically, and with little attention to the complexities of the process. Teaching reading is also like teaching a language that one speaks as a native—and on crucial dimensions quite distinct from teaching math or history. For most of us, reading with comprehension and speaking our native languages are fully automatized processes; we have little memory of having learned to do them or of where we struggled while learning. We have practiced literacy and language skills for thousands of hours, to the point where the process of producing language or reading is transparent. It is, thus, hard to understand why children stumble over certain words, to predict what texts they will find difficult, to appreciate the added complexity for them associated with a novel font or an unfamiliar word—just as it is hard to understand why second-language speakers find certain sounds hard to produce or persist in making certain errors in English. In these respects, reading and a native language are for primary teachers quite different from math and social studies, which came originally in pedagogically defined units and topics, and with which many adults have not achieved fluent and transparent usage.

Learning to teach reading (or English as a second language) requires, in effect, learning what is hard about a process one finds easy and remembering when it was impossible to do what one knows how to do so well. Furthermore, children approach reading with widely varying domains of strength and weakness, capable of producing errors or encountering blocks that have never been noted before. So the teacher must not only be prepared for lots of possible kinds of performance, but also be prepared to understand and diagnose those various performances and then to plan instruction on that basis. This is a highly challenging task for which in general we have not bothered to prepare teachers, and we are still quite unsure how best to do so (see Fillmore and Snow 1999, for a discussion of the challenge). Figuring out how to do this is the next challenge—redesigning teacher education and in-service professional development to ensure universal access to sufficient knowledge about literacy.

References

Adams, M. 1990. *Beginning to Read: Thinking and Learning about Print*. MIT Press.

Bredekamp, S., C. Copple, and S. B. Neuman. 1999. "Learning to Read and Write: Developmentally Appropriate Practices for Young Children." A joint position statement of the International Reading Association and the National Association for the Education of Young Children. Washington: NAEYC.

Burns, M. S., P. Griffin, and C. E. Snow, eds. 1999. *Starting Out Right: A Guide to Promoting Children's Reading Success*. Washington: National Academy Press.

Chall, J. S. 1967. *Learning to Read: The Great Debate*. McGraw-Hill.

Fillmore, L. W., and C. E. Snow. 1999. "What Educators—Especially Teachers—Need to Know about Language: The Bare Minimum." Available at www.ncbe.gwu.edu/iasconferences/1999/institutes/lep/discussiondraft.htm.

Flesch, R. 1955. *Why Johnny Can't Read: And What You Can Do about It*. Harper and Row.

Gee, J. 1999. "Reading and the New Literacy Studies: Reframing the National Academy of Sciences Report on Reading." *Journal of Literacy Research* 31: 355–74.

Huey, E. B. 1908. *The Psychology and Pedagogy of Reading*. Macmillan.

National Reading Panel. 2000. "Teaching Children to Read: An Evidence-Based Assessment of the Scientific Research Literature on Reading and Its Implications for Reading Instruction." NIH Publication No. 00–4754, U.S. Department of Health and Human Services.

Pearson, P. D. 1999. "A Historically Based Review of *Preventing Reading Difficulties in Young Children*." *Reading Research Quarterly* 34: 113–21.

Smith, F. 1983. *Essays into Literacy*. London: Heinemann.

———. 1994. *Understanding Reading: A Psycholinguistic Analysis of Reading and Learning to Read*. Mahwah, N.J.: Lawrence Erlbaum.

Snow, C. E. 2000. "On the Limits of Reframing: Rereading the National Academy of Sciences Report on Reading." *Journal of Literacy Research* 32: 113–21.

Snow, C. E., S. Burns, and P. Griffin, eds. 1998. *Preventing Reading Difficulties in Young Children*. Washington: National Academy Press.

Snow, C. E., H. Scarborough, and M. S. Burns. 1999. "What Speech-Language Practitioners Need to Know about Early Reading." *Topics in Language Disorders* 20: 30–40.

Strucker, J., and C. E. Snow. 2000. "Lessons of *Preventing Reading Difficulties in Young Children* for Adult Learning and Literacy." In the *Annual Review of Adult Learning and Literacy*, vol. 1, edited by J. Comings, B. Garner, and C. Smith, 25–73. Jossey-Bass.

CHAPTER TWELVE

Contemporary Reading Instruction

MARGARET MOUSTAFA

Today's controversy in reading education—often framed as whole language versus phonics—is not over whether to teach letter-sound correspondences but how letter-sound correspondences are best taught. In traditional reading instruction,[1] children are taught letter-sound correspondences and print words out of context and are then provided with stories written on the basis of letter-sound correspondences and whole print words that have been taught. In contemporary reading instruction,[2] children are taught to read stories with familiar language via shared reading and then taught letter-sound correspondences in the context of the stories they have learned to read.

In the following pages the discussion focuses on traditional reading instruction, contemporary reading instruction, and the current policy shift away from contemporary reading instruction back to traditional reading instruction.

Traditional Reading Instruction

Traditional reading instruction uses a parts-to-whole approach. It begins by teaching children letter-phoneme correspondences. The problem with

1. The term *traditional* is used because the assumption that we learn to read by learning letters dates at least as far back as Socrates.
2. The term *contemporary* is used rather than *whole language* because the latter term is often confused with *whole word*, a very different conception of early reading instruction.

this approach is that children who have not yet learned to read have difficulty dividing spoken words into their constituent phonemes. For example, they have difficulty dividing the spoken word *went* into its constituent phonemes /w/ + /e/ + /n/ + /t/ (Bruce 1964; Liberman et al. 1974; Rosner 1974; Treiman 1983, 1985).

Some would address this problem by teaching phonemic awareness (for example, Adams 1990; Foorman et al. 1998; Stanovich 1986). Once children can separate spoken words into individual phonemes, they would then teach letter-phoneme correspondences. They point to a large body of research that shows a high correlation between children's ability to read and their ability to consciously divide spoken words into their constituent phonemes. They say phonemic awareness *predicts* reading ability.[3]

The problem with this line of reasoning is that correlation does not establish causation. For example, there is a high correlation between being in a hospital bed and being sick, but being in a hospital bed does not cause sickness. In statistics, the word *predicts* means nothing more than that there is a high correlation between two phenomena.

Research does not support phonemic awareness training. Bus and van Ijzendoorn (1999) found that phonemic awareness training in kindergarten accounts for 0.6 percent of the total variance in reading achievement in the later primary years. Troia (1999) reviewed thirty-nine phonemic awareness training studies and found no evidence to support phonemic awareness training in classroom instruction. Krashen (1999a, 1999b) conducted similar reviews and had similar findings. Taylor (1998) points out that while children's early cognition develops from concrete experiences to abstract understandings, phonemic awareness training begins with abstract exercises.

In fact, rather than phonemic awareness being a prerequisite to literacy, literacy contributes to phonemic awareness (Scholes 1998; Treiman 1983, 1985). We use our knowledge of how words are spelled to figure out how many phonemes are in a word. When phonemes do not have a one-to-one correspondence with letters literate adults are less competent at analyzing spoken words into phonemes. If asked, most would say there are three phonemes in the word *box* rather than the four that there are.

3. See also G. R. Lyon, testimony before the Committee on Education and the Workforce, U.S. House of Representatives, July 10, 1997; G. R. Lyon, *Newsweek*, October 27, 1997, p. 60.

Another problem with teaching children letter-phoneme correspondences out of context is the incredible complexity of the system. Clymer (1964) examined the best stated phonics generalizations and found that altogether they worked only about 50 percent of the time. Put another way, traditional phonics instruction misleads learners about 50 percent of the time. Clymer's finding have stood the test of replication studies (Bailey 1967; Burmeister 1968; Emans 1967).

In an unsuccessful attempt to create better phonics generalizations, Berdiansky, Cronnell, and Koehler (1969) found that English letters correspond to English phonemes in more than two hundred different ways. Sounds can be represented with multiple letters (for example, the /u/ in *blue, shoe, to, too, two, new, view, through*, and *rendezvous*) and letters can represent multiple sounds (for example, the *o* in *no, to, won, towel*, and *woman*). This leads to mind boggling complexities, such as the vowels in *know* and *now* are written the same but pronounced differently, while the vowels in *know* and *no* are written differently but pronounced the same.

Adding to this complexity is the fact that letter-sound correspondences vary from dialect to dialect. *Mary, marry*, and *merry* are pronounced the same in some dialects but differently in others.

Finally, traditional reading instruction asks children to read stories limited to letter-sound correspondences and whole print words that have been taught. These stories are called decodable stories, phonics stories, or controlled vocabulary stories. The problem with limiting children's reading materials to letter-sound correspondences and print words that have been taught is that the language of the stories becomes contrived, unnatural, and, as discussed in the next section, difficult for children to understand. Consequently, decodable stories give children learning to read the implicit message that reading is a meaningless activity. Allington (1997) surveyed the research on decodable text and found that no well-constructed research supports the use of decodable text.

Contemporary Reading Instruction

Contemporary reading instruction uses a whole-to-parts approach. It begins by teaching children to read stories with familiar language via shared reading and then teaches them letter-sound correspondences in the context of the stories that they have learned to read, as explained below.

Reading Materials for Beginning Readers

Experimental research has consistently found that early readers read stories with familiar language better than print words out of context or stories with unfamiliar language. In his seminal work Goodman (1965) took words from children's stories and put them in lists. He then asked first-, second-, and third-grade children to read the words in the lists and then to read the stories. He found that the children frequently read words that they had missed in the list correctly in the story. For example, they might have read *horse* as *house* in a list but read it correctly in a story about cowboys. Goodman's findings have stood the test of replication studies (Nicholson 1991; Nicholson, Lillas, and Rzoska 1988; Stanovich 1991, 431).

In other seminal work Ruddell (1965) asked fourth-grade children to read two types of text: (1) text where the language was typical of children's spoken language, and (2) text where the language was typical of written language but not children's spoken language. He found the children were able to comprehend the passages where the language was typical of their spoken language much better than the passages where the language was not typical of their spoken language. Ruddell's findings, like Goodman's, have stood the test of replication studies (Kucer 1985; Rhodes 1979; Tatham 1970).

In a variation of Ruddell's study, Rhodes (1979) asked first-grade children to read a predictable story and a decodable story. Predictable stories, by definition, have language that is familiar to children. To three of the thirteen children Rhodes studied, the type of story made no difference in their oral reading or their retelling of the story. However, the other ten children had better oral readings and retellings of the story with the familiar language—the predictable story—than the story with the unfamiliar language—the decodable story. No child did better with the decodable story.

Why do early readers read and comprehend stories with familiar language better than words out of context or stories with unfamiliar language? To understand this, read these sentences:

They live in New York.
They broadcast live from New York.

Even though *live* was written exactly the same in both sentences, it is pronounced one way in the first sentence and another way in the second.

Your knowledge of the English language told you which pronunciation of *live* to use in each sentence.

When children first begin to read, they know much more about spoken language than they know about letter-sound correspondences. Language is their strength. Text with familiar language enables children to use what they know—language—to learn more. It also starts children on the road to reading with the implicit message that reading is making sense of print.

Reading Instruction for Beginning Readers

In contemporary reading instruction, early readers are started on the road to independent reading through shared reading with stories with language familiar to children. Shared reading, also known as the shared book experience, was first developed by Holdaway (1979, 1982). In shared reading, the teacher reads a story with language familiar to the children while pointing to the words in full view of the children (Fayden 1997; Heald-Taylor 1987; Holdaway 1979, 1982; Moustafa and Maldonado-Colon 1999; Slaughter 1983; Trachtenburg and Ferruggia 1989). This is done repeatedly over consecutive days, typically with an oversize book.

In the first few weeks of shared reading the teacher also teaches one-to-one spoken-word/print-word matching, also known as one-to-one matching, or tracking. Taught a few minutes each day, every day, one-to-one matching is typically acquired in one to two weeks (Moustafa and Maldonado-Colon 1999). Once children have acquired one-to-one matching, shared reading enables them to use their knowledge of language to quickly and easily learn to recognize lots of print words in the context of a story.

Once children learn to recognize the print words in the context of a story, they are then taught letter-sound correspondences in print words they have learned to read in the story. This helps children deal with the more than two hundred ways English letters correspond to English phonemes and the inconsistencies of the correspondences. Children's knowledge of letter-sound correspondences builds as the cycle of shared reading and phonics-taught-in-context is repeated with more predictable stories.

Other instructional strategies that help early readers become independent readers are guided reading, shared writing, and interactive writing. Over time, through repeated shared reading with multiple predictable stories, phonics taught in context, guided reading, shared writing, interactive writing, and lots of experiences of being read to and opportunities to read and write, children become independent readers.

There is a large body of comparative research that has found that *children with contemporary reading instruction learn to make sense of print better than children with traditional reading instruction* (Anderson, Wilkinson, and Mason 1991; Cantrell 1999; Cohen 1968; Cullinan, Jaggar, and Strickland 1974; Eldredge, Reutzel, and Hollingsworth 1996; Elley 1991; Freppon 1991; Larrick 1987; Mullis, Campbell, and Farstrup 1993; Reutzel and Cooter 1990; Ribowsky 1986; Richeck and McTague 1988; Sacks and Mergendoller 1997).

Cantrell (1999), for example, found primary-grade children in contemporary classrooms that focused on reading for meaning and skills taught in context achieved scores between the 50th and 76th percentile on the Stanford 9 national norms in reading comprehension, spelling, and language, whereas children in classrooms where skills were taught out of context and meaning was not emphasized achieved scores that fell below the 50th percentile.[4] Eldredge and his colleagues (1996) found below-average, average, and above-average second-grade children with contemporary shared reading instruction averaged higher scores on the comprehension subtest on the Iowa Test of Basic Skills than children with traditional round-robin reading instruction (see figure 12-1).

While all children benefit from contemporary reading instruction, lower achieving children especially benefit (Anderson, Wilkinson and Mason 1991; Eldredge, Reutzel, and Hollingsworth 1996; Sacks and Mergendoller 1997).

Many of these same researchers also looked at children's knowledge of letter-sound correspondences. They all found that *children with contemporary reading instruction learn letter-sound correspondences better than children with traditional reading instruction* (Cantrell 1999; Cohen 1968; Eldredge, Reutzel, and Hollingsworth 1996; Elley 1991; Freppon 1991; Reutzel and Cooter 1990; Ribowsky 1986; Richeck and McTague 1988; Sacks and Mergendoller 1997).

Freppon (1991), for example, found that first-grade children with contemporary reading instruction did not have to sound out words as often as children with traditional reading instruction, but when they did, they were almost twice as successful as children with traditional reading instruction at sounding out words (see figure 12-2). Cantrell (1999) found that primary-grade children in contemporary classrooms outscored children in traditional classrooms in word analysis on the Stanford 9. Eldredge, Reutzel,

---

4. On a norm-referenced test such as the *Stanford 9*, the 50th percentile is average.

Figure 12-1. *Second-Grade Children's Comprehension with Traditional and Contemporary Reading Instruction*

Iowa Test of Basic Skills (maximum = 61)

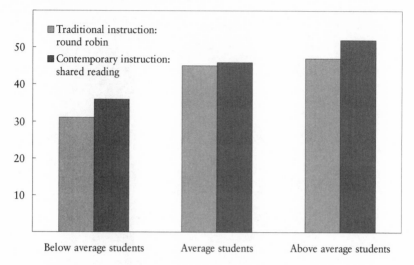

Source: Eldredge, Reutzel, and Hollingsworth, 1996.

and Hollingsworth (1996) found that below-average, average, and above-average second-grade children with contemporary reading instruction outscored children with traditional reading instruction in word analysis on the Iowa Test of Basic Skills.

There is also a large body of research that has found that *children with contemporary reading instruction become fluent readers better than children with traditional reading instruction* (Cantrell 1999; Eldredge et al. 1996; Elley 1991; Freppon 1991; Ribowsky 1986; Richeck and McTague 1988; Sacks and Mergendoller 1997).

Cantrell (1999), for example, found that primary-grade children with contemporary reading instruction read more fluently than children with traditional reading instruction and that they have fewer errors in their oral reading. Similarly, Eldredge and his colleagues (1996) found that below-average, average, and above-average second-grade children with contemporary reading instruction read more fluently than children with traditional reading instruction and that they have fewer errors in their oral reading (see figure 12-3).

Figure 12-2. *First-Grade Children's Correct Sounding Out of Unfamiliar Print Words with Traditional and Contemporary Reading Instruction*

Percent correct

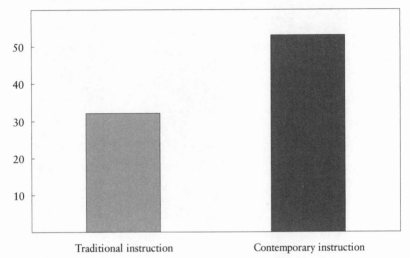

Source: Freppon 1991.

Phonics Instruction

While the 1960s, 1970s, and 1980s brought new types of beginning reading materials and new ways of teaching beginning reading, the 1980s and 1990s brought new understandings of how children learn letter-sound correspondences and new ways of teaching letter-sound correspondences.

Traditionally we have assumed that children learning to read an alphabetic script become independent readers by learning letter-phoneme correspondences. In her seminal research Goswami found that young children make analogies between familiar and unfamiliar print words to pronounce unfamiliar print words (Goswami1986, 1988; Goswami and Bryant 1990; Goswami and Mead 1992). She showed five-, six-, and seven-year-old children pairs of print words that shared a common sequence of letters. Using print words the children did not know in the pretest, she told the children one of the words in each pair and asked them to read the other word in the pair. She found that once the children knew the first word in the pair, children who had begun to read were often able to pronounce the

Figure 12-3. *Second-Grade Children's Oral Reading Fluency with Traditional and Contemporary Reading Instruction*

Words per minute

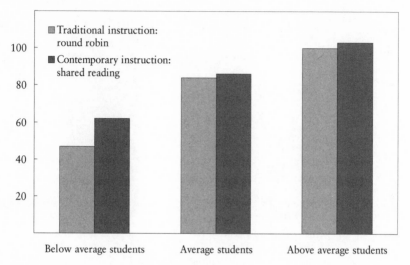

Source: Eldredge, Reutzel, and Hollingsworth, 1996.

second word in the pair when the shared letters represented a common onset or rime.

Onsets are any consonants that may occur before the vowel in a spoken syllable. The onset in *mile* is /m/; the onset in *smile* is /sm/. Rimes are the vowel and any consonants that may occur after the vowel in a spoken syllable. The rime in *smile* is /il/; the rime in *smiles* is /ilz/.

Goswami reasoned that the more print words children recognize, the better position they are in to figure out new print words by analogy to print words they already recognize. A reanalysis of Tunmer and Nesdale's data shows exactly that. Tunmer and Nesdale (1985) studied six first-grade classes, three that emphasized instruction in letter-phoneme correspondences and three that ignored instruction in letter-phoneme correspondences. They found that the children who knew more print words figured out the analogous made-up words that the researchers gave them better than children who knew fewer print words, regardless of whether they had had instruction in letter-phoneme correspondences or not.

Figure 12-4. *Explanations of How Children Sound Out New Print Words*

Percent correct

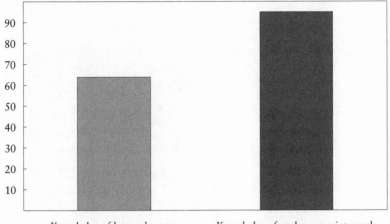

Knowledge of letter-phoneme   Knowledge of analogous print words
correspondences

Explanations

Source: Moustafa 1995.

In my study (Moustafa 1995) I also found that the more print words children recognize, the better they figure out new print words. I further found that children's knowledge of familiar print words accounted for their pronunciation of the unfamiliar words better than their knowledge of letter-phoneme correspondences (see figure 12-4). The data suggest that when children appear to be using their knowledge of letter-phoneme correspondences to pronounce unfamiliar print words, they are actually using their knowledge of other print words they already recognize.

If the more print words children recognize, the better they are able to figure out new print words, then the question is: What is the most effective way to help children learn to recognize lots of print words? The most effective way now known to reading professionals is shared reading with predictable text. Shared reading with predictable text helps children to quickly and easily learn to recognize lots of print words in context.

One way to help children learn letter-sound correspondences is to write print words they have learned to recognize via shared reading on pieces of paper with a logo from the story, highlight a letter or letters that represent an onset or a rime in each word, and group together the words that have

Figure 12-5. *An Example of Contemporary Phonics Instruction Using Stories Children Have Learned to Read via Shared Reading*

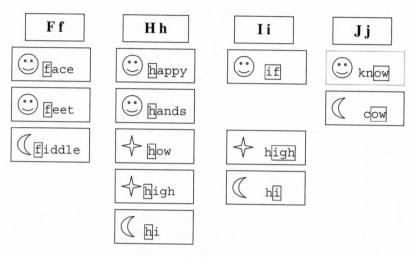

Note: The words in this example come from the children's poems *If You're Happy and You Know It, Twinkle Twinkle Little Star*, and *The Cow and the Fiddle*.

the same highlighted letters (Moustafa 1997; Moustafa and Maldonado-Colon 1999). (See figure 12-5.) As children learn more and more letter-sound correspondences in more and more stories, the logos help them remember the context the words were taken from. Grouping words that have the same highlighted letters helps children make letter-sound generalities based on their own experiences. More important, they are never misled by inconsistent letter-sound rules.

Beyond Instruction: Access to Books

While instructional materials and instruction are important, they are not sufficient. Children and their caretakers need access to engaging, age-appropriate books. Children who are read to become better readers (Feitelson and Goldstein 1986; Feitelson, Kita, and Goldstein 1986; Heath 1982, 1983; Wells 1985, 1986). Children who read more, become better readers (Anderson, Wilson, and Fielding 1988; Mullis, Campbell, and Farstrup 1993).

All this requires books. Children in poor communities in the United States have less access to age-appropriate books both at home and in school and public libraries (Kozol 1991; McQuillan et al. 1997; Smith, Constantino, and Krashen 1997). Smith, Constantino, and Krashen (1997), for example, found children living in Watts and Compton, two economically depressed areas in the Los Angeles area, had an average of .04 and 2.67 age-appropriate books in their homes while children living in neighboring Beverly Hills had an average of 199.2 age-appropriate books in their homes (see figure 12-6). They also found that the school and public libraries serving these economically depressed communities had far fewer books than the libraries serving the high-income community.

Access to age-appropriate books is a powerful predictor of reading achievement (Elley 1992; Krashen 1995; McQuillan 1996). Krashen (1995), for example, found a significant positive correlation between the quality of each state's school libraries and its 1992 fourth-grade National Assessment of Educational Progress (NAEP) reading score, regardless of how much money the educational system spent per pupil. When students with limited access to books are provided with access to books, there is significant growth in literacy (Elley 1991; Elley and Mangubhai 1983; Gambrell 1996).

The Shift Back to Traditional Reading Instruction

As research was making new discoveries about how children learn to read, education policies consistent with contemporary reading instruction were coming into place. An example of this was the California 1987 English language arts framework written by practicing reading-language arts specialist educators. However, beginning in 1995 government policies began a rapid shift back to traditional reading instruction. The two most influential instruments in this shift were the 1992 and 1994 NAEP reading scores and National Institute of Child Health and Human Development (NICHD) Houston study on reading.

National Assessment of Educational Progress Reading Scores

In 1993 the NAEP began reporting fourth-grade reading scores state by state rather than as a single national score. When the 1992 and 1994 NAEP reading scores were disaggregated state by state, California fared poorly relative to the other participating states. California's contemporary reading instructional policy, first in place in California in 1990 when textbooks consistent with contemporary reading instruction were first

Figure 12-6. *Number of Age-Appropriate Books per Home by Neighborhood*

Number of books

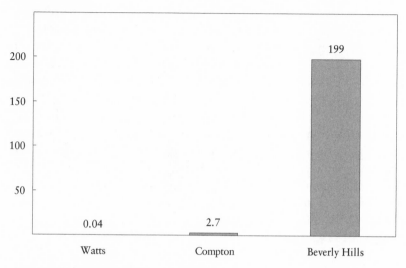

Source: Smith, Constantino, and Krashen 1997.

available in the classrooms, was blamed for California's low NAEP reading scores.

California's 1992 and 1994 NAEP scores were used to discredit contemporary reading instruction and promote traditional reading instruction in California and around the nation. The scores were used to abruptly withdraw California's contemporary language arts framework and begin a process that led to a new framework that advocates decodable stories in lieu of predictable stories. The scores were cited when California laws designed to implement traditional reading instruction were written.

Since the states that had the highest NAEP reading scores in 1992 and 1994—New Hampshire in 1992 and Maine in 1994—also had contemporary reading instructional policies, the reasons for California's poor showing relative to the other participating states must lie elsewhere. With the exception of New Mexico, California has the largest percentage of students who are nonnative speakers of English of any state that participates in the NAEP. While 24 percent of California's students are limited English proficient, fewer than 2 percent of the students in most states are limited English proficient. It takes five to seven years, under ideal circumstances, for nonnative speakers of English to achieve in English at levels equal to their native English-speaking peers (Collier 1989). Yet, the NAEP includes the scores of limited English-proficient children who have been in U.S. schools three or more years with the scores of native speakers of English. Because, by definition, limited English-proficient children do not do as well as English-proficient children in tests in English, including the scores of a large number of limited English-proficient children with those of English-proficient children affects California's scores on the NAEP reading assessment.

Evidence that California's NAEP reading scores are affected by the inclusion of the limited English-proficient children's scores with those of nonlimited English-proficient children's scores can be seen in California's statewide assessment. When the state-mandated Stanford 9 reading scores of the nonlimited English-proficient students are disaggregated from the scores of the limited English-proficient students, the average statewide scores of the nonlimited English-proficient students are at national norms (Moustafa 1999).[5]

The National Institute of Child Health and Human Development Houston Study on Reading

During the 1994–95 school year, under the auspices of the NICHD, Foorman and colleagues studied the effect of various types of reading instruction on the reading achievement of low-achieving, economically disadvantaged, first- and second-grade children in a school district near Houston, Texas. Foorman, a professor at the University of Texas-Houston Medical Center, and her associates used a research design where teachers were trained to use one of three reading instruction programs and data were collected on three to eight children in each of the classrooms of the teachers that had been trained. The programs the teachers were trained in were: (1) Collections for Young Scholars, commonly referred to as Open Court Reading (1995), a traditional parts-to-whole program that emphasizes phonemic awareness, phonics rules taught out of context, and decodable text; (2) the researcher's version of Hiebert and colleagues' (1992) program; and (3) the researcher's version of the district's contem-

5. Test data on California's annual statewide assessments are released every June 30; scores for July 1998–July 2001 are available from the California Department of Education, www.cde.ca.gov.

porary instruction in place before the time of the study. Other classrooms in the district continued using the contemporary instruction in place in the district before the time of the study.

Foorman and her colleagues found the children in the study receiving the Open Court instruction improved in word reading at a faster rate than the children receiving the other types of instruction. Based on this finding, they concluded that the "[r]esults show advantages for reading instructional programs that emphasize explicit instruction in the alphabetic principle for at-risk children."

There were many problems with the research. One problem was the groups were not comparable: the classrooms using Open Court instruction were mostly in schools where fewer students were economically disadvantaged than the classrooms using the other types of instruction, especially the ongoing contemporary instruction. Consistent with this, the children in the classrooms with Open Court instruction had higher pretest scores than the children in the other classrooms. Another problem was the data on the different groups were intermingled. The data on second-grade students who had been in the district's ongoing contemporary classrooms when they were in first grade but in the Open Court classrooms in second grade were averaged into the data of the students who had received only the Open Court instruction (Foorman et al. 1998, tables 1, 3, 4, and 5, and all figures). Most problematic of all was the operational definition of reading employed by Foorman and her colleagues. They equated pronouncing print words out of context with reading.

At the end of the six-month study, despite their greater economic disadvantage and their lower pretest scores, the children in the ongoing contemporary instruction classrooms answered comprehension questions about narrative and expository text they had read silently better than the children in the Open Court classrooms (Foorman et al. 1998, table 5). If reading is pronouncing print words, it could be concluded that traditional reading instruction is more effective than contemporary reading instruction. However, if reading is making sense of print, the Houston study demonstrates that contemporary reading instruction is more effective. Coles (2000), Taylor (1998), and Taylor and colleagues (2000) offer more in-depth analyses of the Houston study.

Before the Houston research had been peer reviewed and before its central finding had been replicated, it was widely reported in the press, presented to the California State Assembly Education Committee, and used to influence policy across the nation. One typical newspaper article entitled

"Study: Phonics Is the Best Way of Learning to Read" quoted Foorman as saying: "We discovered that (phonics) children were 6.03 times as likely to be reading more than one word at the end of the year than whole-language children."[6] In May 1999, a year before it was submitted for peer review to the Journal of Educational Psychology, Foorman and G. R. Lyon, chief of the Child Behavior and Development Branch of the NICHD, presented it to the California State Assembly Education Committee. Shortly after that California passed a law requiring professional development for K–3 teachers to focus on traditional phonics instruction. A year before it was published it was used as the research basis of the Reading Excellence Act, a federal law that also promoted traditional phonics instruction.

The research community was not allowed to review the Houston research, despite repeated requests, until after it had been used to justify legislation (Taylor 1998). The purpose of peer review is to identify problems in research. Taylor et al. (2000) point out that findings from the study that were presented before its publication were apparently called into question during the peer review since they did not appear in the published version of the study.

The Houston study, like the NAEP reports, has been used to marginalize replicated research and the expertise of practicing reading-language arts specialist educators. In 1996, when reading-language arts specialist educators in California recommended that Open Court not be put on the list of state-adopted textbooks, the California State Board of Education overruled the specialists and added Open Court to the list. Newspapers proclaimed Open Court and other traditional parts-to-whole reading programs research-based and urged their adoption for schools with low test scores.[7] Many schools with low standardized test scores have done so.

This policy shift has not been inconsequential. The major finding of the 2000 NAEP reading assessment is that the scores of the children in the bottom 10th percentile were significantly lower in 2000 than in 1992. The authors of the 2000 NAEP reading assessment stated that "this indicates that lower-performing students have lost ground" (Donahue et al. 2000).

---

6. "Study: Phonics Is the Best Way of Learning to Read," *Oakland Tribune*, February 19, 1997, p. A–5.

7. For example, see K. M. Downey, M. Parks, and J. Clayton, "Reading Plans That Work," *Los Angeles Times*, Orange County editorial section, August 8, 1999, p. M4.

Conclusion

Independent, replicated research has produced new instructional techniques that have the power to propel us forward to new levels of literacy achievement. However, in an era where the government is paying more attention to education, all too often money is being spent to support less effective rather than more effective reading instruction, especially for our lowest performing schools. Money that could be spent, for example, on providing classrooms with predictable books for beginning reading instruction or on providing economically disadvantaged children access to engaging, age-appropriate books is instead being spent on traditional reading instructional materials and teacher training in traditional reading instruction.

Traditional reading instruction did not promote universal literacy in the past. It will not promote it now. If we do not use what we have learned from independent, replicated research, we are doomed to repeat the past. In the short term, children in schools with low test scores will lose the most. In the long term, we all will lose.

References

Adams, M. 1990. *Beginning to Read: Thinking and Learning about Print*. MIT Press.

Allington, R. 1997. "Overselling Phonics." *Reading Today* 15 (August/September): 15–16.

Anderson, R. C., I. A. G. Wilkinson, and J. M. Mason. 1991. "A Microanalysis of the Small-Group Guided Reading Lesson: Effects of an Emphasis on Global Story Meaning." *Reading Research Quarterly* XXVI: 417–41.

Anderson, R. C., P. T. Wilson, and L. G. Fielding. 1988. "Growth in Reading and How Children Spend Their Time Outside of School." *Reading Research Quarterly* XXIII: 285–303.

Bailey, M. H. 1967. "The Utility of Phonic Generalizations in Grades One through Six." *Reading Teacher* 20: 413–18.

Berdiansky, B., B. Cronnell, and J. Koehler. 1969. "Spelling-Sound Relations and Primary Form-Class Descriptions for Speech Comprehension Vocabularies of 6–9 Year Olds." Technical Report No. 15. Los Alamitos, Calif.: Southwest Regional Laboratory for Educational Research and Development.

Bruce, D. J. 1964. "The Analysis of Word Sound." *British Journal of Educational Psychology* 34: 158–70.

Burmeister, L. E. 1968. "Usefulness of Phonic Generalizations." *Reading Teacher* 21: 349–56.

Bus, A. C., and M. H. van Ijzendoorn. 1999. "Phonological Awareness and Early Reading: A Meta-Analysis of Experimental Training Studies." *Journal of Educational Psychology* 91 (3): 403–14.

Cantrell, S.C. 1999. "Effective Teaching and Literacy Learning: A Look Inside Primary Classrooms." *Reading Teacher* 52 (4): 370–78.

Collier, V. P. 1989. "How Long? A Synthesis of Research on Academic Achievement in a Second Language." *TESOL Quarterly* 23 (3): 509–31.

Clymer, T. 1964. "The Utility of Phonic Generalizations in the Primary Grades." *Reading Teacher* 16: 252–58.

Coles, G. 2000. *Misreading Reading: The Bad Science That Hurts Children.* Portsmouth, N.H.: Heinemann.

Cohen, D. 1968. "The Effect of Literature on Vocabulary and Reading Achievement." *Elementary English* 45: 209–13, 217.

Cullinan, B., A. Jaggar, and D. Strickland. 1974. "Language Expansion for Black Children in the Primary Grades: A Research Report." *Young Children* 29: 98–112.

Donahue, P. L., R. J. Finnegan, A. D. Lutkus, N. L. Allen, and J. R. Campbell. 2000. *The Nation's Report Card: Fourth-Grade Reading 2000.* Washington: National Center for Education Studies.

Eldredge, J. L., D. R. Reutzel, and P. M. Hollingsworth. 1996. "Comparing the Effectiveness of Two Oral Reading Practices: Round-Robin Reading and the Shared Book Experience." *Journal of Literacy Research* 28 (2): 201–25.

Elley, W. 1991. "Acquiring Literacy in a Second Language: The Effect of Book-Based Programs." *Language Learning* 41 (3): 375–411.

———. 1992. *How in the World Do Students Read? The IEA Study of Reading Literacy.* The Hague, Netherlands: International Associations for the Evaluation of Education Achievement.

Elley, W., and F. Mangubhai. 1983. "The Impact of Reading on Second Language Learning." *Reading Research Quarterly* XIX: 53–67.

Emans, R. 1967. "The Usefulness of Phonic Generalizations above the Primary Grades." *Reading Teacher* 20: 419–25.

Fayden, T. 1997. "What Is the Effect of Shared Reading on Rural Native American and Hispanic Kindergarten Children?" *Reading Improvement* 34: 22–30.

Feitelson, D., and Z. Goldstein. 1986. "Patterns of Book Ownership and Reading to Young Children in Israeli School-Oriented and Nonschool-Oriented Families." *Reading Teacher* 39: 924–30.

Feitelson, D., B. Kita, and Z. Goldstein. 1986. "Effects of Listening to Series Stories on First Graders' Comprehension and Use of Language." *Research in the Teaching of English* 20: 339–56.

Foorman, B. R., D. J. Francis, J. M. Fletcher, C. Schatschneider, and P. Mehta. 1998. "The Role of Instruction in Learning to Read: Preventing Reading Failure in At-Risk Children." *Journal of Education Psychology* 90 (1): 37–55.

Freppon, P. 1991. "Children's Concepts of the Nature and Purpose of Reading in Different Instructional Settings." *Journal of Reading Behavior* 23 (2): 139–63.

Gambrell, L. B. 1996. "Creating Classroom Cultures That Foster Reading Motivation." *Reading Teacher* 50 (1): 14–25.

Goodman, K. 1965. "A Linguistic Study of Cues and Miscues in Reading." *Elementary English* 42: 639–43.

Goswami, U. 1986. "Children's Use of Analogy in Learning to Read: A Developmental Study." *Journal of Experimental Child Psychology* 42: 73–83.

———. 1988. "Orthographic Analogies and Reading Development." *Quarterly Journal of Experimental Psychology* 40 A (2): 239–68.

Goswami, U., and P. Bryant. 1990. *Phonological Skills and Learning to Read.* Hillsdale, N.J.: Lawrence Erlbaum.

Goswami, U., and F. Mead. 1992. "Onset and Rime Awareness and Analogies in Reading." *Reading Research Quarterly* 27: 150–62.

Heald-Taylor, G. 1987. "How to Use Predictable Books for K–2 Language Arts Instruction." *Reading Teacher* 40: 656–61.

Heath, S. 1982. "What No Bedtime Story Means: Narrative Skills at Home and School." *Language in Society* II: 49–76.

———. 1983. *Ways with Words.* Cambridge University Press.

Hiebert, E. H., J. M. Colt, S. L. Catto, and E. C. Gary. 1992. "Reading and Writing of First-Grade Students in a Restructured Chapter 1 Program." *American Educational Research Journal* 29: 545–72.

Holdaway, D. 1979. *The Foundations of Literacy.* Portsmouth, N.H.: Heinemann.

———. 1982. "Shared Book Experience: Teaching Reading Using Favorite Books." *Theory into Practice* 21: 293–300.

Kozol, J. 1991. *Savage Inequalities.* Crown.

Krashen, S. 1995. "School Libraries, Public Libraries, and the NAEP Reading Scores." *School Library Media Quarterly* 23: 235–37.

———. 1999a. "Effects of Phonemic Awareness Training on Delayed Tests of Reading." *Perceptual and Motor Skills* 89: 79–82.

———. 1999b. "Training in Phonemic Awareness: Greater on Test of Phonemic Awareness." *Perceptual and Motor Skills* 89: 412–16.

Kucer, S. B. 1985. "Predictability and Readability: The Same Rose with Different Names?" In *Claremont Reading Conference Forty-Ninth Yearbook*, edited by M. Douglass, 229–46. Claremont, Calif.: Claremont Graduate School.

Larrick, N. 1987. "Illiteracy Starts Too Soon." *Phi Delta Kappan* 69: 184–89.

Liberman, I., D. Shankweiler, F. W. Fischer, and B. Carter. 1974. "Explicit Syllable and Phoneme Segmentation in the Young Child." *Journal of Experimental Child Psychology* 18: 201–12.

McQuillan, J. 1996. "SAT Verbal Scores and the Library: Predicting High School Reading Achievement in the United States." *Indiana Media Journal* 18 (3): 65–70.

McQuillan, J., N. LeMoine, E. Brandlin, and B. O'Brien. 1997. "The (Print-) Rich Get Richer: Library Access in Low- and High-Achieving Elementary Schools." *California Reader* 30 (2): 23–25.

Moustafa, M. 1995. "Children's Productive Phonological Recoding." *Reading Research Quarterly* 30 (3): 464–76.

———. 1997. *Beyond Traditional Phonics: Research Discoveries and Reading Instruction.* Portsmouth, N.H.: Heinemann.

———. 1999. "Report Card on California's Standardized Testing and Reporting (STAR) Program: When Is Public Information Misinformation?" *California Reader* 32 (3): 26–27.

Moustafa, M., and E. Maldonado-Colon. 1999. "Whole-to-Parts Phonics Instruction: Building on What Children Know to Help Them Know More." *Reading Teacher* 52 (5): 448–58.

Mullis, I., J. Campbell, and A. Farstrup. 1993. *NAEP 1992 Reading Report Card for the Nation and the States*. Washington: National Center for Education Statistics.

Nicholson, T. 1991. "Do Children Read Words Better in Context or in Lists? A Classic Study Revisited." *Journal of Educational Psychology* 83: 444–50.

Nicholson, T., C. Lillas, and M. A. Rzoska. 1988. "Have We Been Misled by Miscues?" *Reading Teacher* 42: 6–10.

Open Court Reading. 1995. *Collections for Young Scholars*. Chicago and Peru, Ill.: SRA/McGraw-Hill.

Reutzel, D. R., and R. B. Cooter. 1990. "Whole Language: Comparative Effects on First-Grade Reading Achievement." *Journal of Educational Research* 83: 252–57.

Rhodes, L. K. 1979. "Comprehension and Predictability: An Analysis of Beginning Reading Materials." In *New Perspectives on Comprehension*, edited by J. Harste and R. Carey, 100–30. Monograph in Language and Reading Studies. Bloomington: Indiana University School of Education.

Ribowsky, H. 1986. "The Comparative Effects of a Code Emphasis Approach and a Whole Language Approach upon Emergent Literacy of Kindergarten Children." Ph.D. dissertation, New York University.

Richeck, M. A., and McTague, B. K. 1988. "The 'Curious George' Strategy for Students with Reading Problems." *Reading Teacher* 42: 220–26.

Rosner, J. 1974. "Auditory Analysis Training with Prereaders." *Reading Teacher* 27: 379–84.

Ruddell, R. B. 1965. "The Effect of Oral and Written Patterns of Language Structure on Reading Comprehension." *Reading Teacher* 18: 270–75.

Sacks, C. H., and J. R. Mergendoller. 1997. "The Relationship between Teachers' Theoretical Orientation toward Reading and Student Outcomes in Kindergarten Children with Different Initial Reading Abilities." *American Educational Research Journal* 34 (4): 721–39.

Scholes, R. J. 1998. "The Case against Phonemic Awareness." *Journal of Research in Reading* 21 (3): 177–89.

Slaughter, J. P. 1983. "Big Books for Little Kids: Another Fad or a New Approach for Teaching Beginning Reading?" *Reading Teacher* 36: 758–61.

Smith, C., R. Constantino, and S. Krashen. 1997. "Difference in Print Environment for Children in Beverly Hills, Compton, and Watts." *Emergency Librarian* 24 (4): 8–9.

Stanovich, K. E. 1986. "Mathew Effects in Reading: Some Consequences of Individual Differences in the Acquisition of Literacy." *Reading Research Quarterly* 21 (4): 360–406.

———. 1991. "Word Recognition: Changing Perspectives." In *Handbook of Reading Research*, vol. 2, edited by R. Barr, M. L. Kamil, P. Mosenthal, and P. D. Pearson, 418–52. Hillsdale, N.J.: Lawrence Erlbaum.

Tatham, S. 1970. "Reading Comprehension of Materials Written with Select Oral Language Patterns: A Study at Grades Two and Four." *Reading Research Quarterly* V: 402–26.

Taylor, B. M., R. C. Anderson, K. H. Au, and T. E. Raphael. 2000. "Discretion in the Translation of Reading Research to Policy." *Educational Researcher* 29 (6): 16–26.

Trachtenburg, P., and A. Ferruggia. 1989. "Big Books from Little Voices: Reaching High Risk Beginning Readers." *Reading Teacher* 42: 284–89.

Treiman, R. 1983. "The Structure of Spoken Syllables: Evidence from Novel Word Games." *Cognition* 15: 49–74.

———. 1985. "Onsets and Rimes as Units of Spoken Syllables: Evidence from Children." *Journal of Experimental Child Psychology* 39: 161–81.

Troia, G.A. 1999. "Phonological Awareness Intervention Research: A Critical Review of the Experimental Methodology." *Reading Research Quarterly* 34 (1): 28–52.

Tunmer, W. E., and A. R. Nesdale. 1985. "Phonemic Segmentation Skill and Beginning Reading." *Journal of Educational Psychology* 77: 417–27.

Wells, G. 1985. "Preschool Literacy-Related Activities and Success in School." In *Literacy, Language and Learning*, edited by D. R. Olson, N. Torrance, and A. Hildyard, 229–255. Cambridge University Press.

———. 1986. *The Meaning Makers*. Portsmouth, N.H.: Heinemann.

CHAPTER THIRTEEN

Does State and Federal Reading Policymaking Matter?

RICHARD L. ALLINGTON

There seem few contested areas of education that can equal the "reading wars" in various attributes: its sheer *longevity*, which is the topic of Diane Ravitch's discussion in chapter 10 of this volume; the *vitriol*, which William Lowe Boyd and Douglas Mitchell focus on in the chapter that follows here; and its *importance*, which has been aptly described in P. D. Pearson's "The Politics of Reading Research and Practice" (1997). Every thirty years or so, it seems, a very public yet personal debate about the nature of appropriate reading instruction emerges in the media and in the policy talk in legislative venues (Langer and Allington 1992). This "code-emphasis" versus "meaning-emphasis" dichotomous debate wears on the teaching profession at the same time that it sells newspapers and advances political careers and agendas.

Once again the education profession and the larger public are enmeshed in the latest incarnation of this long-standing debate. Once again policymakers can be found crafting mandates for particular types of instructional materials and particular pedagogies. But to what end?

The recent research on educational policymaking and, especially, the research on policy implementation and impacts provides at least a glimpse of the likely impact the flurry of recent policies may have on educational practice. And that glimpse suggests that current educational practice will survive largely unaltered except at the margins (McGill-Franzen 2000).

The Recent Policymaking Context

A most significant but hardly discussed shift in American education policy is embedded in the new content standards, which mandate that the new standards apply to all students, not just the college bound. The goal of achievement of high academic standards for all students represents, perhaps, the most significant shift in educational policy of the twentieth century. For most of the century educational policy was dominated by the expectations of the "normal curve." For most of the century high academic achievement was expected only from a small proportion of the student population—perhaps 25 percent of all students—and educational practice followed a "slow it down" policy for students whose intellectual capacity was deemed "below average" (Allington 1991). This policy meant reduced academic expectations and a watered-down core curriculum for many students. When high-stakes assessments were initiated in the 1970s, they were minimum competency assessments designed to ensure that most students achieved some very basic curriculum goals. But meeting even these minimum goals—a third-grade reading level at the end of sixth grade, for instance—proved impossible for some students. No state education agency ever reported that all students achieved the minimum basic skill standards, but most states reported slow, steady progress toward that goal. Nonetheless, in most states at least one in five students failed to demonstrate even the basic skill proficiencies.

Perhaps because progress in meeting the older basic standards was proceeding ever so slowly, educational policymakers dramatically shifted the goals. The most influential move may have been the modification of the National Assessment of Educational Progress (NAEP), along with the concomitant development of the new reporting policies (Pellegrino et al. 1999). The reading assessment was reconfigured with an emphasis on assessing "thoughtful literacy," primarily through extended response items that required students to summarize, analyze, and evaluate the information provided in the longer, authentic texts that now composed the reading test. The modification of the NAEP texts and tasks produced a new sort of assessment that was substantially different from the multiple-choice focused traditional standardized test of reading achievement. It was a shift from locating and matching information found in the test texts to tasks that focused more on student understanding of the texts and their ability to organize and evaluate the textual information they encountered.

The shift from simply reporting average student performances on the NAEP to reporting achievement in terms of the percentage of students who achieved the newly created proficiency standards produced dramatically more negative media accounts of American student achievement (Berliner and Biddle 1996). American students' reading achievement did not actually decline, but only about one-quarter of the students were reported meeting the new "proficient" standard and fewer than half met the "basic" standard. Of course, the new benchmarks were simply wishful thinking on the part of policymakers—wishful in that there was no evidence that such standards could be achieved by all students (or even most students)—and the process of standard setting was, itself, deemed substantially flawed by the National Research Council (NRC) and the General Accounting Office (Pellegrino et al. 1999; GAO 1993). But promoting higher achievement was high on policymakers' agendas.

A variety of proposals was developed to foster achievement of these new standards by all students. The federal report, *Time to Learn* (National Committee on Time and Learning 1994), proposed extending the school day and school year for lower-achieving students in order to provide the additional instructional time thought needed by some students to acquire the desired proficiencies. The report noted that, traditionally, instructional time was a constant across students and, thus, learning outcomes varied. In seeming recognition of the tradition of the normal curve, the report argued that to achieve high common academic standards would require that schools provide some students with larger quantities of instructional time through after-school and summer school programs. This represented a shift from the "slow it down" policies that had dominated educational planning (and expectations) for students who found school learning more difficult than many of their peers.

Shortly thereafter the National Commission on Teaching and America's Future released their report, *Doing What Matters Most: Investing in Quality Teaching* (Darling-Hammond 1997), which argued that achieving the new standards would only occur if there was a substantial investment in modifying both preservice and in-service teacher preparation and support. At the crux of the argument was the assertion that few teachers knew how to create classroom environments that fostered the new standards and few school organizations were designed to foster such learning. A second, and implicit, theme of that report was that doing more of the same—adding a few extra hours of traditional instruction each week—was unlikely to produce the desired broader achievement of the new higher standards.

At the same time such proposals were being released there was a flurry of policymaking at the state and federal levels targeted to improve reading achievement. The reauthorization of both the Improving America's Schools Act and the Individuals with Disabilities Education Act (IDEA) stimulated legislative actions that both upped the ante for programmatic demonstrations of positive effects on student achievement and also broadened the population of students who were to achieve these standards. Testimony provided during both reauthorization debates featured an emphasis on using "scientifically proven" practices and "systemic reform" models to better deploy federal funding (for example, Sweet 1997). Passage of the Obey-Porter Comprehensive School Improvement Act restricted funding to those agencies targeting "proven programs." Added into this mix was a steady push for allowing federal funds to be used in any of several plans to increase "parental choice" through the use of federal funds as vouchers or to introduce "free market" economic principles in support of the development of charter schools.

In 1997 federal legislation was passed creating a National Reading Panel that was charged with the responsibility to "assess the status of research-based knowledge, including the effectiveness of various approaches to teaching children to read." In 1998 the NRC released its report, *Preventing Reading Difficulties in Young Children,* which called for a "truce" in the "reading wars" and offered what was dubbed a "balanced" view of the nature of effective early reading instruction (Snow, Burns, and Griffin 1998). *Teaching Children to Read,* the report of the National Reading Panel (2000), continued that theme but neither report quelled the long-standing debate (compare with Garan 2001, Gee 1999).

The NRC report was followed by passage of the Reading Excellence Act (REA) that provided competitive funding for innovations developed from "scientifically based reading research." In addition to the federal actions, legislation concerning early reading instruction was also on the agenda at the state level with more than one hundred bills legislating particular sorts of beginning reading instruction introduced during the 1990s (Paterson 2000). Often similar themes—research-based, explicit and systematic teaching, high standards—were mirrored in this legislation. In much of this policymaking one can locate the assumption that there exists a research base on effective reading instruction that has been largely ignored by curriculum developers, teacher educators, administrators, teachers, and policymakers.

However, little evidence has been provided that supports the assertion that research-based principles have been ignored in the design of beginning reading instruction or in the preparation of elementary school teachers. On the other hand, there has been a masterful public relations campaign that has "fabricated" or "manufactured" a media consensus supporting such assumptions (Allington 1999; Allington and Woodside-Jiron 1999; Coles 2000; Dressman 1999; Taylor 1998).

This sketch of key policymaking activity focused on improving American reading achievement illustrates the intense interest in this policy arena. Much of the legislation and policymaking has focused almost solely on redesigning beginning reading instruction. That is, little interest has been shown in the nature of reading instruction provided to older elementary, middle school, or high school students (or adults). Personally, I find this early emphasis odd if for no other reason than the fact that American elementary students fare far better in international comparisons of students' reading achievement (and also in math and science achievement) than do older students (Elley 1992). The fact that American nine-year-olds ranked second in the world on reading proficiency (while older students ranked far lower) in the most recent international assessment suggests that elementary students in this country are reading reasonably proficiently compared to international peers. Likewise, there have been significant improvements in fourth-grade students' reading performances on the NAEP since 1990. At higher grade levels the reading gains are neither as consistent nor as large as those achieved by elementary school students (Donahue et al. 1999).

These data might suggest that policies on beginning reading implemented earlier were having a positive effect on achievement. This would include the shift (between 1985 and 1995) away from more heavily scripted instructional approaches with their emphasis on traditional, segmented skills teaching to beginning reading materials that emphasized an integrated approach to reading and language arts curriculum design along with an emphasis on reducing vocabulary controls so that better quality texts could be used in beginning reading instruction. Thus, between the 1989 California and the 1993 Texas reading textbook adoptions, virtually all the large textbook publishers shifted to curriculum materials that offered integrated language arts instruction with an emphasis on providing students with access to high-quality children's literature, as required by the curricular mandates in those states. By the 1994–95 school year, almost all commercial curriculum materials reflected this trend. In addition, there was a small movement away from relying primarily on commercial curriculum packages as the framework for delivering reading and language arts instruction. In a series of surveys of elementary teachers it was consistently reported that about 20 percent of teachers made little, if any, use of commercial materials; they relied, instead, on children's literature as the primary curriculum (Baumann et al. 1998; Canney 1993; Strickland and Walmsley 1994). But about 80 percent of the teachers reported that they did use commercial reading series, although most reported some blending of use of both the reading series and children's books in their lessons.

So, if American elementary students' reading achievement has been rising, and it has, why all the concern about changing beginning reading instruction on the part of policymakers? There are four explanations that seem most viable.

First, while American elementary school students' reading achievement has been improving, there remain large numbers of children who still are failing to acquire real reading proficiency (as is the case in all nations). These children are most often poor and, because children from ethnic minority groups are more often poor, minority children are overrepresented in the pool of lower achieving students. In addition, the largest concentrations of poor children reside in our urban centers, the major media markets. Thus the difficulties that urban school districts, especially, have in promoting high levels of achievement have been highlighted in the media.

Second, the widespread misunderstanding of the reconfiguration of the NAEP and the shift in reporting results created the impression that reading achievement has declined. That is, when federal agencies report that approximately half of the students tested failed to achieve the "basic" level on the NAEP in reading, public concern is heightened (the difficulties with the proficiency levels notwithstanding).

Third, many of the earlier reforms violated the "grammar of schooling" (Tyack and Cuban 1995). When Johnny suddenly stopped having weekly spelling tests, when "emergent" writing was fostered and the misspellings were not marked in red ink, when talking about the story read replaced many of the worksheets that children had long labored over, and when cooperative activities began to replace competition, many parents questioned the legitimacy of the new instructional designs. The public preference for educational design would likely have beginning reading instruction that looked more traditional—more like what most adults had experienced. When the media misreported the low ranking of California on the NAEP state-by-state comparisons[1] to mean that reading achieve-

1. McQuillan (1996, 1998) and others have provided several analyses of the California NAEP reports and noted that ranking near the bottom of the participating states is not the

ment in that state had experienced some precipitous decline with the advent of this new instructional design, public concern about the effectiveness the integrated, literature-based curriculum plans emerged. These concerns were particularly evident in organizations of "cultural conservatives" who had long worried about the direction of American education (Gaddy, Hall, and Marzano 1996; Paterson 1998).

Fourth, there is the potential for substantial profit that would accrue to some corporations and some individual reform advocates if particular policies are put into place. The potential profits might come from any of several sources. For instance, the four corporations that now dominate reading textbook publishing (McGraw-Hill, ScottForesman, Houghton-Mifflin, and Harcourt) stand to profit from increased sales if the new basal readers series move again into a dominating instructional role and schools replace existing series with the newer ones that reflect the manufactured research consensus. In addition, the reform advocates identified with curricular materials produced by those publishers would also benefit financially from increased sales revenues.

Corporations like the Washington Post Companies, which owns Kaplan, eScore, and other such tutoring ventures, stand to benefit from an increased interest on the part of middle-class parents who want private tutoring to help their children meet the new, higher literacy standards.[2] Advantage Schools, Dreamcatchers, Sylvan, and other companies providing for-profit schooling and other educational services will benefit if confidence in public education is diminished and alternatives such as charter schools, vouchers, and tuition waivers are funded with public education funds. In other words, corporate America seems to have realized the substantial profit potential that exists in the education industry.[3]

In truth, no single-faceted argument adequately explains the current interest in policymaking concerning beginning reading instruction. Suffice it to say that literacy instructional policies are being promoted that are

---

same as declining performance. The NAEP reading performances of California children has remained stable in the assessments since 1992 (NCES 1999, 114–15). The analyses indicate that California has been plagued by low reading achievement since the passage of Proposition 13 in the 1970s. That legislation reduced education funding and effectively resulted in larger class sizes, lower teacher salaries, and more restricted access to libraries and books.

2. D. Machan, "Dr. Cram," *Forbes*, January 24, 2000, pp. 134–35.

3. P. Vine, "To Market, to Market: The School Business Sells Kids Short," *Nation*, September 8, 1997, p. 265.

not reliably supported by the research, and often the new policies are replacing older policies with little serious attention to the potential impacts of the policies being replaced or documenting the impacts of the new policymaking (Allington 1999; Coles 2000; McQuillan 1998; Pearson 1997; Pressley and Allington 1999; Taylor 1998). An interesting question is whether all this policymaking has the intended effect.

Policy Logic

It seems that educational policymaking proceeds on the assumption that implementing particular policies will have some intended effect. The policy logic for shaping beginning reading instruction seems to go something like this:

> If certain forms of pedagogical knowledge, instructional methods, and curriculum materials are mandated by policy, then (1) teachers will offer a particular type of beginning reading instruction that (2) will positively enhance student reading achievement in the both the short and longer term.

But is there evidence that would support that logic? If not, what sort of studies might provide such evidence? What is the nature of the effects of policy on educational practice? What difficulties will policy researchers have in garnering evidence that would support the attainment of intended effects? These questions are discussed in the sections that follow.

Studies Exploring the Effects of Policymaking in Beginning Reading Instruction

One fascinating aspect of policymaking is that it seems that few policymakers are actually interested in tracking the impact of the policies they create. Few pieces of educational legislation provide funds for the rigorous study of the effects of the policy being promoted. While some legislation includes funding for some sort of evaluation component, rarely is this funding sufficient to examine the intended effects in any rigorous manner. The federal Title I legislation, for instance, has historically required an evaluation component, but the funding available has been miserly and the resultant evaluation studies less than particularly useful (Slavin 1987). The same pattern holds true for the IDEA and the REA funding. Rarely does state education legislation provide any such funding.

Bills have been passed mandating that all teachers pass a test of knowledge of phonics terms and principles (Paterson 2000). But there are no studies that suggest that such legislation will result in teachers who teach differently or that the different sort of teaching that was imagined by the advocates of the policy produces improved reading achievement. And the legislation typically provides no funding to examine the potential relationship between policy and practice.

Likewise, legislation has been passed mandating the use of particular pedagogical approaches or materials in beginning reading with little or no funding to examine whether the mandates effectively altered beginning reading instruction and, if so, whether the altered instruction resulted in improved achievement, short or longer term.

Fortunately, the U.S. Office of Educational Research and Improvement (OERI) has been interested in such questions and has acted to fill the void in funding for studying the impacts of educational policymaking. Over the past decade OERI has funded a number of studies on the relationship between policy and practice, and some of those studies have focused on policies related to reading instruction.

Rand Change Agent Study

Perhaps the classic study in this area is the RAND Change Agent Study that examined beginning in the late 1970s the implementation of federally funded education initiatives (McLaughlin 1991). This multiyear, multisite study found that "it is exceedingly difficult to change practice" (147). There was little evidence that federal initiatives were implemented consistently or faithfully. Central to the problem was the limited capacity that many school organizations had for implementing the expected changes in educational programs. In other words, limited expertise hindered local education agencies even when federal funds were allocated to support innovation in the design and delivery of intervention programs for lower-achieving children and youth. McLaughlin concluded, "Policy can't mandate what matters. What matters most to policy outcomes are local capacity and will" (1991, 147). Timar and Kirp summarized the problem similarly: "Excellence cannot be coerced or mandated" (1987, 309). They argued that institutional capacity for implementing new educational initiatives had been seriously overestimated (alternatively, policymakers had underestimated the difficulty of building local capacity).

In many respects the RAND study reiterated Wildavsky's earlier admonition: "Telling people they have not achieved intended objectives does not necessarily help them discover what should be done" (1979, 7). He noted that if "school districts and their teachers, parents, and administrators really knew what would work and what wouldn't . . . and refused to put the successful strategies into effect, they would deserve condemnation" (312). Of course, the problem was that neither school district personnel nor policymakers had any clear evidence on just what would alleviate the problem of underachievement though. As Timar and Kirp noted, policies had been crafted, seemingly, from anecdotal evidence—from a "handful of success stories" to use their words (1987, 314). The problem as noted by Adam Urbanski, president of the American Federation of Teachers union in Rochester, New York, was that the needed "change in education is difficult. It means doing things differently, not just doing longer and harder what we already do. . . . The challenge of reform is not merely to buttress the schools we have but to invent schools we've never had" (1991, 29). And the available research rarely offers much evidence on what such schools might look like.

Much of the early policy implementation work was well summarized by Cohen and Spillane (1992), who argued that American traditions of decentralized educational decisions and distrust of centralized authority often undermined attempts to reform from a distance. But they also noted that there was little evidence that the press for more standardization in educational planning would actually result in higher achievement, especially achievement of higher-order learning goals. They concluded that the evidence suggested that even with common curriculum goals and common textbook usage teachers varied substantially on what was taught and how they taught. Ultimately, they argued, a "logic of confidence" replaced good evidence of rational relationships between educational resources, instructional processes, and achievement outcomes. In other words, there was little actual evidence of what worked to produce broad achievement of the new higher standards and less evidence that what worked in one locale was transportable to other locales.

Consortium for Policy Research in Education Studies

The early studies of policy effects produced a second wave of educational policy studies. The largest effort was carried out by the Consortium for Policy Research in Education (CPRE) with one series of studies examining the efforts to reform elementary school reading instruction (Elmore, Peterson, and McCarthy 1996). Three schools that had restructured in an attempt to foster higher achievement, particularly focused on developing children's thoughtful literacy proficiency, were studied extensively. The research team conducted sustained classroom observations combined with interviews and analyses of student learning in an attempt to better understand the efforts to reform. What they found was substantial reorganization of the schedule and patterns of assignment of students to classrooms but only modest modifications to the core instructional activities. In other words, the schools had moved to multiage assignment of students to classrooms, to larger blocks of time allocated to specific subject matter, and often to a more integrated approach to curriculum. But these changes in organizational patterns had minimal impacts on teaching. In most cases the teachers continued to teach in ways that they were familiar with—traditional teaching.

Elmore summarized the findings by noting that "it is unlikely that teachers who are not intrinsically motivated to engage in hard, uncertain work will learn to do so in large, anonymous organizations that do not intensify personal commitments and responsibilities" (1996, 25). But changing instructional practice is a demanding, risky business in a high-stakes assessment environment (Johnston et al. 1998; Miller 1995). Elmore noted that changing aspects of schooling that are distant from the core activities of teaching were more likely to be readily adopted than changes in those aspects central to the teaching and learning.

The Michigan Educational Policy and Practice Studies

This series of studies involved analyses of how school district personnel interpreted and implemented Michigan's new reading curriculum framework and the aligned high-stakes assessment that accompanied it. A central aspect was developing a better understanding of local variation in the implementation of the same policy mandate. Spillane (1998) points to the importance of individuals' beliefs about the nature of appropriate reading instruction in their interpretation and implementation of the policy mandates. In addition, different participants had access to different information sources on the policy mandate that influenced their understanding of what was to be done. But different participants who had access to the same sources of information often interpreted the policy differently based upon the particular situation they occupied and the beliefs they held about teaching and learning to read.

Jennings suggested that it was more appropriate to consider policy implementation as "an incident of teaching and learning, rather than as a process by which ideas are filtered through an educational system and enacted by practitioners" (1996, 107). In this case, the curricular framework was aligned with the new assessments, but the framework itself had little to offer teachers about the selection and use of texts during reading instruction. This assessment-driven reform then relied on teachers inventing instructional practices that led to improved achievement on the new assessments. The state's attempts at providing teachers with models of this new instruction, in Jennings's view, were largely fraught with problems as policymakers themselves disagreed on what instruction might look like and the explanatory sessions that were offered typically employed "old pedagogies and pieces of changed reading practices, not a coherent picture" (17).

Standerford (1997) studied implementation of the Michigan reforms in two school districts over a three-and-a-half-year period. She reported that "although all participants were making instructional changes, those changes were uneven and scattered within and across classrooms and districts" (84). The teachers reported, and were observed, attempting to understand the new model for reading instruction, but none felt that adequate information or support had been provided and changes attempted were rarely inconsistent with the teacher's prior knowledge or beliefs about the best ways to teach reading.

Again, these studies point to the difficulty of faithful policy implementation. Even when curricular frameworks are aligned with assessments and when a substantial coordinated effort is made to inform the public and the profession about the new policies, faithful implementation was difficult, at best. McGill-Franzen summarizes these studies by noting that "policymakers must find ways for policies to educate . . . teachers need opportunities to learn from policy. But what they learn from these opportunities depends also on what they bring to policy—their own knowledge and beliefs" (2000, 900).

The Texas Basal Adoption Studies

Texas has long had state-level control of the textbook adoption process. In 1993 Texas required the new reading series to (1) provide opportunities to read connected text rather than isolated skill workbooks; (2) provide an anthology of quality unabridged children's literature; (3) integrate reading with writing, listening, and speaking; along with (4) a systematic presentation of phonemic awareness (Hoffman et al. 1998). Analyses of the new series selected for adoption in Texas revealed that, compared to the older, skill-based series in use, vocabulary control had been largely abandoned in the newer series; thus the new series was found to be more engaging but also posing greater decoding difficulties for beginning readers. In addition, new procedures for introducing the story, for pacing the lessons, for grouping students, and for assessing student progress were also evident in the newer series (Hoffman and McCarthy 1995). Clearly, the adoption of the newer reading series posed challenges for teachers.

Hoffman and his colleagues (1998) studied the reading instructional beliefs and practices of teachers in four school districts while they were using the older skills-based series and after the adoption of the newer integrated, literature-based readers. They found significant differences in the instructional practices of individual teachers in both phases of the study. Instructional practices represented a continuum according to the use and role of various types of curriculum materials. Some teachers never used the reader series in either phase of the study. Some of these teachers relied on children's literature, others on isolated skills work materials. Other teachers followed the instructional manuals accompanying the series in both years, while others dipped into the manual and the series only occasionally. Some supplemented the reader series with children's literature and others supplemented with additional isolated skills work.

In addition, after the adoption of the new reader series some teachers continued to use the older series, while others used the newer series but ignored the instructional guidelines and offered lessons following the instructional model offered in the older reader series. Others continued to use children's literature exclusively and let the new series sit on the shelf.

Teachers' epistemological orientations were "determining factors" in how they organized reading instruction and how they responded to the changed curricular guidelines. Changing the curricular materials had little impact on epistemological orientations. Interestingly, the teachers commonly reported that the new materials had an impact on their students. But this impact was viewed as more motivational than achievement related. The teachers felt their children were no more skilled than in earlier years, but that the children were more interested in reading and reading independently.

Hoffman and his colleagues (1998) also noted that while school districts invested substantial funds in the purchase of new materials, none of those districts invested any significant funds in professional development activities intended to build teacher expertise about effective reading instruction. The typical teacher in their study participated in a single one- to three-hour publisher-sponsored workshop as preparation for implementing the new instructional framework.

Policy Analysis for California Studies

California policymaking has been much discussed, but the most coherent and informative studies of California policymaking and the effects of those policies have come from the Policy Analysis for California (PACE) research team. Carlos and Kirst (1997) provide a far-reaching descriptive analysis of the California educational policymaking across a decade. More focused on the political environment that fostered the policymaking than many policy studies, they describe the struggles between the state superintendent of instruction, the state board of education, the legislature, and the governor for control of educational policymaking. They note that the net effect was a reduced role for the Department of Education as legislative acts became more specific and state board directives more controlling. Carlos and Kirst note that "California's recent struggles in carrying out a continuous and coherent education reform agenda can be attributed largely to a fractured governance structure and the partisan conflicts and alliances that arise with each election" (19). California's reform effort has been a moving target that leaves teachers wondering just what the next "quick fix" might be.

Chrispeels (1997) argued that the earlier California policy initiatives (particularly the 1987 curriculum framework and the associated assessment development) had created a decade-long coherent policy environment that had an impact on practice. However, Freeman and Freeman (1998) offer a less optimistic view. They note that relatively few teachers participated in the capacity-building initiatives sponsored by the earlier California Literature Project—the primary effort to foster teacher understanding of the 1987 frameworks. They point out that while California school districts adopted the integrated, literature-based reading series the framework called for, many teachers misinterpreted the "whole language" framework to mean whole class instruction and had all children reading the same selection at the same time. In addition, because so much money had been allocated for the purchase of the new readers, little funding was available to build classroom collections of children's books and less was available to upgrade the quality of school library collection—collections that ranked among the poorest in the nation (McQuillan 1998).

In short, there is no clear evidence that suggests that the earlier California framework for reading was ever consistently implemented, although opponents have made much of assertions to the contrary. We do know that only a limited number of California teachers participated in any substantive professional development activity designed to enhance their capacity to teach in the manner envisioned in the 1987 framework. There seem to be no studies that assessed, on any large scale, the impact of that policymaking on instructional practice, just as there seems to be no such effort assessing the impact of the more recent California policymaking that represents what seems to be a complete about-face in policy direction.

The Center for Literature Teaching and Learning Studies

As educational policymakers moved to push the use of high-quality children's literature to the forefront of educational practice, the OERI funded the Center for Literature Teaching and Learning to engage in research on the impacts of literature-based instruction. A five-year study of the implementation of literature-based reading instruction in four higher-poverty school districts was completed. This study (Allington et al. 1996; Johnston et al. 1998) was unique in that the design was a 2 × 2 crossed model where two districts selected literature-based basal reader series and two elected to use children's literature as the primary curriculum materials. In addition, two districts (one basal and one books) were identified as operating under centralized decisionmaking, while the other two districts (one basal and one books) were identified as more decentralized in the decisionmaking patterns, especially as concerned the selection of curriculum materials and frameworks. This design was intended to separate the relative impact of organizational factors from curricular factors in the study of educational reform.

As in the CPRE study (Elmore et al. 1996), much of the "reform" involved restructuring schedules and student assignments to classrooms and providing different curriculum materials. However, in the long run it seems that organizational patterns of decisionmaking were more important than the nature of the curriculum materials. That is, in the districts where decisionmaking was more centralized there was less change and reading achievement actually declined modestly over the five-year study period. One district mandated the use of a commercial reader series, while the other mandated the use of children's literature. In the districts where decisionmaking was more decentralized—where large teacher committees made decisions about curricular issues—more consistent and positive change was observed and small improvements in reading achievement followed.

Nonetheless, even in the more decentralized settings, the pace of change in core instructional activities was limited. There was an observed decline in time allocated to low-level skills work and an increase in the amount of reading and writing that students completed. But even the most changed classrooms still looked remarkably similar in most respects after five years of reform activity. At the same time, professional development opportunities targeted to enhance teacher instructional capacity were enormously limited in three of the four districts. For instance, in neither district implementing a children's literature-based curriculum was there any professional development focused on enhancing teacher awareness of children's books (even though teachers indicated that a lack of familiarity was a significant problem for them).

Kentucky Educational Reform Act Studies

There were others who studied educational reform and arrived at similar conclusions. Holland (1998) reported on the responses of educators to the ambitious Kentucky Educational Reform Act (KERA). She noted that "change is not just about policies, or programs, or promises. It is an intensely personal decision to try something new. And to work, change depends on a broad belief that doing something differently will make it better" (26). But, in this case, policymakers changed direction "faster than a weather vane caught in a hurricane" (xxv). The shifting policy directives left teachers, administrators, and parents in a dither.

Guskey and Oldham (1997) provide a comprehensive review of the KERA policies and studies that suggests that there were literally no studies of the effects of reform policies on achievement. They also note that multiple individual KERA reforms were mandated with no evidence that the various components would actually work effectively when implemented as part of a systemic reform package. Indeed, the various components were often inconsistent with each another and implementation was uneven, distorted, and difficult. Wolf and her colleagues (2000) noted that human capital, in the form of curricular and instructional expertise, was inextricably linked to social capital, in the form of trust and risk-taking capacity, in those Kentucky schools where the reform efforts leveraged substantial change in local practice. In the end, however, shifts to multiage classes and the use of tables rather than desks were better documented than shifts in core instructional practice (Bridge 1994).

Other Smaller Scale Studies of Policy Implementation

Scharer (1992) reported on a study of teacher implementation of literature-based instruction following a district mandate. All teachers fell in the "skills emphasis" category of an inventory of teacher pedagogical orientation. She noted a gradual shift in instructional activities such that time allocated to isolated skills worksheets decreased as time allocated to independent, self-selected reading increased. Likewise basal reader series began to occupy less time as reading of children's literature occupied more. But teachers' lack of familiarity with children's books, the limited opportunities for collegial interaction and visits to other classrooms, their limited repertoires of organizational and instructional strategies, their preoccupation with "coverage" of basals or books, and the difficulties with evaluating students for report cards all proved substantial obstacles to implementation of new models of instruction. Limited local capacity (limited expertise, limited organizational support) effectively undermined even motivated efforts to change reading instructional practice.

Pace (1992) studied teachers in four school districts who were involved in "grassroots" implementation of "whole language literacy instruction." She suggests that "the tension between individual innovators and other teachers may be the most important factor to address in accomplishing classroom reform" (471). In every case she presents, teachers involved in the grassroots reform were powerfully affected by the responses of their peers. Half of the participants changed schools or grade levels or left teaching in order to avoid the conflicts involved in teaching differently. The remaining teachers curtailed their reforms and continued to struggle with their beliefs while continuing to use at least some traditional practices as an accommodation to their peers. As Pace notes, little attention has been paid to the influence of peers in the professional work environment on reforming educational practice.

Finally, Datnow and Castellano reported one consistent finding in their careful study of the implementation of a highly structured reform initiative. "Almost all teachers made adaptations to the program in spite of developers' demands to closely follow the model" (2000, 775). The abundant adaptations observed involved omitting complete lesson segments, adding lesson components, extending or reducing mandated instructional time allocations, and so on.

These small-scale studies reflect the findings of the larger studies of school and curricular reform, while also providing close examination of the process of reform. Together, the larger- and smaller-scale studies of attempts to alter classroom reading instruction suggest the substantial complexity involved in attempting to craft educational policies that will result in the intended changes and in attempting to study the effects of policy development.

Summary of the Studies of Policy Implementation

Most studies of the effects of educational policymaking have investigated only the first aspect of the policy logic: how policies affect instruction. The preponderance of the evidence available suggests that educational policymaking rarely, if ever, reliably achieves the intended shifts in instructional processes. If the policy logic set out earlier reflects the intention of policymakers, then the evidence available fails to support that aspect of the logic that suggests that mandates produce intended instructional changes. It seems that policymakers inevitably underestimate the difficulty of fostering complex change in large bureaucratic entities such as schools. Changing schools, especially changing the core aspects of instruction, is an enormously complex undertaking. Most studies of policy implementation never actually address the second aspect of policy logic: changed instruction will produce enhanced student achievement. Perhaps that is because the findings on implementation so consistently suggest that few policies are faithfully implemented.

How to Study the Effects of Policymaking on Student Achievement

Given the enormous interest in improving the academic achievement of American students and the enormous investments of money, time, and individual effort that accompany policymaking in this arena, it would seem that more attention might be paid to the design and funding of studies that address the impact of policymaking on student outcomes. However, such efforts will be complicated and expensive. A brief consideration follows of a few of the design concerns that must be addressed in order to effectively research the relationship between policymaking and student achievement.

Policy Consistency and the Problem of Time Lag

In much of research on educational policymaking, as illustrated by the studies of reading policymaking reviewed earlier indicate, the problem of "policy collisions"—policymaking that produces contradictory policy mandates—seems an important issue. That is, before the impact of one set of policies can be evaluated, a new set of policies that work at cross purposes is proposed. For instance, in both Texas and California earlier policies on beginning reading instruction were replaced by new policies that largely voided the earlier policies. In Texas reading achievement had risen steadily under the older policies, while in California there was no clear evidence on the effects of the earlier policy on student achievement (except perhaps that reading achievement was not rising significantly). In neither case was there much good evidence that the earlier policies had actually been widely and faithfully implemented.

Efforts to change instruction through policymaking are beset by the problem of time lag. In both Texas and California the guidelines for new instructional materials are developed several years in advance of the textbook adoption in order to allow publishers the opportunity to create instructional materials that respond to the new frameworks. The 1987 California framework led to the 1989 adoption of the integrated, literature-based reader series so that by the 1990–91 school year virtually all schools provided teachers with instructional materials that reflected the framework mandates. But the professional development opportunities designed to build local capacity to respond appropriately to the instructional dimensions of the framework had barely touched most teachers at that point. The 1993 release of state-by-state comparisons on the 1992 NAEP produced concern that the new framework was having negative effects on fourth-grade student achievement. By 1995, when the 1994 NAEP results were released, policies substantially altering the 1987 framework were already in the works.

Likewise, in Texas the new integrated, literature-based instructional materials required by the 1990–91 textbook proclamation arrived in classrooms for the 1993–94 school year. By 1995 the Texas State Board of Education was already enmeshed in debates about the need for substantially altering the state curriculum framework, and by 1996 statewide conferences on the topic were being held—while student achievement continued to rise (Ellis 1998).

It would seem that many of those interested in touting the impacts of educational policymaking seriously underestimate the time lag between the emergence of new policies and when the implementation of these policies is initiated. Beyond that there is the problem of the time lag between initial implementation and widespread, faithful implementation of the policies.

Evaluating Fidelity of Policy Implementation

Little of the research to date suggests that educational policies are ever widely implemented as envisioned by the policymakers. Perhaps this conclusion has more to do with the instability of the policy environment than anything else. In other words, there have been few long-term studies (seven to ten years) of policy implementation, in part because educational policymaking continues rather hyperactively, with many policies replaced well short of any ten-year timeline. My point here is that it should not be surprising that studies of policy implementation early in the process find that implementation is less faithful than hoped. It takes time for policies to reach schools and even longer to reach classrooms.

If we were truly interested in the effects of policymaking on student achievement we could design studies that evaluated such impacts, if any exist. The Hoffman et al. (1998) study offers one of the few good examples of such a study on the impact of state policies on literacy instruction. One key was documenting the nature of instruction before the new policy was implemented. The point is that without reliable information on the nature of the instructional environment before a new instructional policy is implemented it will be impossible to assess effects on practice. In the Hoffman et al. study, data on instructional practice were gathered as a baseline and then again in the initial year of implementation of the new instructional materials. That study suggested that fidelity of implementation varied widely. Unfortunately, there was no direct assessment of reading achievement (although teachers were asked about student growth compared to earlier years).

Nonetheless, the Hoffman et al. (1998) study is unmatched because it developed baseline information so that instructional changes could be documented. Many other studies attempting to document policy effects lacked such baseline information. And, of course, policymakers often imagine such data exist. In California, for instance, policymakers seem to have accepted assertions about the implementation and negative effects of the 1987 framework even though the available evidence, scant as it was, suggested that assertions about widespread and faithful implementation were wrong. At a 1997 American Educational Research Association session key California policymakers admitted as much, but this seemed not to diminish their enthusiasm for the shifting policy agenda.[4]

Ideally, policy implementation and effect studies would begin by developing baseline data prior to the implementation of any new policy and continue through documentation of fidelity of implementation. Considering fidelity of implementation as a continuum would be a first necessary step in such research. A multimethod research design might use surveys, observations, teaching instructional time logs, interviews, and other methods to estimate implementation fidelity. A stratified random sampling of teachers across a state, for instance, would provide useful evidence for estimating whether particular state policies produce the intended effect on instructional processes. But since policy implementation takes time, such studies would need to be designed as longitudinal efforts.

Evaluating Trends in Student Achievement

After documenting the process of policy implementation, including varied levels of implementation fidelity, investigators could then move on to attempting to estimate the effects of implementation on student achievement. Treating fidelity of policy implementation as a continuous variable in the research design should allow for reasonable estimates of effects on achievement across the range of policy implementation.

But how should student achievement be assessed? Currently there are few guidelines for making such decisions. Claims can be found of achievement effects on reading, where children's achievement was estimated by their performance on a test of pseudo-word decoding (for example, boj).

---

4. When questioned about the availability of reliable information on implementation of the 1987 framework, Bill Honig and other panelists admitted that there were no data available on scope or fidelity of implementation.

But if policymakers are interested in children's development of higher-order literacy proficiencies (for example, summarizing the main argument and supporting details), then achievement estimates would necessarily involve assessing those proficiencies more directly. Such an interest in higher-order literacy proficiencies stimulated the redesign of the NAEP in the 1980s. Unfortunately, little of the policy research, or intervention research, has to date actually employed assessments of higher-order literacy in estimating literacy achievement. In other words, there exists a fundamental need for substantially better data on how particular instructional models or materials impact the development of higher-order literacy skills and strategies (Taylor et al. 2000).

For instance, the much ballyhooed "proven programs"—Success for All, direct instruction, Open Court reader series—provide absolutely no evidence, positive or negative, of the impact of these programs on the development of the sort of higher-order literacies that are central to the NAEP estimates of student reading proficiency. At best, the evidence points to slim positive effects on traditional standardized reading tests (see Pressley and Allington 1999; Pogrow 2000; Stahl, Duffy-Hester, and Stahl 1998; Venezky 1998; Walberg and Greenberg 1998 for discussions of the poor quality of the evidence supporting these programs). The redesign of the NAEP was intended to provide the sorts of evidence long absent from traditional tests that emphasized lower-level skills of word recognition and information locating and matching. But no one has reliably linked particular sorts of instruction to NAEP estimates of proficiency, although several commentators have noted some interesting correlational data (for example, Goodman 1998; McQuillan 1998). A few recent studies of classroom reading instruction have assessed achievement using evaluations of higher-order reading proficiencies (for example, Knapp 1995; Pressley et al. 2001). A few states (such as Michigan, Maryland, New York, and Wisconsin) have developed their own assessments that tap such skills, but many states (including California, North Carolina, and Texas) have state assessments that tap primarily lower-order skill proficiencies.

A critical aspect of any study attempting to evaluate the effects of educational policymaking on achievement is building or selecting a system for assessing student achievement of the new high academic standards and the higher-order literacy proficiencies. Ideally, such an assessment would be administered at the beginning and end of each school year. The problem with a single annual assessment is the difficulty of accounting for the demonstrated differential effects of summer reading loss. As Cooper et al.

(1996) have demonstrated in their meta-analysis of the available studies, children from lower-income families experience a substantial loss of reading skills over summer vacation periods, losses not found among children from more advantaged families.

Entwisle, Alexander, and Olson (1997) demonstrated just how powerful this summer reading loss is when attempting to estimate school effects on achievement. They found no significant differences in the effects of different schools on student achievement even though the average achievement in schools serving primarily students from lower-income families lagged several years behind the achievement of schools serving more advantaged students. The more than two-year difference in average achievement at the end of the elementary grades was wholly accounted for by a combination of initial achievement differences (observed when students began school) and the cumulative effects of the differential summer reading loss. They also noted that without the twice yearly assessments, differences in school achievement patterns are easily misinterpreted as located in differences in instructional effectiveness. They summarize their findings by noting that policymakers need to realize the enormous impact of summer reading loss in higher poverty communities.

Additionally, attempting to sort the effects of extended time program participation (after-school, summer school) from the effects of regular education programs becomes complicated when participation in such programs is inconsistent across the student population being studied. Similarly, if parents of more advantaged students are more likely to provide children with outside tutoring, school and policy effects become muddied. But it would not be especially difficult to gather such data and estimate effects on achievement.

Who Gets Assessed?

In designing a study of policy effects attention must be paid to the consistency and comprehensiveness of student population participating in the assessments designed to evaluate achievement. Two common problems exist in most current assessment plans, and both must be adequately addressed in order to reliably estimate achievement patterns over time.

First, there is the problem of student mobility. If a policy is implemented throughout a school system (statewide or districtwide), then this problem may be largely ameliorated. However, this is only true if policy implementation is largely consistent throughout the system. When a policy is implemented in only some schools—lower-achieving schools, for instance—it becomes more difficult to estimate policy effects. If some schools have stable student enrollments while others have more mobile populations, the comparisons of effects are muddied. One potential solution to this problem is to again use the idea of a continuum and disaggregate achievement data based on the number of years of schooling students receive in the schools implementing the intended policy. For example, one might reasonably expect different effects, positive or negative, on those students enrolled in a school for three consecutive years than on students who arrived at the school a few months before the administration of the achievement test.

Second, there is the problem of consistency in the assessment pool. It has been demonstrated that an increasing pool of students identified as pupils with disabilities produces artificially inflated improvements in achievement (Allington and McGill-Franzen 1992b; McGill-Franzen 1994). In both cases, this increased identification meant that more lower-achieving students were exempted from the state assessments, thus reducing the number of low-achieving children tested and, thereby, raising average achievement levels. Likewise, Allington and McGill-Franzen (1992a) demonstrated how increased retention in grade artificially inflated reports of improving achievement, as retaining lower-achieving students removed them from the cohort assessment pool. Thus achievement was misinterpreted as improving, and the schools were mistakenly considered to be more effective instructionally. One solution to this problem is replacing grade-level assessment with cohort assessment. In other words, the assessment plan would continually assess and report the achievement of any cohort of students who began school in the same year regardless of what grade they were in over time.

Isolating the Effects of an Individual Policy

Finally, and importantly, studies of policy implementation and effects must attempt to isolate the impact of a particular policy on student achievement. Because a plethora of factors have been identified as having effects on student achievement it will be important to design evaluation studies that attempt to account for factors known to be related to achievement. The recent flurry of policymaking in California will make it more difficult to isolate policy effects. Class size reduction, new mandated instructional materials, an end to social promotion, mandatory summer school attendance for lower-achievers, enhancements in pre- and in-service teacher preparation, and increased per-pupil spending are all recent policy shifts affecting California education.

If there is a general improvement (or decline) in the reading achievement of California students, sorting out any causal relationships between policies and achievement will be a complicated affair. The available evidence suggests that class size reduction alone should improve early literacy development, as should access to more expert instruction and increased per-pupil spending (Achilles 1999). Ending social promotion will artificially enhance reading achievement, at least initially, and the mandated summer school program may improve achievement over the long run. However, as Lindblom and Woodhouse (1993) note, such trial-and-error policymaking is often high-cost policymaking. They suggest an approach that would promote limited policy implementation as studies of effects are completed. Perhaps one or two of the policies would be implemented on a trial basis at different sites, with a more gradual reallocation of funds as evaluation studies provided better estimates of the effects of the various policy components.

Summary

Too little reliable information has been collected on the effects educational policymaking has on student achievement. Such studies could be designed if policymakers are interested in the effects of their policymaking. But the design of such studies will be complicated, and gathering reliable information on achievement patterns will be a relatively expensive undertaking. But that expense is modest in comparison to the funding allocated for almost any educational reform.

Some Final Considerations

Tyack and Cuban (1995), in their book-length review of American educational reform activity across the twentieth century, argue that "it is policy talk, we suggest, that cycles far more than practice" (40). The research on the effects of policymaking focused on reading instruction seems to support that conclusion. Just as the faithful implementation of "whole language" policies (with all the attendant problems of defining just what a "whole language" policy might be) seems to have been widely exaggerated in the policy talk, so too may policymakers' expectations for the implementation of "phonics" policies be overly optimistic. Lindblom and Woodhouse conclude, "When educators view policy demands as inappropriate, they are skilled in finding ways to temper or evade their effects" (1993, 79). The Datnow and Castellano (2000) study documents the validity of their assertion even in the case of the highly structured, closely monitored reform models.

Research suggests that implementation of educational policies entails individual teachers' translation of the policy and its intended impact on instructional processes (McGill-Franzen 2000). But teaching is a complex activity, and teaching well involves more than technical skill. Studies of teaching and teachers, especially expert teachers, point to the myriad of nontechnical components of exemplary instruction (Ladson-Billings 1994; Pressley et al. 2001; Ruddell 1995; Spencer and Spencer 1993).

Two issues deserve consideration. First, even the technical aspects of teaching are rooted in beliefs about teaching and learning. The crux of the reading wars is located in differing beliefs about how best to teach—beliefs buttressed by particular interpretations of particular research. Individual teachers may rely more on personal experience than published research, but even that experience is influenced by beliefs about the nature of teaching (Johnston, Woodside-Jiron, and Day in press). As a California teacher told McGill-Franzen and her colleagues, "Teachers are independent and you cannot tell them how to think and feel. Because if you don't believe in a program . . . it's not going to happen. Because when you go in that classroom and you close that door, you're going to teach what you feel and believe is right and what you feel and believe you can do" (2000, 906).

A second consideration is the question of institutional and individual capacity. This is, perhaps, the more technical end of things. But even the capacity for offering high-quality instruction is more than simply a technical matter. However, as Loveless notes, "If policy intends to help teachers who are incapable of effective instruction, state proclamations will not likely provide much assistance" (1998, 300). The unfortunate truth of the matter is that materials do not teach. Instructional materials of different quality may have some modest impact on the nature and quality of teaching but only if and when teachers elect to use those materials and use them in the ways imagined by the developers and policymakers. Throughout the policy implementation studies reviewed here the constant problem has been the fidelity of implementation—even with instructional materials that offered detailed designs for how instruction should proceed.

So how might policymaking become more productive? In actuality little is known about how educational policies might be successfully developed or implemented; the research to date largely documents the difficulties of achieving faithful implementation. Given the substantial funding of public education and the costs of the various policy proposals, it is surprising how little attention policymakers seem to have paid to the implementation process or the research available. There is little evidence that either aspect of the logic that seems inherent in policymaking is ever fulfilled.

For educational policymaking to become more productive, better information on policy impacts will be needed. But there has been little interest among policymakers on reliably documenting the effects of their policymaking. Perhaps this can be changed. But maybe there is less to educational policymaking than meets the eye. Perhaps the real goal of policymakers is to have "done something," particularly something that public opinion polls support (Allington 1999). In this case the policymaking is an end unto itself that will likely result in a continued avalanche of educational policies that offer no coherent or continuing vision of how schools might improve.

References

Achilles, C. M. 1999. *Let's Put Kids First, Finally: Getting Class Size Right.* Thousand Oaks, Calif.: Corwin.

Allington, R. L. 1991. "The Legacy of 'Slow It Down and Make It More Concrete.'" In *Learner Factors/Teacher Factors: Issues in Literacy Research and Instruction* (40th Yearbook of the National Reading Conference), edited by J. Zutell and S. McCormick, 19–30. Chicago: National Reading Conference.

———. 1999. "Crafting State Educational Policy: The Slippery Role of Research and Researchers." *Journal of Literacy Research* 31: 457–82.

Allington, R. L., S. Guice, N. Michelson, K. Baker, and S. Li. 1996. "Literature-Based Curriculum in High-Poverty Schools." In *The First R: Every Child's Right to Read,* edited by M. Graves, P. van den Broek, and B. Taylor, 73–96. Teachers College Press.

Allington, R. L., and A. McGill-Franzen. 1992a. "Does High-Stakes Testing Improve School Effectiveness?" *ERS Spectrum* 10 (2): 3–12.

———. 1992b. "Unintended Effects of Educational Reform in New York State." *Educational Policy* 6: 396–413.

Allington, R. L., and H. Woodside-Jiron. 1999. "The Politics of Literacy Teaching: How 'Research' Shaped Educational Policy." *Educational Researcher* 28 (8): 4–13.

Baumann, J. F., J. V. Hoffman, J. Moon, and A. Duffy-Hester. 1998. "Where Are Teachers' Voices in the Phonics/Whole Language Debate? Results from a Survey of U.S. Elementary Teachers." *Reading Teacher* 50: 636–51.

Berliner, D. C., and B. J. Biddle. 1996. *The Manufactured Crisis: Myths, Fraud, and the Attack on America's Public Schools.* White Plains, N.Y.: Longmans.

Bridge, C. A. 1994. "Implementing Large-Scale Change in Literacy Instruction." In *Multidimensional Aspects of Literacy Research, Theory, and Practice,* 44th yearbook, edited by C. Kinzer and D. Leu, 257–65. Chicago: National Reading Conference.

Canney, G. 1993. "Teachers' Preferences for Reading Materials." *Reading Improvement* 30: 238–45.

Carlos, L., and M. Kirst. 1997. *California Curriculum Policy in the 1990's: "We Don't Have to Be in Front to Lead."* San Francisco: WestEd/PACE.

Chrispeels, J. H. 1997. "Educational Policy Implementation in a Shifting Political Climate: The California Experience." *American Educational Research Journal* 34: 453–81.

Cohen, D. K., and J. P. Spillane. 1992. "Policy and Practice: The Relations between Governance and Instruction." In *Review of Research in Education,* vol. 18, edited by G. Grant, 3–49. Washington: American Educational Research Association.

Coles, G. 2000. *Misreading Reading.* Portsmouth, N.H.: Heinemann.

Cooper, H., B. Nye, K. Charlton, J. Lindsay, and S. Greathouse. 1996. "The Effects of Summer Vacation on Achievement Test Scores: A Narrative and Meta-Analytic Review." *Review of Educational Research* 66: 227–68.

Darling-Hammond, L. 1997. *Doing What Matters Most: Investing in Quality Teaching.* New York: National Commission on Teaching and America's Future.

Datnow, A., and M. Castellano. 2000. "Teachers' Responses to Success for All: How Beliefs, Experiences, and Adaptations Shape Implementation." *American Educational Research Journal* 37: 775–99.

Donahue, P. L., K. E. Voelkl, J. R. Campbell, and J. Mazzeo. 1999. *NAEP Reading 1998: Reading Report Card for the Nation and the States.* Washington: National Center for Education Statistics, Office of Educational Research and Improvement, U.S. Department of Education.

Dressman, M. 1999. "On the Use and Misuse of Research Evidence: Decoding Two States' Reading Initiatives." *Reading Research Quarterly* 34: 258–85.

Elley, W. B. 1992. *How in the World Do Students Read? IEA Study of Reading Literacy.* The Hague, Netherlands: International Association for the Evaluation of Educational Achievement.

Ellis, L. 1998. "We'll Eat the Elephant One Bite at a Time: The Continuing Battle for Control of Literacy Education in Texas." In *In Defense of Good Teaching: What Teachers Need to Know about the "Reading Wars,"* edited by K. Goodman, 87–105. York, Maine: Stenhouse Publishers.

Elmore, R. F. 1996. "Getting to Scale with Good Educational Practice." *Harvard Educational Review* 66: 1–26.

Elmore, R. F., P. L. Peterson, and S. J. McCarthy. 1996. *Restructuring in the Classroom: Teaching, Learning, and School Organization.* Jossey-Bass.

Entwisle, D. R., K. L. Alexander, and L. S. Olson. 1997. *Children, Schools, and Inequality.* Westview Press.

Freeman, D., and Y. Freeman. 1998. "California Reading: The Pendulum Swings." In *In Defense of Good Teaching: What Teachers Need to Know about the "Reading Wars,"* edited by K. Goodman, 73–85. York, Maine: Stenhouse Publishers.

Gaddy, B. B., T. W. Hall, and R. J. Marzano. 1996. *School Wars: Resolving Our Conflicts over Religion and Values.* Jossey-Bass.

Garan, E. 2001. "Beyond Smoke and Mirrors: A Critique of the National Reading Panel Report on Phonics." *Phi Delta Kappan* 82: 500–06.

Gee, J. 1999. "Reading and the New Literacy: Reframing the National Academy of Sciences Report on Reading." *Journal of Literacy Research* 31: 355–74.

General Accounting Office. 1993. *Educational Achievement Standards: NAGB's Approach Yields Misleading Interpretations.* GAO/PEMD–93–12. U.S. General Accounting Office.

Goodman, K. S. 1998. "Who's Afraid of Whole Language? Politics, Paradigms, Pedagogy, and the Press." In *In Defense of Good Teaching: What Teachers Need to Know about the "Reading Wars,"* edited by K. Goodman, 3–37. York, Maine: Stenhouse Publishers.

Guskey, T. R., and B. R. Oldham. 1997. "Despite the Best Intentions: Inconsistencies among Components in Kentucky's Systemic Reform." *Educational Policy* 11: 426–42.

Hoffman, J., and S. McCarthy. 1995. "The New Basals: How Are They Different?" *Reading Teacher* 49: 72–75.

Hoffman, J. V., S. J. McCarthy, B. Elliott, D. Bayles, D. Price, A. Ferree, and J. Abbott. 1998. "The Literature-Based Basals in First-Grade Classrooms: Savior, Satan, or Same-Old, Same-Old?" *Reading Research Quarterly* 33: 168–97.

Holland, H. 1998. *Making Change: Three Educators Join the Battle for Better Schools.* Portsmouth, N.H.: Heinemann.

Jennings, N. E. 1996. *Interpreting Policy in Real Classrooms: Case Studies of State Reform and Teacher Practice.* Teachers College Press.

Johnston, P., R. L. Allington, S. Guice, and G. W. Brooks. 1998. "Small Change: A Multi-Level Study of the Implementation of Literature-Based Instruction." *Peabody Journal of Education* 73 (3): 81–103.

Johnston, P., H. Woodside-Jiron, and J. P. Day. In press. "Teaching and Learning Literate Epistemologies." *Journal of Educational Psychology.*

Knapp, M. 1995. *Teaching for Meaning in High-Poverty Classrooms.* Teachers College Press.

Ladson-Billings, G. 1994. *The Dreamkeepers: Successful Teachers of African-American Children.* Jossey-Bass.

Langer, J. A., and R. L. Allington. 1992. "Curriculum Research in Writing and Reading." In *Handbook of Research on Curriculum,* edited by P. W. Jackson, 687–725. Macmillan.

Lindblom, C. E., and E. J. Woodhouse. 1993. *The Policy-Making Process,* 3d ed. Prentice-Hall.

Loveless, T. 1998. "The Use and Misuse of Research in Educational Reform." In *Brookings Papers on Educational Policy,* edited by D. Ravitch, 280–300. Brookings.

McGill-Franzen, A. M. 1994. "Is There Accountability for Learning and Belief in Children's Potential?" In *Getting Reading Right from the Start: Effective Early Literacy Interventions,* edited by E. H. Hiebert and B. M. Taylor, 13–35. Allyn-Bacon.

———. 2000. "Policy and Instruction: What Is the Relationship?" In *Handbook of Reading Research,* edited by R. Barr, M. Kamil, P. Mosenthal, and P. D. Pearson, 891–908. White Plains, N.Y.: Longmans.

McLaughlin, M. W. 1991. "The RAND Change Agent Study: Ten Years Later." In *Education Policy Implementation,* edited by A. Odden, 143–55. Albany: SUNY Press.

McQuillan, J. 1996. "Whole Language in California: A Failed Experiment?" In *Visions and Realities in Literacy: Yearbook of the 60th Claremont Reading Conference,* edited by P. H. Dreyer, 17–26. Claremont, Calif.: Claremont Graduate School.

———. 1998. *The Literacy Crisis: False Claims, Real Solutions.* Portsmouth, N.H.: Heinemann.

Miller, S. D. 1995. "Teachers' Responses to Test-Driven Accountability: 'If I Change, Will My Scores Drop?'" *Reading Research and Instruction* 34: 332–51.

National Committee on Time and Learning. 1994. *Prisoners of Time.* U.S. Government Printing Office.

National Reading Panel. 2000. *Teaching Children to Read: An Evidence-Based Assessment of Scientific Research Literature on Reading and Its Implications for Reading Instruction.* Available at www.nationalreadingpanel.org.

Pace, G. 1992. "Stories of Teacher-Initiated Change from Traditional to Whole-Language Literacy Instruction." *Elementary School Journal* 92: 461–76.

Paterson, F. R. A. 1998. "Mandating Methodology: Promoting the Use of Phonics through State Statute." In *In Defense of Good Teaching: What Teachers Need to Know about the "Reading Wars,"* edited by K. Goodman, 107–25. York, Maine: Stenhouse Publishers.

———. 2000. "The Politics of Phonics." *Journal of Curriculum and Supervision* 15: 179–211.

Pearson, P. D. 1997. "The Politics of Reading Research and Practice." *Council Chronicle* (September): 8.

Pellegrino, J. W., L. Jones, and K. Mitchell. 1999. *Grading the Nation's Report Card.* Washington: National Academy Press.

Pogrow, S. 2000. "Success for All Does Not Produce Success for Students." *Phi Delta Kappan* 82: 67–80.

Pressley, M., and R. L. Allington. 1999. "What Should Educational Research Be the Research Of?" *Issues in Education: Contributions from Educational Psychology* 5: 1–35.

Pressley, M., R. L. Allington, R. Wharton-McDonald, C. C. Block, and L. Morrow. 2001. *Learning to Read: Lessons from Exemplary First-Grade Classrooms.* New York: Guilford.

Ruddell, R. B. 1995. "Those Influential Teachers: Meaning Negotiators and Motivation Builders." *Reading Teacher* 48: 454–63.

Scharer, P. L. 1992. "Teachers in Transitions: An Exploration of Changes in Teachers and Classrooms during the Implementation of Literature-Based Reading Instruction." *Research in the Teaching of English* 2: 408–43.

Slavin, R. E. 1987. "Making Chapter I Make a Difference." *Phi Delta Kappan* 69: 110–19.

Snow, C. E., M. S. Burns, and P. Griffin. 1998. *Preventing Reading Difficulties in Young Children: A Report of the National Research Council.* Washington: National Academy Press.

Spencer, L. M., and S. M. Spencer. 1993. *Competence at Work: Models for Superior Performance.* Wiley.

Spillane, J. P. 1998. "A Cognitive Perspective on the Role of the Local Educational Agency in Implementing Instructional Policy: Accounting for Local Variability." *Educational Administration Quarterly* 34: 31–57.

Stahl, S. A., A. Duffy-Hester, and K. Stahl. 1998. "Everything You Wanted to Know about Phonics (But Were Afraid to Ask)." *Reading Research Quarterly* 33: 338–55.

Standerford, N. S. 1997. "Reforming Reading Instruction on Multiple Levels: Interrelations and Disconnections across the State, District, and Classroom Levels." *Educational Policy* 11: 58–91.

Strickland, D. S., and S. A. Walmsley. 1994. "School Book Clubs and Literacy Development: A Descriptive Study." Report no. 22. Albany, N.Y.: National Research Center of Literature Teaching and Learning.

Sweet, R. W. 1997. "Don't Read, Don't Tell: Clinton's Phony War on Illiteracy." *Policy Review* (May/June): 38–42.

Taylor, B. M., R. C. Anderson, K. H. Au, and T. E. Raphael. 2000. "Discretion in the Translation of Research to Policy: A Case from Beginning Reading." *Educational Researcher* 29(6): 16–24.

Taylor, D. 1998. *Beginning to Read and the Spin Doctors of Science: The Political Campaign to Change America's Mind about How Children Learn to Read.* Urbana, Ill.: National Council of Teachers of English.

Timar, T. B., and D. L. Kirp. 1987. "Educational Reform and Institutional Competence." *Harvard Educational Review* 57: 308–30.

Tyack, D., and L. Cuban. 1995. *Tinkering toward Utopia: A Century of Public School Reform.* Harvard University Press.

Urbanski, A. 1991. "Real Change Is Real Hard: Lessons Learned in Rochester." *Education Week* (October 23): 29.

Venezky, R. L. 1998. "An Alternate Perspective on Success for All." In *Advances in Educational Policy,* vol. 4, edited by K. K. Wong, 145–65. Greenwich, Conn.: JAI Press.

Walberg, H., and R. Greenberg. 1998. "The Diogenes Effect." *Education Week* (April 8): 60.

Wildavsky, A. 1979. *Speaking Truth to Power: The Art and Craft of Policy Analysis.* Little, Brown.

Wolf, S. A., H. Borko, R. L. Elliot, and M. C. McIver. 2000. "That Dog Won't Hunt! Exemplary School Change Efforts within Kentucky Reform." *American Educational Research Journal* 33: 349–95.

CHAPTER FOURTEEN

The Politics of
the Reading Wars

WILLIAM LOWE BOYD
DOUGLAS E. MITCHELL

"No American school would knowingly withhold a vaccine from students that would prevent a childhood disease like measles. Yet this is, in effect, what is happening when it comes to the teaching of reading."

—"Reading: The First Chapter in Education" (1996)

"School-induced illiteracy spurs spending explosion: One in three public school students in remedial classes."

—Headline in *School Reform News* (1999)

Today's "reading wars" are only the most recent chapter in a periodic and historic struggle over reading instruction in America's public schools. The conflict today, however, has clearly eclipsed the scope and intensity of earlier battles. Unprecedented political efforts have been undertaken since 1990 to resolve the dispute between "phonics" and "whole-language" advocates, both through state legislation and, especially, through the passage of the federal Reading Excellence Act in October 1998 (Paterson 1998a, 1998b; Rothman 1990a, 1990b; Weaver 1990). The quotes above convey some of the intensity of this war. The story accompanying the second quote, for example, reports that the director of statistical research for the National Right to Read

Foundation claims that "the vast majority of students in remedial classes—
15 million children—are there because of . . . 'school-induced illiteracy':
the continuing failure of regular instructors to teach them how to read."
The article goes on to say that "remedial teachers would be unnecessary
. . . if regular teachers did what they are paid to do." As this quote, and the
chilling notion of "withholding a vaccine" show, strong rhetoric is common in the reading wars. Indeed, the unspoken motto of the most vocifer-
ous antagonists seems to be "take no prisoners."

In this chapter, without taking sides in the war, two central questions
are explored: (1) How did something that appears to be a technical matter—teaching children to read—become a political issue and, indeed, a
war? (2) How did the advocates of phonics gain such a strong political
advantage, in the late 1990s, over the many professional educators committed to the "whole-language" approach?

At first blush, the answer to why the "phonological decoding" approach
associated with phonics has gained ascendancy over the "meaning-
centered" whole-language approach seems simple: test results and scientific research over the past decade have made its superiority clear (Fletcher
and Lyon 1998; Sweet 1997). Key policymakers and members of the news
media have accepted this view. Thus, Representative Bill Goodling, in
introducing the legislation for the federal "Reading Excellence Act," on
October 6, 1997, stated that:

> [H]earings before my Committee on Education and the Workforce
> have pointed out that the fact is we first have to teach teachers how
> to teach reading based on reliable, replicable research on how chil-
> dren learn to read. Dr. Reid Lyon, Chief of the Child Development
> and Behavior Branch at the National Institutes of Health, testified
> before the Committee that fewer than 10 percent of our nation's
> teachers have an adequate understanding of how reading develops
> or how to provide reading instruction to struggling readers.

A closer examination of this issue, however, reveals a more complex
picture. Contrary to popular opinion, some strong arguments have been
presented that the evidence from recent scientific research, and certainly
from test results, is far less conclusive than has been claimed (McQuillan
1998; Pressley and Allington 1999; Rothstein 1998; Taylor 1998).

At the same time, as many have noted about the reading wars (for example, Chall 1992; Coles 1998a, 1998b; Lemann 1997), the struggle is
about much more than a dispute over teaching approaches or test scores.

Deeply embedded in the conflict is a clash between the philosophies and goals of child-centered progressive education (a view aligned with whole language) and traditional, more conservative teacher-centered education (a view associated with skills-based approaches such as phonics). More broadly still, the reading wars touch upon many of the issues and fears associated with America's national identity, increasingly globalized economic and social relationships, and domestic "culture wars" precipitated by rapid social change and the growing ethnic diversity. These philosophical and social issues associated with the reading wars help explain why numerous calls to end the war, by employing a "balanced" or "integrated" approach combining the strengths of both the phonics and whole-language methods, have failed to resolve the conflict (Diegmueller 1996; Hoff 1998; Manzo 1998, 1999; Rothman 1990a; Snow, Burns, and Griffin 1998).

Viewing the reading wars as a struggle between "progressive" and "conservative" educational philosophies is particularly helpful. Following Davies and Guppy (1997, 443), we define progressive education as

> an umbrella term for the pedagogical ideals that emphasize child-centered learning, critical citizenship, missions of social justice, and equality and downplay student competition and quantitative evaluation.

Since its inception in the works of John Dewey, the progressive education movement has attracted controversy and has waxed and waned in popularity (Semel and Sadovnik 1999). Traditional teacher-centered education, on the other hand, represents popularly accepted beliefs about what schooling should look like: a more top-down, individualistic, competitive "drill for skills" education, in contrast to the more bottom-up, active-learning, egalitarian, and social reformist goals of progressive education (Metz 1990). By conservative education, we refer to the traditionally teacher-centered classroom control and instructional processes advocated in Durkheim's (1961) *Moral Education* and described in Willard Waller's (1932) classic *The Sociology of Teaching*.

If the reading wars are viewed as not only a dispute about reading pedagogy but also a conflict between progressive and conservative education philosophies—exacerbated by anxieties emerging from national identity and security concerns—challenges to progressive education and the ascendancy of phonics clearly have been greatly aided by the shift in zeitgeist brought about by the forces of globalization. These forces drive utilitarian concerns about educational excellence for economic competitiveness (which tend to override concerns for equality and social justice) and redistribute authority and power in ways that challenge the beliefs, expertise, and control of professional educators. The forces and consequences of globalization are central to the theoretical framework that will be employed in analyzing the reading wars.

Our analysis is presented in four parts. First, an historical perspective is taken—tracing the continuing struggle between "progressive" and "conservative" philosophies of public education and anchoring the contemporary reading wars controversy in this ongoing historical debate. Second, the "battlefronts"—the broad theaters of operation where the reading wars combatants are waging political and scientific warfare over reading pedagogy—are examined. Third, the widely publicized "California Story" is scrutinized—examining the rise and fall of whole-language instructional policies in the nation's most populous state. Finally, an analytic perspective is adopted to explore why this battle is so fierce and so essentially political in character.

Historical Background

To fully understand the intensity and persistence of today's reading wars, it is necessary to briefly review the historical development of reading instruction in the United States. Conflict over proper reading instruction started almost as soon as the modern system of public schools was founded. Although Horace Mann complained about the practice as early as the 1850s, the earliest reading programs gave steady emphasis to the phonics of letter and word sounds until about 1920 (in addition to emphasizing rote memory of biblical, patriotic, and other moral "character-building" materials).

The picture changed early in the twentieth century, in conjunction with the emergence of educational psychology as a central discipline for the study of educational programs and practices. As a consequence of the work of educational psychologists—most notably Edward Thorndike—schools shifted from reliance on moralistic and phonics-oriented primers to the use of "basal readers" designed to emphasize "look-say" learning of a "sight" vocabulary (Foshay 1990). The basal readers utilized a sharply limited vocabulary (a few hundred words in the earliest readers), high rates of repetition of new words and substantial use of pictures and other contextual supports to help children identify and remember words as they are being learned. Rather than emphasizing phonic decoding, the basal readers were predicated on the assumption that fluent readers rely on repetition and contextual clue interpretation to build up a basic reading vocabulary.

From the 1920s through the end of the 1960s the basal reader approach dominated early reading instruction. Basal readers were developed through a systematic study of vocabulary development and what later came to be called "readability." As Foshay (1990, 25) summarizes,

> The student was to learn to use all the available cues to extract meaning from the page—immediate recognition of words, cues from the context, cues from illustrations, and, finally, phonetic analysis.

> Research evidence indicated that the average child required fifty-seven exposures to a word before recognizing it on sight. Hence, the repetitive and simplified "Look, look. See, see." patterns in the text.

The near unanimous professional commitment to basal readers came under attack in the mid-1950s. Rudolf Flesch stimulated a virtual firestorm of basal reader criticism with the publication of his popular treatise, *Why Johnny Can't Read* (1955). This book, which was on the national bestseller list for thirty weeks, made two telling criticisms of the basal reader approach, arguing that they were: (1) essentially dull, uninteresting, and meaningless texts that failed to engage children in a desire to read, and (2) responsible for creating reading disabilities because they failed to provide children with an opportunity to learn the phonetic skills needed to become independent, self-guided readers.

The first criticism was certainly not new. For nearly half a century the Progressive Education Association had been urging educators to provide children with more meaningful, natural, and interesting text materials in their reading curricula. However, it was the second criticism—a scathing denunciation of the "look-say" method of vocabulary development—that most people remembered. This criticism of nonphonic (orthographic) vocabulary development can be credited with framing the contemporary debates over method that have come to be called the "reading wars." The phonics versus whole-language meaning aspect of the wars developed rather slowly over the next two decades, however, because most educators and scholars dismissed or ignored Flesch's criticisms, and basal reader publishers continued to dominate the field.

Flesch's initial criticism—that the basal readers were essentially dull and meaningless—was picked up by Progressive scholars and professional educators who urged development of a reading program consisting of rich and imaginative literature and encouraging the engagement of children in personally meaningful reading and writing experiences. In the 1960s this approach was known as the "language experience approach" to reading instruction. During the 1970s the phrase "whole language" replaced "language experience" as the name for programs of reading instruction that believe and emphasize that children learn to recognize and use words as a consequence of encountering them in authentic and meaningful communication settings. For the language-experience/whole-language educators, Flesch's second, methodological, criticism was rejected in favor of emphasizing the role of students' and teachers' natural interest in communication in generating the motivation as well as the occasions to read and write printed text.

One of Flesch's most potent critics was Harvard University's Jeanne Chall. Her seminal book, *Learning to Read: The Great Debate* (1967), was responsible for framing the issue of reading instruction as a choice between code-centered (phonics) and meaning-centered (whole-language) interpretations of how children learn. Having framed the issue in these terms, Chall argued persuasively that a code-centered approach was not only helpful for all students and essential for many, but that it was present in most basal reader programs. She also argued for the appropriateness of using meaning-centered approaches, however, and urged combining the code-breaking emphasis with significant improvements in the meaningfulness of elementary school reading materials. Thus, while criticizing the scholarly merits of Flesch's work, Chall acknowledged the validity of both of his central criticisms.

In addition to clarifying and framing the debate over reading instruction methods, *The Great Debate* had a substantial impact on the evolution of basal readers and on the preparation of elementary school teachers. When updating this book in 1983, Chall noted that there had been a substantial change in basal reader curriculum materials, involving a marked shift toward inclusion of direct instruction in phonics. She also documented growth in attention to phonics in teacher preparation textbooks.

Nevertheless, under the leadership of scholars like Kenneth Goodman (1986) and Frank Smith (1983), the whole-language approach developed a large and loyal following. These followers were professionals who saw reading instruction as an expression of a philosophy of education and a grass-roots school reform movement—much more than just a theory of literacy acquisition. The watchwords of this movement were *authenticity* and *empowerment*. Authenticity meant an insistence that children would become naturally fluent readers when invited to utilize reading and writing instruction in settings, like telling their own stories or interpreting truly engaging literature, where they were authentically motivated to communicate content rather than decode text. Empowerment meant an insistence that teachers and students should control the content and occasions of reading and writing rather than having to cope with material chosen by curriculum writers or school officials. The movement focused on creating holistic and "natural" literacy learning processes in which teacher and students could "take control" of what had become an alienating and debilitating experience under the fragmented "drill and kill" impact of basal reader and phonics instructional methods (Goodman 1986).

In short, advocates for the language-experience/whole-language approach to reading instruction accepted Flesch's first criticism of basal readers—that they were dull, boring, and meaningless—but rejected his idea that the solution lay in providing children with direct phonics instruction so that they could decode a richer vocabulary. Instead, these theorists argued, the issue of meaning should be attacked directly by lowering the emphasis on phonological decoding and concentrating on engagement in the communicating act itself. In this respect they followed the thrust of the by-then defunct Progressive Education Association and recalled the early days of emphasis on the social and cultural content of the reading curriculum.

Throughout the 1980s the split between phonics-centered and meaning-centered reading programs became increasingly pronounced. State education agencies became the battlegrounds for these contesting views with the result that several state agencies, most notably California, Texas and New York, adopted statewide curriculum and staff training programs supporting one side or the other. Still, during much of the 1980s whole language was more popular with educators than phonics. This, according to Chall, is because the ebb and flow of educational thinking has tended to favor the romantic ideas of progressive education over more conservative basic skills approaches:

The values and ideology . . . briefly depicted can be found to underlie most reading programs from the 1920s on. From time to time there is a greater acceptance of the need for teaching skills and tools when it is realized that many children are falling behind—particularly those from low-income families, from minority groups, and those at risk for learning disability. Historically, however, these periods seem to be short-lived. Such a period existed during the 1970s, but by the 1980s the thrust was once again toward the more romantic, charismatic, and global methods—methods seen as natural and joyful. These methods are valued so strongly because we want them to solve not only our curriculum problems but our economic, political, and social problems as well. (1992, 326)

As the 1980s unfolded, public educators committed to whole language devoted substantial energy to criticizing standardized achievement tests as inappropriate instruments for assessing authentic student learning. Increasingly, however, they found their convictions out-of-step with the mounting political pressures for academic performance improvement that accompanied awareness of the intense competition for market share in an increasingly globalized economy. Media criticism of the public schools and demands for improved school and student performance facilitated campaigns by conservative interest groups and critics determined to root out progressive education and to replace whole language with phonics. International studies of achievement, particularly in mathematics, were used to declare public schooling a failure. Scores from the prestigious National Assessment of Educational Progress (NAEP) were interpreted as documenting sweeping inadequacies in both reading and mathematics among American school children.

An influential new group of researchers came on to the scene during the early 1990s. Supported by substantial funding from the National Institute of Child Health and Human Development (NICHD), these researchers began a coordinated program of inquiry into the reading attainment of young children, with special emphasis on the difficulties of children who were failing to become fluent readers. NICHD funding was concentrated on studies emphasizing mental processing of information and phonetic decoding of text. The results have been widely interpreted to provide strong and conclusive support for phonics-based reading instruction. Moreover, these studies appear to provide definitive evidence refuting the whole-language movement's assertion that reading is as natural as speaking.

As interpreted by G. Reid Lyon, chief of the Child Development and Behavior Branch at the NICHD, these studies show that about 40 percent of all children do not have a natural grasp of the phonological linkage between print and speech and thus do not gain needed decoding skills through simple exposure to meaningful text (Fletcher and Lyon 1998).

Specifically, NICHD study interpreters insist that a central tenet of the whole-language model—that readers *rely on context* to learn the meaning of words—is wrong. As Share and Stanovich put it, "the common interpretation that children are plodding (recognizing words slowly) *because* they are not using context—is false" (1995, 6). The research they review leads to "just the opposite conclusion"—poor readers do not use the context because they are plodding (that is, decoding inefficiently). Even skilled readers begin to plod when they encounter unusually difficult text, and when they do so their comprehension tends to go down. That is why even highly trained research scholars must read difficult works more than once.

This interpretation of the NICHD studies has been challenged, however. Regie Routman reports that "while children who are taught lots of phonics may have an early advantage *as measured by standardized tests*, that advantage disappears by sixth grade when we look at comprehension" (1996, 92, emphasis in the original). In other words, early phonics instruction may serve primarily to bring up decoding ability during the first year or two of instruction, but it may not deliver the ultimately crucial ability to comprehend reading material in a mature way. Indeed, one of the NICHD researchers, Ehri, speculates that "phonemic awareness may be part of learning to read rather than something that is developed beforehand" (1987, 26, as cited in Dressman 1999). In other words, phonological skill might be as much the *result* of learning to read as a prerequisite building block.

Similarly, other whole-language researchers are fighting back. Daniels, Zemelman, and Bizar assert that the reading wars are:

> peculiar for the role that research has played in the struggle. Decodable text advocates have parlayed a few recent and unreplicated studies into support for their approach—even legislation, in a few states. Yet when we look at the broad, still-accumulating body of educational research, we see that holistic approaches in literacy clearly remain our best documented, most reliable, and most thoroughly proved ways to teach reading to the majority of children. Whole Language works. The proof is massive and overwhelming. Sixty years of research—yes, real scientific research—conclusively shows it to be a superior way [to teach reading]. (1999, 32)

Goodman complains that Reid Lyon has used his ties with the American Academy for the Advancement of Science and other illustrious groups to convince policymakers and the press that NICHD research is the "only scientific research on reading" and that it "all leads to a single conclusion: phonics is the essence of successful reading programs" (1998, 17). Whole-language defenders accuse Douglas Carnine and Bonita Grossen, of the National Center to Improve the Tools of Educators, of a systematic "disinformation" campaign exaggerating and misrepresenting the NICHD findings (Allington and Woodside-Jiron 1998, 1999; Goodman 1998, 21). To this, Denny Taylor (1998) has added an impassioned and decidedly conspiratorial account of what she sees as a vicious political campaign to advance the NICHD research and discredit whole-language instruction.

Nevertheless, despite these passionate objections, the NICHD research findings have gained broad acceptance and have been widely cited in efforts to move states toward phonics programs or legislation. The frequent use of such phrases as "reliable replicable research" and "scientifically based research" in arguments supporting passage of the federal Reading Excellence Act (1998) not only has had the effect of establishing the NICHD research as a model for scientific research, but also has contributed to the growing crisis of confidence in most other educational research (Loveless 1998; Viadero 1999a, 36–37, 1999b).

Clearly, the resolution of the many technical arguments about reading and reading instruction will have to come from the experts on reading—if they can ever agree. What should be stressed here is the fact that, with Congress's passage of the Reading Excellence Act, the NICHD research seems to have won the reading war, at least at this point in time.

Battlefronts in the Reading Wars

Like military wars, the reading wars are being fought on several different fronts simultaneously. Space does not permit a detailed review of all the various theaters of operation, but eight major battlefronts can be identified, each with its own key players and unique dynamics. Arrayed along these eight battlefronts are three different types of combatant "armies."

The most obvious combatants are recruited from the ranks of the education professionals: classroom teachers (and their professional unions); university-based teacher trainers; staff development specialists working in federally supported research and development laboratories, as free-lance independents, or in school district staff positions; school administrators; and a fairly large number of prominent research scholars.

A second set of contending partisans is found among government officials and agencies: state departments of education, governors, state and federal legislative bodies and their staffs, research funding agencies (primarily the U.S. Department of Education and NICHD), and most recently, the president and key members of his administration.

The third source of reading wars partisans consists of the diverse set of public and private interest groups that make literacy an important social issue. This group includes parents and local community groups concerned with the effectiveness of the public schools, but also includes an array of textbook and test publishers for whom reading policy has an immediate economic impact. Even more important are the broad-based cultural groups whose interests include the moral significance of what children are reading (or failing to read) and the overall legitimacy of the educational system and the professionals who operate it.

Partisans can be found on all sides of the pedagogical debate within each of three combatant groups. While there are conflicts *between* professionals and governmental officials, *between* professionals and public or private interest groups, and *between* governmental officials and various public or private interests, the debate is equally vitriolic *within* each of these three different partisan groups. Strategic advantages accrue to the various factions as battles shift from one arena to another. Professional researchers, for example, are favored when the battle is over research methods and findings, but public or private interest groups are favored when the conflict enters the opinion pages of the nation's mass media. A brief review of the major battlefronts shows the lines of cleavage and the relative advantage to the various combatants.

1. *The scientific and scholarly fronts where professionals vie for public and governmental legitimacy.* As previously noted, the most obvious point of conflict over reading instruction is whether scientific study has clearly identified the best approach to reading instruction and, if so, just which instructional model is the most promising. On this battlefront, the key actors are university-based research scholars and those who interpret their work to other professionals and the public and policy communities. Despite the existence of a large number of credible research studies aimed at illuminating the basic parameters of learning to read, warfare on this front remains both murky and highly contentious. An increasing number of scholars are recognizing that scientific issues are closely tied to philosophical and political considerations. It is not accidental, for example, that the contemporary resurgence in phonics-oriented reading methods coincides with the shift from "equity" to "excellence" themes in overall education policy debates, a shift that, as argued below, is connected to economic

globalization. Whole language, as its advocates emphasize, involves a commitment to teacher and student empowerment and is based on the assumption that learning to read starts with the motivation to communicate rather than the acquisition of the skills needed to recognize words.

For the meaning-centered scholars, weak reading performance by students is not so much a matter of inability as a lack of engagement in a community of readers. They are sensitive to the fact that poor reading is usually aligned with family ethnicity and socioeconomic status. Moreover, the whole-language scholars argue, middle-class children from the majority culture are in danger of learning to dislike reading, even as they are mastering the skills needed to do it. For these scholars, it is less important whether readers can recognize or phonetically decode words than that they are motivated to pursue the power of written communication. Further, in empowering students as readers, they wish to promote critical thinking and reflective citizenship, not the creation of docile servants for the status quo (Shannon 1992).

Researchers studying issues related to word recognition and the development of fluent decoding and rapid comprehension of printed text are typically less interested in issues of student motivation. They concentrate, instead, on issues of skill. Since it is obvious that one cannot read at all without recognizing letters and words, it is reasonable to believe (and research evidence confirms) that fluent decoding of text will mean more rapid reading and more immediate comprehension. From this perspective, reading instruction appears to hinge on effective access to the "phonological decoding" of printed text—that is, recognizing how to pronounce the sounds associated with print in order to connect them with a large repertoire of oral language.

Currently, the dominant view is that direct training in the precursor skills of phonic decoding is the way to solve reading problems for most children. But the whole-language scholars remain unconvinced—they see the issue in civil rights terms because they are deeply convinced that learning to read is driven by empowerment and the motivation to communicate, with skills quickly evolving once motivation is established.

2. *The research-funding front where government officials seek to direct professional scholarship.* Closely related to the scholarly front is the research-funding battle, but this theater of operations involves other key players whose work helps to determine what kind of research will be conducted and how broadly findings from that research will be disseminated.

Most important to the reading wars are two streams of funding from the federal government.

One stream of multimillion dollar support, beginning in the 1960s, comes from the U.S. Department of Education. This funding sponsored the seminal first-grade studies in the 1960s and provided substantial funding for the creation and support of a national center on reading.

The other significant federal funding stream has come through the National Institute for Child Health and Human Development. This stream has provided more than $280 million to support tightly structured inquiry into the problems of poor readers (and how those problems compare with how fluent readers acquire this skill). For the most part, U.S. Department of Education funding has supported work on alternatives to basal readers, pursued by scholars who have emphasized the importance of comprehension and meaning development. NICHD funding has been concentrated on studies of phonological decoding that have been interpreted to demonstrate the fundamental significance of direct instruction in phonics. Judging from the research designs utilized and the conclusions drawn, it would appear that the whole-language side, until recently, captured key decision points in the U.S. Department of Education, while phonologically oriented forces have dominated thinking at NICHD.

3. *The curriculum materials front where government officials and private economic interests seek to control professional influence.* Both curriculum materials and student-testing systems are implicated in the adoption of a reading instruction program. While a few states (most notably California, Texas, and Florida) have traditionally exercised strong centralized control over school district instructional materials, in most states local school officials select curriculum materials. Here, the basal readers have loomed large. According to the *Report Card on the Basal Readers* (Goodman et al. 1988), at the zenith of their popularity about 80 percent of all dollars spent on basal readers went to just six publishers. A substantial portion of the purchase price of these books went to advertising and lobbying for their adoption, giving the publishers tremendous leverage on the definition of good reading instruction.

The development of alternative reading instruction models has stimulated tremendous growth in the number and variety of curriculum materials published. Many of the leading research scholars involved in arguments over the scientific power and reliability of alternative reading models are also reaping significant income from the marketing of their own instructional materials designed for classroom use. Allegations abound about such self-interest being one of the driving forces in the reading wars (see, for example, Goodman 1998).

Beyond the authors and publishers of materials, substantial power over reading curriculum materials development is in the hands of state and district curriculum reviewers and approval agencies. Additionally, the nonschool market has become influential as parents anxious about their children's reading readiness are purchasing phonics-oriented reading instruction materials, such as "Hooked on Phonics," in large quantities.

4. *The student assessment front where government seeks professional accountability, competing professional factions seek control of test form and content, and private economic interests pursue profits.* Student assessment is one of the core technologies of public education, a basic tool for management and policy making. Until well into the twentieth century, student assessment was left entirely to teacher judgment (with a lot of advice from parents, school administrators, and boards of education). With the emergence of educational psychology as a field of scholarly inquiry came the development of standardized testing programs aimed at generating data that could be used to make comparisons among students and across instructional programs. Like the textbook market, student-testing programs are heavily influenced by the marketing strategies of a small number of private testing firms. Also like the textbook case, student tests tend to be produced by university-based scholars who have a direct involvement in the scientific debates regarding alternative reading instructional strategies.

Also similar to the textbook situation, student assessment is sharply influenced by a handful of state and federal agencies, with occasional intrusion onto the scene by international projects aimed at comparing student achievement across national borders. The most important national testing program, by far, is the NAEP, which is conducted every two years by the National Center for Education Statistics. Despite the notable problems identified with NAEP's achievement standards, its findings are taken very seriously.

Standardized tests, periodically scaled to reflect average attainment among all school children, have provided the benchmark data for virtually every study of reading program effectiveness. All the major standardized test programs provide one or more measures of word recognition and reading comprehension. Thus they can be used as broad gauge indicators of the successful mastery of both phonetic decoding and meaning comprehension. Unfortunately, despite standardization on similar student groups, there is substantial variability in what these tests measure (scores on one test maker's examination may correspond to as little as 60 percent of a student's ability when measured on a different test). Nevertheless, it is generally believed that these tests can be trusted to evaluate program differences. Support for this belief is not evenly distributed, however.

Meaning-centered whole-language advocates resist trusting standardized achievement test data. In part, they resist these tests because they shift power and influence away from classrooms and into the hands of administrators, policymakers, and politically active community groups. More often, they argue that their resistance springs from the fact that standardized tests provide students with only sterile reading exercises and disembodied text passages, rather than the kind of authentic text and opportunities for creative expression they believe is essential to the motivation of fluent reading. According to Patrick Shannon (1999), in the 1980s whole-language advocates not only sought legislative mandates for their programs but also began to attack standardized testing, which was viewed as "the last straw" by their opponents.

In recent years, notable efforts have been made to generate alternative measures of language learning. These alternative assessment systems bear such names as "running records," "miscue analysis," "kid watching," and "portfolio assessments" (Goodman 1996; Goodman and Burke 1972). The most significant effort at developing a more meaningful and authentic language-oriented student assessment system was the short-lived California Learning Assessment System. It was developed in the early 1990s at substantial state expense, but only administered to students twice before it became the object of intense political controversy and was retired by the governor. Among the most important sources of new approaches to assessment is the federally supported Center for Research on Evaluation, Standards, and Student Testing, located at UCLA.

5. *The teacher preparation front where professional factions seek to standardize and perpetuate their views.* College and university schools of education are the places where the nation's teachers are trained in how to think about student learning and what methods to use to teach reading. University professors are the authors of most of the teacher training textbooks, and they regularly participate in professional conferences where alternative approaches to reading are analyzed and debated. The whole-language movement has been successful in persuading university professors of teacher education that this approach could be used to enhance the

enjoyment of reading and to engage the interest of millions of children who are failing to become fluent readers. Now, however, education schools are under fire for failing to teach teachers how to effectively teach reading (Bradley 1998). The predominant view now, dramatized by the endorsement of both major national teachers unions, is that systematic direct instruction of decoding skills is a necessary part of a "balanced" approach to reading, along with an emphasis on reading comprehension and a rich exposure to literature. Accepting the NICHD view that teaching reading is a complex activity that too few teachers understand well, both major unions have literally stated that, in fact, "teaching reading *is* rocket science" (American Federation of Teachers 1999; Chase 1999).

6. *The professional development front where government agencies seek to arbitrate professional commitments.* Professional development or inservice training for teachers has become big business in the years since the federal government became an active advocate for school desegregation, curriculum reform, and special programs for educationally disadvantaged or disabled students. Professional development specialists are found in large numbers in federally supported educational research and development laboratories; on university campuses; and working for local school districts, state departments of education, and intermediate-level educational service agencies. A large number of private educational consultants also provide staff development services to local school districts. The staff development system has been an important arena for conflict in the conduct of the reading wars. Staff development programs are screened for their support of favored reading instruction models and are frequently utilized to provide teachers with an ideological commitment to one view or another as well as technical training in how to implement a particular instructional model.

Key to the battle dynamics on this front are the state and local agency officials who control the expenditure of staff development resources and who influence the participation of classroom teachers. California adopted a major initiative in 1996 that forbade the use of state funds to pay for teacher staff development programs that take the whole-language approach. In response, Flippo notes, some of those attending the 1999 convention of the International Reading Association in San Diego wore black T-shirts with the words "Banned in California" across the front:

> If a reading specialist or a researcher has a whole-language philosophy, he or she is not allowed "in." Instead, only those who empha-

size phonemic awareness and decoding skills above all else are allowed to give workshops to California teachers. This McCarthy-like
militance—in effect blacklisting—is just one example of how some
politicians, aided by the media's need for sensational news and topics, have kept the reading wars going. (1999, 38)

7. *The mass media front where professional conflicts are defined and
arbitrated for government officials and the public.* The mass media have
played a critical role in the reading wars. *Education Week,* the *New York
Times,* the *Wall Street Journal, Newsweek,* and other major national opinion makers legitimate the sides and arbitrate public opinion on the issues.
This is not a particularly new phenomenon. For much of the twentieth
century, education policy issues have been the objects of widespread popular
interest. Rudolf Flesch's critique of basal readers was on the national best-
seller lists. His later work, "Why Johnny *Still* Can't Read," was picked up
by *Family Circle* magazine in 1979.

Although the media live on controversy and are quick to report findings critical of current practices, they also tend to develop an overall bias
toward one side or the other when issues persist the way reading instruction has. Persuaded by the NICHD research, the media have taken a tilt
toward the phonological approach to reading, opining that meaning-
centered whole-language approaches have contributed to an overall decline in reading ability. As Goodman writes,

It's the movement of the controversy into the mainstream media
that has had the greatest impact on the image of whole language.
That, in turn, has encouraged the far right to step up its attack at
state and local levels, waving newspapers in front of boards, super-
intendents, and legislators that purportedly tell the story of the failure of whole language in California and, by implication, everywhere.
(1998, 27)

8. *The public policy front where government officials arbitrate private
interests and professional beliefs.* Statutory and regulatory control over
reading programs and practices is another key arena of conflict and struggle.
Usually the state education agencies have taken the lead in endorsing specific approaches to reading instruction. They have acted to regulate textbook content and curriculum frameworks, adopt student assessment
programs, develop and disseminate teacher training materials, and in extreme cases take over local schools or school districts where reading per-

formance is very low. Until about 1990 most state legislatures avoided taking sides on the question of reading instruction. Pressured by conservative interest groups and school reform advocates, and influenced by mass media proclamations of public school failure, many state legislatures now have become actively engaged in the regulation of reading instruction. California, as noted above, has gone the farthest in this, by "blacklisting" whole-language consultants to prevent them from influencing staff development. Paterson's (1998a, 1998b, forthcoming) investigation of state legislative activity shows that three states—Arizona, New Mexico, and Ohio—enacted "phonics" statutes prior to 1990. Legislative activity increased from 1990 to 1998, however, with 101 phonics bills proposed and 28 more bills passed, adding Alabama, California, Delaware, Louisiana, Idaho, Oklahoma, Mississippi, North Carolina, and Wisconsin to bring the total to twelve states with phonics legislation by the end of 1997.

It was not until passage of the 1998 Reading Excellence Act that the U.S. Congress became significantly involved in arbitrating reading policy. The Reading Excellence Act endorses the phonics approach to reading instruction and, as noted at the outset, was clearly and heavily influenced by findings from the NICHD research program. The dominance of the phonics point of view in formulating this act is striking. It was represented not only by Reid Lyon's central role, but also by the fact that Representative Bill Goodling, chairman of the House Committee on Education and the Workforce, had employed on his staff Robert Sweet (1996, 1997), the cofounder of the National Right to Read Foundation.

Working in the background to promote state and federal legislative successes for the phonics approach has been a plethora of interest groups, especially conservative ones. These groups and activist parents have skillfully employed a variety of communications and publicity techniques, including direct mail, e-mail, websites, and "op-ed" pieces in newspapers to make their case both well-known and influential.

California: A Case of the Rise and Fall of Whole Language?

California provides an important case study in the politics of the reading wars because it is widely held that the whole-language approach had a period of ascendancy (1987 through 1995) only to decline dramatically in favor of phonics-oriented instruction beginning in 1996 (California State Board of Education 1997, 7). Defenders of whole language question whether whole language was ever a widely used pedagogy in California. They point out that California's curriculum frameworks never used the term *whole language* and instead called for a "literature-based" approach to reading. Further, they claim that so little in-service training was given to teachers that it would have been impossible for a new pedagogy like whole language to be widely implemented. Nevertheless, the California experience became a turning point for whole language because many policymakers and members of the news media concluded that whole language had failed there.

Battles over reading instruction policy in California have been waged across at least five of the eight "battlefronts" described above: state policy, curriculum materials, teacher preparation, staff development, and student assessment. Historically, it should be noted that state-level interest in elementary school education was so keen in the nineteenth century that California began publishing school textbooks in 1890 and continued to publish all the official textbooks for public elementary schools until the 1950s, when the state gradually shifted to a policy of textbook approval rather than state publication. The primary reason for this shift was the growing desire for local schools and districts to be able to select from a variety of curriculum materials. Thus textbook publication was replaced by textbook adoption—providing local schools with a list of approved texts that could be purchased from private publishers with state funds. This proliferation of available texts was, no doubt, a contributing cause to increasing debate over whether schools in California were utilizing the most appropriate materials for reading instruction.

By 1962, when Max Rafferty ran for state superintendent of public instruction, conflicts over reading instruction, following the lines laid out in Rudolph Flesch's *Why Johnny Can't Read*, were in full swing. Rafferty ran, and won, on a platform of bringing phonics back into the elementary school reading instruction program. While Rafferty's populist rhetoric was widely reported, he had remarkably little direct impact on school instructional processes and practices.

Nonetheless, California reinforced its commitment to state level involvement in reading instruction by adopting the landmark Miller-Unruh reading program in 1965, which funded reading specialists to work with teachers and with students having difficulty learning to read. This legislative program continued to provide local schools with direct access to reading specialists until it was folded into a block-granting program for special services in 1987.

With the election in 1970 of Wilson Riles, California's first and only African American superintendent of public instruction, curriculum and pedagogical issues turned from a focus on effectiveness to an emphasis on equality of educational opportunity. Riles created a "Compliance Committee" with independent curriculum materials review authority, charged with the responsibility of making sure that state-adopted curriculum materials gave suitable attention to the contributions of women and racial and ethnic minorities and did not portray these groups in prejudicial ways. This was the period when California was making substantial progress in responding to the mandate of the courts to root out racial and ethnic prejudices in public institutions. As a result of this emphasis, the power base of the state superintendent's office shifted sharply toward the legislature and away from the community of professional educators and university scholars who had previously dominated issue-definition and program development. This tendency toward legislative domination of education policy was dramatically reinforced when California passed its infamous property tax reform measure, Proposition 13, which moved education funding out of the hands of local school districts and into the state's general fund. This shift in taxation for education was widely interpreted as meaning that the state legislature was now responsible for the quality of school programs and the efficacy of its practices.

By about 1980 the equity movement had run its course. In California, as in the rest of the nation, the conviction that the public schools were more characterized by low quality than by inequality began to spread among key research scholars, policymakers, and the popular media. In 1982 Bill Honig was elected state superintendent on a platform of restoring excellence to a school system painted as having slipped badly in its ability to teach children. Honig's views were echoed by the melodramatic *A Nation at Risk* report released by the federal government in 1983. But he had already been working closely with key California legislators to produce the omnibus Hughes-Hart educational reform package (SB 813, 1983) that set in motion massive reforms in California's school programs.

From the perspective of reading instruction, the most important fruit of this reform was the development of a new literature-based English Language Arts Framework, released in 1987 (California State Department of Education 1987). The 1987 framework represents the high-water mark for whole-language instruction in California, although the term *whole language* was kept out of the framework document at the insistence of Superintendent Honig. At the time, the whole-language elements incorporated into this language arts framework seemed an ideal blend of equity and excellence interests. The framework encouraged decentralization of control over reading and the utilization of diverse and meaningful reading materials, while also focusing attention on the importance of all children learning to read during their first few years in school. The framework was followed by a new textbook adoption cycle in 1988, with the first purchases of materials fitting the framework being made by school districts in 1989, some of them for use in the 1989–90 instructional year.

Assessment was soon brought to center stage. In 1990 the governor "blue penciled" funding for the state's widely acclaimed California Assessment Program tests, on the grounds that this matrix-sampled test was not able to report accurately on the progress of individual children and thus did not provide the information needed to hold families and children accountable for their academic progress. By the next year a new test format—the California Learning Assessment System (CLAS)—was under development. During the two years it took to prepare the CLAS test, the California legislature supported a diversity of local assessment testing programs by providing a flat $5.00 per child for local districts to use for implementation of any testing program they wished to select from a state-approved list of private assessments. The CLAS test was aligned with key whole-language concepts, in that it emphasized problem solving, performance tasks, critical thinking, and constructed answers to open-ended questions rather than recall of specific information. These design features provided students being tested with what the test developers believed to be challenging and meaningful text material that inquired into their ability to think and analyze experiences and events.

It was on this score, however, that the CLAS test ran into a firestorm of criticism. Citizen groups, especially religious conservatives, accused the test makers of inappropriately inquiring into private feelings and family experiences. They charged that the test inappropriately directed children's thinking toward morbid and unwholesome topics. The CLAS test was given only twice—in 1993 and 1994—and was then abandoned under pressure. The death knell for the test was an investigative report published in the *Los Angeles Times* accusing the state of releasing school-level performance reports based on a hopelessly inadequate sampling of the students within those schools. The *Times* report stimulated the formation of a state-level special commission to review the technical adequacy of the test. That commission, headed by Stanford University professor Lee Cronbach, noted that the *Times* report was overly harsh but nevertheless confirmed the inadequacy of the sampling used to construct school performance scores.

While the CLAS test results declared California school children to be inadequate in their ability to read with comprehension, it was the release of test data from the NAEP in 1992 and 1994 that led eventually to the abandonment of the 1987 language arts framework. As discussed in more detail below, the NAEP test scores showed a decline in test performance between 1992 and 1994, but the meaning and significance of this decline is debatable. Despite the fact that a national decline in NAEP scores was almost comparable in size to the California decline, the results were immediately seized upon as evidence that the whole-language elements of the 1987 framework were responsible for California's low performance. Additionally, the NAEP scores were interpreted without giving serious attention to the dramatically changing proportions of English-language learners and the rapid growth of children in poverty in the California schools.

Kirst and Mazzeo (1996) analyzed the demise of the CLAS test and pointed out that a major factor keeping it from gaining broad support, and seriously complicating efforts to design its replacement, was the fact that key policymakers were seeking to pursue three distinct and, to some extent, incompatible goals. State superintendent Bill Honig and his staff were seeking to promote performance rather than recall assessments; state senator Gary Hart was seeking to preserve and promote the assessment of schools and school programs (so as to guide reforms as well as to hold educators accountable for student success); and Governor Pete Wilson was championing the importance of producing individual student achievement scores so that students and families could appraise educational progress and accept their share of the responsibility for high achievement.

Faced with a widely perceived decline in performance (even though close examination of the evidence does not support this interpretation), and confronted with divergent goals on the part of key policymakers, California needed to develop a new approach to both reading instruction and student assessment. At this point a crucial event occurred. Charged with financial irregularities, Superintendent Honig was forced to resign from office, leaving his office unable to defend itself against the growing criticism of the CLAS test and the 1987 language arts framework.

In 1996 a new reading initiative was adopted. Consistent with Governor Wilson's convictions and priorities, this initiative called for a number of critical changes. First, the lion's share of the new money made available to education was spent for class size reduction in grades K–3, both in the hope that this would enhance reading instruction and because it kept the new education funding away from collective bargaining. Second, a new language arts framework was developed (released in 1997) that eliminated most of the whole-language concepts of the 1987 framework. Third, it was made illegal to use state funds to pay anyone offering professional staff training who used certain key phrases associated with the whole-language movement. Fourth, an individual-level testing program was adopted (the Stanford Achievement Test, version 9). Fifth, a multiple measures accountability program was adopted requiring schools to certify the number of children achieving at grade level. Sixth, a program of subject matter and grade-level standards adopted by the State Board of Education was implemented.[1]

The social context in which California's abandonment of whole language occurred deserves comment. First, as previously noted, there was a dramatic growth in the number of children from non-English speaking homes and a soaring number of children living in poverty attending California schools. Not only does this explain much of the decline in measured educational attainment, but it also represents a dramatic growth in the number of families and children who present special needs to both public and private institutions throughout the state. Significantly, the shift away from whole language was also accompanied by voter approval of three highly controversial statewide referenda. Taken together, these three propositions leave the unmistakable impression that the state seeks to end any sort of preferential treatment for the enormous number of immigrants and their children. Proposition 187 adopted in 1994 sought to outlaw access to public education and other public services by the children of illegal immigrants. The central provisions of this proposition were defeated in a court battle, but the anti-immigrant sentiments expressed by the large margin of support for it at the polls have not been lost on professional educators or the policymaking community. The second was Proposition 209 (1996), which ended the state's commitment to affirmative action in employment (following a highly publicized end to affirmative action in

---

1. The initiative also included some additional items: a new teacher induction program was expanded to include all new teachers; a new law forbids "social promotion" of students not making grade-level progress in academic subjects; and in 1999 an accountability program for low-performing schools was implemented that threatens to remove principals and redeploy staff if the state's lowest performing schools do not make regular and substantial progress toward bringing children's achievement up to grade-level standards.

student admissions adopted by the University of California). The third, Proposition 227 (1998), sought to outlaw bilingual education programs and to require that English language learning students be given English immersion instruction for only one year before moving into mainstream educational programs.

Clearly the most important single event in the collapse of whole language in California was publication of the 1994 NAEP achievement test scores (Williams 1995). Media and political attention focused on a five-point decline in average statewide reading scores between 1992 and 1994, interpreting it as evidence of the failure of the 1987 language arts framework and endorsement of whole-language by teacher educators across the state. While it is true that this decline was larger than a three-point decline experienced nationally, it could be largely explained by a dramatic rise in the number of California children in poverty and coming from non-English speaking families during this period. According to California Department of Education figures, the National School Lunch Program population of poor children rose by 18.4 percent between 1992 and 1994 to a staggering 42.8 percent of all California school children (the rate had risen by more than 33 percent since the adoption of the framework in 1987). Department figures also indicate that the number of English-language learners rose by 12.5 percent between 1992 and 1994 to more than 22 percent of all children (the number jumped by more than 46 percent from 1987 to 1994). Mitchell and Mitchell (1999) estimated that poverty and limited English proficiency are each independently responsible for more than a 10 percent decline in reading performance as measured by the Stanford Achievement Test, Version 9. Moreover, they found that the proportion of poor and limited English-proficient students within a classroom significantly predicts the achievement of their classmates. If the impact on NAEP testing is similar to that for the Stanford Achievement Test, the dramatic growth in these factors could account for about 80 percent of the California NAEP decline. In short, after controlling for the population changes, California scores declined less than the national average.

Beyond the largely ignored demographic changes, three other problematic features of the presumed link between California's 1987 literature-based curriculum framework and the 1994 NAEP test scores deserve attention. First, the decline in 1994 included eighth and eleventh graders as well as fourth graders. Thus children who had completed their early elementary schooling well before the 1987 program changes could have affected their instruction were just as likely to show lower reading performance as were those who were in the first cohort exposed to the new program emphasis.

Second, the 1994 NAEP report, which proclaimed that 40 percent of California's school children did not meet the "proficient" standard of reading fluency (Williams 1995), employed a new and controversial standard that had been developed in 1992 and not used in earlier tests (Educational Testing Service 1994; Rothstein 1998; Viadero 1993a, 1993b, 1993c). As a result, the widely reported finding of deficient reading ability was not primarily a change in student performance but the injection of a new and debatable standard used by NAEP officials to interpret the meaning of the test scores. Rothstein (1998, 72) comments about this:

> On the 1990–91 reading test administered by the International Association for the Evaluation of Educational Achievement, America's nine-year-olds scored second-highest in the world (the Finns were first). But if the NAEP achievement levels established by the NAGB [National Assessment Governing Board] are to be believed, only 30 percent of U.S. nine-year-olds are proficient in reading. This is simply not plausible, and it raises questions about how the proficiency levels are determined by the National Assessment Governing Board before they are broadcast to the American people in support of a "failing schools" story. The procedure for defining these achievement levels, in reality, is both ideologically and technically suspect.

Rothstein bases his conclusion on two highly critical reviews of the NAGB's standard setting. First, a study by the U.S. General Accounting Office (1993) concluded that the cutoff scores for "basic" and "proficient" levels of achievement should have been set substantially lower than they were. Second, a study by the National Academy of Education (1993) agreed with the GAO findings and concluded that "the procedure by which the achievement levels had been established was 'fundamentally flawed' and 'subject to large biases,' and that the achievement levels by which American students had been judged deficient were set 'unreasonably high'" (Rothstein 1998, 73, referring to National Academy of Education, 1993, xxii, 148; see also Viadero 1993a, 1993c).

The third problem with the presumed link between California's 1987 literature-based curriculum framework and the 1994 NAEP test scores is that this interpretation assumes that the intended whole-language approach actually was widely implemented in California schools within a short space of time (Daniels 1996). This assumption flies in the face of one of the best-documented findings about educational reform: implementation studies have consistently found that implementation of intended reforms is nearly always uneven and weak initially (Fullan and Stiegelbauer 1991; Louis, Toole, and Hargreaves 1999). It usually takes at least three to five years before new programs can be put into practice, and even then the intended reform often is not widely and faithfully practiced. In the case of California's literature-based curriculum framework, many school districts did not even receive the new textbooks needed for it until a year or two after it was adopted.

Despite all these problems and others—such as California's drastic underfunding of its schools and libraries (see McQuillan 1998)—in the absence of other test data the NAEP scores were widely interpreted, by policymakers and journalists, as proof that California schools were not only failing but were rapidly declining as a result of the decision to use a literature or meaning-based approach, rather than a phonics or decoding approach, to the teaching of reading. More valid evidence might have been found in California's CAP (California Achievement Program) testing data, which covered all students, but it had been stricken from the state budget in 1991. Dressman (1999, 280) points out, however, that the CAP scores for the years 1984 through 1990 do not offer any reason to suspect whole language of interfering with reading attainment (if, in fact, a whole-language approach had been widely implemented by then, which is questionable). He notes that "the most salient feature of the CAP scores is their stability from 1984 to 1990. In fact, the raw scores for this test show a slight (although probably not statistically significant) gain for 3rd, 6th, 8th, and 12th graders from 1984 to 1990." Thus "there is no indication that the policies of 1987 had any demonstrable effect at all on the state's reading achievement scores."

Analysis

Accounting for the politics of the reading wars requires more than reviewing their historical evolution, enumerating the arenas within which the battles are being fought, or elaborating the unique California experience. We must also identify the forces at work to shape and control the dynamics of the conflict. As we have already noted, conflicts over reading instruction do not follow the logic of technical disagreement: development of competing conceptions of how to increase fluency followed by straightforward comparisons among alternative methods. Persistent and acrimonious arguments over educational goals and philosophies, assessment techniques, analysis of evidence, the influence of money, the role of political alliance networks—and even the motives of participants in the reading wars debates—have made it abundantly clear that this issue touches deep political divisions in our society and serves as a focal point for conflicts about issues much larger than instructional technique. Cultural clashes in education and disputes over how to teach reading have a long history, as noted earlier. However, we believe that new circumstances have added to and escalated the reading war conflicts. Two key concepts from recent studies of large-scale trends in social and economic organization, *globalization*, and *neo-institutionalism*,[2] provide the basis for a theoretical framework that facilitates an understanding of the contemporary character and intensity of these conflicts. A simplified presentation of key elements of these two core concepts is outlined in tables 14-1 and 14-2.

Globalization

The fundamental changes being brought about by global developments in technology, culture, and economics are now widely recognized. Davies and Guppy (1997), for example, provide a convincing analysis of the forces responsible for the convergence in the timing and content of a large number of educational reform policies sweeping through all the Anglo-American democracies in recent years. The globalization they describe involves much more than the penetration of national borders by multinational corporations, international markets, electronic communications, and the emergence of English as the common language of commerce and governance. Globalization, they argue, also promotes a simultaneous centralization and devolution of authority in ways that reduce the power of middle-level authorities in all types of organizations. This process goes on in governments, corporations, and the public bureaucracies responsible for planning and delivering public services.

The globalization process makes necessary centralization of power within the executive structures of both corporations and governments in order to manage the political and market risks that are associated with

2. Unlike Davies and Guppy (1997), from whom this analytical approach is borrowed, the new institutionalism is employed more broadly than what they call "global rationalization," which they view as an alternative to economic globalization for explaining the wide diffusion of similar school reform ideas internationally.

Table 14-1. *Globalization and the Politics of the Reading Wars*

Theoretical idea	General applicability	Application to reading wars
Simultaneous centralization and devolution of authority, squeezes middle-level authorities.	Electronic information exchange changes the pace and character of technology dissemination, economic market development. and individual rights legitimation.	Reading fluency is seen simultaneously as prerequisite for global participation and a source of both social and technical power for individuals and nations.
Domains Technical	Flexible, rapid response is more important than brute force technologies; knowledge is the key to development.	Information-based technologies require advanced reading skills for problem solving and innovation.
Social	Human rights are globally recognized and legitimated.	Protection of individual rights and access to political and social influence depend on linking thought and feeling to text decoding.
Economic	A new order of competitiveness and standardization of expectations makes adaptability to market crucial.	Access to the labor market and adaptability of production processes depend on reading.

thoroughly integrated political and economic systems functioning in rapidly changing environments. At the same time, constituency and client groups demand substantial devolution of authority so that governments and corporations can accommodate their increasingly diverse preferences and demands. Thus, Davies and Guppy (1997, 459), conclude:

Globalization is transforming education by *squeezing power from the middle*. As power is being wrested from education professionals, teachers unions, and ministry officials, it is being redistributed upward to more senior state officials *and* downward to [more active and assertive] local groups. . . . The conjunction of shifting economic conditions, the energetic pursuit of educational control by high-level state officials, and the loud demands of community associations adds up to a massive challenge to professional educators.

Table 14-2. *Neo-Institutional Theory and the Politics of the Reading Wars*

Theoretical idea	General applicability	Application to reading wars
The legitimacy of action dominates productivity considerations.	Organizations are linked symbolically to their environments.	Mobilizing support for a reading theory is as important as proving its scientific merit.
Environmental Forces Profession	Standards of practice and rationality for systems of production are provided.	Traditionally the domain of policy debate uses scientific vocabulary for deliberation.
Government	Organizational processes and transactions are regulated, and, in the case of public organizations, productivity resources are provided.	Government moved into reading policy because of the significance of globalization of technology, markets, and social standards.
Community	Community provides the values and norms of acceptable action and expects choice and autonomy of action.	Community members have become active in exercising choice and insisting on using value preferences in addition to technical or organizational considerations in selecting instructional programs.

The "information age" is more than a cliché; it reflects the fact that increasingly high-quality electronic information interchange has changed the fundamental character as well as the pace of technology dissemination, market development, and cultural identity formation (compare with Barber 1995). When television brought the Vietnam War into American homes in living color, it created the conditions needed for sustained protest. By the time Desert Storm was being fought in the Middle East, however, it was clear to military officials that they needed to dramatically centralize control over news dissemination about strategic military operations, while allowing CNN to televise radically decentralized coverage of individual cruise missile attacks.

Globalization has evolved in three overlapping waves. The first wave was technical. Transportation and information interchange networks created the infrastructure of globalization. But their potential was not realized until advanced information technologies became routine parts of production, finance, and government operations. With the incorporation of information technologies into machine control, financial transaction processing, government planning, and regulation enforcement, it became clear that flexible and rapid response techniques are much more important than brute force technologies for successful participation in the new world order. Knowledge, even more than material wealth, is now the key to future development. In previous generations those who owned raw materials (like oil or coal) or manufactured sophisticated products (like military armaments or automobiles) accumulated the greatest wealth. In this generation, those who control information processing technologies (like computer hardware and software) or use these technologies to manipulate information in the mass media or financial dealings are accumulating the wealth. Hence, the strategic importance of education has escalated.

Shortly after technological globalization began to be recognized for what it had become—an irreversible turning point in human history—social and cultural relationships throughout the advanced industrial world began to undergo rapid globalization. Academic and popular reflection on the barbarities of totalitarian governments gave rise throughout the decade of the 1960s to a centrifugal redistribution of political power away from the traditional centers and into the hands of cultural and ethnic subcommunities. The legitimacy of governmental authority was challenged and the moral legitimacy of corporations and armies was questioned. Indeed, social globalization made it possible for citizens of one country to feel more akin to those of another than to the more powerful members of their own society. Social globalization is responsible for the empowerment of individuals who now are more likely to believe that they have a basic right to liberty as well as a choice among products and individualized services to meet their unique preferences and needs. This global empowerment is the driving force behind insistence that the new information technologies be used to go beyond economic mass production in order to differentiate goods and services on the basis of preferences and needs.

The new economic order of competitiveness and rising standards in the marketplace associated with economic globalization is widely recognized. The critical point, however, is that globalization has created fundamental structural changes in social relationships throughout the world. The new technical, social, and economic structures are far more robust and unavoidable than the left-wing/right-wing ideological commitments that have defined politics for the century and a half since Marx's early writings.

Both formal governmental structures and the cultural norms that define local communities are undergoing reconstruction to fit the new globalization by embracing new norms of competency, new ethics of participation, and the refocusing of power and authority through a simultaneous centralization and devolution that squeezes middle levels of control in virtually all organizations.

Globalization, then, has more than a little to do with the character and intensity of the current reading wars. First, recognition of the technical and structural character of the new globalized environments has led to a widespread realization that reading fluency is simultaneously a prerequisite for global participation and a critical source of social and technical power for individuals and nations. For a social group or a nation to compete in the new global environment, everyone has to read, and read with critical understanding and an ability to utilize nuanced meanings to analyze issues and solve problems. Technical globalization focused attention on the use of reading skills to adapt to the new information technologies. Increasingly, poor readers are left out of the social systems that guarantee human rights and the economic systems that provide personal income.

The social globalization of the 1960s and 1970s raised the awareness that reading was essential for the protection of individual rights and for access to political and social influence—processes that increasingly depend on linking thought and feeling to the meanings derived from decoding printed text. With social globalization came awareness that the social stratification of reading is a major impediment to the democratization of social relationships. It was not accidental, in other words, that the whole-language movement's emphasis on empowerment of students and teachers came during this intense period of social globalization. Unfortunately, for democratic reformers, economic globalization, with its centralized control, usually takes political precedence over democratic globalization of egalitarian social relationships.

Awareness of economic globalization has renewed attention to the technical importance of learning to read. The new economic environment with its highly competitive, rapidly changing, and insistently adaptive marketplace can only be accessed successfully by individuals who can read fluently and understand what they read. Under the influence of the new information technologies, machines are able to easily out-think and out-perform poor readers. They can only be guided into meaningful production tasks by workers who have a more comprehensive and subtler grasp of the printed word (Reich 1991).

The growing importance of educational achievement in international economic competition has greatly increased the importance of standard-ized testing and quantitative research and outcomes measures in educa-tion. These popular instruments of centralized assessment and control are inconsistent with both the philosophy and more qualitative and holistic evaluation techniques associated with the whole-language approach. More holistic, "portfolio" assessment is generally viewed as too cumbersome and expensive for statewide assessments. Furthermore, policymakers and the public would still want the results somehow converted to numbers for easy comprehension and use.

Neo-Institutionalism

The effects of globalization have contributed to the need for organiza-tional theorists to reconceptualize the essential character of social institu-tions. Institutional theorists have noted that both governments and corporations are behaving in ways that defy the logic of classical theories of formal organization. In contrast to classical organization theory, which sought to account for organizational structures and behaviors in terms of the internal functional prerequisites of organizational coherence and stability—neglecting the importance of environmental forces—neo-institutional theories emphasize the existence of active forces of constraint and control located within these critical environments. The key elements of neo-institutional theory are outlined in Table 14-2.

The line of sociological analysis called the "new institutionalism" be-gan with the now classic essay of Meyer and Rowan (1977), which was given popular currency in the work of DiMaggio and Powell (1991) and was reviewed at some length in the 1995 yearbook of the Politics of Edu-cation Association (Crowson, Boyd, and Mawhinney 1996). Analytically, the new institutionalism calls attention to two previously neglected as-pects of complex social organizations: the importance of organizational legitimacy and the influence of environments.

Neo-institutional theory was born in the recognition that modern or-ganizations often put symbolism and institutional legitimacy ahead of tech-nical rationality and productivity. When this happens, organizational behavior is grounded in social norms and values that establish boundaries for acceptable actions and define the moral, traditional, rational, and le-gal grounds that can be offered and accepted as the basis for actions pro-posed or taken. That is, organizational behavior is not just a matter of "realistic" pursuit of identified goals. Indeed, what counts as rational or realistic behavior is defined by the legitimated social norms and values that become the defining characteristics of the organization itself.

Environmental forces are significant in shaping organizational structure and behavior. All complex social organizations exist, neo-institutional theory notes, in dynamic tension with three distinct environments: (1) a web of professional societies that define standards and legitimate production techniques for organizational workers and leaders; (2) governmental structures that provide regulations, procedural legitimacy, and critical resources; and (3) a broad array of client groups and attentive publics who define core values and demand responsive products and services.

Professional control relies on technical language systems (seen by outsiders as arcane jargon) to deliberate about optimal approaches to task performance. Professional associations legitimate new concepts and ideas, through systems of research and research knowledge dissemination. Through professional networks, professional norms and standards are disseminated and adopted internationally.

Governments create the network of rights and responsibilities necessary to sustain social organizations. This network consists of contractual enforcement and regulation of civic behavior for both individuals and organizations. Government influence is based on legitimate coercion; definition of and legitimate authority for administration and policy; symbolic ratification of interests, policy problems, and policy solutions; and allocation of substantial fiscal resources.

Community environments directly influence institutional priorities and practices by bringing popular interests to bear on the norms of acceptable action, the range of choices that can be left to experts, and the autonomy of action that is left to institutional employees. Community pressures are most successful when they are transmitted privately and subtly, but they can also be expressed as threats to disrupt institutional functioning.

The key ideas of organizational legitimacy and environmental influence combine to explain why organizations sometimes adopt and implement policies and practices that are not rationally linked to any production technology and may not be coherent with one another or with the organization's nominal goals. When, for example, the federal government adopts a policy urging reading programs to be based on "reliable and replicable research" and accompanies that legislation with a declaration that testimony before the adopting committee indicates that there have been "scientific breakthroughs" in our knowledge that support direct phonics instruction, the result is a powerful legitimation of phonics-based instruction, quite independent of the extent to which this body of research is complete, accurate, or unchallenged.

Implications

Globalization and neo-institutionalism thus converge as a set of core ideas for explaining key aspects of the politics of the reading wars. Globalization provides the sense of urgency to reading improvement—a sense of urgency that is quite independent of the adequacy of our pedagogical knowledge base. Neither nations nor corporations can now imagine continued social and economic success if their members do not read—regularly, fluently, and with understanding. Globalization also sets key parameters for responding to this urgent imperative.

To fit the globalized zeitgeist, reading policies must be technically flexible and adaptive, socially responsive to individual needs and preferences, and focused on developing the skills needed to improve economic productivity and competitiveness and assure political participation and national identity. Moreover, globalized reading policies will likely encourage centralized control exercised by the public and private officials responsible for positioning nations and corporations within the globalized technical, social, and economic systems. In short, reading policy will be seen as far too important to be left to educators, far too technically complex to be left to well-meaning but unscientific practitioners, and far too precious to subcultural or ethnic groups and the unique purposes of families and children to be undertaken without some adaptation to local needs.

The core ideas on neo-institutional theory explain how this urgency and these parameters are turned into specific policy proposals, and how those proposals become the objects of political conflict and struggle. Education professionals can be expected to interpret reading pedagogy as a matter of rationally implementing programs and policies that have acquired the status of "legitimate professional practice"—ratified by peer review through professional training programs, conferences, and peer review of program and practice implementation. Globalization undercuts this time-honored professionalism, however, by highlighting the risks and urgency for action that outstrip the capacity of professional deliberations to keep pace.

Globalization also encourages popular community opinion and highly centralized governmental authority to become detached from professional judgment. The mass media play a particularly powerful role, identifying scientific "breakthroughs" and bringing them to the attention of public opinion leaders and key governmental actors. This provides these nonprofessional environmental groups with the language and, above all, the sense of legitimate understanding of the critical issues needed to challenge professional control over policy and practice. Of course, tensions between professional expertise and control versus public or lay control over education policy are a classic and central theme in the literature on the politics of education (Benveniste 1997; Boyd 1976, 1978; Iannaccone 1967). However, the shift in the 1980s from an *input* to an *outcomes*-orientation toward education, and toward what has been called the "politics of excellence and choice," began a period of steady decline in the influence of professional educators (Boyd 1992; Boyd and Kerchner 1988). As epitomized by the famous *A Nation at Risk* report in 1983, the forces of social and economic globalization precipitated this shift and decline.

In order to strengthen their leverage over professional judgment, opinion leaders begin to focus on those members of the profession that are incompetent or uncommitted to their mission and begin to assert that the entire profession is characterized by sloth or incompetence. The next step is for members of the profession, themselves, to seek influence through the popular community or through centralized governmental agencies by becoming "policy entrepreneurs" who are "on the circuit" of popular culture venues or government testimonials. Ultimately, then, the professional group itself begins to see itself as another special interest group needing to mobilize popular and governmental authority in order to reinforce its weakened professional authority. Once this happens, the focal policy question, in this case reading pedagogy, becomes a "political football"—an issue used to develop and test values and social and political influence, rather than an issue for which deliberation over realistic means/ends rationality is able to control political support for policy proposals.

Conclusion: From "Religion" to "Rocket Science" in a Global Economy

Emphasizing the ideological disputes over reading instruction, P. David Pearson (as quoted in Rothman 1989) cautioned the governing board of the NAEP in 1989 that "reading is more a religion than a science." By 1999, however, because of wide and persuasive dissemination of the new NICHD research findings, the world of reading policy had shifted dramatically. As noted earlier, the predominant view now, dramatized by the endorsement of both major national teachers unions, is that systematic direct instruction of decoding skills is a necessary part of a "balanced" approach to reading, along with an emphasis on reading comprehension and a rich exposure to literature. Both major unions have accepted the NICHD view that teaching reading is a complex activity that too few teachers understand well, and have literally stated that "teaching reading *is* rocket science" (American Federation of Teachers 1999; Chase 1999).

Although near-religious attachments to the opposing views of how reading should be taught remain evident, and defenders and practitioners of whole language continue to maintain their positions, the evidence at this writing points to a sweeping victory for the advocates of skills-based instruction. The federal Reading Excellence Act and numerous state laws urge the use of reading methods supported by "reliable, replicable scientific research" (unequivocally meaning skills-based phonics instruction); the American Federation of Teachers (1999) commissioned an NICHD researcher to write their "Teaching Reading *Is* Rocket Science" document; and mandates for phonics increasingly drive teaching training and new required courses for current teachers. One can ask, though, is this a permanent victory? What will the future hold?

We believe that the proclamation that reading is "rocket science" can be interpreted not simply as a technical, pedagogical response, but also as a strategy for strengthening professional control in the wake of the "pulling away" of authority from the middle levels generated by globalization. And the "near religious attachment" of the professional advocates can be interpreted, at least in part, as a display of professional anxiety due to the way globalization is making education "too important" to be left to the educators alone. In the face of the triumph of centralizing forces (the Reading Excellence Act and others), we can also speculate that the other force of the globalized market—insistence from clients and attentive publics that production be individualized and adaptive rather than standardized— still will generate pressures to let the choice of reading strategy be decentralized to the classroom level, at the same time it is centralized to the state and federal level. Some parents, as well as educators, no doubt will still favor a holistic approach to reading instruction. How will this tension between the need for centralization and decentralization be resolved in education policy?

This tension lies at the heart of the debate over our pursuit of national standards and systemic reform. In our democratic society it implicates a perplexing intersection of competing values (Strike 1998). Can one size fit all (Ohanian 1999)? One wing of the national standards debate calls for high standards that consistently apply to all and can be easily measured by conventional standardized tests. Another wing favors national standards but wants flexibility for local and regional adaptation and believes a more nuanced "authentic" assessment approach is needed. And, of course, a variety of opponents resist national standards for a variety of reasons (Arons 1997). Significantly, the flexibility and authentic assessment wing of the standards movement runs up against globalization's pressures for standardization and ease of assessment. By the same token, it is an irony of whole language that one of its key goals—capturing the full meaning of texts—is consistent with the information processing needs of globalization, but its emphasis on nuanced "authentic" assessment is not (see Adams and Bruck 1995, 18).[3]

The reading wars began as a dispute about competing instructional methods—means rather than ends—but they clearly are also very much about goals, standards, and outcomes: whether all children will learn to read and the extent to which they will become thoughtful and critical readers empowered to construct their own meanings from texts (Shannon 1992). Whole-language advocates intensely oppose what they see as the "drill-and-kill" robotics of direct instruction. In a thoughtful assessment of the reading wars, Stahl (1999, 20) advocates a balanced approach and agrees that reaction against whole language frequently has gone too far, mandating "more phonics than has ever been taught, and more phonics than children need to know in order to automatically recognize words." However, Stahl also decries the highly ideological and politicized approach of many whole-language advocates, which has contributed to the "radical swing away from whole language [which] also uses political means. Whole language is treated as opposition and demonized, just as whole language advocates had demonized those associated with direct instruction or basal readers."

Stahl (1999) calls for efforts to arrest the swing between extreme positions and the pursuit of a balanced approach combining the strengths of both whole language and phonics methods. To the extent that a "balanced" or "integrated" approach combining the strengths of both whole

3. In theory, nuanced authentic assessment might be made consistent with the needs of globalized standards, if the powers of modern information systems were fully connected to more sophisticated standards definitions. At present, it appears that less complex assessment data are required.

language and phonics can be widely agreed to, the need for a choice of reading methods will be lessened. But the ideological division and tension between the extremes of the warring camps is such that many whole-language advocates are suspicious of the claims for "balanced" approaches. Thus the need for local choice of methods will remain, both for this reason and because of the need for differentiated approaches to meet the learning styles and requirements of an increasingly diverse student population. Perhaps charter schools and education voucher plans will meet part of this need for flexibility and adaptation. The unmet needs, however, will produce pressures for centralized systems to be modified to allow more flexibility.

To sum up, we have argued that the reading wars should be viewed as a part of a continuing conflict between progressive and conservative education philosophies that has been exacerbated by the forces of globalization. While national cultural disputes have long been played out in the arena of education, the contemporary shift away from progressive education seen in the ascendancy of phonics has been sharply accelerated by the shift in zeitgeist brought about by the forces of globalization. These forces drive utilitarian concerns about educational excellence for economic competitiveness that demand accountability and lead to a different view of what is required for equality and social justice. Further, they redistribute authority and power in ways that challenge the beliefs, expertise, and control of professional educators. Clearly, globalization is an irreversible force (short of a catastrophe that ends civilization as we know it). This will mean that educators, along with other professionals and policymakers, will need to discover a new balance between professional rationality, governmental authority, and adaptation to popular needs and preferences. This suggests that the reading wars will not be won or lost; rather, they will be adaptively superseded by the need to make the entire range of educational services respond to the simultaneous centralization of policy control and adaptive adjustment to needs and interests. The rancorous disputes over reading methods are probably only the first of a number of new "school wars" (Ravitch 1974) to be fought—wars that will reach every aspect of education that is touched by the process of globalization. The recent spread of the curriculum wars into more "value-free" technical domains, such as mathematics, seems consistent with this proposition. Educators thus seem likely to continue to live in "interesting times."

References

Adams, M., and M. Bruck. 1995. "Resolving the 'Great Debate.'" *American Educator* 19, 2 (Summer): 7, 10–20.

Allington, R. L., and H. Woodside-Jiron. 1998. "Thirty Years of Research in Reading: When Is a Research Summary Not a Research Summary." In *In Defense of Good Teaching: What Teachers Need to Know about the "Reading Wars,"* edited by K. S. Goodman. York, Maine: Stenhouse Publishers.

———. 1999. "The Politics of Literacy Teaching: How 'Research' Shaped Educational Policy." *Educational Researcher* (November): 4–13.

American Federation of Teachers. 1999. "Teaching Reading Is Rocket Science: What Expert Teachers of Reading Should Know and Be Able to Do." Prepared by Louisa C. Moats. Washington.

Arons, S. 1997. *Short Route to Chaos: Conscience, Community, and the Re-Constitution of American Schooling.* University of Massachusetts Press.

Barber, B. R. 1995. *Jihad vs. McWorld: How Globalism and Tribalism Are Reshaping the World.* New York: Ballantine Books.

Benveniste, G. 1977. *The Politics of Expertise,* 2d ed. San Francisco: Boyd and Fraser.

Boyd, W. L. 1976. "The Public, the Professionals, and Educational Policy-Making: Who Governs?" *Teachers College Record* 77, 4 (May): 539–77.

———. 1978. "The Changing Politics of Curriculum Policy-Making for American Schools." *Review of Educational Research* 48, 4 (Fall): 577–628.

———. 1992. "The Power of Paradigms: Reconceptualizing Educational Policy and Management." *Educational Administration Quarterly* 28, 4 (November): 504–28.

Boyd, W. L., and C. T. Kerchner, eds. 1988. "Introduction and Overview: Education and the Politics of Excellence and Choice." *The Politics of Excellence and Choice in Education* (1987 yearbook of the Politics of Education Association), 1–11. New York: Falmer Press.

Bradley, A. 1998. "Ed. Schools Getting Heat on Reading." *Education Week* (February 18). Available at www.edweek.com/ew/1998/23read.h17.

California State Board of Education. *Learning to Read: Two Day Workshop.* Sacramento: Comprehensive Reading Leadership Program [AB 3482], 1997.

California State Department of Education. 1987. *English-Language Arts Framework for California Public Schools: Kindergarten through Grade Twelve.* Sacramento.

Chall, J. S. 1967. *Learning to Read: The Great Debate.* McGraw-Hill (updated edition 1983).

———. 1992. "The New Reading Debates: Evidence from Science, Art, and Ideology." *Teachers College Record* 94, 2 (Winter): 315–28.

Chase, B. 1999. "President's Viewpoint: Read across America Returns!" *NEA Today Online* (January 1). Available at www.nea.org/neatoday/9901/presview.html.

Coles, G. 1998a. *Reading Lessons: The Debate over Literacy.* Hill and Wang.

————. 1998b. "No End to the Reading Wars." *Education Week* 18, 14 (December 2): 52, 38.

Crowson, R. L., W. L. Boyd, and H. B. Mawhinney, eds. 1996. *The Politics of Education and the New Institutionalism: Reinventing the American School.* London: Falmer Press.

Daniels, H. 1996. "Is Whole Language Dead?" *The Voice*, newsletter of the National Writing Project (Summer). Available at www.-gse.berkeley.edu/NWP/Voice/sum96/sum96pg9.html.

Daniels, H., S. Zemelman, and M. Bizar. 1999. "Whole Language Works: Sixty Years of Research." *Educational Leadership* 57, 2 (October): 32–37.

Davies, S., and N. Guppy. 1997. "Globalization and Educational Reform in Anglo-American Democracies." *Comparative Education Review* 41, 4 (November): 435–59.

Diegmueller, K. 1996. "The Best of Both Worlds." *Education Week* (March 20).

DiMaggio, P., and W. W. Powell, eds. 1991. *The New Institutionalism in Organizational Analysis.* University of Chicago Press.

DiIulio, John. 1999. Speech presented at conference on civil society issues, carried on C-SPAN (Spring).

Dressman, Mark. "On the Use and Misuse of Research Evidence: Decoding Two States' Reading Initiatives." *Reading Research Quarterly* 34 (1999): 258–85.

Durkheim, E. 1961. *Moral Education: A Study in the Theory and Application of the Sociology of Education.* Translated by E. K. Wilson and H. Schnurer. Edited with an introduction by E. K. Wilson. Free Press.

Educational Testing Service. 1994. *Data Compendium for the NAEP 1992 Reading Assessment of the Nation and the States.* Washington: Education Information Branch, OERI, U.S. Department of Education.

Flippo. R. F. 1999. "Redefining the Reading Wars: The War against Reading Researchers." *Educational Leadership* 57, 2 (October): 38–41.

Flesch, Rudolf. 1955. *Why Johnny Can't Read.* Harper and Row.

————. 1979. "Why Johnny *Still* Can't Read." *Family Circle* (November 1): 26, 44, 46.

Fletcher, J. M., and G. R Lyon. 1998. "Reading: A Research-Based Approach." In *What's Gone Wrong in America's Classrooms*, edited by W. M. Evers. Hoover Institution.

Foshay, Arthur W. 1990. "Textbooks and the Curriculum during the Progressive Era, 1930–1950." In *Textbooks and Schooling in the United States* (89th yearbook of the National Society for the Study of Education), edited by David L. Elliott and Arthur Woodward, Part I, 23–41. University of Chicago Press.

Fullan, M., and S. Stiegelbauer. 1991. *The New Meaning of Educational Change.* Teachers College Press.

Good, H. G. *A History of American Education.* Macmillan, 1956.

Goodman, K. S. 1986. *What's Whole in Whole Language?* Portsmouth, N.H.: Heinemann.

————. 1998. "Who's Afraid of Whole Language? Politics, Paradigms, Pedagogy, and the Press." In *In Defense of Good Teaching: What Teachers Need To*

Know about the "Reading Wars," edited by K. S. Goodman. York, Maine: Stenhouse Publishers.

Goodman, K. S., P. Shannon, Y. S. Freeman, and S. Murphy. 1988. *Report Card on Basal Readers.* Katonah, N.Y.: Richard C. Owen.

Goodman, Y. M. 1996. *Notes from a Kidwatcher: Selected Writings of Yetta M. Goodman,* edited by Sandra Wilde. Portsmouth, N.H.: Heinemann.

Goodman, Y., and C. Burke. 1972. *Reading Miscue Inventory.* Macmillan.

Hoff, D. J. 1998. Riley: "It's Time to Move Past Education Policy Wars." *Education Week* (February 25).

Iannaccone, L. 1967. *Politics in Education.* New York: Center for Applied Research in Education.

Kirst, Michael W., and Christopher Mazzeo. "The Rise, Fall, and Rise of State Assessment in California, 1993–96." *Phi Delta Kappan* (December 1996): 319–23.

Lemann, N. 1997. "The Reading Wars." *Atlantic Monthly* 280, 5 (November): 128–34.

Louis, K. S., J. Toole, and A. Hargreaves. 1999. "Rethinking School Improvement." In *Handbook of Research on Educational Administration,* 2d ed., edited by J. Murphy and K. S. Louis, 251–76. Jossey-Bass.

Loveless, T. 1998. "The Use and Misuse of Research in Educational Reform." In *Brookings Papers on Education Policy: 1998,* edited by D. Ravitch. Brookings.

Manzo, K. K. 1998. "NRC Panel Urges End to Reading Wars." *Education Week* (March 25).

———. 1999. "Reading Experts Question If 'Balance' Is the Answer." *Education Week* 18, 35 (May 12): 8.

McQuillan, J. 1998. *The Literacy Crisis: False Claims, Real Solutions.* Portsmouth, N.H.: Heinemann.

Metz, M. H. 1990. "Real School: A Universal Drama mid Disparate Experiences." In *Education Politics for the New Century,* edited by D. E. Mitchell and M. E. Goertz. London: Falmer Press.

Meyer, J., and B. Rowan. 1977. "Institutionalized Organizations: Formal Structure as Myth and Ceremony." *American Journal of Sociology* 83 (2): 340–63.

Mitchell, Douglas E., and Ross E. Mitchell. 1999. "The Impact of California's Class Size Reduction Initiative on Student Achievement." California Educational Research Cooperative, School of Education, University of California, Riverside.

National Academy of Education. 1993. "Setting Performance Standards for Student Achievement: A Report of the National Academy of Education Panel on the Evaluation of the NAEP Trial State Assessments—An Evaluation of the 1992 Achievement Levels." Stanford, Calif.

Ohanian, S. 1999. *One Size Fits Few: The Folly of Educational Standards.* Portsmouth, N.H.: Heinemann.

Paterson, F. R. R. 1998a. "The Christian Right and Prophonics Movement." Paper presented at annual meeting of the American Educational Research Association, San Diego, Calif. (April).

———. 1998b. "Mandating Methodology: Promoting the Use of Phonics through State Statute." In *In Defense of Good Teaching: What Teachers Need to Know about the "Reading Wars,"* edited by K. S. Goodman. York, Maine: Stenhouse Publishers.

———. Forthcoming. "The Politics of Phonics." *Journal of Curriculum and Supervision.*

Pressley, M., and R. Allington. 1999. "Concluding Reflections: What Should Reading Instructional Research Be the Research of?" *Issues in Education: Contributions from Educational Psychology* 4.

Ravitch, Diane. 1974. *The Great School Wars: New York City, 1805–1973; A History of the Public Schools as Battlefield of Social Change.* Basic Books.

"Reading: The First Chapter in Education." 1996. In *Learning to Read . . . Reading to Learn: Helping Children with Learning Disabilities to Succeed.* National Center to Improve the Tools of Educators. Available at www.ldonline.org/ld_indepth/reading/ltr-cec/ltr2-cec.html.

Reading Excellence Act of 1998. 1998. 105 Cong., 2 sess., Senate H.R. 2614. U.S. Government Printing Office.

Reich, R. 1991. *The Work of Nations: Preparing Ourselves for 21st-Century Capitalism.* Knopf.

Rothman, R. 1989. "NAEP Board Is Seeking a Consensus on Reading." *Education Week* (September 27).

———. 1990a. "Balance between Phonics, 'Whole Language' Urged." *Education Week* (January 10). Available at www.edweek.org/ew/1990/09200040.h09.

———. 1990b. "From a 'Great Debate' to a Full-Scale War: Dispute over Teaching Reading Heats Up." *Education Week* (March 21). Available at www.edweek.org/ew/1990/09310040.h09.

Rothstein, R. 1998. *The Way We Were? The Myths and Realities of America's Student Achievement.* New York: Century Foundation Press.

Routman, R. 1996. *Literacy at the Crossroads: Crucial Talk about Reading, Writing, and Other Teaching Dilemmas.* Portsmouth, N.H.: Heinemann.

School Reform News. 1999. "School-Induced Illiteracy Spurs Spending Explosion: One in Three Public School Students in Remedial Classes." Heartland Institute, vol. 3, no. 2 (February): 1, 6.

Semel, S. F., and A. Sadovnik, eds. 1999. *"Schools of Tomorrow," Schools of Today.* New York: Peter Lang Publishing.

Shannon, P., ed. 1992. *Becoming Political: Readings and Writing in the Politics of Literacy Education.* Portsmouth, N.H.: Heinemann.

———. 1999. Interview by author (April 27).

Share, D. L., and Keith E. Stanovich. 1995. "Cognitive Processes in Early Reading Development: A Model of Acquisition and Individual Differences." *Issues in Education: Contributions from Educational Psychology* 1: 1–57.

Smith, F. 1983. *Essays into Literacy.* Portsmouth, N.H.: Heinemann.

Snow, C., M. S. Burns, and P. Griffin, eds. 1998. *Preventing Reading Difficulties in Young Children.* Committee on the Prevention of Reading Difficulties in Young Children, National Research Council.

Stahl, S. A. 1999. "Why Innovations Come and Go (and Mostly Go): The Case of Whole Language." *Educational Researcher* (November): 13–22.

Strike, K. 1998. "Centralized Goal Formation and Systemic Reform: Reflections on Liberty, Localism, and Pluralism." *Education Policy Analysis Archives* 5, 11. Available at www.epaa.asu.edu.

Sweet, R. W., Jr. 1996. "Illiteracy: An Incurable Disease or Education Malpractice?" Washington: National Right to Read Foundation. Available at www.nrrf.org/essay_Illiteracy.html. [A document with the same title was widely disseminated by a Senate Republican Policy Committee in 1990; see Weaver 1990.]

Sweet, R. W., Jr. 1997. "Don't Read, Don't Tell: Clinton's Phony War on Illiteracy." *Policy Review* (May-June): 38–42.

Taylor, D. 1998. *Beginning to Read and the Spin Doctors of Science: The Political Campaign to Change America's Mind about How Children Learn to Read.* Urbana, Ill.: National Council of Teachers of English.

U.S. General Accounting Office. 1993. "Educational Achievement Standards: NAGB's Approach Yields Misleading Interpretations." GAO/PEMD–93–12.

Viadero, D. 1993a. "GAO Blasts Method for Reporting NAEP Results." *Education Week* (July 14). Available at www.edweek.org/ew/1993/41gao.h12.

———. 1993b. "Students' Reading Skills Fall Short, NAEP Data Find." *Education Week* (September 22). Available at www.edweek.org/ew/1993/03read.h13.

———. 1993c. "Yet Another Report Assails NAEP Assessment Methods." *Education Week* (September 22). Available at www.edweek.org/ew/1993/03naep.h13.

———. 1999a. "New Priorities, Focus Sought for Research." *Education Week* 18, 41 (June 23): 1, 36–37.

———. 1999b. "What Is (and Isn't) Research?" *Education Week* 18, 41 (June 23): 1, 33–36.

Waller, W. W. 1932. *The Sociology of Teaching.* John Wiley.

Weaver, C. 1990. "Weighing Claims of 'Phonics First' Advocates." *Education Week* (March 28). Available at www.edweek.org/ew/1990/09320010.h09.

Williams, Paul L. 1995. "1994 NAEP Reading—A First Look: Findings from the National Assessment of Educational Progress." Prepared by the Educational Testing Service. Washington: U.S. Dept. of Education, Office of Educational Research and Improvement, Educational Resources Information Center.

Contributors

Richard L. Allington
University of Florida

Richard Askey
University of Wisconsin-Madison

Michael T. Battista
Kent State University

William Lowe Boyd
Penn State University

Gail Burrill
National Research Council

Adam Gamoran
University of Wisconsin-Madison

David C. Geary
University of Missouri-Columbia

E. D. Hirsch Jr.
University of Virginia

Tom Loveless
Brookings Institution

Douglas E. Mitchell
University of California,
Riverside

Margaret Moustafa
California State University,
Los Angeles

Diane Ravitch
New York University

Roger Shouse
Penn State University

Catherine E. Snow
Harvard University

Index